C0-AVA-655

PUBLIC AND PRIVATE ENTERPRISE IN A MIXED ECONOMY

Public and Private Enterprise in a Mixed Economy

Proceedings of a Conference held by the
International Economic Association
in Mexico City

EDITED BY
WILLIAM J. BAUMOL

St. Martin's Press   New York

338.74
P 976

189143

© International Economic Association 1980

All rights reserved. For information write:
St. Martin's Press, Inc., 175 Fifth Avenue, New York, N.Y. 10010
Printed in Hong Kong
First published in the United States of America in 1980

ISBN 0-312-65397-2

Library of Congress Cataloging in Publication Data

Main entry under title:

Public and private enterprise in a mixed economy.

Includes index.
1. Government ownership – Congresses. 2. Government business enterprises – Congresses. I. Baumol, William J. II. International Economic Association.
HD3842.P87   1980   338.7'4   79-24732
ISBN 0-312-65377-2

Contents

List of Participants

M. Michel Felix Albert, Chef adjoint du Service des Etudes Economiques
   Générales, Direction Générale, Electricité de France
Professor Benito Acosta, Research Professor, CIDE, Mexico
Professor Armando Arancibia, Research Professor, CIDE, Mexico
Mr Tulio Arroyo, Instituto Politedinico Nacional, UPIICSA/SEGI, Mexico
Professor Haim Barkai, Professor of Economics, Hebrew University, Jerusalem
Professor William J. Baumol, Professor of Economics, Princeton and
   New York Universities, USA
M. Marcel Boiteux, Directeur Général, Electricité de France
Dr José Casar, CIDE, Mexico
Mrs Mercedes Salcedo Chávez, Conasupo, Mexico
M. Pierre Dreyfus, Ancien Président et Directeur Général de la Régie Renault
Mr Eibenschutz, CIDE, Mexico
Mrs Carmen Espinoza, CIDE, Mexico
Professor Luc Fauvel, Secretary General, International Economic Association
Professor Dietrich Fischer, Department of Economics, New York University
Dr Tomás Galán, Director of Planning, Instituto Nacional de Industria, Madrid
Mrs Elma González, CIDE, Mexico
Professor Oscar González, CIDE, Mexico
Professor Luis Gutiérrez, Research Professor, CIDE, Mexico
Professor Lord Kaldor, King's College, Cambridge, UK
Dr Rodrigo Keller, Director of Studies, Instituto Nacional de Industria, Madrid
Dr Armando Labra, President of the Collegio Nacional de Economistas,
   Mexico
Professor David Levhari, Department of Economics, Hebrew University,
   Jerusalem
Mr Manzuilletes, CIDE, Mexico
Dr Ernesto Marcos, Director de Coordinación de Industria Paraestatal
   Secretaría de Patrimonio y Fomento Industrial, Mexico
Dr V. Ajmone Marsan, Director of Economic Studies, Instituto per la
   Ricostruzione Industriale (IRI), Rome
Lic Trinidad Martínez-Tarragó, Director of Studies, CIDE, Mexico
Professor Isaac Minian, Research Professor, CIDE, Mexico
Mrs Ifigeniai Navarrete, CIDE, Mexico

Dr Rezsö Nyers, Director of the Institute of Economics of Hungarian
  Academy of Sciences
Professor Bernardo Palomera, Research Professor, CIDE, Mexico
Dr Richard Pryke, Department of Economics, University of Liverpool, UK
Dr Antonio Sacristán Colás, President of CIDE, Mexico
Lic Emilio Sacristán Roy, Director Adjunto de Empresas y Fideicomiso de
  Nacional Financiera, Mexico
Mr Sánchez, CIDE, Mexico
Professor E. S. Savas, Professor of Public Systems Management and Director,
  Center for Government Studies, Graduate School of Business, Columbia
  University, NY, USA
Professor Hans K. Schneider, Direktor, Energiewirtschaftliches Institut,
  University of Cologne, FRG
Professor T. N. Srinivasan, Indian Statistical Institute, Delhi, and Special
  Adviser, Development Research Center, World Bank, Washington, USA
Mr Christian Stoffaes, Assistant to the Director General of Industry,
  Department of Industry, Paris, France
Dr Márton M. Tardos, Head of Department, Institute for Economic and
  Market Research, Budapest, Hungary
Carlos Tello, ex-Secretary of the Secretaria de Programacion y Presupuesto,
  Mexico
Professor Pedro Uribe, Research Professor, CIDE, Mexico
Professor William Vickrey, McVickar Professor Political Economy, Columbia
  University, NY, USA
Professor Pedro Vusković, Research Professor, CIDE, Mexico

Observer
Mr Peter Ruof, Program Officer, International Division, European and
  International Affairs, the Ford Foundation, New York, USA

Introduction

William J. Baumol
PRINCETON AND NEW YORK UNIVERSITIES

This volume reports the discussion at a conference held in Mexico City in January 1978. A conference on the role of public and private enterprise in mixed economies was first proposed to the International Economic Association by Lord Kaldor. A distinctive feature of any meeting devoted to this subject is the absence of any large body of theory or empirical evidence on which the discussions can be based. Thus, unlike many other conferences sponsored by the IEA, we could not hope to start from an accepted analytic base well known to all the participants. The conference could not hope to take stock of any systematic body of knowledge and devote itself to exploration of the most felicitous directions for its augmentation. Our work, then, had to devote itself to an earlier phase of the analysis of our topic – the determination of the issues and the hypotheses to which future research could usefully address itself. Our agenda, then, was the preparation of an agenda for future students of the subject.

In saying this I should not imply that the functioning of public and private enterprise is entirely *terra incognita*. There exist both theoretical and empirical materials of high quality that relate to the subject and that in some cases go to the heart of the matter. For example, there is an extensive literature on optimal pricing and investment policies for nationalised firms, almost all of it dominated by the pathbreaking work of Marcel Boiteux. There is also some systematic empirical work on the performance of public and private enterprise in particular industries or particular geographic areas. Here, the work of E. S. Savas and Richard Pryke is particularly noteworthy. Finally, there is a body of experience, of knowledge derived by observation in the course of managerial activities, which is waiting to be brought together and organised. In short, the conference dealt with an area about which considerable knowledge has been accumulated, but it seems never to have been brought together and shaped into a coherent body of analysis. Part of the task of the conference, then, was preliminary exploration of this body of information to estimate its dimensions and indicate its character in a way that would be useful to future students of the subject. This goal helped considerably in determining the list of speakers invited to the conference, as is clearly confirmed by the list of contents of this volume.

A second theme ran persistently through our discussions. This was the distinction between the less developed and the industrialised economies. There was a widespread feeling that nationalised enterprise has a special role to play in some stages of industrialisation of a developing economy which is quite different from its potential contribution in an industrialised society. This issue is, of course, of prime importance to a number of Latin American countries as well as to many LDCs throughout the globe and was perhaps a main source of interest to the Mexican sponsors of the conference. A number of the papers consequently addressed themselves to the subject of economic development and its implications for the role of public enterprise.

The shadow that hung over the discussion was, of course, the danger that ideological precommitment would preclude dispassionate analysis and that participants would come determined to preach rather than to study and learn. Inevitably, there were occasional manifestations of this malaise but they were, happily, rare. In most cases dedication and concern were kept distinct from partisanship and the discussions consequently did generate some light and little heat. This volume contains papers which to me were remarkably informative. For example, the descriptions and evaluations of the experiences in Hungary, France, Italy and Germany I found extremely illuminating and in several cases led me to revise a number of views I had held before. The discussion of the kibbutz in Israel strikes me as a model of analysis of the experiences accumulated by a particular type of enterprise. I stop at this point, leaving deliberately incomplete the list of papers I consider particularly valuable, for fear of being driven to replicate the book's table of contents in order to avoid giving offence to anyone.

Finally, I turn to the pleasant task of repaying debts of gratitude. First, I must thank the Programme Committee whose members, Herbert Giersch of the University of Kiel, José Encarnacion of the University of the Philippines, Lord Kaldor of King's College, Janos Kornai of the Hungarian Academy of Sciences, David Levhari of the Hebrew University, Jerusalem, Alan Peacock of the University of York, Rodolfo Becerril Straffon of Colegio Nacional de Economistas, Jorge Tamayo of Colegio Nacional de Economistas, and William Vickrey of Columbia University, were most helpful in their suggestions and were most patient with me during the slow process of programme formulation. Second, it is a pleasure to thank Professor Luc Fauvel and Miss Mary Crook of the Paris office who did everything they could, and more, to facilitate the process of organising the conference. I owe much to their judgement and experience, and the guidance they offered.

Lord Kaldor was a fertile mine of ideas who contributed excitement and substance to both the planning process and the conference itself. Without him it would have been a much duller and less fruitful enterprise.

Our Mexican hosts – the Centro de Investigacion y Docencia Economicas – under the able and energetic leadership of Lic Trinidad Martínez-Tarragó provided the necessary facilities, arranged most effectively for our physical comforts, and, above all, contributed through its own members and via other Mexican participants many valuable ideas and much information about the special problems of enterprise in developing economies. Obviously, the success of the conference is in large part to be ascribed to the work of Mrs Martínez-Tarragó and her associates. The Mexican organisations which played a crucial role for the conference were the Secretaría de Patrimonio y Fomento, which supported the conference; the Colegio Nacional de Economistas, which sponsored it; and the Centro de Investigacion y Docencia Economicas which co-ordinated it.

Finally, I come to two debts, left until last both because of their magnitude and because of my feelings toward the persons to whom they are owed. Professor Dietrich Fischer took upon himself the task of keeping records of and summarising the discussions and in the process making sense and order of their meanderings and convolutions. Only he could have done this so effectively and so quickly. Carolyn Riportella undertook the assembly of the manuscript including editing, communication, diplomacy and handling of crises. She seems to have come out of it unscathed. Certainly, it is thanks to both of them that I escaped undamaged.

The Issues

1 Public or Private Enterprise – the Issues to be Considered

Nicholas Kaldor
PROFESSOR EMERITUS, CAMBRIDGE UNIVERSITY

INTRODUCTORY

The subject matter of this meeting concerns the relative advantages of public and private enterprise in mixed economies.

This problem has a large number of aspects and it is one that cannot be analysed universally without taking into account the framework of political and social institutions, traditions and history, and the stage of economic development, of the particular country to which the analysis is applied.

For good or ill the world is divided into separate states which differ from one another in many things, not just in language, culture and historical image, but also in the nature of their political and social institutions which are a legacy of their past history. It is usual to distinguish among three broad groups of countries: socialist, capitalist and those of the 'third world'.

I. THE SOCIALIST COUNTRIES

In the first group we have the so-called Socialist states or 'centrally-planned economies' such as the USSR and the Peoples' Democracies of Eastern Europe, as well as China and some other countries of South-East Asia. The main feature of these countries is that private enterprise has more or less been abolished except perhaps in agriculture and in small enterprises employing not more than one or two workers. Yet, as one of the papers before us shows, the question of the type of enterprise to be preferred and to be expanded is a live problem even in the case of these economies, since, apart from state enterprises, they contain a large sector of co-operatives which, to a greater or lesser degree, are under the self-management of their worker-members, who are also collectively the owners of the enterprises though they cannot 'withdraw' their share individually. Within limits the members of the co-operatives, directly or through their elected committees, decide on the main policy issues

concerning the type of products to be produced and the types of activity to
which the enterprise should extend, as well as on the share of the current
income which should be ploughed back into the enterprise rather than
distributed. There are no clear principles to determine where the boundary line
between state enterprises and co-operative enterprises should be drawn. The
fact that co-operative enterprise is dominant in agriculture whilst state
enterprise dominates industry and services is the outcome of a historical
development which leaves open the question whether the co-operative type of
enterprise should be extended to the industrial field or state enterprise be
extended to agriculture, or whether it would be best to have both types of
enterprise in all the main sectors of the economy, operating side by side. The
Socialist countries also possess a privately owned sector producing for the
market, but consisting mainly of small enterprises or of people working on their
own account. Here again there is the question whether the limits of private
enterprise should be constrained or loosened and what are the types of
activities or the sectors of the economy for which they are best suited. All these
matters are the subject of continuing discussion.

II. THE DEVELOPED CAPITALIST COUNTRIES

The mixed economies of the rest of the world raise problems of a different
character. The world of the developed capitalist states of Western Europe,
North America and Oceania is one in which private enterprise is dominant but
where some public enterprise is also universal – they necessarily exist in those
institutions which are charged with law and order, defence, public
administration, and so on. In most countries they also extend to education,
health and related social services, communications by road, rail, air and sea
and public utilities. Many of these services could be (and partially are) provided
by private enterprise – for example, education and medical services – others
are a public monopoly mainly on the ground that they are natural monopolies,
or that they can best be provided by a single organisation on a national scale –
such as the provision of post and telecommunications, electricity, gas, railways,
as well as the services which are generally provided by local authorities such as
water supplies, sewage systems, street lighting, etc.

In addition to all these which we might broadly denote under the name of
'infrastructure', there is also in most countries public ownership of a varying
number of industrial enterprises which are either directly or indirectly in
competition with private enterprise, and where the question whether public
enterprise performs better or worse than private enterprise is a matter of
considerable controversy. In some countries (as in France at the present
moment) the expansion of this 'optional' public sector (if I may use that term)
is in the forefront of political discussion.

The individual capitalist countries show a great deal of variation in respect
of the importance of this 'optional' public sector. At one extreme there are
countries which have had a Social Democratic Government for a very long

period and yet refrained from nationalising private enterprise or creating public enterprise in sectors where it would compete with private enterprise. The best example of this is Sweden which had a Socialist Government in power continually for forty-four years, during which the country was brought to the forefront of all others in the matter of the provision of public education and health services, social security, etc., but where the state refrained from either taking over existing firms or creating new public enterprises in competition with private ones. At the opposite end of the scale is Italy, which never had a Socialist or even a Social-Democratic government (though Social-Democrats or Socialists were often part of a coalition dominated by non-Socialists) but where nevertheless the state-owned sector of industry is very large and extensive, as we shall learn from Dr Marsan's paper.

Then we have countries which occupy a mid-position: such as Austria, France and Britain, each of which has an important group of publicly owned enterprises. In the case of Austria, which is perhaps economically the most successful of these countries, the public sector (resulting from large-scale nationalisations immediately after the war) extends to the three largest banks and to the 'heavy industries' – coal, iron, steel, engineering, shipbuilding, oil refineries and the heavy chemicals. The industrial state enterprises are thus complementary to rather than competitive with the private sector and they have provided through their own steady expansion the indispensable base for a large expansion of manufacturing industry in general. (It is not, perhaps, generally known that next to Japan, Austria had the fastest rate of economic growth since the Second World War, and the fastest increase in real income per head – in sharp contrast to the inter-war period when her economy was stagnant through most of the period, with heavy unemployment.) The public sector of Austria, accounting for 16 per cent of all employees, 20 per cent of total output and 25 per cent of exports, is the largest (in relative terms) among the developed countries of the West.[1]

Then there is the case of France and Britain where the nationalised sector of industries is mostly the product of the post-war period. Both in Britain and France the 'infrastructure' services – electricity, gas, railways and air services – were mainly nationalised after the Second World War. In addition, in Britain the first post-war Labour Government nationalised the coal industry and also the steel industry, though the latter was later denationalised by a Conservative government, only to be renationalised again – though with a much narrower scope – by the Labour Government of 1964–70. In addition, the British National Oil Corporation is a recently created state-owned enterprise for the production and distribution of North Sea oil, operating in co-operation with private firms. The Government has also recently nationalised the shipbuilding and aircraft industries. The road haulage industry has also been partially nationalised. In France, in addition to the public utilities – gas, electricity,

---

[1] In Great Britain the nationalised industries and enterprises account for 10 per cent of output and of employment.

railways and air services – nationalisation extended to parts of the oil-producing and refining industry, the chemical industry, the aeronautical construction industry and the motor car industry as well as some of the large banks and insurance companies. Two enterprises discussed in detail in M. Dreyfus's paper are La Régie Renault and Elf-Aquitaine, both of which are in direct competition with privately owned enterprises.

The individual firms which are nationalised in France, like Renault, are mainly the historical result of their having been owned by collaborators with the enemy during the war. In Britain on the other hand there is a group of state-owned firms where state-ownership has much more in common with the state-owned firms of Italy – that is to say, it is public ownership 'by default', occasioned by the insolvency or bankruptcy of important enterprises which would have ceased to exist unless they were taken over by the state; and where their continued existence was considered to be a national interest. This is the case of Rolls Royce, one of the largest aero engine manufacturers of the world, and the motor car firm of British Leyland, which only recently was the largest producer of motor cars in Britain and the only large motor car firm in British ownership.

In both these countries, Britain and France, the question of whether nationalisation should be extended or otherwise is a matter of acute public discussion. In France the parties of the Left are united in wishing to extend nationalisation considerably, the acute difference between the Socialist and Communist parties concerns only how large this extension should be. In Britain on the other hand the professed aim of the Tory party is to restrict the scope of public enterprises, but (apart from the BNOC), as far as I know, they have no concrete plans for the denationalisation of any particular part of the existing public sector.

The evidence concerning the relative efficiency of the public sector varies according to country, period and the particular criteria chosen. In Britain, for example, according to Mr Pryke, the public sector had a clear lead over the private sector in terms of output and productivity growth up to 1968[1] while according to his present paper, the experience was the reverse one for the period after 1968. The same appears to be true of Italy and for much the same reasons: with the deterioration of the economic situation and the acceleration of inflation, the State enterprises became the recipients of open-ended subsidies (mainly to hold down prices) with the usual demoralising effects on management and workers which that involves. There can be no doubt, however, of the success of the public sector in Austria and (at least partially) in France. In Austria the growth of output of the public sector was more than sixfold, and the growth employment threefold in 30 years.[2]

---

[1]See his book, *Public Enterprise in Practice: British Experience over Two Decades* (London, 1971).
[2]For France, cf. the evidence in M. Dreyfus's paper.

III. THE DEVELOPING COUNTRIES

The experience of the countries of Western Europe with public enterprise is, however, only of limited relevance for the question which should be at the centre of our discussions this week – the question, that is, how far the 'third world countries' of Latin America, Asia and Africa should develop their industries through public enterprise or through private enterprise.

This is a highly complex question, and all I can do within the compass of an introductory paper is to indicate which, in my view, are the main considerations relevant to the issue.

I assume that the main aim of all these countries is to have a maximum attainable rate of economic development so as to raise the standard of living of their populations. It is also agreed that such development is not attainable without a large manufacturing industry capable of absorbing a considerable part of the available labour force.

The main issues to be considered are:

(1) *The extent and continuity of development.* Here the argument in favour of nationalisation is that state enterprise can take its decisions on long-run considerations and these are not, or need not, be governed by the profit motive which should not necessarily be regarded as relevant from the point of view of investment decisions.

(2) *National or foreign ownership of large industrial enterprises.* While in principle this is independent of the choice between public or private enterprise, in practice in many of the developing countries, private enterprise means enterprise under the control of foreign countries.

(3) *Efficiency of operation.* Both from a technological and a managerial point of view.

(4) *Long-run effects on the general social structure.* I.e. the degree of equality or inequality in the distribution of wealth and power.

I would like to say something on each of these four points.

(1) Public enterprise and economic development

Private enterprise is actuated by the profit motive. Firms only invest in a particular 'project' when the profit which they expect from it (looked at either in isolation or as part of an interconnected plan of investments) is at least as high as any alternative way of investing the same funds. There are a number of reasons which can be adduced to show that such profit-guided investment will tend to be smaller than the social optimum.

(i) The profitability associated with the project is based on expectations, and as the future is uncertain these may be heavily discounted on account of uncertainty. This is particularly true in cases where it is a question of extending enterprises into a 'new field', either into a new industry which comes into existence as the result of new technical knowledge, or into a country in which an industry, existing elsewhere, has not yet been developed, and where the circumstances surrounding its future operations are uncertain (availability of skilled labour, management supporting public services, etc.). It normally cannot take into account either the static or dynamic economies which result from the expansion of the scale of industrial activities.

(ii) The theory which suggests that the profit criterion secures the best allocation of resources is only applicable under highly unreal assumptions under which the market mechanism operates perfectly, where both the amount of labour available for employment and the amount and the size of funds available for investment are to be taken as given, and where the profit resulting from any particular investment provides a measure of the net addition to the national output which can be attributed to that investment. There are a number of powerful reasons for rejecting such postulates. The additional flow of output which results from a given amount of investment may be very much greater than the stream of profits which result from it, and may be more reasonably measured by the value of the net output stream (or the stream of 'value-added') which results from that investment. When productive capacity is enlarged, it will in general be possible to increase the volume of employment, or to transfer labour from occupations where its net contribution to the national output is very small or zero to a new employment where its productivity is positive and large and where the earnings of labour are also much higher. For these reasons the measure of social profitability should not be the profit that is imputed to the owners of the capital invested in an enterprise, but should comprise also the addition to other types of income generated by the new investment. In principle, therefore, public investment can make use of better criteria for deciding on the amounts and kinds of investment to be undertaken than is the case with private investment.

(iii) This will be true also on account of the fact that when public investment is part of a national plan it is possible to take all kinds of criss-cross effects (or indirect effects) into consideration which would not be possible with private investment. Keynes once said that in the face of complete uncertainty investors generally rely on a convention that the future will be just like the present, and for that reason 'the effects of the existing situation enter, in a sense disproportionately, into the formation of long-term expectations'. Hence capacity is only likely to be created in so far as its use appears to be profitable at the *existing state of demand*. Since the demand for commodities depends on the level of incomes which are generated in production, the additional production generated in the future by the sum of the investment decisions of the present will itself increase the demand for commodities in comparison with the present level – a factor which private investors cannot take into account (or can do so only very imperfectly) since they take their decisions independently of each other. Investment by public enterprise, on the other hand, can take the comprehensive effect of all investments into account in judging the social profitability of any particular investment project. (It should be noted, however, that a State Plan is capable of doing this even when investment is undertaken by private enterprise, as the Japanese example shows. What is required is that there should be a fairly comprehensive state investment plan for industrial development, and that the state should be capable of giving effect to this plan, through the 'administrative guidance' of privately owned firms – provided that, as in Japan, these are native and not foreign-owned firms.)

(2) National or foreign ownership

In principle the question whether a particular country's industries should be developed by national or by foreign enterprise is a different one from whether the enterprise should be privately or publicly run. In some countries (such as Japan or Sweden) the scope for foreign-owned or foreign-controlled enterprises was firmly restricted from the start. However in the developing countries the standards and attainments of education are not normally sufficient for self-generated development of modern industry by native entrepreneurs, since they lack the knowledge and ability to run such enterprises, and/or the willingness to bear the risks. Hence, in practice, public enterprise may be the only alternative to foreign-owned and foreign-controlled private enterprise. It should be pointed out, however, that the absence of the necessary know-how presents an obstacle to the development of industry under public enterprise in the same way as to native private enterprise, i.e. that public enterprises will also be dependent on foreign know-how for their operation, so that in practice it may not make so much difference whether an enterprise is formally owned by the state or whether it is owned by a foreign parent company. It is also argued in favour of a foreign-controlled private enterprise that there will normally be much greater willingness to provide the necessary know-how for efficient operation – both from a technical and a managerial point of view – to a subsidiary than to provide the same in the form of technical assistance for the running of a nationalised enterprise.

In my view this presents a very real dilemma to many developing countries. It is generally agreed that foreign domination of a country's industries leads to highly undesirable results, both socially and politically, and may be creative of tensions, both domestic and international. There are several distinguished economists in the United States (such as Professor Hirschmann) who advocate that the United States should divest itself entirely from the enterprises it owns in Latin American countries, and that this is an essential prerequisite for the development both of more satisfactory international relationships and also for the sound evolution of political institutions within the countries. The best solution might be (a suggestion once made by Myrdal) that the governments of developing countries should aim at the creation of *joint enterprises* in which the developing country would provide the greater part of the capital, while the parent company of the developed country would provide the technical and managerial know-how, and they would both have equal participation in the shares of, and equal say in the running of, the enterprise, but with the proviso that the government of the developing country should have the option of acquiring the foreign parent country's share of the enterprise after a stated number of years.

(3) Efficiency of operation

The strongest argument in favour of private enterprise in developing countries is that it is generally better managed and technically more efficient than public enterprise. In the developed countries, as we have seen, there is no clear presumption on present evidence one way or the other. But it could be argued that the case against public enterprise is stronger on efficiency grounds in the less developed countries where considerations other than fitness and efficiency for a job may play an important role in appointments for the top posts in state-owned enterprises – these may be decided as a matter of political patronage, in the same way as the top posts in government services. (This does not mean that private enterprise is free of such patronage; in the case of enterprises owned or controlled by the family of the founder, family members receive undue preference for top appointments.) However, I think on balance it would be conceded that in less developed countries privately run firms may be more efficient in that they involve less bureaucracy and have a better quality of management than public enterprises.

Both this consideration and the one preceding may argue in favour of private enterprise or of joint private and public enterprises as the main vehicle for development. But it should be kept in mind that any such judgement can only be made on the basis of the existing situation the continuation of which cannot be taken for granted. It is possible for a country to develop native talents to a high degree of technical skill through education in the same way as a number of countries such as Japan or the USSR have done and it is possible also to develop a cadre of administrators both for government services and for the running of public enterprises who would bring to their task the same qualities of selfless devotion and incorruptibility as that of the public servants of many of the developed countries of Western Europe.

(4) Long-run considerations

While it cannot be demonstrated that private enterprise is superior to public enterprise in the majority of cases and the majority of countries, there are reasons for supposing that public enterprise is inferior in terms of efficiency of operation, technical dynamism etc. in countries which are less developed economically and also less mature politically – these two things generally go together.

It would also not be contested by unbiased observers that the establishment of fully fledged socialist states in the Soviet Union and various countries of Eastern Europe has not produced the results which were expected of it, not only by those who were the fervent advocates of a Socialist state, but of the more numerous group of Western intellectuals who looked favourably on the idea of a socialist state, and who hoped that the countries where such régimes were established would provide, through their success, an example for others to follow.

The Soviet Union has now been in existence for sixty years. Very few people would have expected that after such a long period the results should be so meagre – either in terms of an increase in living standards of the working classes or in terms of the creation of a free society in which the powers of compulsion exercised by the state authority have vanished or at least were reduced to a minimum. No one (certainly not Lenin) expected that the 'dictatorship of the proletariat' would last for sixty years or anything like it. Some Communist leaders, like Rosa Luxembourg, questioned the need or the justification for such dictatorship from the start. And no one expected that a Socialist society would retain so many features of the class conflict of capitalist states. (Some of the difficulties and complications that beset the organisation and control of production of a centrally-run socialist state are well brought out in the analysis of Rezsó Nyers and Márton Tardos relating to the economic reforms of Hungary.)

In some fields no doubt the Soviet Union has made enormous strides – in the development of science-based technology in certain fields (mainly those related to defence); in others, however, there is a surprising lack of technical dynamism and continued dependence on western technology to secure industrial progress. Hungary is probably the most successful of the Socialist countries economically and manages to run its affairs with less restriction on individual freedom than is the case with other socialist countries of the Warsaw Pact. Yet in terms of the increase in real income per head over the last 20–25 years Hungary's record with 65 per cent of employees in state enterprises is much inferior to that of neighbouring Austria which is a mixed economy in which the share of employees in state industry is only 16–20 per cent. In the period after the Second World War there can be no doubt that the mixed economies of the type of Austria and Sweden have proved far more successful than the socialist economies of Eastern Europe – irrespective of whether success is judged purely by the criterion of the increase in material living standards, or also by the criterion of the general freedom and contentment of the population, and its effective participation in decision-making.

The greatest problem of the Socialist countries which has not so far been resolved is connected with the centralisation of power which appears to be an inevitable adjunct of universal state ownership. Again, I do not think that many people would dissent from the view that centralisation of power is undesirable in human society, as it generally leads to both moral and material corruption of those who exercise power.

On the other hand, looking at the development of capitalism since the Second World War, one cannot believe that the kind of society which has emerged in the developed countries of the West (and which is imitated with greater or lesser success in the developing countries) is either viable or desirable as the destination of humanity. The concentration on material welfare of the successful modern consumer societies in the West is not only highly wasteful in terms of exhaustible resources, but creates a socially restless and basically frustrated competitive society which fosters a scale of values that moralists and religions throughout human history have regarded as reprehensible. Moreover it also leads, through the process of industrial concentration – which in some of the leading countries of the West has accelerated considerably since the Second World War – to a concentration of power in the hands of the owners and managers of giant enterprises which is no less distasteful than state power: indeed in some ways it is more so, since it is power without responsibility. I cannot see that there is any long-run future for a society where some men are extremely powerful in relation to their fellow men simply because they possess a great deal of money or have the power of dismissal or patronage over a large number of employees. The more capitalism develops into a corporate state dominated by a small number of giant enterprises the less likely it is that it can survive. As biological evolution shows, nature abhors giantism.

It is the power conferred by the possession of wealth, far more than the inequalities of living standards occasioned by it, which makes modern capitalism so unsatisfactory as a method of organisation of human societies. (Capitalist consumption, though highly conspicuous, may not amount to much, at least in the developed countries, in terms of consumption foregone by wage and salary earners.) For that reason, it is at most inconceivable that it should continue to exist indefinitely. Sooner or later it is inevitable that it should give way to, or be replaced by, or develop into, something else. But in the light of the history of the present century it is far less clear than it appeared at the end of the nineteenth century what that something else is going to be. In the light of the experience of the Communist countries of Eastern Europe (perhaps it is too early to come to any definite judgement on the Chinese experiment) it can confidently be predicted that it will not be centralised Socialism that provides the alternative.

IV. WORKERS' CO-OPERATIVES

There is a small but growing group of people who put their faith in workers' co-operatives operating through the framework of a regulated market economy as the best solution to the problem of the economic organisation of human societies.

There are a number of isolated examples suggesting that it is possible to run enterprises under workers' control and/or ownership, and that this form of organisation avoids the main defects of both capitalist enterprise and of a centrally directed Socialist economy. For it secures a high degree of decentralisation in decision-making, and avoids the conflict of interest between workers and capitalists or workers and management – which events have shown can be the plague of state enterprise in Socialist states or of the public sector of mixed economies as well as of capitalist private enterprise. Among the Socialist countries, Yugoslavia alone has been entirely restructured along co-operative lines. The intention has been to create a system of 'self-management' of business undertakings by their workers and this has recently been extended to include the separate control of 'work units' within an enterprise. However, the workers are not the owners of the enterprises – the initiation of a co-operative is the task of the local authorities and the workers have no beneficial interest in the assets of the enterprises. Hence under that system the material incentive to develop through reinvestment of profits is a weak one. Moreover, it is not clear how far in the case of Yugoslavia the decentralisation of decision-making in the economic sphere has led to an abatement in the exercise of centralised power in the political sphere.

Co-operatives exist in the agricultural sector of most Socialist countries, and in at least one, Hungary, they have proved more successful in improving productivity and real earnings than State-operated manufacturing industry. Agricultural co-operatives extend also in the field of banking in a number of countries where production is in the hands of individual private enterprises. The co-operative Credit Agricole of France is the largest bank in Europe and the third largest bank in the world. In Germany also co-operative banking has made great strides since the Second World War through the Bank fuer Gemeinwirtschaft. In Britain, under the recent Labour Government some industrial enterprises have been rescued from extinction through the creation of workers' co-operatives as in the motor bicycle factory, Meriden, and the Kirkby engineering factory. These enterprises now appear to have reached a stage at which they can operate without loss; and in both cases they secured the full identification of the workers with the success of the enterprise which ended demarcation disputes or union squabbles which mar the rest of British industry. There is also the much publicised Basque experiment at Mondragon (near Bilbao in Spain) started by a Basque priest, Jose Maria Anizmendi (who died in 1976). Thanks to him, fifty-eight industrial co-operatives have been created in the last twenty years with a combined turnover of roughly $300 million a year and a labour force of nearly 14,500.

And last but not least there is the experience of the Kibbutzim of Israel going back over fifty years which shows (as Professor Barkai's paper relates) that co-operative enterprise, given the right ideological motivation, is capable of producing results in terms of output and productivity growth which are comparable with the best results of capitalist enterprise in manufacturing and not just in agriculture.

In comparison with the huge enterprises of modern industry, publicly or privately owned, the size of most workers' co-operatives is very small. Experience also tends to suggest that the effective involvement of workers in the management of enterprises – which is essential to their success – is only possible when the number of workers involved in decision-making is not too large. This fact alone makes it improbable that workers' co-operatives could effectively displace other forms of enterprise within a measurable period of time. There is also the fact that this type of enterprise appears more promising when it emerges in replacement of other types of enterprise which have failed – whether capitalist (as in Britain) or Socialist (as in Yugoslavia). Thus even if co-operative enterprises were to be regarded, *faute de mieux*, as the most promising ultimate solution of the problem of organising human societies, this is not likely to obviate the need of developing countries having to choose in the interim stages between public ownership or private enterprise or of forms of joint control of the state and private interests.

Discussion of Lord Kaldor's Paper

Dr Pryke said that one advantage of public enterprises mentioned by Lord Kaldor was that in planning they could take a longer term perspective than private enterprises. But this was not necessarily always an advantage. For example, the British Government tried to jump ahead of the United States in aircraft technology with the Concorde. But the result was an unmitigated financial disaster. Similarly, British investments in coalmines in the expectation that demand would pick up in the future were probably not advisable. There was consistent overoptimism in governments' forecasts of the future.

Professor Vickrey pointed out that politicians did not always use a longer time horizon in their decisions than managers of private enterprises. For example, previous mayors of New York City had made settlements with labour unions which were very generous in terms of pension plans, and such practices had shifted financial problems to their successors. He also said that politicians generally had a taste for grandiose projects, and had long-term visions when it came to public works, but adopt a rather short-term perspective in regard to their financing.

Professor Srinivasan agreed that the typical time horizon of politicians is the time until the next election. But public enterprises were normally managed by bureaucrats with a relatively secure position, who could take a longer term perspective. But it was doubtful whether managers of public enterprises were more successful in forecasting the future than those of private enterprises.

Professor Uribe said that discount rates used depended more on the size of an enterprise than whether it was in public or private hands. He suggested that very large private corporations (such as IBM or General Motors) used low discount rates, like large public enterprises, while smaller enterprises whose lifespan was more uncertain tended to use higher discount rates in their financial calculations.

Mrs Martínez-Tarragó mentioned that Kaldor had made a distinction between the role of public enterprises in developed and less developed countries. But she saw no basic difference between the two cases though their role may differ in degree with differences in the level of development. In both cases, public enterprises may be established for political or economic reasons or both, the purpose being the pursuit of social goals, in the absence of or by competition with private enterprises.

Lord Kaldor replied to Pryke that it was true that a long-term perspective could sometimes lead to mistakes, such as the Concorde. But without a long-term view nothing much would happen at all. He quoted Pigou as having said in 1931 under the impact of the great depression, 'When in doubt, don't contract – expand'. He said he would like to reformulate this proposition as 'when in doubt, *do* something'. He stressed that the alternative to an investment project was usually not investment of the same money in some other project, but no investment at all. The state has the capacity to invest in risky ventures and to set up 'pilot enterprises' (*entreprises pilotes*) in areas where private capital is too timid. He admitted that this involved some risks, but said that the alternative was usually to do nothing. In answer to the question raised by Mrs Martínez-Tarragó, he said that public enterprises in developing countries often suffered from growth pains such as political patronage, or were not professionally led. He quoted the paper of Mr Sacristán, Jr. in which he had said that some public enterprises had failed through corruption. As a remedy he proposed the training of a core of administrators, as France had done in her 'Grandes Écoles,' who were beyond corruption, selfless, devoted and competent.

Professor Baumol concluded the discussion by saying that one could find examples for almost everything. There were cases of intelligent foresight and lack of foresight, efficiency and inefficiency, in both private and public enterprises. One could not generalise from examples. He stressed that the central purpose of the discussion should be to find mechanisms which could insure that the long-term perspective was properly taken into account. He was sceptical about the creation of perfect, incorruptible human beings and saw a solution rather in institutional mechanisms on which one could rely.

Part One
Less Developed Countries
and the Role of Public Enterprise

2 Development Planning in a Mixed Economy

T. N. Srinivasan[1]
DEVELOPMENT RESEARCH CENTER, WORLD BANK
AND INDIAN STATISTICAL INSTITUTE

I. INTRODUCTION

The term 'mixed economy' can be defined in several different ways, depending on the criterion used: organisation of production, resource allocation or ownership of means of production. Thus an economy in which *production* activity is carried on in both private and public units is a 'mixed' economy. However, once we admit the provision of services in the set of production activities, every economy in the world where there is a government becomes a mixed economy by this definition, though the extent of public production (say, as measured by the share of value added by public sector in national income) varies between economies. Henry Tulkens (1976) defines a mixed economy as an organisation of society in which the resource allocation decisions belong *in part* to the private domain and are determined by personal tastes and opportunities and *in part* to the public domain in which groups of individuals take decisions that affect other individuals who are nevertheless bound by these decisions.[2] This too, is not altogether satisfactory since a class of decisions which are private in everyday usage, such as decisions in a household or a family, become similar to public decisions according to this definition, since these are taken either by groups of elders of the household or by the household head and all members of the household are bound by them. By the criterion of

[1] The views expressed are personal and not necessarily those of the World Bank and the Indian Statistical Institute. I wish to thank Montek Ahluwalia, Mrinal Datta Chaudhuri, John P. Lewis, Bagicha Minhas, Suresh Tendulkar and Oktay Yenal for their valuable comments on an earlier draft.

[2] Tulkens attempts by this definition to distinguish unambiguously the private and public components of a mixed economy and to develop a set of behavioural and institutional characterisations of the public sector that will serve as building blocks of a theory of mixed economy that will be comparable to the Arrow–Debreu theory of the neo-classical private ownership economy. This appears to be a very ambitious venture and certainly it is still too early to claim much progress.

ownership of means of production, a mixed economy is one in which there are substantial amounts of both private and public ownership (Grossman, 1974). To the extent that organisation of production is determined by the ownership of means of production, there is a substantial overlap between the two criteria. However, ownership differences by themselves may be unimportant, if the criteria as well as the mechanism by which the use of these assets is determined are broadly similar.[1] For instance, a price-regulated private monopoly and a state monopoly may take the same decisions regarding the operation of the enterprise, as long as the state tries to achieve the same objective (and faces the same production conditions) whether through price regulation or through state production. Thus the fact that the enterprise is privately owned in one case and publicly owned in the other makes little difference in its operation. It does make a difference, however, in that the operating surpluses accrue to the private owners in the former case and to the state treasury in the latter. Even this difference disappears if the state has 100 per cent profit taxation as a feasible policy instrument. This suggests that in the 'ideal' case in which the state has in its policy arsenal enough (in an appropriate sense) instruments so that it can achieve its objective in a way that does not distort incentives and disincentives to private decision-making, the 'mixed' character of an economy under any of the above definitions raises no major analytical or policy issues. It is precisely because the 'ideal' is unattainable in most real world economies that interesting analytical and policy issues do arise.

At this stage, it may be worth noting that a 'mixed' economy is often said to serve a political purpose, above and beyond its economic performance. Thus, in a plural society dedicated to democratic values, the diffusion of 'economic power' that goes with the mixed economy acts as a check against any tendencies towards concentration of 'political power' that might subvert the democratic system. In the documents and pronouncements of politicians in power of the Indian Five-Year Plan, this has often been claimed as a virtue of the Indian mixture of public and private sectors.[2] Of course, a case for 'capitalism' is often made on the grounds that it promotes political freedom.[3] However, the political implications of an economic system (capitalist, socialist, mixed, etc.) will not be pursued here except in so far as they have some relevance for economic planning.

In this chapter, it is not proposed to offer yet another definition of a mixed economy. Instead, the following 'facts' about the nature of the economy and its planning will be assumed. By failing to define the term explicitly, one runs the risk of implicitly defining it to mean simultaneously several different things,

---

[1] Grossman's comparative approach to economic systems in terms of performance criteria and social values is perhaps the most operational, though as he himself recognises, very often some economic systems tend to attach values, both to means of achieving certain ends and to those ends. This may arise because the distinction between ends and means may be blurred either in an objective sense or in the perceptions of the public as well as policy-makers.

[2] Almost every five-year plan document has some words to this effect.

[3] Grossman (1974), *op.cit.*, p. 13.

such as mixtures of public and private sectors, of perfect and less than perfect markets, of modes of production and even the so-called 'dual economy'. This risk is unavoidable since all these are present to some degree in any real world developing country.

Supply and demand generation

The production of goods and services will be assumed to take place in units that may be owned by individuals, families, partnerships, shareholders with limited liability, workers, or local, state and central authorities. The management of the unit, i.e. authority to make decisions regarding its operation as well as its expansion or contraction through investment and disinvestment, may be in the hands of the owners, family heads, professional managers, under the control of shareholder representatives, workers' representatives or bureaucrats with or without managerial and professional experience. The production activities will include foreign trade activities as well. The ownership and the management characteristics of a unit will determine the process by which demands for intermediate goods, for primary factors, and for investment (including inventories) are generated. This leaves out private and public consumption as well as export demand. Private, i.e. household consumption decisions (except over any publicly provided goods and services) are taken by households. Public consumption as well as provision of goods and services to households on a non-market basis are determined by public authorities at various levels. Of course, export demand originates abroad.

Broadly speaking, in such an economy, the public sector is of significance in large-scale manufacturing industry, transport and public utilities. While the mode of production in the private sector manufacturing industry is likely to be essentially capitalistic, in agriculture, semi-feudalistic, co-operative as well as capitalistic modes will often co-exist. However, government intervention in some form or other takes place in virtually every sector. The policy problem of the state in such an economy has been described as one of trying to achieve socialistic objectives subject to the constraints of an essentially capitalistic economy.

Planning

The planning task in this economy is assumed to consist of drawing up, essentially, an investment plan for the economy for a period, usually of five years. This so-called five-year plan may be part of a long-term perspective plan covering a period of fifteen to twenty years and annual plans may be drawn up for each of the five years of the plan. Though the investment plan will, in principle, cover the entire economy, the state or public authorities will have direct control only over that part of the plan relating to the public sector. While the investment or capacity creation part of the plan is basic to it, the plan will also usually elaborate production targets for crucial sectors, foreign trade targets in respect to major categories of exports and imports, as well as targets for some major items of public consumption. The plan, at least on paper, will be feasible in that, first, the targets of production and imports will be consistent with the end use planned for the same commodities; second, there is macro-consistency such that planned investment in the aggregate equals domestic savings plus planned capital inflow; third, the sectoral pattern of investment and its time phasing is consistent with the production targets, so that capacity utilisation ratios stay within feasible and desired limits. The feasibility of the plan may have been achieved, in part by 'norm forcing', i.e. by assuming optimistic performance in respect to productivity growth, raising domestic savings, ability to raise exports or save on imports and so on. The question whether the plan is intended to be 'optimal', i.e. whether it maximises some objective or welfare function subject to feasibility constraints, is deferred for later discussion.

Public policy instruments

The instruments of public policy will consist of: taxes (and subsidies), quotas, public sector production, procurement from private production and distribution, public investment and consumption, issuing of fiat money and control of monetary sector, issuing of permits (licences) and prohibitions of various kinds. As stated earlier, the structure, domain of operation and the effectiveness of these instruments of public policy, as well as the cost of acquiring information, are assumed to preclude a 'command economy' (Grossman, 1974). Implicit in all this is a political framework that is pluralistic with several layers of authority and which can be characterised, if not as a full-fledged representative democracy, at least as a non-dictatorship that permits orderly expression of political and economic grievances.

The rest of the paper is organised as follows. In Section II some broad issues of development strategy are discussed, with particular reference to India. Section III takes up the planning of agricultural development to be followed by planning of the industrial, and foreign trade and service sectors in Sections IV and V, respectively. The final section offers some concluding observations. Though, in some ways, a better organisation of the discussion would have been to separate the analytical issues involved in planning in a mixed economy (as well as the nature of research needed to clarify them) from the major issues of planning in an actual economy, i.e. the Indian economy, it seems more instructive to raise the analytical issues as and when they arise in a natural context. Since writing the paper, I became aware of Professor Tsuru's (1968) stimulating paper on India. His discussion is similar in many aspects.

II. PLAN FORMULATION

Only in the cloud-cuckoo land of computable multi-sector, inter-temporal, optimising models of development planning do 'optimal' plans emerge, as it were, out of the ashes of computer cards.[1] In the formulation of a plan in a real world mixed economy, purely economic considerations play only a part, the political considerations being far too important to be ignored altogether. Indeed, the objectives and goals of planning as well as the means of implementation of a plan once it is formulated reflect the political realities of the society. These realities reveal themselves as constraints on the use of public instruments and create a gap between 'rhetoric' and 'reality' or equivalently between 'declared' and 'revealed' objectives.

A view of the role of planners in a mixed economy would be to suggest that they serve two important purposes. First, just as ideal civil servants are supposed to do, they accept the premises and goals of their political superiors in power, lay bare their economic implications and map out the feasible economic policy space in which the politicians can attempt to implement them. Second, the planners themselves may take part, perhaps indirectly, in the political process so that the political support to desirable economic policies is strengthened and opposition to them weakened. Indeed, if the expertise of the planners commands respect, the political leaders in power can use it to diffuse opposition.

It is trite to observe that there is unlikely to be a single overall objective to planning. The problem is not just that the objectives of planning will often include – besides income growth – employment, reduction of inequality, regional balance, etc., etc. In principle, the trade-offs in 'production', so to speak, among these could be quantified.[2] If one were to accept the idea that an optimal plan is one that maximises a planner's welfare function, one could attempt to arrive at the trade-offs among these objectives in the planner's welfare function, as for instance Raiffa (1969) tries to do. But once it is granted that more than one set of preferences are involved, the question of aggregation of preferences arises. There is by now a vast literature on this and the interested reader is referred to Sen (1977). It is fair to say, however, that as yet this literature has little to offer to the practice of planning.

Early development plans, such as India's first five-year plan, placed per capita real income growth at the centre of the planning exercise. Subsequent plans added additional goals, such as employment generation, self-reliance in the sense of being able to pursue the development goals without concessionary foreign assistance, provision of a minimum standard of living to the entire population by a certain specified time point, etc. By and large, a development strategy that was evolved under the influence of Professor P. C. Mahalanobis during the second five-year plan has continued to hold sway with minor variations. Two aspects of this strategy have received most critical attention in India and abroad. These were the importance given to the development of

---

[1]The state-of-the-art of development planning models as of 1973 is described in Blitzer *et al.* (1975). The paper by Janos Kornai in this volume is particularly relevant for the present discussion.

[2]Some of the computable planning models have been successfully used for this purpose. Perhaps this is their greatest strength.

domestic capital goods industry and to the public sector. By and large, a substantial portion of the projected heavy industrial production was reserved for the public sector. Import substitution was the dominant factor in the industrial development promoted under this strategy, both in the public and private sectors.

Space does not permit a detailed discussion of the Indian development strategy except to note the connection between the 'mixed' character of the Indian economy and the strategy. Minhas (1974a, 1974b) provides a perceptive discussion of many of the issues. Apart from ideological preference for the public sector, planners believed that (i) private investors may demand a higher risk premium for investment in some industries than would be socially justified; (ii) the scale of investment effort in heavy industries may be beyond the capital-raising capacity of the private sector; (iii) the public sector, through appropriate price policy for its output, will generate profits for further investment in the economy; (iv) by production and/or distribution of crucial inputs, the state will be able to control the private sector and (v) the employment and wage policy of the public sector can be directed to benefit disadvantaged groups in the society. These considerations were additions to the standard 'market' failure issues relating to pervasive economies of scale, externalities, etc. It is worth noting that, while in principle one can think of alternative policies other than public production (as for instance interest subsidies for risky investment, loans to private investors, taxation of profits and incomes, wage subsidisation, etc.), the fact that public production was chosen as the policy to be pursued indicates a perceived limit to the use of the other policy instruments to the required extent. This is not to suggest that such perceptions were necessarily based on the objective circumstances nor can it be argued *ex post facto* that the public sector enterprises did, in fact, achieve all the objectives for which they were set up.

It will not be a distortion to argue that the Indian development planners (and indeed planners in similar mixed economies) have preferred (i) direct allocational controls to indirect controls, such as intervention in market price determination through taxes and subsidies and (ii) intervention in income generation by influencing the pattern and mode of production to attempts at redistributing income through taxes and transfers. While the limited efficacy of fiscal instruments may have been the cause of this preference, given that the actual beneficiaries of direct interventions were not the ones for whom they were ostensibly intended, it can be argued that this preference reflects the interests of the political power structure. A more charitable view would attribute it in part to the unrealistic expectation that direct interventions will be effectively enforced by an incorruptible bureaucracy (and that, indeed, all economic agents could be made to put the 'social interest' as perceived by the planners ahead of their private interests), in part to an exaggeration of the limits to intervention through the market and, of course, in part to the political and ideological considerations. Regardless of the origins of such a preference, the fact that it exists has important implications for planning in a mixed economy. These are understood better in the context for sectoral planning, to which we now turn.

III. PLANNING AGRICULTURAL DEVELOPMENT

Agriculture is one of the most important sectors in the densely populated, less developed countries. It often accounts for more than half of the value added and employs more than sixty per cent of the labour force. Most of the wage goods, some of the major exports and quite a few of the raw materials for industry originate from agriculture in these economies. It is also one of the most difficult to tackle in planning, as is evident from the experience of Soviet and Eastern European agriculture. Production often takes place under a bewildering variety of organisational forms, depending upon the crop, region, history and tradition. In the case of some export crops, such as tea, coffee, rubber, etc., a significant proportion of output is produced by plantations that are organised like industrial firms, often owned by foreigners. Most other crops, and in particular food crops, are usually produced by individual farms.

In India, the national commission on agriculture (1975) that looked into the development of agriculture, stated that the agrarian economy of India represented a transient and unstable equilibrium among three modes of production: (i) self-cultivation by large farmers, primarily based on a capitalist mode of production, with employment of wage labour, capital, machinery and scientific inputs, with the landowner acting as the entrepreneur and with output intended for sale; (ii) self-cultivation by small and medium-landowning peasants, with production based on family labour and for on-farm consumption, though the hiring of labour and market sales by larger peasants was not ruled out; (iii) feudal and semi-feudal landlordism, consisting of vast areas of land under cultivation by sharecroppers of various kinds. The commission then went on to state that, among three alternative paths of development, i.e. encouraging privately owned capitalist farms, co-operative and collective farming with no private ownership in land and a peasant-proprietor agriculture supplemented, where necessary, by co-operative and collective institutions, the third alternative is the most desirable course of development for Indian agriculture. This is not the occasion to examine this recommendation critically. It is clear, however, that given the existing structure, planning agricultural development is no easy task. It is further complicated in India by a provision in the federal constitution that assigns the task of development of agriculture to the individual state governments.

The major aims of an agricultural development plan would consist of: (i) expanding the production base; (ii) increasing the productivity of inputs through technical change; (iii) ensuring that the pattern of production and end use of output conforms to 'plan'; and (iv) encouraging socially desirable (and avoiding socially undesirable) income distributional effects. The production base can be expanded by investing in land, labour and capital used in agriculture. Investing in land involves bringing new land under cultivation and improving currently cultivated areas through provision of irrigation and drainage facilities, levelling and contour bunding, etc. As is well known, given the large proportion of small holdings and the fact that even a small holding often consists of a substantial number of even smaller scattered parcels, the returns to investment in land will be lower than they could have been had this situation not prevailed. To some extent, the market acts as a partial corrective in that individual owners lease in and lease out land to each other so that each operates a contiguous area. However, the externalities and scale economies involved call for community action. Further, it has been argued since the days of Marshall that if the land is cultivated by a sharecropper, he may not invest in land or use other inputs to the optimal extent unless the costs are shared by the landlord in the same proportion as output.

Major irrigation works built with public funds often remain under-utilised for a long time because the field channels that take the water to individual holdings are often not built, either because the owner of the holding has little investable resources of his own and has little or no access to the credit market, or he has little incentive to build because of lack of awareness of the potentials of irrigated agriculture. To the extent that some inappropriability is involved in the construction of field channels, the absence of institutions for collective action may explain the failure to construct them. Worse still, the irrigation charges by the state often involve substantial subsidies, the benefits of which accrue to the larger and richer peasant who is better able to make use of the facility. Privately owned irrigation facilities, such as tubewells, etc., usually account for a sizeable chunk of irrigation investment. These are often encouraged by subsidised credit, fuel and power, the benefits again accruing to the richer peasants. However, to the extent that some forms of minor irrigation works can be constructed mostly with labour, the smaller holders often construct them with their family labour. For this and other reasons, in India the smaller holdings have a larger proportion of their area irrigated than larger holdings. Of course, if the state can enact and enforce meaningful land reform, many of these difficulties will disappear. In the absence of land reform, taxation of land or income from agriculture can be a redistributive measure. But, at least in India, the rural landlord-based political power structure has not enforced land reform legislation and has prevented the imposition of any significant taxes on agricultural income and wealth.

Expansion of the agricultural labour force, even beyond what is already taking place through population growth, is inappropriate in an economy such as India's. The problem is one of better and fuller utilisation of the labour force. In this context, the issue whether the technical advance that goes under the name 'Green Revolution' has resulted in 'excessive' mechanisation becomes relevant and will be taken up below. To the extent that better utilisation of labour and land involves education in a broad sense (including formal schooling, acquiring functional literacy or dissemination and absorption of relevant knowledge), public sector activities in education and agricultural extension have to be examined for their efficiency as well as adequacy. The literature on private versus social returns to various forms of education, and indeed whether some types of education serve no purpose other than signalling or screening, is now vast.[1] Some have suggested that in India social returns to primary (higher) education are higher (lower) than private returns.[2] Again, to the extent that any externalities inherent in this can, in principle, be internalised through appropriate tax/subsidy schemes, the fact that in practice they are not internalised may either reflect the limits or political considerations of such schemes. In fact, rural primary schools often serve larger areas than urban schools and they are less well-equipped, both in terms of teachers and teaching materials. Apart from this, the resources devoted to agricultural extension services appear to have been inadequate to the task imposed on them in India.

Turning now to the so-called Green Revolution and the associated technical change, it has been claimed, and rightly, that these innovations are scale neutral, in the sense that they do not confer any advantage to the larger farmers as compared to the small – the per hectare yield from the use of the newer varieties of seed is the same in large and small farms as long as inputs used per hectare are the same. But institutions may not be scale neutral – the access to credit markets, irrigation water or administratively allocated inputs may be biased in favour of the larger farms. It has also been suggested that the new varieties, by reducing the duration for which a crop occupies land, have made it possible to increase the number of crops grown each year on a plot of land. This has had the consequence of increasing the demand for labour at certain periods in a year, when a crop has to be harvested and the same land prepared for sowing the next crop within a few weeks. In addition, the opportunity cost of raising fodder for bullocks has risen because of the possibility of increasing income through crop rotation that substitutes grain crops for fodder. It is alleged that these factors have encouraged the bigger landlords to mechanise these operations and the same machinery, once acquired, has been used to displace labour in other seasons of the year when the labour availability is not a constraint. Also, the increased return to self-cultivation, once the new technology is introduced, has resulted in eviction of tenants and sharecroppers, a phenomenon not without historical precedent.

While the burden of the above argument is that the larger landholders have the incentives and means to introduce new yield-raising techniques, it has been argued (Bhaduri, 1972) that in a semi-feudal agriculture where the landlord serves as moneylender and trader as well, he will be reluctant to introduce yield-raising innovations if the added income to the tenant will make him less dependent on the landlord for credit. It has been shown elsewhere that the argument as stated is false (Srinivasan, 1978a). Nevertheless, an important issue for theoretical and empirical research remains. It is the task of developing a theory of inter-related, imperfectly competitive markets with price rigidities and rationing and testing it empirically.

[1] See Arrow (1973), Spence (1973) and Schultz (1972).
[2] See Blaug *et al.* (1969).

There are a number of other issues that bear on the spread of the green revolution, such as its crop specificity (the new varieties relate mainly to the two major cereal crops, rice and wheat), and the limitations on its geographical coverage arising out of the fact that not all areas have the potential for controlled irrigation, so necessary for benefiting from the new technology. With limited geographical mobility of labour and ability to tax the beneficiaries of the green revolution, adequate limitations on the spread of the new technology constrain agricultural planning from the point of view of regional balance and equity.

There is another related area that is beginning to be researched, and that is the nature of the incentive structures underlying some traditional market or exchange arrangements. For instance, equal sharing of output by landlords and tenants has been observed in sharecropping contracts under a wide variety of circumstances. Hurwicz and Shapiro (1977) have shown that as long as the landlord cannot observe (and hence enforce) the intensity of the sharecropper's effort, a 50 per cent share offered to the sharecropper *maximises* the landlord's income under some plausible assumptions about the sharecropper's income-leisure preferences. Of course, other aspects of crop-sharing, such as its sharing of production risks or enabling of the landlord (implicitly) to hire the labour of the sharecropper's family members who may not be available for (explicit) wage labour, have been discussed in the literature.[1] All these arrangements are manifestations of institutional adjustments for the absence of markets or their imperfect functioning. But they do constrain the planning process, in so far as state intervention in the existing institutional set-up either in a partial way, or, worse still, with inadequate understanding of the multiple roles played by these institutions, may and often does fail to achieve the objectives of such intervention.

A few words on the consumption side of agricultural output are in order. Governments often procure (by compulsory levy or other means) food grains from producers or traders, at a price below the market clearing price that would have prevailed in the absence of such procurement, and distribute such food at subsidised prices to poor urban consumers. The balance of food grains left with the producers or traders is sold in an open market. It can be shown that under certain assumptions such a policy could raise the weighted average of the procurement and open market price to a level above the equilibrium price with absence of procurement, thus, in effect, amounting to taxation (implicitly) of rich consumers to subsidise both *producers* and poor urban consumers of food (Ahluwalia and Srinivasan, 1978). Presumably the fact that government opts for procurement rather than explicit tax/subsidy policies implies that the latter are infeasible or have other (undesired) effects. There are interesting and important issues relating to stabilisation (prices, incomes, revenues, etc.) policies. It will take us too far to discuss them here.

The development literature has devoted considerable theoretical and

---

[1] See Stiglitz (1974), and Bell and Zusman (1976).

empirical attention to issues relating to rural-urban migration, in response to a fixed minimum wage exceeding the market clearing wage in the urban (manufacturing) sector. This is again a problem that arises from the 'mixed' character of an economy which permits occupational and residential choice to individuals. The problem is diminished, for instance, in China where rural-urban migration without state permission is prohibited, though some observers have reported such migration even there. Given that the problem exists, its effect has to be taken into account in planning.

There is an important political task with enormous economic implications in agricultural planning in countries such as India. While a long line of distinguished economists have identified the labour surplus in such economies as a potential for capital formation, the efforts to realise this potential have not occurred on a large scale because of administrative and resource constraints. Also, in so far as those employed in such projects are not adequately compensated in the form of wages, they should have a role in the choice of the assets to be created with their labour and in sharing the benefits accruing from the assets. Otherwise, an adequate supply of labour will not be forthcoming. The importance of the participation of such groups in the decision-making aspects of planning in a mixed economy cannot be overemphasised.

In some states of India there have been attempts at utilisation of the labour surplus through what are known as employment guarantee schemes, in which those who want work are guaranteed employment at a wage somewhat below the ruling market wage. However, it appears that the projects in which the surplus labour is employed are not often chosen with sufficient thought to enable them to yield productive assets. Since these schemes have been in operation in limited areas and for not too long a period, it is too early to attempt an evaluation.

IV. INDUSTRIAL AND FOREIGN TRADE PLANNING

We have already referred to the fact that establishment of production capacity in the public sector in some industries has been a feature of the development plans of many mixed economies including that of India. The instruments of policy used in India in an attempt to make the private sector industrial investment conform to the plan have been industrial capacity licensing and almost-automatic protection against foreign competition through a system of import quotas and tariffs. The licensing system has two main objectives: first, to ensure that no more capacity than targeted in the plan was established in any industry and, second, to prevent concentration of economic power in large concerns. The import licensing reinforced the industrial licensing by ensuring that imports were disallowed in areas where adequate domestic production capacity had been created. The exchange control and allocation system ensured that exporters surrendered their foreign exchange earnings to the authorities at the official exchange rate and foreign exchange was allotted only to import licence holders and other permitted users. With local variations, such a system existed and continues to exist in a number of developing countries.

The economic consequences of such industrialisation and foreign trade regimes have been extensively documented in a set of studies sponsored by the Organisation for Economic Co-operation and Development (OECD) and the National Bureau of Economic Research (NBER).[1] The picture that emerges from all these studies is that of high-cost, inefficient industrialisation, with a bias against export promotion and in favour of import substitution. The NBER studies also document some attempts at liberalisation, many of them unsuccessful.

From the point of view of the present chapter, two developments are worth noting. The first is the literature on the theory and practice of project evaluation or appraisal.[2] The other is theoretical and empirical work on effective protection and the related concept of domestic resource cost of earning (or saving) foreign exchange. While in the development literature, in particular that on planning models, the concept of a 'shadow' price of a commodity or resource as distinct from its market price has had a long history; the project appraisal literature explicitly places the computation and use of shadow prices in a mixed economy context. In other words, the problem can be posed as follows: given that an initial equilibrium of an economy consisting of private and public sectors is characterised by non-removable distortions (such as tariffs, quotas, factor price differentials, etc.), and an investment project is being considered (either in the public sector or for licensing in the private sector), how should the social worth of the project be evaluated? This amounts to asking (i) how the inputs (including primary factors) and outputs of the project ought to be valued given their domestic market prices are affected by the distortions and (ii) to the extent that other policies for redistributing income once accrued are not feasible, so that the acceptance (or rejection) of a project has distributive consequences, how should these be reflected in the evaluation of the project? The literature on welfare economics, while recognising the existence of the second question has avoided it, sweeping it away by assuming that lump-sum and other non-distorting transfers between individuals are feasible. On the other hand, the project appraisal literature has not always clearly recognised the conceptual distinction between the two questions. A number of recent contributions to the theory of optimum taxation (surveyed by Mirrlees, 1977) have, however, considered situations in which optimal lump-sum transfers are assumed to be infeasible.

The literature on effective rates of protection (ERP) and domestic resource costs (DRC) of earning or saving foreign exchange, strictly speaking, is

---

[1] The OECD studies on Industrialisation covered Brazil, India, Mexico, Pakistan, Taiwan and the Philippines. The NBER studies on Foreign Trade Regimes covered Brazil, Chile, Colombia, Egypt, Ghana, India, Israel, South Korea, the Philippines and Turkey. For the India studies in these two series, see Bhagwati and Desai (1970) and Bhagwati and Srinivasan (1975).

[2] See Little, I. and Mirrlees, J., (1974), and United Nations Industrial Development Organisation (1972).

addressed to the problem of resource allocation in production. By ranking activities according to their rates of effective protection or, equivalently, their domestic resource costs, an attempt is made to infer the resource-pull effects of the system of existing distortions or any proposed change in them. Only under a rather restrictive set of assumptions do such inferences seem to hold.[1] In spite of its theoretical weakness, some have advocated the use of ERPs (or DRCs) for project appraisal and choice in a mixed economy. Even if the theoretical weaknesses were not there, it is clear that this method of project appraisal addresses itself only to the first of the two questions raised above.

The vast literature on the theory (and practice) of multi-level planning as well as on decentralisation procedures and algorithms has not been touched upon here, for the reason that, as yet, its practical relevance to problems of planning in a mixed, less developed economy is not apparent, though undoubtedly it has had an impact on recent economic reform in the centrally planned economies of eastern Europe. For the same reason, recent work on the theory of labour-managed economies (Dreze, 1976) is not considered here.

V. PLANNING EDUCATION, HEALTH AND OTHER SERVICE SECTORS

It is well known that externalities of various kinds abound in the provision of education, health and sanitation services. A possible divergence between private and social returns to investment in education has already been mentioned. There is a significant complementarity among health, sanitation, water supply and nutrition programmes. In the absence of a safe water supply and control over communicable diseases, improving the nutritional status of the population may be ineffective and costly. And in the absence of adequate nutrition, resistance to diseases will be lower and the cost of curative health programmes higher. Concern about some of these problems has led some to propose a so-called Basic Human Needs Approach to development planning. Some conceptual, measurement and policy issues relating to this approach have been discussed elsewhere (Srinivasan, 1978b).The constraints imposed by the 'mixed' character of an economy in planning these sectors can be illustrated by the example of attempts to improve the nutritional status of children of school age by supplementary feeding at school. This has often led merely to a substitution of food that the child would have been fed at home by the food eaten at school, with little or no gain in nutritional status of the child. Thus, in the absence of means to affect the (private) intra-family allocation of food (other than through a general income supplement, in the hope that some of it will percolate in the form of food to the child or pregnant mother), well-meaning attempts at nutrition improvement have not succeeded. As is well-known, the pattern, nature and rural-urban distribution of health care facilities

[1]See the papers of the symposium on effective rates of protection in the *Journal of International Economics*, 1973.

(even the publicly provided ones) in many less developed countries reflect the preferences of the urban-ruling élite rather than social needs. It is true that many of these problems are not entirely due to the 'mixed' nature of the economy but, nevertheless, the policy choice for their solution is constrained by it.

VI. SUMMARY AND CONCLUSION

In this chapter, the problem of planning in a mixed economy is viewed as one of designing a policy framework which adequately reflects the socio-political constraints of the economy so that socially desirable plans are formulated that can, at the same time, be implemented within the confines of the system. This involves both devising appropriate criteria for choice for the public sector in situations where the private sector operates under a given set of distortions, and the more traditional task of choice among alternative policy instruments. It illustrates some of the issues and indicates areas for further research by drawing upon selected theoretical and empirical studies, as well as the experience of planning in India with respect to agriculture, industry and foreign trade.

In conclusion, a broader problem may be briefly raised. The whole purpose of planning, by definition, is to steer the economy away from a course which it would otherwise take, to a socially more desirable direction. Given our assumption that an essential element of a mixed economy is its non-monolithic political power structure, it is inevitable that some politically powerful groups may stand to lose in the planned development. The art of planning, as contrasted with its science, which was discussed earlier, is to identify and operate on coalitions of political forces that will support or attempt to thwart the plan. In other words, if a 'winning' coalition could be formed (or a blocking coalition could be prevented from forming) on each issue in such a way that few feel that they are members of losing coalitions on all issues, a desirable and feasible plan could emerge. Put another way, in the absence of a 'revolutionary' restructuring of the socio-economic-political framework that does away with the 'mixed' economy, only a reformist strategy of the above type is feasible.

REFERENCES

Ahluwalia, M. S. and T. N. Srinivasan (1978), 'Impact of Procurement on the Free Market Price', (under preparation), World Bank Development Research Center.
Arrow, K. J. (1973), 'Higher Education as a Filter', *Journal of Public Economics*.
Bell, C. L. G. and P. Zusman (1976), 'A Bargaining Theoretic Approach to Cropsharing Contracts,' *American Economic Review*.
Bhaduri, A. (1973), 'Agricultural Backwardness under Semi-Feudalism', *Economic Journal*.
Bhagwati, J. N. and P. Desai (1970), *India: Planning for Industrialization* (London, Oxford University Press).

Bhagwati, J. N. and T. N. Srinivasan (1975), *Foreign Trade Regimes and Economic Development: India* (New York, National Bureau of Economic Research).

Blaug, M. *et al.* (1969), 'The Causes of Graduate Unemployment in India' (London, Allen Lane, The Penguin Press).

Blitzer, C. B. *et al.* (eds.) (1975), *Economy-Wide Models and Development Planning* (London, Oxford University Press).

Drèze, J. (1976), 'Some Theory of Labor Management and Participation', *Econometrica.*

Grossman, G. (1974), *Economic Systems* (Englewood Cliffs, N.J., Prentice-Hall).

Hurwicz, L. and L. Shapiro (1977), 'Incentive Structures Maximizing Residual Grain Under Incomplete Information', (mimeographed) Department of Economics, University of Minnesota.

Little, I. and Mirrlees, J. (1974), *Project Appraisal and Planning for Developing Countries* (London, Heinemann Educational Books).

Minhas, B. S. (1974a), 'Whither Indian Planning', M. N. Roy Memorial Lecture, The Indian Renaissance Institute, Dehradun, India.

———, (1974b), *Planning and the Poor* (New Delhi, S. Chand and Co.).

Mirrlees, J. (1977), 'Theory of Optimal Taxation', (mimeographed) Oxford, Nuffield College.

National Commission on Agriculture (1975), *Agrarian Reforms*, Part XV of the Report, New Delhi, Government of India.

Raiffa, H. (1969), 'References for Multi-Attributed Alternatives,' Memorandum RM–5868–DOT, Rand Corporation.

Schultz, T. W. (1972), *Investment in Education: The Equity Efficiency Quandary* (Chicago, University of Chicago Press).

Sen, A. K. (1977), 'On Weights and Measures', *Econometrica.*

Spence, M. (1973), 'Job Market Signalling', *Quarterly Journal of Economics.*

Srinivasan, T. N. (1978a), 'Agricultural Backwardness Under Semi-Feudalism: Comment', *Economic Journal.*

——— (1978b), 'Poverty, Development and Basic Needs', *Food Research Institute Studies*, Vol. XVI, July.

Stiglitz, J. (1974), 'Incentives and Risk in Sharecropping', *Review of Economic Studies.*

Tsuru, S. (1968), 'Merits and Demerits of the Mixed Economy in Economic Development – Lessons from India's Experience' in *Essays in Economic Development* (Tokyo, Kinokuniya Bookstore Co.).

Tulkens, H. (1976), 'The Publicness of Public Enterprise', in W. G. Shepherd (ed.), *Public Enterprise: Economic Analysis of Theory and Practice* (Lexington, Mass., Lexington Books).

United Nations Industrial Development Organisation (1972), *Guidelines for Project Evaluation* (New York, United Nations).

Discussion of Professor Srinivasan's Paper

Professor Barkai said that Professor Srinivasan's very interesting paper had started with a definition of private and public enterprise, and said he was also tempted to offer a definition. He characterised a public enterprise as one which ultimately relied on the government purse. In that sense, he said, the major American banks were also public enterprises, because, as Kaldor had pointed out, the government would rescue them from a threatening collapse, even in the absence of any formal agreement.

Barkai then raised the issue of the criteria according to which public enterprises ought to be run. A government planning body would have to address two issues, one macroeconomic and one microeconomic.

The macroeconomic problem was to select a rate of investment that was consistent with a desired rate of economic growth. This volume of investment could be financed through domestic savings and/or through net capital imports. Imports of foreign capital were usually under government control. The domestic savings rate could be influenced through the availability of government credits for investment.

The microeconomic problem was the selection of specific projects among which the government's portion of total investment ought to be allocated. Two possible criteria for project selection were either maximisation of net profit (i.e. value of output minus wages paid), or maximisation of total output. In the first case, wages paid to workers were considered a social cost. In the second case, wages paid by an enterprise were considered, rather, as a reallocation of resources, with a loss on one side made up by a gain on another side, and the only goal was to maximise the total product which could be distributed. Barkai simply wanted to raise this issue, which he considered very important, but he refrained from offering a solution.

Finally, he discussed the problem of uncertainty. In every decision, there are risks involved. Government decisions are usually big, and therefore can lead to large errors. If decisions about investments were more decentralised, some would succeed and others fail, but a big disaster was quite unlikely. This might be preferable. As an example he mentioned agriculture. Certain infrastructure services, such as roads, irrigation systems, the availability of productive information through extension services, etc., were best provided by the government. But other decisions, such as the best allocation of labour, could be left to decentralised units.

Mr Gonsález found that the discussion had so far centred on a comparison of private and public enterprise and a dispute about which was 'better'. But he thought that it would be more useful to concentrate on the mutual inter-relationship between the two forms, and how they could best support each other. He also mentioned that public enterprise had a role to play in promoting a more equitable income distribution.

Professor Vickrey addressed two issues, scale economies and discount rates. He said that infrastructure projects are characterised by economies of scale, and that therefore public subsidies are needed to make marginal cost pricing feasible. Whether these subsidies were better given to private or public enterprises was an open question. With regard to interest rates he said that there were institutional factors which led to larger differences in discount rates between private and public enterprises than was justified by differences in risk. He said that, for example, the cross-Florida barge canal was found profitable at the ridiculously low interest rate of $2\frac{7}{8}$ per cent per year, but was abandoned half finished in the 1950s. Also, tax-exempt bonds issued in the United States for the financing of infrastructure projects caused the interest rate actually charged to be artificially low.

Professor Baumol pointed out that universal marginal cost pricing was not feasible, but that we lived in a world of 'second best'. The problem with scale economies was that they led to natural monopoly, and the question to be addressed was how to make a monopoly serve the public interest. Regarding interest rates he agreed that the examples cited by Vickrey were indeed horrible. Nevertheless, he stressed that due to the law of large numbers the public had lower risk than a private enterprise, and could therefore apply a lower discount rate and take a longer view into the future. If society created 1000 new enterprises in a year and a few of them failed, the risks were negligible. But for a single enterprise, the risk of failure was a real threat. In the pooling of risks, central planning had an advantage.

Lord Kaldor said most economists were used to thinking in terms of full employment where the problem was scarcity of labour. In such a situation it was appropriate to choose the proper discount rates carefully in order to compare the profitability of competing projects. But most less developed countries suffered from high unemployment. The alternative to the investment of funds in a project was usually not to invest the freed resources in another, more profitable project, but to do nothing at all. This left precious resources unused. Even in developed countries, the problem was not so much one of *allocating* scarce resources among competing uses, but of *activating* unused resources. If, for example, the American space programme had not been undertaken, the released resources would most probably not have been better used elsewhere, but would simply have remained idle. In Great Britain, the public car firm, British Leyland, had plans to build a new mini car, which would have added to employment, output and exports. But the project failed to meet a profitability criterion, and was dropped. As a result, the 'value added' in manufacturing was much smaller, since there was more unemployment. We should not pay blind respect to profitability criteria. The problem was to maximise output, not profits.

Mr Gutiérrez suggested that the role of public enterprise in most developing countries was not so much to be economically efficient, but rather to help maintain a given political system. Public enterprise has been criticised for being corrupt, inefficient and a drain on public funds. But by alleviating unemployment and some of the most severe forms of inequality, public enterprise has helped to stabilise the political situation and allowed the functioning and growth of private enterprise. In Mexico, for instance, contrary to the 'crowding out hypothesis' of public activities, private investment appears to be positively correlated to the growth of the public sector. The traditional concept of economic efficiency should be widened to include the favourable economic impacts of greater political stability in LDCs.

Srinivasan replied to Kaldor that part of the unemployment in less developed countries could be attributed to distortions in factor prices. If there was a surplus of any resource, such as labour, it should properly be assigned a shadow price that reflected this surplus in cost calculations, not the actual wage rate paid. This was sometimes done. But, shadow pricing can be abused in that almost any project could be shown to generate acceptable rates of return by assigning a low (high) enough shadow price for inputs (outputs). He raised the issue of the corrections that ought to be made in the face of such distortions. He also pointed out that improvements in income distribution might also be achieved through progressive taxation and redistribution, rather than through public employment. Without considering what policy instruments were feasible in any given political context, one could not argue which was best.

Barkai said that one should make a distinction between public enterprises and the government. Public enterprises could not be responsible for maintenance of full employment, but this goal should be achieved through macro policies of the government. British Leyland, for example, should be allowed to maximise its profits like any other enterprise, without being responsible for creation of employment. *Kaldor* replied that public enterprises were the principal instrument through which a government could achieve full employment. In order to fulfil this task, public enterprises needed to consider the additional net output resulting from their activities, not just the additional profits. Alternative policy instruments were budget deficits, but these may be inferior in terms of the resulting additions to output and employment.

Baumol offered a synthesis of these two opposing views by saying that it may be appropriate for public enterprises, like other enterprises, to maximise profits, but that these profits were not to be evaluated simply in dollar terms. They should incorporate social costs and gains. For example, if there were unemployment, wages were to be evaluated at zero. Environmental pollution was to be considered as a social cost. Public enterprises should therefore not be criticised if they made financial losses, as long as they helped to meet important social objectives. But a different issue, which was often raised by opponents of public enterprises, was that they are, allegedly, *inefficient*. Their employees were said to be lazy, there was a lack of proper supervision, appointments were made on a political or personal basis, etc. Was it possible to have it both ways, i.e. to satisfy public policy goals without inefficiency? This was the key issue to be addressed. The question was whether the profit criterion, with appropriate corrections for externalities, was an efficient means by which social objectives could be accomplished.

Professor Uribe agreed that it would be ideal to take social costs and gains into account, but it was difficult to carry out in practice. How should the cost of the noise of Concorde be assessed? Or the entertainment value of the moon programme? Or the extinction of whales? One could always devise a set of prices so that a desired result would emerge. The evaluation of such factors was ultimately a political, not an economic issue. Economists could simply ask the public whether it was prepared to pay such and such an amount for these benefits, which were rather hard to identify. *Dr Pryke* added that if he were put in charge of any public enterprise, he could always make a case that it was socially profitable.

Vickrey illustrated the fact that the financial profitability of an enterprise does not measure its contribution to public welfare, by saying that a monopoly could increase its profits by charging different prices to different customers, but that this practice might well reduce total welfare.

M. Dreyfus pointed out that in France public enterprises were expected to make a financial profit and could not rely on government subsidies. But he said that the rates of profit of public enterprises were usually somewhat lower than those of comparable private enterprises, because public enterprises were required by the government to meet other objectives, such as the location of new plants in economically depressed areas, the purchase of inputs from financially troubled companies, the stabilisation of the cost of living by holding back on price increases, etc.

Srinivasan concluded the discussion by saying that relegating problems from economics to politics was not necessarily always a good solution. It depended on who had power. In some cases, political goals consisted of improving the conditions of the poor and reducing inequality. But he said that in India public enterprises were sometimes abused by the rich, including rich workers, to further their own purposes.

3 Public Enterprise in an Underdeveloped and Dependent Economy

Armando Labra
COLEGIO NACIONAL DE ECONOMISTAS, MEXICO

I. THE NATURE OF THE PROBLEM

The object of this chapter is to review the socioeconomic and political framework that determines the potential role of public enterprise in guiding economy towards development paths that benefit the more populous strata of society, in an underdeveloped and dependent capitalist economy – a so-called 'mixed economy' – in which private ownership of production goods and productive investment predominates and contributes to the persistence of increasing inflationary pressures, unemployment, balance of payments deficits and social inequality.

If the aim of development is to achieve simultaneously sustained increases in production and productivity; equitable sharing of income and levels of employment; increasing access to social security and education within a framework of conscious popular political participation, our basic assumption is that the social organisation that we attempt to analyse fails to attain some or all of these features of development.

Ability to achieve the harmonious progress along all these lines is mainly dependent on the capacity to achieve economic success whose benefits accrue to a majority of the public, for, otherwise, the economic failure simply blocks progress in the remainder of the system. Certainly, social, political and cultural development will not occur during economic stagnation.

Underdeveloped and dependent capitalist economies – or 'mixed economies' – are mixed to the degree that the historic conditions that gave rise to capital accumulation are not present, particularly when they are not characterised by heavy exploitation of labour, restriction of labour organisations and the absence of political commitments to large social groups.

Under these circumstances, in which the state is an endogenous product of the system, the degree of progress or backwardness of social organisation is determined by the degree to which the state overcomes the obstacles or finds substitutes for the favourable conditions that the historic situation in this century no longer offers for spontaneous accumulation of capital.

To the extent that historic conditions favourable to capitalist development no longer occur spontaneously and the 'invisible hand' is conspicuous by its absence, the ability to introduce the guiding hand of the state as a regulating force seems to be the only way of maintaining the accumulation process out of public and private capital in proportions that help to guarantee the political and social survival of the system.

Such ameliorative state intervention has evolved towards further consolidation as public intervention has proved necessary to keep the system afloat, and inevitably reshuffled economic and political power in a manner detrimental to private interests and to the benefit of the public interest. Paradoxically, capital needs the presence of an increasingly powerful state in order to survive, which, in turn, serves to inhibit the private interests.

Within this evolutionary process, the visible hand of the state is shown in public enterprises by means through which it induces the type of permanent and productive investment that private capital does not provide in sufficient amounts, or does not do so efficiently in a wide range of areas which go beyond the traditional role of public expenditure, that of offering administrative, political and infrastructure services to capital.

However, this arrangement can actually produce a web of vices and distortions whose ideological and political role is doubtful, as public enterprise has sometimes become increasingly inefficient – in some cases irreversibly so – subsidising capital for long periods, deterring the statisfaction of its own capital requirements and finally, working to the detriment of the public agency whose funds sustain it.

The structure of the network of public enterprises also complements the rigid type of protectionist economic policy that so frequently seeks to defend infant industries against the industrial countries which supply obsolete technology and financing expensive to the developing lands.

To the extent that the rigidity of protectionist policies creates captive markets and unadaptability in industrial processes and favours a decline in real earnings, in the public sector income and in public investment, the economy is depressed and with it, for lack of economic nourishment, the social, political and cultural structure is adversely affected as well.

As part of this process the economy is subjected to stagflation with unemployment, which it is impossible to overcome by traditional means, using the country's own activities which have lost their dynamism, while external resources, if they are available, incur a great political, social and financial cost.

On arrival at this historic stage, it is necessary to rationalise, to a maximal degree, the allocation of resources, in order to halt the expansion of unemployment, to overcome the shortage of foodstuffs and of foreign currency, all of which otherwise converge to a crisis which leads, in the sorts of countries that we are studying, less to revolutionary solutions than to intensification of repressive actions which threaten democratic forms and support the inception of fascism.

The financial and technological impotence of private capital, a consequence of prolonged overprotection, hampers its self-regeneration. Thus it becomes unavoidable for the process of accumulation to turn to the resources allocated to public enterprise as they become the only source of increased employment, and alone are consistent with priority to foodstuff production and a hierarchy of final uses of foreign currency necessary to shore up real investment.

Only in this way can the management of the external debt be carried out rationally, a programme justified by its economic and social yield and not merely by its static consequences which international financial agencies and certain neo-classical theoretical models emphasise.

However, the utilisation of capital is decreasingly able to offer concrete solutions capable of dealing with pressing economic, political and social problems so long as there persist unemployment, restriction of internal demand, external imbalance, and inflationary pressures all of which serve to exhaust the external financial sources that traditionally shore up the inefficiency of developing economies.

II. THE ECONOMY

In strictly economic terms, capital accumulation by private enterprise in conditions of stagflation is subject to feedback that discourages the investment of surpluses and encourages the monopolisation of productive forces and the exploitation of labour.

This is explained by the fact that insufficiency of investment is caused by, and provokes, inflationary pressures, as a result of which the real rate of earnings decreases and its decline can only be held in check by reducing the level of employment or by raising the level of prices – courses which stimulate the exploitation of labour and add fuel to stagnation as they inhibit effective demand, promoting inflationary restriction of supply and speculative rises in prices – processes which all, in turn, help to consolidate stagnation by undermining real profitability of capital, restricting the scope of the market, and reducing overall saving and investment.

In these circumstances, as spontaneous flows of capital begin to dry up, there is no evidence that stimulus of private interest can restore the pace of growth, except to the extent that private investment, domestic and foreign, is helped by repression of the organisations that speak for organised labour and, for all practical purposes, of every political democratic movement.

In such circumstances, only artificial repression by the economic–political establishment that holds in check any upward movement in the cost of labour can guarantee to private capital a rate of earnings higher than the increase in costs and prices. This can, doubtless, stimulate very short-term growth, but diminishes the possibility that the country's social, political and cultural development can proceed with equity and in a manner that preserves its sovereignty.

To break the vicious circle of stagflationary cessation of investment, the only effective means seems to be encouragement of accumulation of capital through public investment that requires a relatively lower rate of earnings and surplus value and whose structure can be designed to optimise, in economic and social terms, the allocation of extremely scarce resources.

In this note, public enterprise offers a strategic political and social avenue for immediate reactivation of the economy through direct stimulus of employment, improving the distribution of income, and increasing overall supply, as it stimulates the domestic market, which thereby offers favourable prospects to the investor. This implies that public enterprise serves as the backbone of the system as it deals with the most critical of economic issues: employment, production of foodstuffs and foreign exchange.

The provision of the required financial resources is a social necessity, justified not by financial returns but by the aims of public spending, which it is necessary to subordinate to the interests of all productive sectors. Consequently, public policy, acting through the prices and other financial decisions of public enterprises that consolidate overall savings, must be guided by a centralised programme. Both public and private investment must be induced to give priority to employment, production of foodstuffs, and foreign exchange when private capital is insufficient, non-existent or inefficient. In this way the state carries out the task of overcoming the historic deficiencies of capitalist evolution in countries such as those we are analysing.

III. SOCIETY

The capitalist economy's inability to regenerate spontaneously under the conditions just described, aggravates unemployment and maldistribution of income and increases the proportion of the population which does not have adequate income levels.

To the extent that industry and business rely upon intensive use of capital and mass markets, their reliance upon socio-economic structures based on surplus labour and limited markets worsens unemployment and increases inflation, concentration of income, dependence upon foreign countries and, inevitably, the repression of non-conformity in depressed sectors of the economy.

Domestically, the effects of concentration of wealth are not confined only to the distribution of income but also affect the distribution of property and political power, consolidating the power of élites in all social sectors, including labour and peasant organisations.

The process of concentration is reversed as the social benefits of an economic policy sustained by public investment serve to induce widespread redistribution of wealth by providing the sorts of employment that are permanent, productive, necessary and well-paid, thereby strengthening the social fabric.

IV. POLITICS

Economic inefficiency in democratic organisations inevitably induces the system to turn toward fascism, with the support of the middle classes and capital – although historically the former always are, in the final analysis, jeopardised by it.

To the extent that spontaneous behaviour of the market produces inefficiency as the state abstains from an economic role as a result of indecision about guidance of capital and investment, the options of political action are necessarily narrowed as economic monopolisation and political power become entwined.

At this stage, centralised exercise of power undermines effective working-class and trade union organisations and can, eventually, undermine economic and social democracy, by turning to military programmes as the final response to economic needs and the polarisation of class interests.

Its responsibility for the stability of political institutions forces the state to survive by seeking to provide widespread benefits through *political* policies which, in turn, affect economic and social policy in two ways: seeking to provide employment and income to stimulate demand and, through it, public and private investment in a politically stable and progressive atmosphere based on attention to the needs of the majority of citizens.

To the extent that organised capital resists the exercise of political power for the benefit of the majority or undertakes to assume formal leadership of public affairs, a historic stage occurs that is conceivable only to those entrepreneurs moulded by the anachronistic doctrine of the 'invisible hand' or neo-classical Friedmanism.

To sum up, there is historical evidence of lack of adaptability of private capital to the needs of economic, political, social and cultural development in non-industrial, colonised, dependent and over-exploited societies; the fundamental role of the state in these types of society is to make up for the historical deficiencies in the system, which become more complex and cumulative over time and demand growing state participation to guarantee the evolutionary continuity of the economic and social structure.

Consequently, the state has the historical responsibility of sharing in capital accumulation by which surplus value reverts through a rational process to a system guaranteeing a fluid market and sustained improvement in living standards. This is the means by which state enterprise guarantees that production and employment are rendered less vulnerable to crisis, brought about by the erratic behaviour of private capital.

The only alternative to the use of state enterprise as the pivot of public action for overall progress of the system is, nowadays, the elimination of the tenuous forms of democratic life that, even though tenuous, have nevertheless taken root in our countries.

Discussion of Dr Labra's Paper

Mr Stoffaes listed three environments in which public enterprises had a role to play: (i) in industrialised capitalist countries, (ii) in planned economies, and (iii) in less developed capitalist countries. Differences in these environments have to be considered if a reliable judgement is to be made about the efficiency of these enterprises. In advanced capitalist countries the role of public enterprises was marginal, serving only to impose some checks and balances upon the market. Typically they covered industries which were natural monopolies, public services, or areas where substantial externalities caused market failures. They also were sometimes used to maintain employment (for example in the British coal, steel, shipbuilding or automobile industries), to promote regional balance (such as in the industrialisation of Southern Italy), and to encourage investment in new and risky, high-technology industries (e.g. the electronics, nuclear and aerospace industries in France). Alternatives to public enterprises in developed capitalist countries were the regulation of private monopolies, or subsidies, and investment premiums to private companies. There was not sufficient empirical evidence to favour one instrument over the other, at least from the point of view of economic theory.

In planned economies, public enterprises with more or less autonomous decision-making power were called upon to strive to approach market efficiency, while remaining within a socialist framework. Examples were the economic reforms in Hungary, in the Soviet Union (Liberman) and in Yugoslavia.

In the third case, that of less developed countries, public enterprises played a very important role as instruments to promote equity and growth in the economy through capital accumulation. There were two alternative scenarios, populism and fascism. Under a populist, democratic government, labour unions were very strong; this brought about inflation, which lowered profits and reduced private investment, causing lower growth, unemployment and instability. Under the fascist scenario government repression reduced inflation, created favourable conditions for private investment (especially from overseas), led to concentration of ownership, to private capital accumulation, to a lower growth in consumption and was also unstable because of inequity, low growth and political problems raised by the domination of multinational firms. Latin America has shown successions of one scenario by the other, for example, in Chile where Allende was followed by Pinochet or in Argentina where Peron was followed by Videla. Stoffaes admitted that, like every theory, this description was schematic and an imperfect account of reality. But he argued that these considerations could lead to a specific role for public enterprises as a tool of capital accumulation in developing countries. Public enterprises in highly capital-intensive sectors in third world countries can therefore accelerate this development process, relative to the century-long experience of western countries in their nineteenth- and twentieth-century industrialisation, when capital accumulation was left entirely to private capitalists.

He concluded his comments by mentioning an alternative instrument to public enterprises, and listing four criteria for judging the efficiency of either instrument. As a feasible alternative to public enterprises he suggested the regulation of private firms through tariff protection, exchange controls, possibly the prohibition of foreign investment, and subsidies in such areas as education, health, transportation, energy, agricultural infrastructure, etc. To promote equality he suggested the use of taxation and redistribution.

For the evaluation of public or regulated private enterprises he suggested (a) macroeconomic, (b) microeconomic, (c) social, and (d) political criteria. As advantages of public enterprises he listed (a) that profits were reinvested, instead of being partially consumed, promoting macroeconomic growth, (b) that public enterprise could afford to take risks which private investors refused, and that it could be left free to act as a monopoly in markets where competition would be wasteful, (c) that it could negotiate the transfer of technology more successfully (e.g. oil in Mexico) and (d) that it avoided the nepotism of hereditary succession in private enterprise. He said it also avoided excessive control by private enterprises by a bureaucracy that inhibited economic growth in such countries as India or Egypt. It could avoid excessive urban concentration in capital cities with its detrimental externalities; and it could counterbalance the power of domestic and foreign private capital.

As potential disadvantages of public enterprises (and he criticised Mr Labra for mentioning only advantages) he felt (a) that private enterprise was better able to resist excessive wage demands by workers, which in state enterprises were sometimes subsidised at the expense of investment; (b) management of public enterprise sometimes lacked sufficient responsibility and gave in too easily to government pressures and political lobbying, and this resulted in inefficiency; (c) public enterprise was also vulnerable to new forms of nepotism, political appointment of managers, and corruption. This was a serious problem in some developed countries, and even more so in less developed countries; (d) finally, nationalised enterprise was conducive to bureaucratisation. The solution to these problems, in his view, was a tradition of competent, conscientious managers who were free from corruption.

Lord Kaldor stressed that Latin American countries had to industrialise in order to develop. Since their agricultural sectors were not capable of meeting urban requirements, and food had to be imported, these countries had to foster export industries, in order to maintain the balance of foreign trade. He said that private entrepreneurs, who were predominantly foreigners, wanted the local markets and were not interested in exports. Multinational corporations were not altruistic, and that was the essence of the problem.

Professor Sacristán said unemployment, which caused both insufficient demand and a shortage of resources, was the main justification for government intervention in the economy. He said that some industrialised countries were able to export their unemployment and inflation to less developed countries by granting them credits and penetrating their markets with foreign consumer goods. He also pointed out that if profits were exported, instead of being invested, this hampered economic growth.

Dr Pryke said people in Britain complained that multinational corporations exported jobs to less developed countries with low wages and flooded the British market with imported goods. Now we were being told that they exported unemployment. Both could not be true. He suspected that there were non-economic barriers which discouraged multinational corporations from reinvesting more profits in less developed countries, namely the fear of nationalisation.

Professor Vickrey said inflation was like theft while unemployment was like vandalism (since whatever went unproduced was unavailable to *anyone*). The main problem with inflation was not its level, but the *uncertainty* associated with it. If accounting practices were adjusted to a fixed rate of inflation, one could get along well with it. But the rate of inflation was more controllable when it was at 5 per cent per year than when it was 20 to 30 per cent.

Mr Gutiérrez said that development was so important for Mexico that it could not be left in private hands. Traditional Mexican entrepreneurs did not take risks. One problem was a shortage of data and information; others, the feudal attitude towards existing and new ventures, and the large number of family-owned firms. He also said that investment in relatively less developed regions could be financially less profitable than investment in urban conglomerations, but socially preferable.

Mr Marsan agreed with Gutiérrez on the importance of information. He said that Boiteux had cited as one of the principal advantages of the fact that Electricité de France was a public enterprise, the superior information available to the state, which consequently knew the real alternatives.

Dr Labra concluded the discussion by saying that in his opinion there was no alternative to public enterprise in less developed countries. The disadvantages of public enterprise were similar to those of private enterprise, he said. But they might have social advantages. He agreed that industrialisation was important for the solution of Latin America's economic problems, but it was essential to ask 'industrialisation for what and for whom?'. Even more important, and a precondition for industrialisation, was the guarantee of an adequate food supply. He said that at the moment many countries experienced a period of stagnation *and* instability. Ways had to be found to provide growth with stability, in a democratic society.

4 Some Considerations on the Role of Public Enterprise

Emilio Sacristán Roy
DIRECTOR ADJUNTO DE EMPRESAS Y FIDEICOMISO DE NACIONAL
FINANCIERA, MEXICO

I. INTRODUCTION

The essential object of this paper is to analyse the aim of public enterprise in economic development; or, more precisely, it is to evaluate public enterprise as an agent for promoting industrial development.

It should be noted at once that although the considerations presented here do not allude to the actual state of public enterprise in Mexico, they are undoubtedly based fundamentally upon the Mexican experience, to which specific reference will be made at various points throughout the paper.

It is taken that public enterprise can be an efficient agent for the promotion of industry, for, as we shall see later, public enterprise can increase the formation of capital, and it can render technological transfer more efficient and less costly, and it also competes more effectively with the great transnational firms. To the extent that public enterprise has an advantage over private enterprise in these three ways it may be considered as a true agent that promotes industry. This chapter will describe general norms for economic policy which may ensure more effective action by public enterprise.

Finally, it should be noted that this chapter does not deal with public enterprise as a provider of public services or as an organisational mechanism for decentralisation of government functions. Here public enterprise is assumed to manufacture goods, and special attention will be paid to public firms which compete in the same market (or related markets) as domestic private firms or transnationals.

II. PUBLIC ENTERPRISE AND CAPITAL FORMATION

There is a widespread and deeply rooted belief that public enterprise must be relatively less efficient than private enterprise, therefore it must have a lower capacity to generate economic surplus and contribute to capital formation.

Actually, there is no objective reason to support the belief that private firms must be more efficient than public firms; on the other hand, there is ample reason to conclude that distributed profits are greater in private firms, and that therefore the surplus available for reinvestment must be less. To show this we may turn to theory. Contemporary growth theory shows that the instability of the propensity to consume out of profits is the main source of disequilibrium in the growth process. To the degree that the propensity to consume out of profits can be reduced and its stability ensured, the economy may appropriate the optimal golden age of stable growth.

One of the main determinants of the propensity to consume out of profits is undoubtedly the proportion distributed relative to profits retained in firms. The latter generally represents reinvestment in the near future, whereas a large proportion of the former is consumption. It is to be expected that instability and unpredictability of the proportion of profits distributed or accumulated must lead to instability in the propensity to consume out of profits. It is also to be expected that the greater the proportion of distributed earnings the greater the propensity to consume out of profits.

It is to be expected that in private enterprise (in its most orthodox definition) the proportion of distributed profits is greater than in public companies, since the capitalist owner lives from them (consumes them). Erratic behaviour in profits taken out of or reinvested in the firms should also be expected. The orthodox definition applies mostly to small and medium-sized firms, however. Large-sized firms of national or transnational proportions, with great atomisation of the shareholders (many of whom are institutional), display more predictable behaviour with regard to the amount of distributed profits, which, to a certain degree, is independent of realised profits and is merely intended to give the shareholder a percentage return on his holdings which will keep him satisfied. In that case the magnitude of dividends becomes predictable, yet the proportion of distributed profits varies a great deal and may be quite high. It is even possible to show no profits at all and still declare dividends (from profits accumulated previously).

Generalisation about state-owned firms points in the opposite direction. Foreseeable needs for reinvestment have top priority, and only surplus profits which are not reserved for future needs are distributed. The government does not establish a minimum or fixed amount of earnings distribution, except under very special circumstances.

To summarise, we may conclude that public enterprise contributes to capital formation to a greater degree than private enterprise. Furthermore, it does so in a more consistent way, thus making far steadier growth. The propensity to consume out of profits does not vary as much, since the proportion reinvested out of profits is less subject to fortuitous developments.

This conclusion is valid if and when the operation of public firms is as efficient (or inefficient) as that of private enterprise, and the profit margin in each type of firm is similar. This leads us to a new series of considerations.

The traditional argument which is used to show that private enterprise is more efficient is derived from the assumption that the 'profit motive' is the main incentive for the owner-managers. In this respect it should be noted that in a great number of private firms (which generate most industrial production), the profit-receiving owner and the management are quite independent. To the extent that this is true it is exceedingly unconvincing to cite the 'profit motive' as a reason to expect management of private firms to be more efficient. This traditional argument is plausible only for small and medium-sized firms, in which the owners participate in administrative and operational decisions. Actually, large firms have developed a class of professional 'business managers' who are employed by the firms and perform their administrative duties whether or not they have a marginal incentive in profit-sharing. Both private and public firms can and do hire the services of these managers, and in both cases an additional incentive may be related to profits, if it is deemed advisable.

In addition, the view that man's only incentive is pecuniary is quite debatable. Success and power play a very important role and are also strong incentives in administration.

It is also asserted that public-enterprise managers are not as competent (and thus, the operation is less efficient), since they are chosen for reasons other than their capability, most notably for political reasons. It cannot be denied that this contention is sometimes valid, but it is also true that the managers of private firms are selected on criteria other than competence, on grounds such as inheritance, nepotism, friendship and loyalty. We must, however, recognise that administrators are subject to greater control by the board of directors in the private than in the public firms. In sum, there are convincing reasons for expecting the management of a public firm to be less competent than that of a private firm. In other words, it is not possible to conclude from such an analysis that public enterprise is less efficient than private enterprise, so that it will not generate as much economic surplus which can be used for capital formation. Nevertheless, there do exist factors other than the competence of management, which may cause them to be relatively inefficient.

One such factor, which seems to affect public more than private firms, is the ability (or inability) of management to resist labour union demands. In the case of the private firm, labour and management are opposing interests, and this in the long run leads to a degree of equilibrium in collective bargaining. In contrast, the management of a public firm does not serve capitalistic interests but is answerable primarily to the government, and therefore cannot easily check workers' demands. There are numerous examples of public firms whose labour situation has caused them to lose competitiveness. This situation is aggravated when managers must serve the requirements of political expedience.

Corruption is another factor which occasionally makes public enterprise less productive than private enterprise. Not only does it affect the distribution of income; it also reduces capacity for capital formation. Corruption is actually a misuse of resources, which become unavailable for productive wages or for reinvestment; in both cases resources are withdrawn from the productive process, thus decreasing the capacity for capital formation.

When labour is used in production, it generates a surplus which in the capitalistic firm is passed on to its owner or owners in the form of profits, and in the government firm goes into increases in its own endowment or to the public treasury, if that is decided upon. As has been mentioned before, for the economy to function properly, attaining a growth rate which is not only maximal but also stable, is necessary for the greatest possible proportion of the economic surplus to be reinvested in capital formation. This will permit production to increase (through greater labour productivity), as well as making possible higher wages and standards of living.

Optimal growth might be achieved if this surplus could be reinvested totally; yet in an economy such as ours this is not possible, because of capitalist consumption, bond interest charges, intermediary costs, advertising, etc. The greater and more widespread the corruption among public officials and employees, the lower the reinvestable surplus will be, thus depressing the rate of growth of the economy and producing an inequitable distribution of income.

The misuse of the economic surplus may generate serious disturbances and cause disequilibrium. Besides hindering the growth process, it is to be expected that the greater part of resources withdrawn from capital formation will constitute capital exports or luxury consumption (of either domestic or imported goods).

The same holds for corruption in private firms, although in macroeconomic terms surplus is not diminished by as much, since the 'unearned funds' simply pass from one capitalist to another, and the effect is reduced to any added consumption or evasion of capital induced by this 'transfer'. The loss in surplus should not be great if the transfer is between two productive capitalists; but if it goes from productive investors to the commercial intermediaries ('coyotes'), agents, advertising staff, or even bankers, then a substantial loss must be expected, with consequences similar to those resulting from the corruption of public officials and employees.

It seems evident that although corruption does not occur exclusively in the public sector, the opportunities are greater in public enterprise than in private. In some cases corruption reaches such extremes that it may completely offset the natural advantages of public enterprise in capital formation.

There is another way in which corruption can adversely affect public enterprise. In countries such as ours, where industrial activity is extensively controlled and firms are required to deal with innumerable application forms, permits and registers, frequently involving lengthy and tedious procedures, firms may resort to devious means to cut through the red tape; not so much to obtain favourable decisions as to speed up the process. Private firms can use such methods seemingly without restriction. On the other hand, public firms encounter great difficulty in making and accounting for such payments. Unfortunately, this problem cannot be ignored, for in this respect public firms are at a serious disadvantage in their daily operation.

These factors are at least partly offset by the fact that public firms, through political connections and considerations of communal interest, may be able to obtain more favourable treatment from the authorities. Public firms also have certain monopolistic – or monopsonistic – market advantages, *vis-à-vis* both suppliers and clients, if these are also public firms or the government itself. However, it should be stressed that this situation is not as common as private enterprise would pretend.

In view of the above considerations, we may conclude that although public enterprise can contribute more to capital formation than private enterprise, and can be just as efficient in its operation, the special restrictions and conditions to which it is subjected may change the situation. In fact, should additional restrictions be imposed upon it because of its public character, such as regulations designed to maintain price levels or volume of employment, then even if public firms operate at the same level of efficiency as private firms, their surplus generating capacity can be significantly reduced. Besides these constraints, which are the most widespread, the state imposes others which also inhibit capital formation, such as the requirement that the firm continue production of unprofitable goods for the social benefit, that it invest in infrastructure, that it promotes the training of skilled labour, etc.

It may be added that to the extent that public enterprise is subject to specific requirements of various kinds, it is extremely difficult to evaluate the performance of its managers and to judge its operational efficiency.

III. PUBLIC ENTERPRISE AND TECHNOLOGY TRANSFER

Another issue which must be analysed in order to evaluate the role of public enterprise in economic development is its ability to expedite and cheapen the process of technology transfer.

Generally speaking, the greater the bargaining power of local firms *vis-à-vis* foreign supplies of technology, the lower will be the cost of obtaining it. Now, from the national point of view, technology transfer will also be cheaper if at the same time it includes the adaptation of new techniques to the technological and social conditions of the receiving country. Otherwise, unrestricted and technologically unmodified transfer from developed nations may mean excessive costs in terms of capital consumption and imports, thus reducing the generation of employment.

In both cases it must be conceded that public firms are generally in a better position than private firms; that is to say, they are better able to effect technical transfers at a lower direct cost as well as a lower, indirect social cost. In fact, it may be said that through the support of the government, and often even by their own means, public firms generally have stronger bargaining positions than private firms. However, it should be noted that even here corruption can play an adverse role.

As far as adapting technical transfers to the current circumstances is concerned, public enterprise is not only more acutely aware of this need, but it also has easier access to the support of the specialised agencies the government has established for this purpose. It should be mentioned that private firms in many cases do not resort to government aid in this matter, either because of distrust or simple prohibition in the licence or technical assistance contract.

IV. PUBLIC ENTERPRISE AND RESTRICTIONS ON MONOPOLISTIC PRACTICES AND FOREIGN DEPENDENCE

The limited scope of markets in underdeveloped countries along with the modern technology required for mass production, gives rise to a particularly acute problem of monopolistic structure. The traditional corrective, which is simply to prohibit monopoly or oligopoly, does not apply where the market physically cannot accommodate more than a limited number of productive units. It is necessary to recognise that such monopolies must be tolerated, and yet that their adverse effects upon the economy have to be prevented. To achieve this, it is necessary not only to resort to government price controls, quality norms and production quotas, but public enterprise must also participate in these markets in order to serve as a basis for comparison.

If monopoly is in the hands of a public firm, then its restrictive practices may be made to benefit rather than harm the economy. If public firms participate in oligopolistic competition, their mere presence will tend to limit the unfavourable consequences of this type of market.

Closely analogous to this, is another worrying problem for developing countries: the preponderance of firms with foreign affiliations and the incapacity of domestic firms to compete on reasonable terms. In fact, various sectors of our economies are dominated almost completely by foreign interests and transnational firms. The process of domination has occurred not only through the establishment of foreign firms and their advantages in coping with the complexity of modern technology and the huge amount of capital required; the process also involves the sale of already established firms to foreign interests when they cannot withstand the pressure of open competition.

In this respect public enterprise can also play a very important role, for its very nature permits it to compete with transnational firms under more favourable conditions than private enterprise.

V. OTHER CONSIDERATIONS

Aside from the effects which may be expected from public enterprise upon capital formation, technology transfers and industrial competitive capacity, there are still other areas in which public firms can contribute to the process of economic development. For instance, industrial decentralisation can undoubtedly be promoted more effectively through public enterprise.

In most countries, the incipient industrialisation process has generally led to the concentration of industry, giving preference to a few large metropolitan zones. This process of industrial concentration is attributable to the large economies of scale which may be obtained. However, there comes a time when these economies cease to exist. The continuous expansion of industrial centres brings with it great urban concentration, which after a point leads not only to social and sanitary problems, but basically to problems of an economic nature.

The tendency toward increasing returns which causes industrial concentration is then checked and diminishing returns set in. No longer can the best use be made of human resources; the cost of public services becomes quite considerable, the distance to be covered is even greater, the cost of land grows speculatively high, etc. Then decentralisation commences, with the creation of new and more numerous industrial areas. In many countries such as ours, which are undergoing industrialisation, the stage has been reached where it is convenient, and even necessary, for the future of industry, to begin a vigorous process of decentralisation, especially since this process apparently will not occur automatically for the following reasons:

(a) the demand for manufactured goods in many cases arises from the privileged portion of the population concentrated in the cities;
(b) because of agricultural backwardness, industrialisation has relied heavily upon relatively modern techniques which require large quantities of public services and highly specialised human resources;
(c) transportation facilities and their networks are still deficient.

As a result, vigorous decentralisation can only be induced by a series of stimulative actions, both public and private, so that the growth of industry does not begin to yield relatively decreasing returns.

Public enterprise can play a key role here. Reasonable decentralisation criteria can be used in the establishment of public enterprise. In private firms, fiscal and other incentives are frequently insufficient to counteract the preferences and convenience of the owners and managers. However, care should be taken not to sacrifice economics in order to achieve decentralisation, for there are numerous examples of this in our economies.

Just as public enterprise can act as catalyst in decentralisation, it can also become a promoting agent of those activities to which the general strategy of industrial development has assigned top priority. In these activities expected profit is commonly low or at least uncertain, so that fiscal and monetary incentives are insufficient to produce an adequate flow of initial investment funds to ensure that the process will continue by itself. The role of public enterprise is vital in this case. However, it should be kept in mind that there have sometimes been great blunders by public firms in pursuit of this objective.

VI. THE 'MIXED FIRM'

There are various forms that the public firm can adopt to adapt itself to different situations and successfully pursue the objectives that have been mentioned. The most appropriate form should be chosen for the special requirements of each case.

Among the different types of public enterprises, there are first the firms which are wholly public, either because they have deliberately been organised in that way or because all of the shares have passed into the hands of the state or one of its dependencies. This type of firm is generally advisable for the provision of public services or for carrying out functions of the government in a decentralised manner. It is also the proper type of firm to be used in promoting key strategic activities where the presence of foreign or private domestic firms is considered undesirable. However, in Mexico and similar countries, wholly public firms are also found in other fields. Government trust funds are among such firms, and these have developed profusely in Mexico.

Another group of public firms is that which can be called the 'mixed firms'. For our purposes, this is a more interesting group and corresponds more closely to the considerations presented in this chapter.

A 'mixed firm' should be understood here to mean a corporation in which both the state (directly or through a government agency) and private capital participate in the ownership of capital shares, with the understanding that the firm is to operate just as any other corporation in seeking to maximise profit, and is managed by professional administrators who can ensure the fulfilment of these objectives.

Within the framework of this 'joint venture', the state participates actively in production and promotion, while providing the necessary stability and support to private capital; and at the same time, private capital ensures efficient operation according to the rules of the capitalist game, through professional, autonomous management.

In some cases, a majority interest in the joint venture may be owned by the state, and in others by private capital, depending fundamentally upon the particular line of activity of the firm, its role within the economy, the required amount of investment, and the recovery period. The important point, however, is that the shares of each party must be sufficiently significant to provide the attributes of the 'mixed firm' described above. In other words, private capital seeks to ensure entrepreneurial ability and management independent from political interference, while the state provides financial and industrial security and greater bargaining power. Both ingredients are necessary to make certain that the numerous investment projects required by industrial development are reasonably profitable.

Whenever investment requires foreign technology of a complicated nature or critical supplies of foreign origin, the structure of the 'mixed firm' can be modified to permit three-way participation, so that the state and private capital continue to provide the above mentioned ingredients, but are complemented by a foreign firm responsible for transferring technology at minimum cost and effort, assuring its control by the 'mixed firm' and guaranteeing the supply of critical inputs. Furthermore, this three-way formula can facilitate access to international markets through the presence of foreign capital.

It should also be noted that the Mexican experience indicates that it is in many cases advisable for the state participation to be carried out through the Development Bank or through the agency entrusted with industrial promotion. This procedure helps to give the public enterprise the autonomy required for sound and efficient operation.

VII. CONCLUSION AND RECOMMENDATIONS FOR ECONOMIC POLICY RELATED TO PUBLIC ENTERPRISE

Throughout this chapter, the advantages and disadvantages of public enterprise have been discussed, as well as its role in the process of development. It has been shown that public enterprise can be an important agent in promoting industrial expansion, for by its very nature, it has the capacity to generate greater and more stable capital formation, cheapen and rationalise the process of technology transfer, and act to palliate the adverse effects of monopolistic market structures, while equalising the competitive position of domestic enterprise *vis-á-vis* transnational interests.

It has also been established that the process of industrial decentralisation can be accelerated through public enterprise, and activities with priority can be promoted by it.

It should be stressed that to obtain the advantages of public enterprise to permit it to become the key agent of industrial promotion, it is imperative, on the one hand, ultimately to eliminate corruption within and at the expense of public enterprise, and on the other, to free it from excessive restrictions and limitations which hinder its efficient and profitable operation, so that it can maximise the surplus destined for capital formation.

It seems absurd to conclude that one must combat corruption in every possible way, for this is something that should be taken for granted. However, it is also necessary to realise that the various measures for the control and supervision of public enterprise, and of economic policy in general, must permit public firms the degree of autonomy they require for adaptable and efficient operation, so that they can compete effectively with private national or foreign firms.

Moreover, special restrictions and conditions imposed upon public firms to ensure the fulfilment of specific goals should be limited to those firms undertaking very special assignments, and in any case, care should be taken to avoid reducing the capacity to generate surplus for capital formation.

In view of these considerations, it may be suggested that the logical solution in many cases can be the 'mixed firm' formula, where private (national and foreign) interests and those of the public sector coincide, for it has the advantages of public enterprise and at the same time, the necessary conditions and autonomy for adaptable and efficient management.

Discussion of Lic Sacristán Roy's Paper

Professor Srinivasan said that Lic Sacristán's paper had looked at the advantages and disadvantages of public enterprise from a somewhat abstract theoretical viewpoint. This was true of most of the discussions of this issue, particularly in developing countries, as he could confirm from his familiarity with similar debates in India. He stressed that the question of what form of enterprise was the most efficient in any given situation would have to be studied empirically. He doubted whether there was any empirical evidence for the claim that private enterprise tended to consume more out of profits than public enterprise. Conspicuous consumption was to be observed not only among capitalists, but also in the public domain. For example, the latest toys for the airforce or navy, or luxury housing for bureaucrats, did not have very high social value. Regarding Sacristán's reference to the stronger position which public enterprises possessed in negotiating the transfer of technology, he said that if this were indeed the case, then the government could simply require that all such negotiations be done under state auspices. This did not necessarily imply that production itself should also be in public hands. He also doubted whether a bureaucrat in charge of a public enterprise had more knowledge of the available range of choice of technology than a private enterprise. But this again was an empirical issue. Regional decentralisation, which had been mentioned as another advantage of public enterprise, could also be achieved by other means. He said he could see the potential advantages of a 'mixed' enterprise, (called a 'joint' enterprise in India), which Sacristán had favoured. But he also had the nagging fear, which Sacristán had expressed in his last sentence, that it might end up having the disadvantages of both public and private enterprise. He concluded with a plea for a pragmatic point of view in investigating what form of enterprise best suited given social, political and economic circumstances and the developmental stage of a country.

Professor Fischer said he found Sacristán's paper interesting and balanced. He wanted to mention an additional advantage of public enterprises, and one more problem. Sacristán had pointed out that private enterprise tended to lead to higher consumption out of profits, which seemed to be particularly high in many developing countries, and might be less effective in transfer of technology than a public enterprise. In addition to that, as M. Dreyfus had said earlier, public enterprises could afford to undertake risks and innovations for which private enterprise was not prepared. Because of its externalities, private enterprise often had a tendency to invest less in innovation than was socially desirable. He had carried out some calculations with a simple model which showed that if a public firm were operated efficiently, free from corruption, and acted in the public interest, then it tended to invest more in innovation than a private firm, and would make the results of research publicly available. This led to considerably higher economic growth. In fact, the loss to society resulting from an underinvestment in innovative activities by private enterprises turned out to be much higher than the resulting addition to their profits. Concerning the problems of public enterprises he agreed with Sacristán that corruption could be very serious and that every effort should be made to eliminate it. One particular form it took was that employees in public enterprises or government agencies sometimes collected wages without performing much work, occasionally even without showing up except on paydays. It was said that a foreigner touring the capital of some country pointed to a government building and asked how many people worked there. 'About half' was the answer. The fact that this joke has circulated in several countries indicated that the problem was widespread. Personal working experience in a city government had led him to believe that 50 per cent was a rather optimistic figure. There seemed to be little control. People had a tendency to spend public funds, including salaries, more readily than money coming from their own pockets. He asked what means were available to eliminate corruption, including workers' inefficiency. One possibility might be compensation on a piece-work basis, where this was possible, provided the quality of work did not suffer too much. This eliminated the need for constant supervision, since every worker was free to work as hard or as slowly as he liked. But not all types of work could be evaluated in this way. He asked what other arrangements were possible to encourage efficient work, and to eliminate other forms of corruption.

Professor Vickrey said that he was not sure that it was in fact an advantage of public enterprise that a larger share of its profits tended to be used for reinvestment, keeping down any dividend to the state. There was some correlation between an enterprise's ability to create a surplus and its opportunities for expansion, but the correlation was not perfect. For example, telephone companies in developing countries often needed funds for expansion, but were unable to finance it out cf their own profits. This led to waiting times of a year or two to get a phone. Investment funds, whether they came out of profits of public enterprises, or a budget surplus, or government borrowing, should be allocated on the basis of overall objectives. This was more efficient than if they were seized by the particular agency which happened to generate them. If investment funds were retained in the companies which created them, this might lead to a shortage of funds for new and possibly innovative activities.

M. Albert said it was important for an enterprise, whether public or private, to have a management which was responsible for its success or failure, and was independent of the state administration whose part is to define main objectives and criteria. Electricité de France, which was publicly owned but an independent unit, was very efficient. But the French telephone company was run directly by a ministry, an arrangement called *étatisation* in France. In such a system, there was always a risk that nobody wanted to be fully responsible for its operations, and that nobody took the necessary initiative and risks. An enterprise should be subject to some biological risk of extinction, otherwise it lacked the incentive for efficiency. If it were a natural monopoly, the state would have to give some guidance. But as Dr Marsan had pointed out, the possibility of entry and exit should be maintained whenever it was possible.

Dr Marsan took issue with Sacristán's contention that public enterprise should be freed 'from specific restrictions and conditions which hinder its efficient and profitable operation so that it can maximise the surplus available for capital formation'. He admitted that there were cases, such as steel in Italy or oil and petrochemicals in Mexico, where a state enterprise ran at a profit and yet private enterprise did not enter the industry, because the investments required were too huge. But in the normal case, he said, restrictions and constraints would be required by social goals. This was the main purpose for which a government wanted public enterprise, so the real problem was that these restrictions had to be defined clearly beforehand. Missions should be assigned to public firms in a democratic way, after open debate by elected officials. They had the right and obligation to set goals for public firms, but also to pay for them, because they imposed an additional cost. He agreed that sometimes unjustified restrictions were imposed on public firms which had no social goal. For example, in Italy the government had pledged that it would cover the costs of the telephone service by adjusting rates, but refused to do so during an inflationary period, which led to a deficit. Such restrictions were unwarranted, but others were acceptable and necessary. The issue was then to enable management to pursue profitability without being judged inefficient because of the restrictions imposed upon it. Managerial talent and initiative should not be discouraged. It was very important that managers be appointed on the basis of their experience and professional expertise. If there were corruption in appointments, good managers would no longer be attracted. This tended to invite more corruption, producing a vicious circle.

Mr Manzuilletes said that the actions of private enterprises did not meet the goals of social justice. By providing cheap infrastructure services, the Mexican government had subsidised private enterprise. There was a conflict between means and ends. The ends were an increase in the living standard of the majority, but the means used were to allow private enterprise to make high profits. These means often produced results opposite from those intended. Special tax benefits had been given to foreign enterprises, because they had advanced technology. But this had enabled foreign firms to control the key sectors of the economy. It had been expected that because of their rapid growth these firms would create more employment. But in fact they had not. Multinational companies did not produce goods for consumption by the majority, but for a small minority. They employed highly capital-intensive production methods, which had led to the concentration of income in a few hands. Another argument for favoured treatment of multinational companies had been that they helped to improve the balance of payments deficit. But in fact in 1973, 50 per cent of all of Mexico's imports (72 per cent in the manufacturing sector) had been undertaken by multinational corporations. In addition there were payments for foreign services. Resources created in Mexico flowed abroad, and re-entered in the form of foreign loans. This produced a vicious circle.

Lord Kaldor mentioned that the government of Attaturk had created a whole range of public enterprises in Turkey, which invariably operated at a loss. It was not that they operated so inefficiently, but the government compelled them to sell to private enterprises at prices below costs. This was used as a means of transferring profits from public to private enterprises. He disagreed with the statement that governments were less able to resist the demands of unions, saying that in Great Britain the public sector always had to bear the brunt of the incomes policy. While salary increases this year were running at 10 per cent in the public sector, they were at least 15 per cent in the private sector.

Dr Srinivasan said that sometimes government policy instruments generated corruption rather than eliminating it. One example was the allocation of imports through licences, rather than auctions. If licences were allocated at a cost which was below what the market would bear, this became a source of potential corruption. Concerning Fischer's question on how to encourage work effort, he said one method was to design a system which was, in effect, self-policing, such as piece rates. Where the person's effort could not easily be measured, then profit-sharing was another instrument which gave individuals an incentive to maximise their own effort and efficiency, so long as the accounting unit was sufficiently small for an individual's effort to make a difference.

Sacristán objected to Srinivasan's use of the term 'bureaucrat', implying that the person in question lacked initiative, to characterise the managers of public enterprise. He said that incidence of bureaucracy was related more to the size of the enterprise, rather than to its public or private status. He agreed with Albert and Marsan that appropriate decentralisation of decision-making and the independence of managers was important, and that direct control of enterprises by the government tended to produce inefficiency. Here it was necessary to distinguish between the government *per se* and the public sector. He agreed with Vickrey and Kaldor that investment funds should be allocated where they were needed most, not necessarily assigning them to the enterprises which generated them. The issue which he had addressed was high consumption out of profits in private enterprises and the higher savings potential of public enterprises, regardless of where those savings were invested.

5 Design of a Development Policy for Mexico: Industry and Oil

Ernesto Marcos
SECRETARIA DE PATRIMONIO Y FOMENTO INDUSTRIAL, MEXICO

I. INTRODUCTION

The development pattern that Mexico has followed in the last three decades brought with it a high rate of industrial growth. Based on a scheme of import substitutions, production of final consumption goods and an important group of raw materials and intermediate products expanded at a rate higher than 7 per cent per annum.

By the mid-sixties, this growth and development strategy began to show symptoms of exhaustion. In general, these took the form of a declining trend in the long-term rate of growth and the sharpening of certain imbalances in the balance of payments and in sectoral development.

In particular, the increasing struggle in agricultural development, together with the persistence of a high rate of demographic growth, resulted in a gradual loss of capacity to supply foodstuffs and increased unemployment in rural areas. This labour surplus was absorbed at a decreasing rate by the manufacturing and the service sectors, thus raising the total of urban unemployment and, consequently, polarising the community even more than unequal distribution of income would do.

The interrelationship of these factors led to a vicious circle in which the lower rate of expansion of domestic industrial demand reduced investment in the manufacturing sector, aggravating unemployment even more. Industry and services concentrated their expansion on those sectors serving the demands of high-income groups, thereby introducing an additional source of imbalance in the industrial structure of the country.

This was evident in the sharpening of the foreign trade imbalance. In addition to the dependence on imports, the process of indiscriminate substitution had aggravated a tendency to import foodgrains to offset the shortage of domestic production. At the same time, the failure to give priority to manufacturing investment gave rise to a multiplicity of industries with very modest scales of production that, along with limited export possibilities, restricted the capital good markets, rendering its domestic production unattractive.

These real factors that limited economic growth were accompanied by financial factors that resulted in a series of stops and starts, thus aggravating inflationary pressures and accelerating indebtedness to foreign countries as a result of balance of payments pressures.

Governmental policy, particularly since 1969, sought to solve some of these problems, but it did so in a partial way, attending to the most urgent pressures, seeking to use public expenditure to compensate for the gradual fall of the domestic demand. At the same time that investment was promoted in the fields of oil, iron and steel, and rural industries, expenditure in some social services expanded, particularly in urban areas.

In this way, by means of public actions, the government sought to reduce some of the most obvious obstacles to development. But this was carried out under the earlier growth pattern without any change in its general character, maintaining untouched a series of policies, particularly those relating to financial issues and the exchange rate. Thus, public efforts to reanimate development were limited to specific sectors, producing in the economy as a whole a growing lack of congruity which brought about results different from those sought.

In the economy as a whole the general tone was set by policies designed to support the rate of exchange and the intermittent implementation of restricted credit policies, while in specific areas state action was oriented towards eliminating bottlenecks (in energy, fertilisers, iron and steel); raising the level of employment, especially in depressed rural areas; and towards maintaining or increasing the standard of living of some labour sectors.

The result of these actions was the relative success of some sectoral policies and the sustaining of an average level of activity higher than that which could have been expected.

But in the economy overall, increasing difficulties in the behaviour of several crucial variables made it impossible to think of retaining partial policies without readjusting completely the general character of its growth pattern.

One of these troublesome phenomena has been the balance of payments position: although private sector imports have been reduced in relative terms as a result of its lower investment, these were compensated by the growing public imports of foodgrains and by the greater volume of capital goods that the para-state sector acquired abroad. At the same time, the rise in prices that characterised these goods since 1971 affected the total amount of our imports which have reached figures that were never anticipated. Exports, although growing, did not grow quickly enough, primarily because of the orientation of industry towards the domestic industrial market and to the adverse effects that the lower growth in demand had on its cost structure. The maintenance of the parity of exchange made it more difficult to reduce unit costs by means of greater exports.

The increase in the foreign trade deficit led to greater foreign indebtedness which began to rise dramatically. Given the extreme liquidity that characterises the instruments of saving, this growing deficit and indebtedness to foreign countries introduced a speculative atmosphere which, while restricting the reinvestment of profits, made the flight of capital more attractive.

The policy of restriction of domestic credit favoured reduced use of capital by enterprises, making feasible growing substitution of dollar loans as a source of capital, increasing considerably the degree of passivity of Mexican firms. This could induce not only a growing flight of 'liquid' capital accounts, but also the financing in dollars of physical assets, as the indebtedness of the enterprises rose without a concomitant rise in real assets.

The inflationary tendencies which beset Mexico as they did the rest of the world since the beginning of the seventies, have been rendered more acute by various bottlenecks in the Mexican productive sector. Both in agriculture, where an insufficient supply led to rises in prices, as well as in the industrial area where rises in costs caused increased prices, the Mexican inflation rate was raised above rates prevailing in the world generally.

The effects of that inflation on the flight of capital, which theoretically would have had a calming effect on inflation, were counteracted by the severe depression of private investment and, by seeking to maintain the rate of exchange, private indebtedness was stimulated and public indebtedness to foreign countries accelerated. During the long period this process was under way, domestic demand was stimulated. Initially directed mainly toward speculative types of goods, in the late months of 1976 it spread to all types of durable goods.

The impossibility of continuing this process indefinitely led to the devaluation of September 1976. For an economy of the size and complexity of the Mexican one, the magnitude of this measure has no precedent. In less than three months the exchange rate was reduced by half in terms of the former dollar exchange rate. Its inflationary effect was much greater than the price rises recorded in the preceding year. Its impact on all economic activities was devastating, leading to the greatest depression in the entire post-war period.

The devaluation of 1976 concentrated, into a very short period, effects that should have occurred over several years, both because of the measures adopted to prevent it in the previous nine months and because of the psychological effects produced by its magnitude. It is as if, as the last vestige of the stabilising development policy was abandoned, the fictitious character of the economy fostered during an entire decade was suddenly revealed.

The restructuring of the Mexican economic policy will have to be based upon a new strategy of long-term development. This strategy will have to deal with the central problem besetting our growth: the generation of enough employment and the meeting of the basic needs of the Mexican population for nourishment, health and education. The establishment of these priorities determines, to a considerable degree, the specific policies that must be pursued in the various sectors and, what is perhaps more important, modifies the internal mechanism of our growth, seeking consistency between ends and means, avoiding the danger that the latter will be achieved at the expense of production and employment. This implies the subordination of fiscal, credit and monetary policies to the general priorities established; it implies increased production of goods destined to satisfy the basic needs of mass consumption; it implies consolidation of our economic independence by better use of our natural resources. It would be presumptuous to imply that the design of this strategy has been completed, much less that it is in operation.

In a mixed economy like that of Mexico, implementation of such a programme requires in its initial stages high levels of growth in order to permit modification of the existing structure of production and services, orienting any increases in the desired direction.

This work, whose initial stages could in 'normal' circumstances have been completed within two or three years, must be adapted to present conditions. Economic reality imposes serious restrictions upon any such programme. These restrictions are not limited to those stemming from our society but also include those that derive from the international financial position from which Mexico cannot quickly extract itself, but to which it is linked by policies pursued in the past, to a greater degree, than the average of countries similar to ours.

If this modification of our growth and development strategy had been started in the mid-sixties, its implementation would have been characterised by a gradual modification of sectoral policies and a radical change in macroeconomic mechanisms. Under present conditions, major modification of the macroeconomic mechanism is not feasible, we cannot consider transforming it even gradually before the current economic problem has been overcome. Rather, one must co-ordinate such plans with far-reaching changes in sectoral policies that hasten improvement in the present difficult position.

This situation would appear, at first glance, to be similar to that faced by economic policy at the beginning of the seventies, in which modifications of global policy occurred exclusively on a sectoral level. The difference in present policy, in addition to that resulting from experience of recent years, has two key elements:

(a) On the one hand, on a macroeconomic level, we no longer have any artificial objective that must be pursued, as was the case of the parity of exchange and the mechanisms of public and private financing. There are short-term restrictions that have to be taken into account in order to preserve economic stability, but these do not require the adoption of policies based on preconceptions about the functioning of the economy.

(b) The exercise of this freedom is also influenced by the objectives of the new growth and development strategy. In other words, despite the restrictions imposed by the need to deal with economic fluctuations, it is necessary to behave in a manner consistent with the priorities established by the new strategy. It is this bridge between what it is possible to do today and the goals for the future that constitutes the essence of short-term policy for the Mexican government.

From the previous explanation concerning some broad characteristics of the Mexican economy, stems the need to focus our attention on two of the main objectives of the new growth and development strategy:

(1) Food production
(2) Energy production.

These objectives or priorities will be the subject of the second part of my chapter.

In the third part, I shall talk about the programme and incentives required by the priorities. Finally, I will finish the paper with an explanation of the role that public enterprise has to play in order to fulfil the objectives of the Mexican new growth and development strategy.

II. PRIORITIES

In the previous section of this paper I gave some reasons why food and energy are chosen as priority sectors.

(a) Food production

The general growth and development priority assigned to food production involves co-ordination of rural employment with targets in agricultural and fishing production. The former requires revision of policies relating to the holding of land, which has become the scarce factor of our economy; the latter means a revision of the structure of investment and credit mechanisms to be achieved by means of regional differentiation, zones of maximal rural employment with areas of maximum production. The former involves intensive investment in labour power, mainly in capital-intensive activities in the countryside, which has until now specialised in small infrastructure projects and in industrial enterprises oriented towards regional self-sufficiency in basic products.

The latter involves the expansion of a modern food industry that provides capital to and organises agriculture and fishing in order to achieve levels of production and productivity that can assure supplies to urban areas.

One cannot assume that, in the short term, these policies will increase rural employment substantially, although it is feasible for the underemployment index to be lowered, thereby reducing migration to large urban centres. It is obvious that the medium-term solution to the problem of employment lies in the sphere of the industrial and services sector. The required expansion of the markets for both these outputs, however, depends on the achievement of a 5 per cent annual growth rate in income, at a minimum. In other words, current idle capacity tends to limit growth below the average rate of growth needed for the economy. Therefore the industrial development programme is of great importance, particularly for the medium term.

(b) Energy production

The top general priority for industry lies in the energy sector, for it underlies the activities of our economy. It is in the industrial sector that the significance of energy is greatest. Electricity, oil and gas are critical inputs for industry. The industrial priorities that have been established are consistent with the general aims of the new strategy and can be summed-up in terms of the economic sectors that become crucial: basic mass consumption goods including housing construction; capital goods; food; iron and steel; sources of energy, particularly the petrochemical industry, both basic and secondary; and fertilisers.

III. PROGRAMMES REQUIRED BY THE PRIORITIES

Overall consistency of different fiscal, financial and expenditure devices should be achieved by an annual programme that, although limited in its macroeconomic effects, helps to reorient different sectors of the economy toward the desired structure.

Such a programme is absolutely necessary for public enterprise, in order gradually to reduce the restrictions that economic fluctuations impose via the balance of payments and of fiscal deficits, and in order to assure achievement of the established targets at the macroeconomic level, thus providing the necessary basis for greater future growth and development.

The priorities of growth and development require a consistent design in the various means adopted for their achievement; fiscal and customs-duty incentives and financial support for infrastructure expenses. In a mixed economy such as ours it is only through incentives that private investment can be attracted toward the directions required by these priorities, particularly toward those branches of the economy in which the importance of the public sector itself as principal consumer, can guarantee sustained demand.

But the reorientation of industry cannot be limited to the establishment of sectoral priorities. These indicate new fields for expansion. But, at the same time, it is necessary to improve efficiency. As has been pointed out, indiscriminate substitution of imports resulted in the creation of an industry directed almost exclusively toward the domestic market, the establishment of very small plants serving consumers rather than industry, and with excessive vertical integration resulting from an oligopolistic structure.

The indiscriminate use of quantitative controls has favoured price levels that, measured in foreign currency, are higher than those prevalent in international markets. This has reinforced the excessive concentration of industry upon the domestic market and has, at the same time, prevented adequate growth of exports. The balance of payments problems thereby generated, and the resulting reduction in volume of production, have prevented industry from benefiting from the advantages of dynamic scale economies that access to foreign markets can offer.

In this way, a vicious circle has been generated within domestic industry – which is less efficient than that of developed countries in terms of the use of inputs per unit of output – incapable of growing because of lack of expansion of demand, and more important, because of the limited ability and opportunity to compete with other countries.

It is therefore necessary to modify not only the magnitude of protection but also to restructure the devices through which it is granted. Instead of direct protection via prices it is necessary to design a strategy in which protection is granted through production costs: cost reductions relative to the international costs of inputs in general use which the country has in abundance, items such as minerals and combustibles from the oil fields, which enable industry to penetrate not only the domestic market but also the foreign one. This policy should not be driven to an extreme which will weaken state enterprises. This approach can help to compensate for the lower productivity of the industrial process peculiar to a developing country, to increase ability to compete, to accelerate growth and, by taking advantage of scale economies, to eliminate gradually the inefficiency that made protection necessary at the outset.

This all requires greater participation of manufacturers in export, not only to improve the balance of trade but to assure the adoption of more efficient norms and scales of production.

Having explained some characteristics of the Mexican economy, the priorities of growth and development and the programmes required by the priorities, we will finish by analysing the role that the public sector has to play in order to achieve the national goals.

IV. THE ROLE OF THE PUBLIC SECTOR IN THE NEW STRATEGY OF GROWTH AND DEVELOPMENT

One cannot ignore the fact that, as long as the constraints imposed by the state of the world economy endure, the action of the measures just discussed will have a limited effect in stimulating and, consequently, modifying the industrial structure of the country. Private enterprise functions almost exclusively by pursuit of profits and these can only be achieved as part of an overall expansion.

To achieve this, it is necessary to overcome the effects of world recession for only in this way is it possible to reach the employment goal appropriate for the industrial sector and, as a corollary, the service sector.

Hence a first, short-term objective for public enterprise is the gradual reduction in the magnitude of these effects. As these primarily take the form of public deficits and deficits in balance of payments, priority has been assigned to those matters. The problem of the public deficit requires public firms to increase their efficiency in the short run, readjusting costs and prices and raising their own resources for investment. The balance of payments problem requires those firms capable of exporting to do so with great promptness, and those which can provide substitutes for imports, either directly or indirectly, to do so in accord with the available supply.

As Mexico and, in particular, its state-owned firms are producers of minerals and oil, it is in these areas that the export drive should be concentrated. In silver, lead, copper and zinc, mining firms with state participation must in the short run undertake maximal productive efforts in order to raise the total amount of their exports. However, it is the oil sector that offers the greatest opportunities.

The discoveries of oil fields and the accelerated expansion of PEMEX stocks offers the possibility of eliminating, in the near future, the problems of the balance of payments. From this point of view, the export of crude oil and gas is a possible choice but it is necessary to emphasise that it is only a temporary choice. Mexico has already gone beyond the stage in which its future can be confined to the primitive role of exporter of crude oil. Neither in terms of employment nor in terms of income is this a viable alternative in the long term.

Hence the use of resources derived from oil, rather than oil itself, is what is important. It is this new development strategy, and its implications for the use of oil, which offers the prospect of better use of all our resources; of full training for our labour force; of providing capital to the countryside and raising its production; of consolidating our industry and raising its efficiency; of offering more employment and better wages; of satisfying the basic needs of all of our population.

In other words, the importance of oil stems from the role it can play in the new development strategy. Consequently, for public enterprise, including PEMEX, highest priority must be assigned to provision of the basis which will permit the nation in future years to take advantage of the resources derived from the present indispensable exports of crude oil.

For this purpose it is necessary to plan the behaviour of the public sector, not in a casual manner but in a systematic way, to prepare it for its role in accomplishing this task. The planning of the public sector in a mixed economy requires a forecasting model both for the short and medium term, which permits the governing role of public investment to reassert itself, induces private investment in certain sectors, and takes the place of this investment when it does not occur. By this means, not only will sectoral balancing of supply and demand be assured, but also the level of overall investment required to maintain the desired rate of growth in income, employment and exports.

Training of public sector management to enable it to carry out this planning task, as well as the achievement of an organisational structure appropriate for the new strategy, is the reason for the organisational reform introduced by President Lopez Portillo's government.

This restructuring of public enterprise and of the sectoral policies is required by the very essence of the new development strategy; it will permit the economy to emerge from the difficult economic situation in which the country finds itself, but with a different conception of our growth; a new image of the country we want to be and can be.

It is obvious that this course and its double objective involves risks and, above all, sacrifices. Thus, the rate of growth of the economy in 1977 very probably has for a second consecutive year remained below the rate of demographic growth and the forecasts for 1978 lie in the neighbourhood of 5 per cent. The government is aware of the sacrifices these figures reflect in terms of employment and living standards.

But for the next five years greater and increasing rates of growth are considered feasible. It is possible that by 1982 we will be growing at 9 per cent per annum with an average of 7 per cent for the period. The most important thing is that it should be growth of a different kind, one that satisfies basic needs and does not only induce imitative consumption by privileged groups. There is the risk, of which we are aware, that in pursuing this double goal, the immediately urgent tasks will take priority over matters more important for the long run, and the state of the world and national economies will again inhibit the structure of the growth programme.

One cannot rule out this possibility because, by itself, the determination of the Mexican Government is not sufficient to prevent its occurrence. Events often surpass the will of states. But we are convinced that it is possible to achieve our goals: in addition to the political will, we believe we have the capacity to attain them and, above all, we have the solidarity of the Mexican people determined to create an economy that is not only wealthier, but also fairer.

Discussion of Dr Marcos' Paper

Mrs Navarrete gave a brief overview of the historical development of the Mexican economy which led to the current situation. Sustained development began in 1940, and could be divided into three phases. A first phase, lasting from 1940 to 1955, was characterised by inflationary development, with an average annual growth of GNP of 6 per cent, while prices went up by 11 per cent per year on the average. Development was essentially balanced among sectors, with industry growing at 7 per cent per year. New land was irrigated and soil redistributed. The basis for the steel industry was laid during that time. Unemployment decreased. Development was financed essentially by internal resources, and the foreign debt was low. Two devaluations occurred in 1947 and 1954. In the last few years of the first phase, there was increasing concentration of profits, and the first signs of unequal income distribution began to appear. But in spite of these disturbing elements, taken overall, the first phase represented successful development. A second phase lasted from 1956 to 1972. The main goal during that time was to stabilise development and reduce inflationary pressure. GNP rose by 6.5 per cent and prices by 4.5 per cent per year on the average. Multinational corporations entered such industries as food processing and pharmaceuticals. The employment rate diminished. The basic failing of this phase was that investment in agriculture was discontinued, which was to create difficulties later. Agricultural production yielded a surplus, despite hunger in some places. The imbalance in income distribution grew more acute. A third phase, beginning in 1973, was characterised by stagflation. It began with high unemployment. GNP grew by 4 per cent per year, whereas prices rose by 16 to 19 per cent per year. One source of this tremendous inflation was the rise in the prices of imports, while exports did not increase. Only a national economic plan could permit further advance. The past had been characterised by incoherent, conflicting efforts which did not achieve their goal. She agreed with the investment strategy outlined in the paper, which would use oil revenue to finance industrialisation. She asked how the food problem was going to be dealt with, and what policies regarding imports and exports were planned.

Mr González agreed with Dr Marcos and Mrs Navarrete that the basic problem was agricultural. The increase in food production had not kept pace with population growth. He said that enterprises bought the crops from farmers at very low prices and earned high profits, while the farmers had barely enough to survive. 80 to 90 per cent of the companies in rural areas were transnational. He asked whether the government was planning to set up more public enterprises in key industries such as food processing.

Mr Arroyo said that past policies promoting import subsitution had led to investments in capital-intensive industries in Mexico. The promotion of export-oriented manufacturing industries, which was advocated in the paper, also required capital-intensive modern plants so that the products could compete effectively with those of other countries. But this was in conflict with the goal of reducing unemployment. Mexico needed appropriate technology which made the best use of its available factor endowments and reduced unemployment.

Professor Srinivasan said that export-oriented industries could also be labour-intensive, as the successful examples of Korea and Taiwan had shown. Arroyo said that Hong Kong and Singapore could be added to this list. Mexico differed from them in that it had a large potential domestic market. But people had no money. This was a result of the importation of capital-intensive industry. Ways would have to be found to employ the large reserves of unused labour, so as to increase effective demand, and to let them produce goods for the domestic market. This required the development of more adequate technologies.

Dr Marsan said that labour or capital-intensity alone was not a sufficient criterion for the choice of industries. Oil extraction was very capital-intensive, yet Mexico had no choice but to produce oil. *Arroyo* explained that he agreed that the extraction of oil was a useful investment, given the high price of oil and Mexico's endowment of this resource. But he questioned whether investments in a petrochemical industry, which by its nature was highly capital-intensive, were the right thing for Mexico. The same financial resources might better be invested in industries that created more jobs per dollar of investment, and therefore, probably also more value added.

Mr Gutiérrez commented on the suggestion in the paper that industry be supported by low input prices (e.g. for oil), rather than by tariff protection. He said that the growth prospects of Mexican public enterprises producing inputs for industry have been negatively affected by this – never proven – contention that subsidised prices (e.g. energy and steel) promoted industrial development. He added that there were opportunity costs in the form of foregone revenue from the potential export of these inputs and the foregone benefits of the required Government subsidies. A better way to support industry was tax exemption to private industries running on three shifts per day, and to those which were export-oriented. This was more consistent with the employment and foreign exchange objectives.

Mrs Espinoza added that low costs for inputs protected inefficient industries, in the same way as an overvalued currency had protected inefficient industries in the past.

Marcos agreed that this was a potential problem of which one had to be aware. But he said Mexico must take into account the possibility that excessive oil exports might weaken its export price. It might well be in the country's interest to have a domestic price for oil that was lower than the international price.

Dr Marsan said that the Italian government had initially tried to encourage industrialisation of the south through the granting of low-cost loans. But this had created little new employment. Now it had begun to subsidise manpower, and this had an effect on the choice of technology, giving preference to labour-intensive industries. He also said the paper had distinguished clearly between long-term and short-term objectives. To find a proper balance between the two was a perennial problem. In Italy there was general agreement on the long-term objectives of increased employment and growth. But then suddenly the 'urgent' problem of combating inflation prevented pursuit of these goals. He said he hoped that Mexico would be able to adhere to its long-range goals, but that this was not always easy.

Srinivasan said that a pure floating exchange rate permitted macroeconomic policies to be pursued independently of exchange rate considerations. He asked whether Mexico had instead chosen a partial or 'dirty' float in its exchange rate. *Marcos* replied that the exchange rate was used as a policy instrument, and could not be left to move absolutely freely.

Mrs González asked whether public investment in oil would mean a reduction of public investments in health care and education.

Marcos said that success was not measured by the rate of economic growth alone, but by the fulfilment of the objectives of the development strategy, the provision of health, food and education. But to achieve these goals, priority had to be given to the production of food and energy. Therefore, even if the oil industry by itself did not provide much employment, it was important. Jobs could be created in other industries, some of which required energy as an essential input. The proper choice of technology would have to be considered for the industrial system as a whole, not for each sector separately. He also thought that Mexico should have a petrochemical industry. Some countries had oil, others had industry, but Mexico had both. Concerning agricultural policy he said there were the dual objectives of self-sufficiency in food production and of the stimulation of rural employment. He saw the solution in the mechanisation of subsistence agriculture, using comparatively small and inexpensive equipment, with which it could become more productive and supply the food needs of the cities. Regarding trade policy, he said that in the past Mexico had put too much emphasis on export promotion. This had made it necessary to import foreign capital goods, since the domestic capital goods sector had been insufficient to meet the demand. It was now also necessary to provide motivation for exports, and for industrialisation in general. This required greater emphasis on import substitution in capital goods, at least in those areas where it was economically advantageous to do so.

Part Two
Private and Public Enterprise:
Experience in Various Countries

6 Market Structure and Market Organisation in the Electricity and Gas Public Utility Sector of the Federal Republic of Germany

Hans K. Schneider and Walter Schulz
ENERGIEWIRTSCHAFTLICHES INSTITUT, KOLN

I. INTRODUCTION

The electricity and gas public utility sector of the FRG consists of a decentralised system of supply with a considerable degree of concentration of decision-making power. The titles to real estate (including that of the public road system) as well as to the economic resources, both of which are regulated by the civil law, form the legal basis of their supply activities. The owners are the public territorial authorities (states and cities, and, in the electricity sector, also the federal state), private subjects (individual persons and firms), as well as the so-called mixed companies which belong both to private and public owners. The public utilities are essentially free in their investment policy though the *Energiewirtschaftsgesetz* allows far-reaching government intervention which, however, has not occurred to any great extent. Regulation of investments, beyond certain minor measures of control, does not take place. It is true that the construction of oil and gas plants has been restricted in recent years. But this was not part of an overall control scheme in the electricity sector but was only intended to stabilise hard coal consumption in this sector.

The public utilities are essentially free in their pricing policy. Pricing decisions for gas are not subject to administrative controls; according to the dominant philosophy, competition by substitutes is so intensive that there is no need for specific controls. Electricity prices for large-scale consumers are also unregulated, whereas the prices for small customers are, to a certain extent, regulated. However, freedom of price formation has virtually been abolished for pure retailers, because their prices are not allowed to exceed those of the utility from which they buy electricity. Higher prices are regarded as abusive by the *Bundeskartellamt*.

Since concentration in production has continually increased and a growing number of utilities are confined to retailing, the concentration of decision power has increased. Most vital decisions are taken by the *Verbundgesellschaften* who dispose of the greater part of production capacity, as well as the grid, and co-operate closely.

In most cases the electric and gas public utilities in the FRG do not simply pursue short-run maximisation of profits. They rather prefer a policy of output maximisation compatible with a minimum profit which is regarded as being sufficient. The fact that most of the public utilities in the FRG are public or mixed enterprises may have influenced this pricing behaviour; the realisation of economies to scale to the greatest possible extent was, however, probably of greater importance.

In pricing policy, there are great differences between gas and electric utilities. Because of intensive competition in the heat market, gas prices have to be adjusted to fuel oil prices. Therefore, gas pricing is dominated by the principle of charging what the traffic will bear. The rapid penetration of natural gas has been greatly eased by the policy of price discrimination.

The electric utilities attained an average growth rate of electricity production that was 3 per cent higher than the growth rate of GNP and which is at least equal to the growth of electricity production in comparable industrial countries. The gas utilities increased the share of natural gas in meeting the primary energy requirements from 1 per cent (1962) to 14 per cent (1976); on the supply side they managed to set a basis for further expansion, even beyond the year 2000. Throughout the period investments were sufficiently high to permit an overall supply adequate for unrestricted satisfaction of demand. New investments use modern techniques of high standard and the age structure of the capital stock can be considered healthy. The few available investigations which permit a comparison indicate that prices do not seem to be higher than comparable[1] prices in other industrialised countries.

In the FRG there is no centralised energy planning board in which the planning activities of the utility companies are integrated. The energy programme of the Federal Government does not bind firms directly but tries to inform them of the estimated or desired trends of development in energy demands and supplies. In addition to the expected influence on individual decisions by the energy programme, government intervenes according to circumstances either to prevent undesired or to enforce desired developments in the energy sector, if the market mechanism fails. Other interventions have been based on the *Energiewirtschaftsgesetz* (see p. 71) and recently, above all, on the *Gesetz gegen Wettbewerbsbeschränkungen* (law against restraints on trade), the provisions of which are interpreted more and more extensively.

Although the amount, as well as the intensity, of interventions has increased considerably, and although the degree of freedom for the private decision-making process has evidently diminished, the principles of decentralised control of the decision processes in the electricity and gas supply sector are still valid.

[1]In order to carry out a comparison the different tax regulations and subsidies, as well as the effects of price controls, have to be taken into account.

The structure of future development of the existing system cannot yet be discerned. There are no plans for comprehensive reform but only individual proposals which are based mainly on the existing law against restraints on trade. The farthest-reaching proposal is that of the Monopoly Commission which suggests an elaborate centralised control of investments and prices. In view of the existing political checks and balances resulting from the federal system of the FRG, this proposal is unlikely to be carried out. There may, however, be a better chance for some of the proposals, the analysis and evaluation of which will be part of this chapter.

II. THE PRESENT STRUCTURE AND ORGANISATION

Today the electric utilities meet about four-fifths of the overall electricity demand compared to the three-fifths of twenty-five years ago. Electricity production by industry, therefore, has been crowded out. There are two reasons for this development. The power plants of the hard-coalmining industry, which practically feed their total production into the public grid, are regarded in statistics as belonging to the industrial producers of energy, although according to their function they are part of the public supply system. The amount of production of these power plants has decreased in absolute terms within the last few years. At the same time the electricity production of the industrial power plants has grown at a slower rate than public electricity production. The main reason, however, is technical progress and, in connection with it, the economies of scale which reduced production costs of the public power plants more than that of the industrial ones, as most of the stations of the public utility sector are bigger. Besides, the fact that the public utilities act as monopolists may have contributed to the decreasing share of the industry-produced electricity. Anyhow, the representatives of this group of power stations claim that public utilities not only block direct access to the market, but also offer such unattractive conditions for taking over excess electricity, as well as for delivering electricity for reserve purposes, that electricity production by industry is made uneconomic in many cases.

The (public) electricity supply sector can be characterised by a high degree of concentration on the one hand and, simultaneously, by a high degree of fragmentation on the other. According to statistics there are about 1200 public utilities; however, almost half of them are the smallest companies with unimportant market shares. 75 per cent of the rest again consist of small companies. Their share in overall electricity production is only about 0.5 per cent; their shares in delivery of electricity are 12 per cent as far as small customers and 6 per cent as far as large-scale consumers are concerned. If we neglect these small companies too, the number of remaining public utilities is reduced to 168. But even within this group some few companies dominate. 65 per cent of the overall electricity production, 48 per cent of the delivery to large-scale customers (mainly industrial customers), and 28 per cent of the delivery to small customers are concentrated in the biggest nine companies.

Delivery to small customers is dominated by the regional and local public utilities. However, the autonomy of these companies, which only act as retailers, is restricted mainly because their prices are tied to those of the suppliers.

Therefore, the big leading companies have more influence than indicated by their market shares. These firms are, at the same time, owners of the transregional grid. The grid is planned and used according to free co-operation contracts between eight *Verbundunternehmen*.

Today natural gas dominates the public gas sector of the FRG with a market share of 85 per cent. The share of manufactured gas will decrease further, at least as far as the next years are concerned. About 40 per cent of the natural gas comes from indigenous production which probably cannot be increased further. The rest is imported from the Netherlands, the Soviet Union, the Norwegian part of the North Sea, and – in a few years – from Iran and Algeria.

With respect to the gas supply we have to distinguish three steps: (i) the national and international gas supply market; (ii) wholesale markets; and (iii) retail markets. The degree of concentration in indigenous production and imports is very high. The biggest three companies together have a market share of 70 per cent, the biggest six one of 90 per cent.

Three-fourths of overall gas production is sold by integrated transportation and distribution companies. These firms own the transregional pipeline systems, which today are spread all over the FRG. The amount of gas supplied by these companies is almost equally divided among direct deliveries to final consumers (above all customers in the industry and the electricity sector) and deliveries to local distributors. In the transregional pipeline system too, there is a high degree of concentration. The most important company has a market share of some 60 per cent; the market share of the three biggest companies together amounts to 85 per cent.

Almost 500 companies are solely engaged in the distribution of gas on the local level. Forms of co-operation that can be compared to those in the electricity sector do not exist. However, there are joint ventures, in which the importing gas companies work together with various foreign partners.

The public utilities in the FRG are mainly mixed or public companies. In the electricity sector the type of mixed and public companies owned by the states is predominant at the production stage, while at the distribution stage public companies with cities as owners prevail. Purely private firms play an unimportant role.

Gas production is dominated by private companies (with a share of 84 per cent). Private companies also have a share of about 50 per cent in distribution, mainly because delivery to large-scale consumers is reserved for them by contracts. Local distribution is mainly controlled by the public, especially the cities.

At the local stage of distribution, gas and electricity are often supplied by the same firm. Consequently, decisions on investments and prices are not co-ordinated by free competition processes, but internally. As far as one can judge, the internal co-ordination depends on the relative costs and returns of these two forms of energy. However, there are at least two limits to co-ordinated pricing behaviour: gas profit margins are limited by intensive competition with oil and electricity prices have to be tied to those of the suppliers. In general, it is true that restrictive, monopolistic behaviour is rarely found and also can hardly ever be proven.

The integration of gas and electricity supply into one company, which, as the cities argue, serves as a means to decrease overhead costs, has been criticised. The same is even more true for those companies where a deficit division, mostly responsible for public transport, is part of the organisation. In the latter case, returns from the energy division are used to subsidise the deficit division.

III. THE LEGAL FRAMEWORK

The public utility sector has been characterised by contractual barriers to market entry almost right from the start. Most utilities were begun on private initiative and shortly afterwards were taken over by cities. The use of public roads for the distribution system is subject to licensing. By restricting the licence to only one company the market can be closed completely to any entrant. Disputes on market demarcation arose mainly in the course of regional expansion of utility companies but were rapidly settled by contracts. Together with exclusive concessions granted by the cities, these demarcation contracts resulted in a perfect system of barriers to entry.

This state of affairs was sanctioned by the 1935 *Energiewirtschaftsgesetz (Gesetz zur Förderung der Energiewirtschaft)*. The law provides for control of investments and prices as well as the duty of the public utilities to supply all customers according to published tariffs and conditions. In severe cases of misbehaviour the licence to supply can be withdrawn. However, these far-reaching options were not used systematically to change the structure and organisation of the public utility sector. On the contrary, these controls may even have stabilised its traditional structure. Still, the pricing policy of the public utilities was subjected to a number of restrictions – especially with regard to small customers – which later, however, were withdrawn for gas utilities.

The fundamental issue of the *Ordnung* of the public utility sector arose again when the law against restraints on trade *(Gesetz gegen Wettbewerbsbeschränkungen*, passed in 1957) was discussed. The trade-restraining contracts which characterise the public utility sector were exempted from the law. Like the *Energiewirtschaftsgesetz*, the *Gesetz gegen Wettbewerbsbeschränkungen* takes for granted that competition does not lead to satisfactory results in the public utility sector, which thus needs special consideration. The legalised special treatment was declared to be only a provisional solution until a revised *Energiewirtschaftsgesetz* could be created.

To date, however, no legislative steps toward fundamental reform have been taken.

It is quite likely that the law against restraints on trade will have more influence on the future structure and organisation of the electricity and gas sector of the FRG than the *Energiewirtschaftsgesetz*.

It is true that this law excludes these companies from the general prohibition of certain contracts which aim at restraining competition. Thus the law allows the exclusion of direct competition within the supply areas. However, to prevent the firms from misusing their position as a regional or local monopoly the law provides that the *Bundeskartellamt*, which is an independent authority on the federal state level, has a right to intervene in cases of misuse.

As the exclusion of competition aims at a rationalisation of supply, which means lower costs and prices, prices are said to be unjustified if they would be lower without a demarcation contract. Comparison with a hypothetical case of competition is used by the *Bundeskartellamt* as the relevant criterion for misuse. It will have to be characterised here in more detail. A critical analysis will be given later.

More radical is a proposal asking for a change or an extension of existing laws against restraints on trade: by strictly separating the production from the distribution sphere, competition between the companies for 'regional markets' would be established witin thee electricity sector. This proposal will be dealt with first. In between there is a proposal which aims at intensifying competition between existing companies, which will be discussed afterwards.

IV. THE CONCEPT OF NATURAL MONOPOLY AND A PROPOSAL TO INTENSIFY COMPETITION BETWEEN ELECTRIC PUBLIC UTILITIES BY MEANS OF VERTICAL DIVESTITURE

There have always been two reasons for the special treatment of public utilities: they meet a vital need and they are natural monopolies. In Germany it has been believed for a long time that their supply should be guaranteed by public authorities or companies. Today these reasons for special treatment of the gas and electricity sector no longer play an important role. Furthermore, historic experience has shown that public companies *per se* do not guarantee a policy which is dedicated to the 'common weal'. The criterion that is used to justify the special treatment of the public utilities is that of natural monopoly.

This concept has frequently been misinterpreted in economic discussions as justification for a general exclusion of competition in the field of gas and electricity supply. In this context, however, one fails to see that even in the gas and electricity supply sector, natural monopolies are often characteristic of specific branches of activities only and that monopolistic power does not necessarily result from natural monopoly as such.

These issues will be discussed next. They are the core of a recently developed proposal which aims at a fundamental reorganisation of the electricity sector on the basis of competition.

The concept of natural monopoly has been used for a long time by economists to study economic policy in the public utility sector. However, things are simplified far too much if public utilities are just defined as natural monopolies and a legal exclusion of all forms of competition is therefore demanded. Chadwick's[1] distinction between 'competition *for* the field' and 'competition *within* the field' already made it clear that a natural monopoly in the production sphere does not exclude competition for the supply of a market.

A natural monopoly is said to exist if the cost function is strictly subadditive. In case of a one-product natural monopoly the following must then be true:

$$K(\sum_i x_i) \leqslant \sum_i K_i(x_i)$$

for $i = 1 \ldots n$, where x_i stands for the number of units of the product supplied. Since electric and gas utilities are multi-product firms, it is appropriate to use a more general characterisation of the natural monopoly which replaces units of homogeneous product with sets of customers. For any partition of the set N of customers into the subsets S and T (with S, $T C N$, $S - T = 0$) the following is required:[2]

$$K(x^S) + K(x^T) \geqslant K(x^{S+T}).$$

This extension to the case of a multi-product firm permits – in addition to the mere economies of scale – the inclusion of all other 'economies of joint production' which result from the heterogeneity of the products. A typical instance of such economies in gas and electricity supply is the economies of utilisation: a higher degree of utilisation of the capacity can be attained by joint supply of customers with different time profiles of use.

According to this extended concept a natural monopoly is present if only joint use of a capacity by all consumers fully realises all coalition gains. These gains may be increasing even if there no longer are economies of scale (the subadditivity does not exclude increasing costs per unit).

What matters is the fact that in many cases strict subadditivity of the cost function only applies to some fields or some stages of the overall supply system. At the stage of local distribution we are certainly faced with a natural

---

[1]Chadwick, E., 'Results of Different Principles of Legislation and Administration in Europe; of Competition for the Field, as Compared with the Competition within the Field of Service', *Journal of the Royal Statistical Society* (1859). Chadwick's position has turned up again in several articles of Demsetz. Demsetz, H., 'Why Regulate Utilities?' *The Journal of Law and Economics,* Vol. 11 (1968), 55–65; 'Information and Efficiency: Another Viewpoint', *Journal of Law and Economics,* Vol. 12 (1969), 1–22; 'On the Regulation of Industry: A Reply', *Journal of Political Economy,* Vol. 79 (1971), 356–65. Williamson, O.E., 'Franchise Bidding for Natural Monopoly – in General and with Respect to CATV', *The Bell Journal of Economics,* Vol. 7 (1976), No. 1, 73–104.

[2]Faulhaber, G. R., 'Cross-Subsidization: Pricing in Public Enterprises, *American Economic Review,* Vol. 65 (1975), 966–77, 968.

monopoly as the joint use of the capacity by all customers offers the most efficient solution. Electricity production does not constitute a natural monopoly. Given its cost functions, the size of the market permits the existence of a large number of efficient suppliers. In this case the natural monopoly is confined to certain spheres of the overall supply system only, i.e. the 'regional markets'[1] in which competition amongst several suppliers would not be efficient. That does not mean that competition for the supply of the 'regional markets' becomes impossible. Therefore we cannot conclude that a natural monopoly leads to monopoly prices. If competition for 'regional markets' can be established, '. . . the rivalry of bidders has eliminated monopoly power, even though only one firm (because of scale economies) will succeed in securing the contract and producing the product'.[2]

However, there must be a reservoir of bidders on nearby markets in order to secure an efficient competition for the supply of the different 'regional markets'. The electricity sector meets this requirement, since the natural monopoly does not cover the overall supply but only parts of the transportation and distribution system. Electricity producers as well as existing utilities may be potential competitors for the supply of 'regional markets'.

In order to establish competition *for* supply areas, general access to the electricity transportation grid obviously has to be rendered possible. This can be achieved, e.g. by a separation of the grid from other activities so that each electric utility can use the grid at prices which would not discriminate between different categories of users. This is the central idea of a proposal concerning the reorganisation of the electricity sector on a competitive basis in the FRG (Gröner-proposal).[3] According to the Gröner proposal production, transport and distribution should be allocated to different companies, i.e. the private or public transport companies[4] should neither be able to produce nor distribute electricity. They offer their service, 'use of the transportation system', and sign agreements for transportation of electricity with the bidders for the supply of regional markets. According to Gröner, bidders are the producers of electricity. On the demand side cities or districts act as representatives of the regional markets. They invite bids for the supply of their areas for a certain period of time and are obliged to give the contract to the bidder with the cheapest offer. Thus, competition could not only be established amongst a variety of bidders in the production sphere but also in the distribution sphere.

However, the Gröner proposal does not stand a critical test since it is based

---

[1]'Regional markets' are sets of consumers in a more or less extended region which are supplied by a common (distribution) system (cities, counties, but also very big high-voltage consumers). The supply of a 'regional market' is the relevant output unit in investigations about the organisation of the public utility sector.

[2]Demsetz, H., 'On the Regulation of Industry'; *op cit.*, 359.

[3]Gröner, H., 'Ordnungspolitik in der Elektrizitätswirtschaft', *ORDO*, Bd. 15/16 (1965), 333–412; Grundzüge einer Wettbewerbsordnung für die Elektrizitätswirtschaft', *SchdVfS*, NF Bd. 65 (1972), 47–69; 'Die Ordnung der deutschen Elektrizitätswirtschaft', Baden-Baden (1975).

[4]If there are several transportation companies their areas of activities have to be demarcated, in order to avoid duplication of vestment.

on false assumptions about the economics of the electricity sector. It disrupts the economic system which is formed by the set of power stations within an area together with the grid, and assumes that there will be direct connections between the owners of the power plants as suppliers and the 'regional markets' as buyers of electricity.

The smallest possible demand units are the 'regional markets'. The concentration of dispersed demands with different time profiles of use on a high-voltage system realises coalition gains. The optimal degree of concentration of demand occurs if all coalition gains by means of the joint use of production and grid capacities are exhausted. The most important of these gains are: load diversification amongst consumers, the realisation of scale economies in the grid by means of higher levels of voltages or an optimal grading of the levels of voltage, and the realisation of scale economies in production of electricity as well as advantages of specialisation in different types of power plants. The production and grid sphere form a connected system, as investments in the grid can partially be substituted by investments in the production sphere (and *vice versa*): additional investments in the grid which effect a more comprehensive concentration of demand can cause savings in the production of electricity. Within the production sphere the various types of power stations complement one another.

A basic characteristic of the electricity sector is the fact that the single units are integrated into systems on the supply as well as on the demand side. A concentration of demand corresponds to an integration of the various types of plants to a system on the supply side.

The Gröner proposal adheres to the fiction that direct connections amongst the various producing and demanding units can be established. However, there is no economic reason for the owners of power plants to act as bidders for 'regional markets'. For the investment and sales policies of a power company it is of no importance whether and to what extent contracts have been signed to supply specific regional markets. Power companies provide the grid companies with electricity and their sales potential is solely determined by their competitive strength (in the case of unrestricted competition) in the electricity production market itself. Their engagement in supplying 'regional markets' cannot improve their market position. Thus there are no noticeable incentives for directly connecting businesses in these different markets.

Separation of the production, transportation[1] and distribution spheres would rather lead to the following development:

In the production of electricity a large number of competitors (including the constructors of power plants) may emerge. The bidders for power capacity would be confronted on the demand side by only one grid company in each of the larger areas. The grid companies would announce their power demand in the shorter and longer run and the power plants would compete for the

[1]Actually this sphere contains not only transportation but also all tasks of a grid.

demand. It would certainly be up to the grid companies to co-ordinate the planning of stations with that of the grid.

Strict separation of the production and grid spheres would permit intensive competition in electricity production. However, there would be no direct relations between power production and the bidding for regional markets. As business between the grid companies and regional markets is precluded by the Gröner proposal, a bidder for the supply of 'regional markets' could play only a minor part as an intermediary between just one grid company and one or more 'regional markets'.[1] Efficient competition for 'regional markets' would not develop on this basis. That is why the Gröner proposal is not a proper means of establishing a competitive structure in the electricity sector.

V. COMPETITION AMONGST UTILITIES FOR 'REGIONAL MARKETS'

The basic economic obstacle to competition for regional markets by electricity producers is the fact that suppliers (i.e. power plants) as well as buyers (regional markets) are integral parts of larger systems. Therefore there are no direct relationships between a multitude of suppliers and customers which might be determined by market processes. Separation of production, transportation and distribution would permit competition on the production side only. Similarly sweeping measures cannot be realised on the demand side. It is only possible to establish competition amongst existing utilities for regional markets by bidding.

There are several well-known arguments against the admission of such limited competitive relations. Such limited competition is said to be confined to border-districts of the supply areas and to single large-scale customers and is said to lead to unfair advantages to the consumers in these areas, for which the other consumers have to pay. This, however, is true only in the short run, for in the long run borderlines will change and therefore new sales areas will be contested for. Price differentiation between safe and contested markets may provide protection against competitors for a while but cannot prevent a change of the borderlines of the supply areas in the long run. These are problems that impede or may even exclude competition or may demand corrective actions which, however, do not endanger competition as a general principle.

The risk of losing márkets may induce cost and price decreases. Such a favourable development, however, could be compensated for if competition were not able to select the most efficient suppliers. There are actual economic reasons for the exclusion of competition and the demarcation of safe supply areas.

It is convenient to approach this issue with the help of a coalition model. The enterprise is seen as a co-operative game of 'regional markets'. Absolute freedom to form coalitions would be the analogy of the frequently used

[1]Intermediaries may look for several offers only in border-areas between two grid companies.

reference model of perfect competition. Such a state, however, is by no means true to life. Even worse, these conditions may not even prevent a failure of competition.

Today's protected supply areas can be called forced coalitions. It is the alleged effect of rationalisation brought about by the demarcation contracts which serves as a justification for the legal protection of these forced coalitions. If such an effect is really brought about, why then can the supply areas not do without such contracts? If an aggregation of regional markets leads to lower electricity prices by means of rationalisation, there should be an incentive for all customers to maintain this favourable coalition. There would then be no need to protect supply areas as forced coalitions of regional markets, and an immediate competition between utilities for regional markets would allocate regional markets to supply areas in such a way that the structure of supply would be improved. (The practical problems and restraints of competition for regional markets will not be considered here.)

However, it can be shown that even a coalition which maximises the advantages of co-operation can be unstable. This will be true if there is no mode of distributing the co-operation gains, which will give all members an incentive to stay with the coalition. In such cases individual rationality and group rationality are in conflict. Faulhaber has proved this by showing that a natural monopoly can be unstable.[1] In technical terms, subadditivity of the cost function does not guarantee that, if all costs are covered, there will be a price vector which lies in the core. In such a case the lowest cost solution can only be reached by a forced coalition which forestalls inefficient entry. Those members of the coalition who would get better prices as members of another supply arrangement have to be kept from leaving the coalition, since the damage they inflict on the remaining members will exceed the advantage of those who quit.

There are therefore theoretical reasons which, under specific conditions, justify protection of closed supply areas as forced coalitions as well as contracts aimed at exclusion of competition (of course this does not justify the protection of historic supply areas). Free entry (freedom of coalitions) thus does not secure an allocation of regional markets to areas of supply at lowest costs. One counter-example, given by Faulhaber, is sufficient to demonstrate this. However, the counter-example does not tell us anything about the likelihood of such a failure. Baumol et al.[2] showed that under specific conditions even quasi-optimal pricing can keep a natural monopoly stable. This, however, only means that there are conceivable worlds where the

---

[1]Faulhaber, G. R., *op cit.*, 966–77.

[2]Baumol, W. J., E. E. Bailey, R. D. Willing, 'Weak Invisible Hand Theorems on the Sustainability of Prices in a Multiproduct Monopoly', *American Economic Review*, Vol. 67 (1977), 350–65. The fact that the units in which charges are calibrated are the customers (or more exactly: the characteristics of the delivery), while the stability of supply areas is a matter of keeping regional markets together, poses additional problems. We refer to the discussion about the output unit in the public utility and transportation sector, which dates back to the Taussig–Pigou Controversy in the 1913 *Quarterly Journal of Economics*.

'invisible hand' is active, even in a natural monopoly, so that everything turns out for the best.

For the policy-maker it is important to know whether we live in such a world or whether it is at least possible to establish such conditions by economic policy. Further investigations are needed to provide a sounder basis for the far-reaching decision whether the protection of today's supply areas should be eliminated and replaced by making use of the (limited) possibilities of competition for the supply of regional markets. Only by initiating competitive processes can one prove whether competition leads to favourable results or not. Before such an 'experiment' is set up all other means of getting more information about possible consequences should be used. These means may perhaps also help in finding a suitable framework for competitive relations as well as in interpreting the data generated by such an 'experiment'.

To this end a simulation model has been developed which (among other things) will permit us to analyse, whether, under prevailing conditions in the electricity sector in the FRG, price competition will lead to a globally more efficient supply system.

The model handles different types of public utilities (interregional, regional and local public utilities) and, after feeding in the characteristic data of various supply areas, computes the price vectors for different sets of goals of the companies. The essential elements of the model are: (i) effort–cost functions (with different coefficients for the various types of utilities); (ii) corresponding money–cost functions; (iii) principles of pricing which – given the cost functions and the assumed demand conditions – determine the price vector, which corresponds to the goal concerned, as well as (iv) demand functions.

The effort–cost functions show the relations between the characteristic data of the supply areas (size, demand density, structure of demand, etc.) and the capacities in production, transmission and distribution (production capacity and its composition according to the demand duration curve, length of lines and cables at different voltage levels, number of transformers, etc.). Thus, starting with the characteristics of an arbitrary supply area the model determines the quantity relations underlying the cost function. The coefficients of the effort–cost functions were determined by means of a multiple regression analysis. The money–cost functions have been derived from the effort–cost functions in two steps: first, a replacement value for all assets of a utility has been determined by using today's standard values for the specific investment expenses for different components. This value must then be reduced, as the (lower) incremental capital use is relevant to pricing decisions. Therefore a correspondingly lower annuity factor was applied to the replacement value. The fuel costs have been determined from specific fuel consumption rates, losses and fuel prices.

On the demand side customers have been divided into four groups:

(a) distributing companies purchasing electricity wholesale at high-voltage levels;

   (b) high-voltage industrial consumers;
   (c) deliveries in medium voltages to distributing companies and industrial consumers;
   (d) deliveries in low voltages to small consumers.

For each group a linear demand function has been assumed.

If a certain pricing principle is assumed, the price vector can be determined from the cost and demand functions. Alternative principles of pricing have been chosen in the model: maximisation of output (kwh), sales, or the sum of consumers' surplus, pricing according to peak responsibility and a general pricing formula in which the price relations amongst consumer groups were exogeneously determined. Throughout, a zero profit constraint was applied.

The model determines the price vector for any given supply area and the changes in the price vector if the supply area is altered through gains or losses of regional markets. It is used to find out whether price competition for regional markets will change the composition of supply areas in a way that improves the overall supply arrangement. The advantage of such a simulation model lies in the fact that it can handle a great variety of cases with different constellations of data, and thus helps to establish strong hypotheses about the development of actual competitive processes.

The model was used to determine the frequency of market failure, given different constellations of data. There is market failure if the transition of a regional market R from A to B would improve the overall supply arrangement but does not occur because either the prices of B exceed those of A and/or the take-over of R would compel B to raise its prices over previous levels (subsidisation of R in the enlarged coalition B + R). In the former case the transition would be blocked by the customers of R, in the latter case by the customers of B. There is also market failure if a transition that worsens the overall supply arrangement is blocked neither by the customers of R nor by the customers of B.

Thus there are eight different cases:

The take-over from R by B improves the overall supply arrangement and

   (1) is successful, because the consumers of R and B are better off;
   (2) is blocked, because the consumers of R are worse off;
   (3) is blocked, because the consumers of B are worse off;
   (4) is blocked, because the consumers R and B are worse off.

The take-over from R by B worsens the overall supply arrangement and

   (5) is successful, because the consumers of R and B are better off;
   (6) is blocked, because the consumers of R are worse off;
   (7) is blocked, because the consumers of B are worse off;
   (8) is blocked, because the consumers of R and B are worse off.

In cases (2), (3), (4) and (5) there is a market failure; in cases (2), (3) and (4) price competition prevents a potential improvement in the overall situation and in (5) it even leads to worse conditions.

The economic reason for such market failure lies in the fact that price competition for regional markets occurs, not through prices for regional markets (franchise bidding) but rather through the prices final consumers have to pay. However, this alone is not a sufficient reason for market failure. The decisive difficulty stems from the principle of equal prices within the supply area of a utility. This equalisation of prices between areas with high and low costs of supply, which is backed by economic policy, leads to an orientation of final prices towards the average supply conditions. Market failures arise because decisions which should be based on marginal supply conditions are based on average supply conditions.

These general considerations only permit the conclusion that under these conditions price competition *may* give rise to wrong decisions. Such an analysis of possible events, however, cannot determine the presumable frequency of market failure. Therefore the model has been used to analyse a large number of cases where price competition will lead to take-over by the more efficient companies. An improvement of the overall supply arrangement has been measured by the sum of consumers' surpluses. Calculations have been made for fifteen utilities. They were picked so that the whole array of supply situations of the FRG (by size of enterprise and supply area, demand density, composition of consumers, etc.) were covered. Five types of regional markets were picked, which range from the supply of a typical metropolitan area, and a strongly industrialised area, to rural areas with a low demand density. Results have been derived for all possible transitions of these regional markets amongst the fifteen utility undertakings. Furthermore four alternative principles of pricing have also been used in all calculations. Thus the analysis of the frequency of a market failure is based on $15 \cdot 5 \cdot 14 \cdot 4 = 4200$ cases.[1]

Just under 40 per cent of the analysed cases are characterised by market failure. In most of these cases an improvement of the overall supply arrangement could not be realised by price competition. In 7 per cent of the cases competition would even lead to a deterioration. These results show that the proposal of initiating competition for regional markets is of questionable value, if simultaneously the principle of equal prices within supply areas is

[1]About 10 per cent of these 4200 possible categories were not occupied, since sales of some of the selected utilities to one of the four customer groups were less than those of a regional market.

The number of possible cases would be essentially higher if hybrid cases, which are characterised by different principles of price-making of both competing utilities, had also been considered. The inclusion of hybrid cases would, however, further increase the number of those cases in which the price vectors of the competing utilities overlap. In such cases definite evaluations of the overall relative price advantages cannot be carried out. Even so, the majority of cases involved such overlapping of prices. In such cases of partial price advantage it was assumed that total price advantages could possibly be realised in half of the cases by a restructuring of the price vector. (The cases of partial price disadvantages were treated analogously.) The cases of partial internal subsidisation were analysed using the same procedure.

accepted. It can likewise be demonstrated that the market failure is not explained by 'peculiarities' of the electricity industry. The process of selection takes place rather within a wrong framework.

Table 6.1 summarises the frequency and character of market failure for the sample of cases analysed.

TABLE 6.1   OUTCOME OF CALCULATIONS USING THE ELECTRICITY MARKET MODEL

	Percentage of							
	Cases with market failure				*Cases without market failure*			
	(2)	(3)	(4)	(5)	(1)	(6)	(7)	(8)
Improvement of overall supply situation (+) Deterioration of overall supply situation (−)	+	+	+	−	+	−	−	−
Lower prices at B (+) Higher prices at B (−)	−	+	−	+	+	−	+	−
Take over of R by B without internal subsidisation (+) Take-over of R by B implies internal subsidisation (−)	+	−	−	+	+	+	−	−
Percentage values	15	10	6	7	17	8	15	22
			38				62	

VI. SOME GENERAL REMARKS ON THE PRINCIPLE OF EQUAL PRICES

Equal prices for small customers (e.g. households) in large areas with differing supply conditions can be justified because they contribute to the regional policy goal of equalisation of living conditions. However, equalisation of prices for electricity and gas, when these energies serve as inputs in production, leads to distorted decisions on the location of industry.

Because of the high share of joint costs, there is no direct connection between prices and costs of the individual customer. The equalisation of prices further loosens this connection. Price differentials between regional markets served by different utilities are no longer indicators of differences in costs and efficiency but rather depend on the distribution of 'good risks' and 'bad risks'. Price competition and yardstick competition no longer guarantee the selection of efficient suppliers. Furthermore, the detection by the *Bundeskartellamt* of abusive behaviour is rendered more difficult because there are no sharp dividing lines amongst (permissible or desired) price equalisations, abusive price discrimination and excessive prices. Price equalisation in many, but not all, cases implies cross-subsidisation. The abolition of contractual barriers to market entry would lead to the break-up of such undertakings. Cross-subsidisation, which is politically desired, has thus become an important reason for the maintenance of the contractual protection of existing supply areas in FRG.

VII. INTENSIFICATION OF MONOPOLY CONTROL AND THE 'HYPOTHETICAL COMPETITION CONCEPT'

As an alternative to vertical divestiture (Gröner proposal) or price competition for final consumers by the existing integrated undertakings, an intensification of monopoly control can be chosen. The *Bundeskartellamt* has worked in this direction. The exclusion of direct competition in supply areas is upheld; any abuse of the monopoly power which is thereby given to the utilities is to be fought by control measures. The criteria of 'abusive behaviour' are said to be deduced from a 'hypothetical competition concept'.

Two landmark decisions of the anti-trust referees (*Kartell-referenten*) characterise the way in which 'abusive behaviour' is actually determined. The first of these resolutions (vertical resolution of 1965)[1] refers to two utilities, one of which purchases for the other. The prices of the purchasing utility B are judged abusive if they exceed those of the supply utility A and if A could supply the area of B directly at its lower prices if there were no demarcation contract. The courts have sustained this interpretation. In this way the pricing autonomy of purchasing utilities has practically been abolished. Under the second resolution (horizontal resolution of 1967)[2] this interpretation was extended to other cases. The prices of utility B are regarded as abusive if any (adjoining) utility A with lower prices would also be able – in the absence of a demarcation contract – to supply the area of B at lower prices. Higher prices of B are regarded as non-abusive if the supply conditions in area B lead to higher costs, which could not be avoided if the supply arrangement were changed. The *Bundesgerichtshof* (BGH) has specified this by introducing a distinction between structural (*strukturbedingt*) and individual (*betriebsindividuellen*) additional costs of supplying a certain area. [3] The identification of abusive pricing behaviour therefore requires more than a mere comparison of prices. The differences in supply conditions must be identified and shown to imply 'additional structural costs' which justify corresponding price differentials. According to the BGH and *Bundeskartellamt* the identification of different supply conditions has to take into account cost-influencing factors such as the

---

[1] *Tätigkeitsbericht* BKartA (1965), BTDrS V / 530, 61.
[2] *Tätigkeitsbericht* des BKartA (1967), BTDrS V / 2841, 85.
[3] *Wirtschaft und Wettbewerb*, Jg. 22 (1972), 819–24.

character of settlement, topographic characteristics, the composition of demand, etc.

The practical problems of separating 'structural' and 'individual' costs of supply as well as the problems of identifying 'price' differences between utilities, which offer a multitude of different prices and have widely differing demand structures, are not analysed here. Suffice it to point out methodical flaws in price comparisons which imply systematic measurement errors. But even if these problems could be solved with sufficient accuracy, there remain fundamental objections to the method of identifying abusive pricing policies. Prices of utility B are considered excessive if they exceed the prices of the utility A by more than the 'structural cost additions' or, in other words, if the price differences reflect 'individual cost additions'.[1] Since the assumed difference in efficiency cannot be measured the *Bundeskartellamt* suggests an indirect procedure which, however, is economically unsound.

At first sight it may seem unobjectionable to measure differences in efficiency indirectly by the excess of price differentials over 'structural cost additions'.[2] It can easily be shown, however, that the conclusion on which the procedure is based – if price differences exceed the specific structural cost differences, there must be differences in efficiency – does not hold when price and cost differences are measured in the way the *Bundeskartellamt* does.

The starting point of the procedure to identify abusive pricing is the prices of the utility A chosen as the basis of comparison.[3] Thereby the distribution of joint costs, i.e. the vector of profit margins (contribution margins) chosen by A is taken as the basis of comparison. One disregards the fact that the effect of a vector of profit margins on sales revenue depends on the composition of output by consumer groups. Low profit margins in serving a group of customers are the easier to bear the smaller the group; high contribution margins of certain customer groups imply substantial contributions to earnings only if these groups have a large share in total sales. As public utilities differ greatly in composition of output, the effects on revenue of an identical vector of profit margins are quite different. The numerical example of Table 6.2 illustrates the

[1] The asymmetry of applying the abuse test to the higher-pricing utility (instead of the lower-pricing one) is a general characteristic of such control schemes. The initiation of the investigation is similarly biased: the investigation starts if perceptible price differences are observed, though price differences are not *conditiones sine qua non* for abusive pricing as defined above.

　The parallel to the treatment of price discrimination in the Robinson–Patman Act, which also confines itself largely to price differences instead of the solely relevant differences in profits, is surely no accident. Cf. Adelman, M. A., 'Price Discrimination as Treated in the Attorney General's Report', *University of Pennsylvania Law Review*, Vol. 104 (1955/6), 222–42.

[2] This indirect procedure for the measurement of efficiency differences by adjusted price differentials is attractive to the controlling body since it largely avoids direct evaluation of the 'reasonableness' of costs and prices.

[3] The affirmation that the prices of the utility A should only be used for comparison, if they are not themselves abusive does not help much, as long as there are no definite criteria of abusive pricing. If abusive pricing is to be identified by the referred method of adjusted price differentials there is a *petitio principii*.

TABLE 6.2 ILLUSTRATION: TEST OF ABUSIVE PRICING

	Case 1 Customer groups				Case 2 Customer groups				Case 3 Customer groups			
	I	II	III	∅	I	II	III	∅	I	II	III	∅
Company 1												
(1) Attributable costs	8.0	5.0	10.0	7.5	2.0	15.0	15.0	8.5	11.0	4.0	9.0	8.5
(2) Profit margins	12.0	5.0	5.0	8.5								
(3) Prices	20.0	10.0	15.0	16.0	10.0	20.0	25.0	16.0	19.0	9.0	19.0	16.0
(4) Delivery shares	0.5	0.3	0.2									
Company 2												
(5) Attributable costs	10.0	8.0	13.0	10.9								
(6) Profit margins	10.0	13.0	10.4	11.1								
(7) Prices	20.0	21.0	23.4	22.0								
(8) Delivery shares	0.2	0.3	0.5									
Company 2												
(9) Additional structural costs	2.0	4.0	2.8	3.0								
(10) Non-abusive prices	22.0	14.0	17.8	17.5	12.0	24.0	27.8	23.5	21.0	13.0	21.8	19.0
(11) Gain (+), loss (−)				−1.5				+4.5				0.0
(12) Additional structural costs	0.0	0.0	0.0	0.0								
(13) Non-abusive prices	20.0	10.0	15.0	14.5	10.0	2.0	25.0	20.5	19.0	9.0	19.0	16.0
(14) Gain (+), loss (−)				−1.5				+4.5				0.0

consequences this has for the identification of abusive pricing by the method of adjusted price differentials.

Let us suppose that a comparison of the supply structures reveals 'additional structural costs' of utility 2 as high as 3 Dpf per kWh sold. On the basis of an assumed splitting procedure[1] this involves 2.0 Dpf/kWh for consumer group I, 4.0 Dpf/kWh for consumer group II and 2.8 Dpf/kWh for consumer group III.

If one adds additional structural costs to the prices of the reference company 1 one gets, as row (10) shows, the prices of utility 2 which are non-abusive. Thus utility 2 should lower the prices for groups II and III as they are abusively high, but at the same time it is allowed to increase prices for group I.[2] This price adjustment would lower the average revenue of utility 2 by 4.5 Dpf/kWh (from 22.0 to 17.5 Dpf/kWh).[3] Thereby, a loss of 1.5 Dpf/kWh would be inflicted upon company 2 (the non-abusive average revenue is $16 + 3 = 19$ Dpf/kWh).

Let us compare this result with cases 2 and 3, in which other price vectors hold for the reference utility 1. In case 2 the price adjustment would increase average revenue for company 2 by 1.5 Dpf/kWh. The procedure thus leads to a 'non-abusive' average revenue which is even higher than in the original situation (22 Dpf/kWh). Company 2 is allowed an unjustified surplus revenue amounting to 4.5 Dpf/kWh. In case 3 the desired result is reached as a result of a rather particular constellation of data.

This example shows that the proposed procedure *may* lead to serious and undesired consequences, especially if one takes into account the fact that utility companies can follow a pricing strategy which intentionally makes use of the consequences of such a control scheme.

The magnitude of the described consequences determines whether they are to be considered as a mere possibility or as a real danger. Only a model analysing the interaction of the different factors under realistic assumptions about the relevant variables (vectors of delivery, vectors of profit margins, etc.) leads to quantitative statements about possible errors of measurement relative to the probable magnitude of price abuses.

---

[1] The determination of additional structural costs for single groups of consumers requires that the joint costs be split up. As there is no way of splitting up joint costs on a causative basis, one of the conventional methods has to be used. Therefore, in a strict sense, it is not valid to speak of additional structural costs when speaking of single groups of consumers. However, the *Bundeskartellamt* insists upon separate identification of abuse of prices for single groups of customers, and thus has to split up joint costs somehow. Such a concept can be questioned for economic reasons because it offers no criteria to determine under which conditions there is abuse when costs of jointly used capacities are split up. The joint use of capacities in the electricity sector can be characterised as a public or semi-public good, and as one knows there is no convincing economic method of splitting up the costs of public goods among customer groups.

Rows (13–14) of Table 6.2 show that the amount and distribution of additional structure costs does not influence the results of the procedure as measured by the unjustified profits/losses inflicted upon company 2.

[2] Or should one assume that utility 1 should lower the price for consumer group I?

[3] For reasons of simplification a completely inelastic demand is assumed.

The procedure proposed by the *Bundeskartellamt* to detect abusive pricing was simulated by means of the model described above. The assumption was · made that utility companies have to adjust their prices to match those non-abusive prices determined by the procedure described. The example given above shows that 'unjustified' discrepancies from cost recovery can go in either direction. The quality of the control to prevent abuse was measured in the model by the amount of these cost discrepancies.

Measuring errors in the determination of a price abuse can be all the more important, the bigger the differences in the profit margins and in the composition of output between utility companies. If one takes as a basis for the calculation the real delivery situation of the utility companies and the alternative price-setting principles, the usefulness of the procedure under the real conditions can be tested with the aid of the model. Simulation results indicate a margin of error of the order of 10 per cent of the total cost of the public utilities analysed.

This error margin is solely due to methodical flaws in the specification of a price abuse. When making a complete evaluation, one also has to take into account the weakness inherent in the method of measuring the actual price differences and the estimation errors and demarcation problems when determining structurally originated cost differences. Seen as a total, the error margin can well have the same magnitude as the presumed price abuses to be determined.

This detailed analysis of a specific procedure for the control of abuse proves once more that there are narrow boundaries for an official control and regulation of complex economic relationships. All one can hope to do is to prevent striking abuses.

Such control systems should, above all, be considered a preventive measure. Attempts at perfection in order to enlarge decision-making in its range of application introduce the danger of permanently subjugating more and more fields of private enterprise to an administrative control and regimentation. In the present case, the control of price abuse, the step toward general control of costs is not very wide.

A special problem arises in the fact that the indicators used to measure the efficiency and success of such intervention are often misleading. Only experience shows how well an administration solves the problem defined by itself, but not whether the problem has been defined correctly. The analysis of the method proposed by the *Bundeskartellamt* to detect and control abusive pricing is a good example of this more general problem: each enforced adjustment of actual prices is regarded as a success by the administration, yet there is no economic justification for this conclusion in many cases.

VIII. FINAL REMARKS

The preceding analysis shows that, on the one hand, complete exclusion of competition in the public utility sector is not a necessary condition for supply at lowest costs. On the other hand, it is also impossible to open the market to a greater number of competitors. What can be done, however, is to break up the existent system by initiating partial competitive processes. Above all, changes can be brought about in the production sphere. If a strict separation between production and the grid were legally enforced, a variety of companies could enter electricity production. However, it cannot be maintained *a priori* that, compared to the present state, the costs of producing electricity would thereby be lowered.

In the grid sphere such a far-reaching competitive state cannot be brought about. Coalition gains, which were dealt with in this chapter, are the most important obstacle to competition. Existing companies might, however, be enabled to enter the supply areas of others, if there were periodic opportunities to bid for regional markets. These processes should be facilitated by supplementary measures such as access to existing transportation systems and permission to construct transit lines.[1]

It has been argued that the initiation of competitive processes would favour cut-throat competition and cream-skimming; furthermore, it is feared that the principle of equal prices would have to be given up. There is no need to deal with cream-skimming separately, since it will vanish as soon as the principle of equal prices is given up. The danger of cut-throat competition cannot generally be accepted as an argument against partial intensification of competition. Otherwise competition would have to be restrained in many sectors of the economy, where oligopolistic supply structures dominate. From the existence of a natural monopoly, it cannot be deduced that cut-throat competition is inevitable in the public utility sector, for the natural monopoly does not comprise the whole field of supply, as was shown above. The cost functions are not such that the most efficient supply could only be attained if there was only one company.

On the other hand, the danger of cut-throat competition is higher than in other sectors of the economy, not only because there are few competitors but also because the competitive forces are active only intermittently. It might be necessary, moreover, to adjust market structures before abolishing barriers to entry. At any rate, the principle of equal prices in a supply area should be given up. The effect of this principle is that the competitive power depends on whether attractive or unattractive types of delivery dominate in the supply area of a company. Efficient companies, whose supply areas are unfavourable, would have no chance of prevailing over competitors.

It is easiest for the public utilities themselves to discover where additional profits can be made by taking over regional markets because there are cost advantages or because the going prices in an area are excessive. The incentives to search for these opportunities are also highest for the utilities.

[1] Such contractual arrangements already exist in today's system. However, they bind the partners by contract not to enter each other's markets.

The initiation of competition would, moreover, give more and better information to other groups which, besides the direct competitors, exert a noticeable influence on the policy of public utilities. Organisations of energy consumers as well as of the industry, consultants specialising in energy prices and terms of delivery, and others, are part of this system of watchdogs. Thus, the effects of direct partial competition would be passed on to other parts of the system. Furthermore, the relative strength of buyers would increase. Here, too, the contested regional markets would derive benefits from competition. Finally, the information base for the supervising authorities, the control activities of which would be kept in force, would be enlarged considerably. An undesired development in the competitive processes could be detected more easily and corrected more effectively.

Therefore the establishment of partial, direct competitive relations between public utilities should not be judged in isolation, but rather as an initial impulse which will, hopefully, drive the overall system to more dynamic and efficient development.

Discussion of Professor Schneider's Paper

Professor Baumol said he found the paper fascinating, partly because he himself, together with Professor Fischer, was working on an analysis of the choice of industry structure. He had two comments, first a technical and then a substantive one. On the first point he said that in order to decide whether the firms in a given industry should be amalgamated or broken up to minimise production costs, the theory of natural monopoly was relevant. Recent developments in that theory had shown that scale economies were neither a necessary nor a sufficient condition for natural monopoly. The proper condition was what mathematicians called 'subadditivity' of the cost function, meaning that a single firm could produce a given output more cheaply than any collection of smaller firms. The significance of this result was that one could not judge from local information alone whether an industry was a natural monopoly. Usually, information on costs of production was available in a small neighbourhood of the average output combination actually produced in the recent past, and this was quite sufficient to determine whether local scale economies were present, i.e. whether marginal costs were lower than average costs. But in order to test for subadditivity, it was necessary to estimate the cost function also at points far from actual output levels, e.g. at points corresponding to a 75 per cent cut in output. The reason why it was necessary to know the entire cost function between the origin and the output of interest was that it was necessary to make certain that there did not exist a combination of several very small firms which could produce the given output more cheaply. This requirement was difficult to meet, since it called for information well beyond the normal range of experience, but it was absolutely necessary. Failure to make at least a rough estimate would evade the issue. This was a technicality, but very important for decision-makers. He asked Professor Schneider whether he had done this.

Baumol's second point related to the choice between public and private enterprise. It was clear, as had also been said in the paper, that in the presence of natural monopoly some measures had to be taken to prevent monopolistic output restrictions and excess profits. Among such measures were anti-trust legislation, nationalisation or regulation. The first of these, namely the breaking up of large enterprises, was not advisable in the case of a natural monopoly, because it would increase production costs and could be prohibitively expensive. Europe had resorted to nationalisation, while the United States used regulation of private monopolies. Experience had shown that regulation as

currently practised in the United States was far from being an advertisement
for itself. The pressure from the regulator was usually not for firms to reduce
their prices, but to *increase* their prices in order to protect inefficient
competitors who complained that they had been hurt by 'unfair competition'.
Another consequence of regulatory practice was the concentration of talent
among the firm's lawyers rather than among its technicians and managers,
because success in a legal proceeding could contribute much more to the
earnings of regulated companies than increased efficiency in production. He
doubted whether nationalised industries operated more efficiently or paid more
attention to social costs than private monopolies just because they were run by
public servants. This was true in some cases, but not in others. He said that, for
example, the Soviet Union had an abominable record of efficiency, and a
record of extensive damage to the environment by industry. The central issue
was not that private firms had the wrong incentives and public firms the right
ones. The issue was how one could devise effective automatic rules to force
management, whether public or private, to be efficient in its contribution to
social goals.

Mr Stoffaes suggested that in the light of the great variation in performance
of public and private enterprises, economic theory alone could lead us no
further. New insights into the issues of efficiency would probably have to be
found in the fields of sociology and organisation theory – or even history, in
the light of the key factor of the existence of a professional civil service class
for the efficiency of public enterprise. Baumol thought this evaded the issue. He
said there were economic rules which encouraged efficiency, and one should
not rely on better human beings to perform better. He gave two examples.
Pollution charges automatically forced management to take the social cost of
environmental damage into account. The second example was taken from the
regulation of airline rates. The existing transatlantic carriers reacted to the
entry of Laker Airlines by trying to undercut it and drive it out of the market.
To permit maximal competition while preventing predatory pricing, which
temporarily set prices below costs and then raised them again once the
competitor had been driven out of the market, he had proposed that existing
airlines be permitted to lower their fares as far as they want. But once they had
lowered them, they should not be allowed to raise them again, except in
measure with increases in costs *beyond their control* (such as in fuel prices),
and with other demonstrable exogenous changes.

Lord Kaldor asked Baumol whether he would be willing to expand some
more on the notion of subadditivity, which he found intriguing, and explained
why scale economies were neither necessary nor sufficient for natural
monopoly. Baumol said subadditivity of a cost function for a given output
combination simply meant that a single firm could produce that output most
cheaply. A layman would naturally use that characterisation of a natural
monopoly, not the notion of scale economies. Scale economies meant that a
doubling of all inputs, for example, made it possible to produce more than
twice as much of every output. But doubling all inputs was not necessarily

cost-minimising. It might be possible to double outputs by increasing some inputs more than others, without doubling costs. Therefore, scale economies were not a necessary condition for natural monopoly. Neither were they a sufficient condition. A given output combination could be broken up in many different ways. For example there could be scale economies in the production both of cars and trucks. This would imply that two firms which each produced half the cars and half the trucks demanded would have higher costs than a single firm supplying the total demand. But it was still conceivable that two specialised firms, one of which produced all the cars and the other all the trucks, would have lower costs, e.g. because of lower administrative overhead. Therefore, scale economies were not a sufficient condition for natural monopoly either. A sufficient condition for subadditivity was that the cost function showed declining average costs for proportional increases of a given output bundle, and was convex along a cross-section. So far, nobody had produced an illuminating set of necessary and sufficient conditions.

Professor Srinivasan asked whether subadditivity of the cost function corresponded to superadditivity of the production function. Baumol said this was true, and by the duality theorem one could translate every theorem on cost functions into one in terms of production functions. Sometimes it was easier to work with one, sometimes with the other. *Professor Uribe* suggested that information on costs for small outputs near the origin might be estimated by using engineering production functions, and Baumol agreed.

Kaldor said that one should not only take into account the minimum feasible production cost of alternative combinations of firms, but also the rationality with which competition worked. The facts proved that markets did not behave in a rational way. One could, for example, observe that, typically, the elasticity of output with respect to employment was greater than unity. But with a rational allocation of production one should expect just the opposite, for the simple reason that neither labour nor equipment were homogeneous. Different plants had different kinds of equipment, and one could order these in a descending order of efficiency. If the allocation of production was rational, the most efficient equipment, which yielded the highest output per worker, would be used first, and to full capacity, before the next most efficient equipment was used, and so on. An increase in output would thus affect the marginal unit only. On these conditions the marginal output per worker had to be lower than the average, and the elasticity of output with respect to labour input *less* than unity. The fact that employment tended to increase by less than output showed that there was imperfect competition among firms and that a change in demand affected the degree of utilisation of plants of all kinds, not just the least efficient ones.

Dr Pryke was concerned that an electricity supply system which was splintered up as much as the German one would not expand in the 'merit order' just explained by Kaldor. He asked whether the German utilities had set up rules to run in merit order. *M. Boiteux* pointed out that the natural monopoly in electricity was linked to the distribution network, not to the generation of electric power. He mentioned that Electricité de France was required to buy electricity from any producer at 5 per cent below its own sale price.

Professor Savas asked how the electricity industry could be structured to encourage competition and reduce costs.

Schneider replied that the most important step was to facilitate the access of independent electricity producers to the existing power grid. A discussion was now under way in Germany seeking to determine how competition could be increased through easier access to a high voltage grid. He said there was strong co-operation among utilities on a contractual basis. If a utility was short of generating capacity, it bought power elsewhere. He said that, compared to other countries, the FRG had a highly decentralised system of electric utilities. Although it was not perfect, nationalisation was, at the moment, no longer being considered.

7 Public Enterprise and Advanced Planning Techniques: The Experience of Electricité de France

Marcel Boiteux
DIRECTEUR GENERAL, ELECTRICITÉ DE FRANCE

I. INTRODUCTION

The planning and economic studies now being carried out at Electricité de France are the product of constant evolution since the fifties, an evolution which can truly be called the product of a continuous and deliberate conjuncture of economic theory and methodological progress.

The combination of such activities now being carried out was created very gradually: as a development of the theory and practice of marginal cost-pricing, the optimal management of hydraulic reservoirs and long-run programming of the choice of investments. During the sixties the contribution of operational research played a critical role in the improvement of economic computation and extension of its field of application. More specifically, effort was devoted to reduction of the scale of the problems involved. We sought not only to extend our modelling to ever-greater portions of the firm's activity, but also to use our modelling as a means to subdivide the complex problems into subproblems which could be solved more easily. We were thus able to impart a concrete, operational sense to notions of decentralisation, of separability and, more generally, of breakdown of time and space. To the effort of analysis and formalisation necessary for a large-scale approach there was added a constant search for economic interpretation, of which duality in mathematical programming constitutes a special example.

It is not the objective of this paper to describe all the methods and models employed but only to illustrate, by means of the long-term programming of investments, the kinds of approaches and principles which can guide a large public company in the exercise of its role of economic agent seeking to contribute to the social welfare.

II. PRIMARY CONSIDERATIONS IN CHOICE OF ELECTRICAL EQUIPMENT

Investment plays a particularly important role in the electricity sector, currently representing 30 to 40 per cent of its turnover. I am speaking of equipment for the production and transportation of energy (which is very large and has a very high unit cost), or distribution (much of which is practically mass-produced and geographically very dispersed), and shall be referring more specifically to equipment in the first category.

General characteristics of problems to be solved

The supplier of electricity enjoys the thankless privilege of having to deal with several difficulties.

Diversity of possible choices. The techniques of electricity production are in fact very varied: thermal, using petroleum or coal; nuclear; gas-turbines; gravitational hydraulic pumping, etc.

Moreover, the decisions affecting equipment themselves induce a multiplicity of options: the technical characteristics of each particular piece of equipment, location, dates of entry into service and transfer, etc.

Interdependence of decisions. The decision to build more or fewer nuclear power stations, for instance, has an effect on the way equipment in existence or at the planning stage will be run. This decision thus modifies the data that will be needed to estimate the value of services rendered during its lifetime by equipment whose construction is being debated.

But beyond this direct dependence there are also the repercussions of overall decisions related to the total structure of the production plant upon the particular technical choices: for instance, upon the size of pumping stations. The same applies to the decision to connect two centres of production and consumption by a very-high-tension transport line: the presence of this line could well modify the construction of other production centres.

Future uncertainty. Most of the data have a random character, either because of conjunctural fluctuations in demand or stochastic elements affecting supply, such as hydraulic conditions or the availability of equipment.

Since electricity is not an item that can be stored, the repercussions of this randomness become immediate. Moreover, considering how long it takes to manufacture the equipment (5 to 7 years) and the duration of its physical existence (over 30 years), the major uncertainties affecting the future (technological progress, energy costs, etc.) cannot be ignored.

'Upstream' and 'downstream' repercussions of decisions. Considering the relative importance of the electricity sector in the national economy, the

decisions it takes are not neutral, and a company of the size of EDF cannot be termed a small economic agent. We realise, too, that the community will grant it certain monopoly privileges only along with the imposition of conditions which will guarantee from it an appropriate contribution to the social welfare.

Consequences for methods of analysis

The difficulties I have just mentioned, though they have historically been dealt with gradually, have had a profound effect on planning methodology.

Impossibility of a combined approach. In theory, if it were possible to draw up a list of all possible sequences of projects, it would be sufficient to consider each combination of these projects which was 'acceptable' from the point of view of satisfying the demands for electricity, and to choose the best combination, which is to say, the least expensive, all other considerations being equal.

Unfortunately, and here the field of electricity is not an exception, it is very rare that one can draw up an exhaustive list of all possible equipment programmes. Even if one could, the approach would almost certainly not be operational because a combined approach of this kind would have to take into account a vast number of possibilities as a result of the diversity and interdependence of the decision variables.

The inadequacy of a marginal approach to the profitability of projects. Direct study of the profitability of a project presupposes an ability to compare the cost and the value of this project. But the evaluation of the services which a particular project will render obviously depends on the conditions of its future use, and it is heavily affected by the characteristics of the system to which it will be added marginally; moreover, the random nature of the parameters of supply and demand complicates the problem considerably.

In the late forties, the research economists of EDF used an approach that in effect avoided the problem of postulating a kind of measuring standard based upon a fixed reference set of equipment, carefully chosen and capable of being used on an unlimited scale. In particular, the evaluation of hydraulic projects was carried out by calculating the relative profitability of the project considered relative to the thermal combination reference base which was capable of rendering the same services in terms of satisfaction of demand.

In the years immediately following, it turned out to be relatively easy to envisage the scale of operation to which it was necessary to refer in order to define the thermal standard 'equivalent' to the equipment being studied.

But the nature of these key situations can change significantly in the course of the many future years that must be considered, as the character of demand and the production system change. Moreover, as technical progress causes evolution in the 'thermal standard of reference' the use of intuition becomes unreliable.

The need for global studies and the breakdown of problems.   In 1954, mathematical programming – initially linear – was introduced to make crucial global studies possible, the analytic approach being confined to selection and definition of the optimal technical characteristics of the individual projects introduced at the margin.

An element of considerable methodological importance was thus introduced almost naturally: considering the complexity of the system under review, it was quite impossible to take into account in a single model all the decision variables related to the set of possible programmes. It was necessary to introduce separation in the set of these decision variables with the idea of substituting for an overall approach a co-ordination of more circumscribed approaches for which compatibility conditions were specified to guarantee their complementarity.

The 'advanced' programming methods used by Electricité de France are profoundly stamped by this philosophy. The company has at its disposal a system of models, each able to encompass a subgroup of decision variables. It is the best possible combination of these that we are after: the best being defined as that which maximises some criterion of evaluation or objective function. These models, organised to permit a dialogue among them, enable us to define by successive iterations the overall optimum. Moreover, they furnish all the economic indicators (quantities, shadow prices) which the decentralised decision-makers need.

The decisions are 'separated' in accord with their character into the following categories:

(a) 'global' (evolution of the system) or 'marginal' (the choice of magnitudes of particular projects);
(b) tactical (short-term management) or strategic;
(c) those related to problems of location and transport networks or, abstracting from these elements, to a system of production and consumption that we suppose to be located only at one spot.

From a purely conceptual point of view, however, nothing prevents us from imagining the most general formulation of the problem raised by the choice of investments. It is in reference to this fictitious model that the considerations which follow will be discussed, before we return to examine in greater depth methods of breakdown and their economic interpretations.

Our character as a public enterprise has led us to take into account the cost to the community of an unsatisfied demand, and to use a normative discount rate in our calculations. We shall return to these considerations later.

III. THE GENERAL FORMULATION OF THE PLANNING OF INVESTMENTS AT EDF

Since we are speaking about a public company which cannot use the market for reference nor allow itself to profit from its position as a monopoly, the rule of management which guarantees – in a sector with globally increasing returns – the proper contribution to the social welfare is 'satisfaction of demand at the lowest cost', recognising that this is the demand elicited by the company's practice of marginal cost pricing.

The above formulation shows that the problem can be expressed quite naturally in terms of mathematical programming. It is, in fact, a matter of minimising a cost function (the unknowns are the decision variables of investment, of operation, etc.), under various constraints (in particular, that require demand to be met).

Modelling – economic interpretations and methods of solution

The evolution of our work can be described with the help of a rather artificial distinction between two periods in the evolution of our planning methods.

The period emphasising mathematical programming and duality. After the initial use of linear models from 1954 to 1961, non-linear programming made for an important advance by the introduction in the evaluation function of failure costs, transport losses and the effects of diminishing returns in hydraulic equipment. The methods of solution, based at first on the algorithms of G.B. Dantzig, afterwards called upon other, faster methods (Wolfe's 'reduced gradient'), enabling us to begin taking more particular phenomena into account at the level of production system management and the introduction of new types of equipment such as hydraulic pumping.

There were many ways in which the economic interpretation of dual variables was able to be used. Thus the dual variables associated with the constraints requiring the meeting of demand during the different 'time-periods' under consideration (years, seasons, hours of the day) could easily be interpreted in terms of the marginal costs to be used in pricing and the calculation of the equipment's revenue value.

The revenue value of a piece of equipment is, in fact, by definition – with the exception of its running costs – the sum total of the services rendered by this equipment for the duration of its life. The value of these services is exactly equal to their marginal cost, at each moment the equipment is in operation (this is another implication of the models).

The calculation of the revenue value of a new piece of equipment – or of the variation in this revenue value relating to alterations in the characteristics of the equipment – has thus become the basis of decentralised studies of the choice of projects and the determination of their dimensions, complementarity being completely guaranteed by the global approach of long-term programming. Another immediate use of revenue values relates to the problem of transfer of old equipment and its depreciation costs: this work enabled us to advance towards a normative accountancy, for the creation of decentralised management analyses based on surpluses in global productivity.

Thus, the study of duality was very rich in information and imparted operational content to a number of the properties of the economic optimum.

The present formulation in terms of optimal control. The formulation now being used, inspired by the theory of optimal control, is employed not only in the long-term programming of investments but also, especially in certain operation models, related to the hydraulic system. This formulation has the advantage of providing a clear synthesis and making perfectly clear the relations in time between the variables. It gives directly, year by year, not only the values of the control variables (the quantities of equipment of various kinds to be put into operation) but also the revenue values of this equipment and their evolution in time. The dynamic character of investment decisions is, moreover, more easily taken into account.

Articulation of the models with the economic environment

Leaving aside for the moment the problem of articulation 'downstream', that is to say, with the company's decentralised sublevels, to which we shall return, let us look at the way in which the external economic environment was taken into account, obviously from the viewpoint of the desired contribution to the social welfare.

Sectoral limits.   An attempt to include explicitly the interactions of the company's decisions with those of other economic agents can lead to the construction of enormous economic models in which everything affects everything else and *vice versa!* There, too, the temptations of the model builder may run into conflict with the practical possibilities: a preferable solution is to be sought in the interaction of submodels. Thus, for instance, an iterative interplay between two sectorial models: one related to the electricity sector, the other to the oil sector, was preferred to a large-scale cybernetic model of the energy sector.

The introduction of a cost of failure.   Considering the random elements already mentioned, the term 'meeting demand' must be formulated in probabilistic terms. It is evident that an increase in productive capacities sufficient to avoid failure in any area must lead to waste: but where should one stop?

Initially, criteria of probability were first formulated in terms of the capacities of the system in certain typical situations. Interpretation, with the aid of duality theory, of these constraints indicated the implicit cost attributable to unguaranteed supplies. At present, the model's evaluation function includes a term for failure cost, to which a very clear economic interpretation has been assigned. In effect, this concept enables us to examine the quality of Public Service in terms of the social welfare: we knew, from the implicit dual measure, what the prevention of one kilowatt-hour of failure really cost; what remained was to measure this value against what the community was prepared to pay, as a consumer of electricity, in order to avoid that cut. A macroeconomic approach and various surveys showed that the values on which EDF relied were compatible with external failure valuations, which enabled us, in a way, to interpret the failure term in the evaluation function in terms of external effects.

At present in EDF extensive use is being made of the concept of failure cost, which is at the base of the decentralised economic calculations carried out at the level of electricity distribution.

Inclusion of the role of demand via pricing. The validity of the approach employed rests on the fact that, as has been indicated, the demand introduced into the large-scale investment model is that which results from the use of marginal-cost pricing.

From a practical point of view, price elasticity of demand and levels of electricity prices are not easy to determine. Until a recent period corresponding to the evolution of the production plant toward adaptation to demand, which is to say, toward a state persistently close to the optimum, we were justified in not taking the effects of prices (at marginal cost) on demand explicitly into account. We based our consumption forecasts on econometric models in which the prices of different forms of energy did not figure among the explanatory variables.

Since the crisis this no longer holds good, nor has the system evolved as an adapted structure for several years. Concomitantly, studies have been undertaken to verify that the structure of marginal costs unbalanced by massive recourse to nuclear power would still correspond closely in the intermediate term to equilibrium prices compatible with our hypotheses about demand. In the same spirit, there have been various studies on the interest, from the community's point of view, of developing certain uses of electricity in competition with other forms of energy.

IV. TIME AND SPACE IN THE PLANNING OF INVESTMENTS AT EDF: THE BREAKDOWN AND TREATMENT OF UNCERTAINTY

In the preceding pages, I have emphasised the continuing interest in the proper breakdown of problems rather than their solution by models bordering on the gigantic. This is preferred not only for operational reasons, it being impossible to arrive at their solution by the present means of calculation, nor for aesthetic ones, although 'clever' solutions are intellectually more pleasant than approaches involving solid hard work.

On the contrary, this choice rests upon a philosophy. Over and above the economics of this calculation it is in effect dictated by the presence of autonomous events and men.

Events fluctuate, sometimes foreseeably. It is important to preserve a capacity for rapid adaptation to cope with the occurrence of unforeseen, and sometimes major, events.

Men constitute a multiplicity of decision centres. It is impossible to imagine that a complex organisation can function for a single planning centre, and decentralisation is an absolute necessity. But it is only possible under certain conditions relating to the data supplied to the decentralised decision-makers.

On the basis of these general conditions, I shall speak more concretely about the functioning of the planning system at Electricité de France as applied, in particular, to a breakdown in time, a breakdown in space and the treatment of uncertainty.

Methods of breakdown in time and in space

It is the interdependence of all decisions spread over time and space which has made necessary their integration into a large-scale model. Breakdown constitutes a move in the reverse direction: one returning to decisions their attributes as individual actions and guaranteeing their consistency for an appropriate contribution to social welfare.

As we have seen, the global approach enables the supplier of electricity to satisfy three objectives through the solution of a dynamic optimisation problem:

(a) to define as a function of the values of the economic parameters the optimal evaluation of the production system;
(b) to help prepare programme decisions;
(c) to supply elements necessary for precise specification of particular projects.

Closer examination of points (b) and (c) was the objective of the breakdown in time and space respectively.

Breakdown in time.   Every year Electricité de France must define the exact size of the different kinds of equipment whose construction is to be undertaken. This procedure, to which all investments are subject, is called at EDF the 'adjustment of equipment programmes'.

A decade ago, the ideas of F. Bessière on the concept of separability in economics had led us to see the necessity of this kind of approach, solved up to that time only in a very pragmatic way. Long-term programming models did not, in fact, produce satisfactory answers, because of the inevitable crudity of their formulations. In fact, it seemed necessary to construct a short-term investment decision model capable of guaranteeing the coherence of its results with those of a long-term model within the general optimality framework of the economic criterion.

The solution was sought, rather, in co-ordination between two optimisation models, the short-term model using as 'input' valuations, or shadow prices, obtained from the long-term model.

The formulation in terms of optimal order is, in relation to this, extremely enlightening since Pontryagin's maximum principle supplies us with an instrument to deal with separability in time.

The subproblem reduced to the decisions to be taken during the first year (that is to say, the adjustment decisions) can, in fact, be separated from the long-term global problem if one can correctly formulate the criterion function to be used. But the theory of optimal order has shown that this criterion function is Hamiltonian for the first period of the global problem, which one can form from the optimal value of the joint or dual variables available once the long-term problem has been solved. These joint variables are the revenue values of various kinds of equipment, and the economic interpretation of the preceding is simple: the adjustment model can be limited to writing an equation which states that the anticipated cost of 1 Kw of power of a piece of equipment under consideration is, at the optimum, exactly equal to the variation of its revenue value (which represents the value of services rendered over the one-year period being considered).[1]

From the economic point of view, the conditions of methodological coherence are thus specified, and from the practical point of view, we were able to move from the solution of a dynamic optimisation problem to that of a succession of static optimisation problems, of which only the first was of immediate interest and for which one need only write the optimality conditions.

Decomposition in space.   In dealing with the problems of co-ordination between a planning 'centre' and a 'periphery' made up of decentralised economic agents, our work on separability enabled us to apply the classic findings of Kuhn and Tucker's work on duality or that of Dantzig and Wolfe on the breakdown of mathematical programmes.

(a) The most characteristic example at EDF of 'centre periphery' interaction in the area of investment is that mentioned at the beginning of this report, of marginal decisions concerning individual projects, once the adjustment of programmes has been defined.

To the 'price' signals obtained from the economic interpretation of global models and sent out by the Central Office, the Regional Equipment Offices reply with quantity information. In this case corresponding financing-need figures are obtained by summation of profitable projects listed in diminishing order of interest. A procedure can thus be initiated, with the Centre possibly adapting the large-scale model to take account of the 'feedback quantities' when not compatible with the data introduced into the large-scale model (for example, limits upon financing).

(b) Another interesting example is that of the management of hydraulic equipment, the problem for which Pierre Massé provided the first contribution

[1]Given that the decision period considered is one year.

in his book *Reserves, or Regulation of the Future*, in the late forties. Although not directly concerned with equipment decisions, it is relevant because it refers at the same time to breakdown in space (geographically dispersed reservoirs) and breakdown in time (weekly decisions within an annual cycle corresponding to climatic periodicity).

The method is based on a procedure involving communication among three submodels run either at the regional level (in this case an entire valley containing a series of several reservoirs, each with an influence upon the other) or at the local level (the reservoir).

The information exchanged concerns shadow prices (marginal costs by hour . . .) and quantities (weekly supplies of energy from the various pieces of equipment . . .).

The treatment of future uncertainty

Special provision must be made for the treatment of uncertainty in economic decision-making.

In short-term management, the uncertain generally assumes a manageable form whenever objective probabilities can be used, and the treatment of random processes, within the framework of the approaches which were mentioned earlier, does not raise any major conceptual problem; satisfactory solutions have been found which are already classic.

However, there exists another class of uncertain events which obstinately refuse to be reduced to the laws of probability. These are the elements with which we have no experience and in which we can find the essence of the differences between tomorrow and today or yesterday. The same holds for technological evolution, political or economic influences which govern the evolution of the prices of raw materials, primary sources of energy or the labour force, economic growth and its relations to future needs for energy, etc.

Even though the oil crisis has enabled us to see this more clearly, the situation is not new, and as Paul Valéry said: 'The future is like everything else, it isn't what it used to be'.

In such cases, we find ourselves faced with an 'uncertain' future, and we realise then that we have no obvious decision criterion at our disposal. On this subject one need only recall the lively debates of twenty years ago on the approaches of Von Neumann and Morgenstern, the criteria of Savage and the ten axioms of Milnor.

In the sixties, Electricité de France used an approach based on an evaluation of the stakes associated with various possible decisions, by supposing that such and such an event should occur.

The parametric solution of mathematical programming models has shown clearly the decisions to be faced given those major uncertainties that are the consequence of developments in nuclear power costs and oil prices.

More or less simultaneously with the preceding approaches, and parallel to them, another line of thought was developed within EDF, focusing upon the economic evaluation of the system's capacity to adapt.

The more uncertain the future, the more severe is the penalty attached to an error when we are dealing with decisions involving a long period of inactivity and decisions which are practically irreversible.

In investment, for example, the possibility of using means which are more quickly put into operation (gas turbines or the delayed retirement of older power stations) enables us to reduce the effect of future uncertainty by modifying the system's capacity to respond.

We were thus able to evaluate the interest of a two-year sequential adaptation policy limited to a relatively small fraction of the equipment programmes, programmes consisting essentially of equipment which required four to five years to put into operation.

This methodological advance has benefited, since the beginning of the seventies, from the gradual evolution of the 'classic' operational research approach towards thinking in terms of dynamic regulation and, more precisely, optimal order.

In effect, the nature of the problem is the same as that of the breakdown in time mentioned above. To every hypothetical future, or rather 'futures' (short-, medium- and long-term) there is a corresponding chain of successive decisions. An immediate commitment to the complete series of these 'optimal' decisions, thus making a wager on the realisation of hypothesised futures is neither possible nor desirable, since it would amount to a refusal to leave open the possibilities of adaptation which we have at our disposal.

The introduction of these possibilities of adaptation obviously entails a supplementary cost. We can see that there is an optimal course between the extremes in this area, the waste of resources – by the optimist prepared to wager on an easy future by counting too much on his exceptional ability to adapt, and by the pessimist inclined to overequip himself with protective options. The search for this optimal course must lead to a distinction between those portions of a plan involving weighty decisions which cannot easily be reversed and those permitting rapid adaptation.

New ideas are now being employed in the design of so-called 'strategic' methods using a 'decision branch' formulation, in which, unlike the so-called classic policy methods, we take into consideration the growth of information, on the states of nature, as time passes.

V. A CRITICAL LOOK AT THE METHODOLOGICAL EVOLUTION – PERSPECTIVES

The preceding discussion emphasised the main characteristics of Electricité de France's approaches and the major developments made possible during the last twenty years by advances in methods and in means of calculation.

I have shown how we have been able, without foundering in unworkable immensity, to simulate production activity more and more accurately while taking into account future uncertainty, the dynamic character of decisions and their spatial dimension.

But there is another side of things, which is more difficult to control given it does not deal with the production function itself, but with circumstances outside the company's 'black box' and which, moreover, often lies in that part of the domain which is not yet quantified and measurable.

I have mentioned, in brief, that the use of a normative discount rate, the inclusion of failure cost in economic calculations and pricing at marginal cost have enabled EDF to impart to the signals exchanged with the economic environment content consistent with realisation of an overall optimum.

However, current modifications in certain mechanisms or manifestations of economic growth imply that resources which were until now considered free and unlimited have today been raised to the level of economic goods. These include the aesthetic environment, air and water. The fact that the public sector's economic calculation procedure, as practised until now, is in no position to respond to everything immediately has led some people to doubt the quality of the service it can render to society and to envisage limiting its use to daily running decisions, the rest being left as a matter for political decision. The existence of external effects which are complex and for which it is difficult to establish norms, added to problems of forecasting, threaten to remove all practical significance from a construction whose logic is not in question but which rests on excessively partial consideration to permit the evaluation. French studies and experience in decentralised planning, in fact, lead us to be very modest in evaluating the capacity of an organisation to generate a system of normative prices which indicate its true utilities and disutilities correctly.

But the Public Authorities sometimes make up for such deficiences by statutes establishing norms and other circumscribing indications. Should one not see in that the beginnings of an iterative dialogue with the users of these resources?

Public companies certainly have a role to play in this area and a system of valuation must be sought for a variety of non-commercial benefits.

A producer of electricity, for example, uses up some of the water and heats the rivers on whose banks he places his power stations. Thus he enters into competition with the other users of the water: factories, conglomerations, etc. Rather than be satisfied with a set of norms related to the maximum damage permitted, to temperatures and level of oxygen in the used water, etc., we can envisage an approach by all users of a basin, the aim of which, taking into account the form of each one's production functions and a criterion of social cost (the function of oxygen and temperature levels, etc.) would be to define optimal stocking, cooling and purification for the entire basin. Interpretations through duality, analysis in the framework of such an approach, would enable us to give precision to the notion of the 'value of the water' and to inform the decentralised decision-makers of the cost to the community of the harm they are doing. It would be up to them to make the best decisions locally: to restore the water suitably depolluted or to pay the social cost and leave the task of depollution to the community.

This is only an example but it shows clearly the nature of the challenge facing public sector economists: either real progress can be made through this sort of approach or else authoritarian action will prevail without any guarantee that it will entail no serious waste of resources. The difficulty of real progress through the course I have mentioned obviously lies in the necessity of organising the dialogue among all present and future users of the resource: the longevity of public companies and the fact that they are obliged to make long-term plans for their activities are additional factors calling for the role the Public Authorities should assign to them in this area.

I have not mentioned the inclusion of other considerations such as the contribution of the choices of public companies to the realisation of the goals of the state in the macroeconomic sphere relating to problems of employment, external balance, economic stabilisation or, in another sphere, town and country planning or redistribution, which these days are generally tackled in a very imperfect fashion, by means of analyses based on a multiplicity of criteria.

It is evident that decentralised economic calculation cannot solve every problem and that there is doubtless little hope that one day we shall be able to define democratically the single-social utility function which would, by appropriate decomposition, guarantee the consistency and optimality of all macroeconomic choices. We know, too, that decentralisation through prices does not always lead to optimal decisions, although special procedures enable us in certain instances to take into consideration cases of non-convexity (increasing returns) and public goods. There exists, moreover, along with public companies, a more or less important sector which does not operate under perfect competition and whose evaluation function, when it is made clear, does not necessarily correspond to the same system of prices as the public sector's.

VI CONCLUSIONS

These, in brief, are the main elements of recent planning developments showing the joint evolution of problems and methods in a large public company. This example – a very partial one – should obviously be considered only as a particular case, but certain ideas which I have tried to stress have more general significance.

The problems facing electricity suppliers are, in effect, of the same kind as those which economists in all of the public sector have to solve, and it is therefore not surprising that, from these problems, we can begin to extend our thoughts to economic regulation, problems of decentralisation, the optimal allocation of resources and pricing.

Some of these issues have been relatively well formalised and analysed by economic theory, supplemented by mathematical programming. The latter, of course, goes some way beyond the solution techniques that it calls upon: in fact, it supplies – by means of simplified models of the economic system – a structure encompassing the interrelation of values and quantities which permits us to advance towards a more coherent and more relevant description of the system itself.

But it would be foolish to suppose that the problems of the public sector, like those of a large company which is not a marginal component of the production system, can be solved fully by the optimal solution of large-scale models. The title of an article which appeared a few years ago in the USA makes this clear: 'Requiem for large-scale models'.

Guidance for optimal functioning of large organisations must be sought, above all, in proper breakdown of their problems and the definition of the best normative signals within these organisations, or between them and their exterior environment. This is the path along which Electricité de France has tried to advance in the last thirty years.

The task is far from completed and exchange of ideas is essential to progress in an area in which the leading role taken in the past by public companies must continue.

REFERENCES

1 Massé, P., *Les réserves ou la régulation de l'Avenier*, 2 vols. (Hermann: Paris, 1946).
2 Boiteux, M., 'Le Choix des Equipments de Production d'Energie Electrique', *Revue Française de Recherche Opérationnelle*, No. 1 (1956).
3 Boiteux, M., 'Sur la gestion des Monopoles Publics Astreints à l'Equilibre Budgétaire', *Econometrica* XXIV, 1 (1956).
*4 Massé, P. and R. Gibrat, 'Applications of Linear Programming to Investments in the Electrical Power Industry', *Management Science*, No. 3 (1957).
5 Boiteux, M., 'La Tarification des Demandes en Pointe: application de la Théorie de la Vente au Coût Marginal', *Journal of Business*, XXXIII, 2 (1960).
6 Boiteux, M. and F. Bessière, 'Sur l'Emploi des Methodes Globales et Marginales dans le Choix des investissements', *Revue Française de Recherche Opérationnelle*, No. 20 (1961).
7 Boiteux, M., 'L'orientation Rationnelle des Consommations d'Energie Electrique par la Tarification', Symposium de la 'Commission Economique pour l'Europe' (Varsovie, 1962).
8 Massé, M., *Le Choix des Investissements*, ed. Dunod (Paris, 1964).
9 Albouy, M., 'Politique d'Adaptation Séquentielle des Moyens de Production a la consommation d'Energie Electrique', IVème conference de l'Ifors (1966).
10 Bessière, 'La Méthode des Modeles Elargis: Application à un Problème de Choix des Investissements', IVème conference del' Ifors (Boston, 1966).
11 Albert, M., and P. Larivaille, 'Utilisation de Modèles globaux pour le Choix des Opérations de Programmes d'Electricité de France', Congrès Ifors (Helors, Athens, 1968).

*These titles are available in English.

12 Breton, A., and F. Falgarone, 'Gestion Optimal des Réservoirs d'une Vallee Hydraulique', Colloque de l'Iria (Versailles, Dec. 1973).

*13 Balasko, Y., 'On Designing Public Utility Tariffs with Applications to Electricity', Congrès de la Société de'Econométrie (Toronto, Aug. 1975).

*14 Bergougnoux, Mm., Garlet, Merlin and Saumon, 'Modèles globaux pour l'Etude d'un Schéma Directeur a Long Terme de l'Evolution d'un Système de Production-transport d'Electricité' (Cambridge, Sept 1975).

*15 Balasko, Y., 'A Contribution to the History of the EDF Green Tariff: its Impact and its Prospects', Conférence de l'Institute of Public Utilities' (Detroit, May 1975).

*16 Francony, M., and J. D. Levi, 'Amortissement et Tarification', Colloque Unipede (Madrid, 1975).

*17 Breton, A., and M. Cremieux, 'La Séparabilité dans le Temps du Problème de Choix des Equipments de Production à Electricité de France', Congrès ORSA/TIMS (Philadelphie, April 1976).

*18 Garlet, M., E. L'Hermitte and D. Levy, 'Methods and Models used by EDF in the Choice of Investments', TIMS XXIII (Athens, July 1977).

19 Bernard, P., 'Où en est l'Application de la Méthode des Comptes de Surplus á Electricité de France?', A paraître dans la revue de l'Andese: *Vie et Sciences Economiques* (1977).

Discussion of M. Boiteux's Paper

In his opening remarks, *M. Boiteux* indicated that Electricité de France invested about 4 billion dollars per year, and the gestation lag until these investments generated income was up to 6 years in the case of nuclear power plants. In making investment decisions of that order of magnitude, intuition could be useful to some extent, but was insufficient by itself. Mistakes were very costly, and sophisticated planning models played an essential role in reducing costs.

Professor Vickrey said that the nature of the scale economies of public goods, such as electricity or other infrastructure services, took the form of *economies of density* rather than economies of market size *per se*. Average costs could be reduced if more customers were added in the same local region, but not if several geographically distant areas were served by the same company. He proposed to take advantage of that by having a relatively large number of monopolies, each limited to one region, to provide services such as electricity. He even favoured the splitting off from a national postal service of the local pick-up and delivery service for performance by more or less independent local agencies, which would vary the quality of service according to local preferences.

As a means to finance infrastructure services, Vickrey proposed a tax on the value of land. If electricity had to be transmitted past a piece of land, or a mailman had to walk by it, the owner of the land should pay for this, even if he used the land only as a tennis court and did not consume any of these services directly.

Vickrey also discussed the interest rate to be used in choosing among alternative investments. For example, a high interest rate would favour thermal power plants, with relatively lower construction costs but higher operating costs, while a low interest rate would favour hydroelectric projects, with higher construction costs but very low operating costs. In a time of immediate capital shortage, such as after a war, for example, should a (lower) long-term interest rate be used, simply because the projects had a long life, or should not rather a (higher) short-term rate be applied, since a project not undertaken immediately may be undertaken a year or two later when interest rates will be lower?

Regarding the problem of centralised vs. regionalised decision-making, *Boiteux* responded by saying that, for distribution to the low- and medium-voltage customers, EDF was divided into about 90 regional divisions which purchased electricity at the same prices as big industry from the central generation and transmission department which is supplying power to high-voltage customers. He said also that these divisions were autonomous in terms of financial accountability. He asked whether one should go further and also give these units juridicial independence. If it were up to him, he said, he would rather make them subsidiaries under somewhat stricter central control, in order to make sure that where there is 'naturally' high profitability they did not waste money. But this would bring problems of its own. As long as the regional directors were competent and cost-minded, the current organisation was probably the best.

Regarding interest rates, Boiteux said that he agreed with what Vickrey had said, but that it was not always easy to explain this to the government. He said that long-term discount rates were used in selecting the type of equipment to be built. Presently, a real rate (constant money) of 9 per cent per year was used, together with a study of the sensitivity both to a rate of 11 per cent and to a rate of 10 per cent up to 1990, and 7 per cent later on. For decisions on the timing of investments, short-term discount rates – higher than long-term ones – were to be used.

Mr Eibenschutz asked whether EDF included estimates of future price increases in its economic calculations. If the government adjusted its decisions to future rates of inflation, he saw a danger that this would by itself create more inflation.

Boiteux answered that EDF eliminates from its computations the effect of inflation, and that nominal interest rates used to select investments were presently close to 20 per cent per year, corresponding to the real rate of 10 per cent fixed by the government. In answer to a question by *Dr Pryke*, asking how the 10 per cent annual discount rate had been arrived at, *Boiteux* said that it was prescribed by the government, because it was estimated, rightly or wrongly, to be the average marginal profitability of capital for the French economy over recent years. He also said that electricity prices had increased less rapidly than the average price level, and considerably more slowly than labour costs. He said that if EDF were to set prices equal to marginal costs, it would theoretically incur a deficit, because scale economies meant that marginal costs were lower than average real costs. As a matter of fact, due to inflation, he said that the difference between prices charged and marginal costs was only of the order of 5 to 10 per cent. He also pointed out that marginal cost analysis was aimed less at fixing the general level of rates than at establishing a rational differentiation of the prices of power according to the voltage level (high, medium or low) and the timing of the demand occurrence (winter or summer, peak or low-load hours . . .). For instance, the difference between the highest peak price for the highest rate and the lowest off-peak price per kilowatt hour of electricity for the lowest rate was about a factor of 10.

Vickrey asked how the cost to consumers of service interruptions was estimated. *Boiteux* said this was one of the most difficult figures to estimate. For example, in one case in a mountain village electricity was interrupted and nobody wanted to spend the coin required to notify the utility by telephone. On the other hand, an interruption in a city would provoke a storm of complaints that food had spoiled in refrigerators, etc. *Professor Srinivasan* said that an added difficulty was that customers had an incentive to misrepresent the true cost to them of a service interruption. Mountain villagers might fear a rate increase if they appeared too anxious to have service restored. *Pryke* mentioned that in England gas users were free to choose between cheaper interruptible service and more expensive service which had preference in case of a system overload. He said this system of self-selection by customers made estimation of the economic cost of an interruption less urgent. *Eibenschutz* asked whether EDF or other electric utilities offered insurance against service interruption. *Boiteux* said not at present, but the question might merit study. *Vickrey* mentioned the problem of 'moral hazard' in insurance, in the sense that customers had little incentive to minimise their losses from a power failure if insurance against damages was available. *Srinivasan* pointed out that there might be insufficient diversification of risk to make insurance worthwhile, since a blackout affected all customers in a wide area simultaneously.

Professor Baumol asked whether the sophisticated planning methods of EDF had something to do with its being a public enterprise, or were a mere coincidence. Did a public enterprise have an advantage over private enterprise in its ability to use advanced planning techniques? *M. Dreyfus* said that without directly answering Baumol's question he wanted to point out something which Boiteux's modesty had prevented him from saying, namely that it was the sophisticated planning methods introduced by Boiteux, Massé and others which made France's rapid postwar reconstruction possible.

Dr Pryke said he thought that *planning* in Great Britain was just as sophisticated as in France but that lower performance had to be attributed to problems such as overstaffing, failure to convert to large-scale generators, etc. His hypothesis was that France's success was not so much due to better planning as to better *management.*

Eibenschutz said that EDF was known as an innovator in planning. He felt the main reason for this was the fact that EDF had to compete with other government agencies for investment funds, and had to justify its expenditures carefully. He said that private electric utilities in the United States had less motivation to reduce costs, since the regulatory system permitted them to increase their rates whenever their costs increased. *Boiteux* agreed that the reason for the use of advanced planning methods in EDF was its competition for funds with other government agencies, and the supervision exercised by the government.

Addressing Baumol's question whether EDF's leading position in planning was connected with its being public, *Mr Gutiérrez* suggested that the goals of a public enterprise were more complex than those of a private enterprise. By its very nature, a public enterprise had to be concerned with societal objectives apart from its *raison d'etre*, with questions such as the creation of employment, the saving of foreign exchange, purchasing from domestic suppliers with idle capacity, even if their prices were relatively higher than those of foreign competitors, etc. A public enterprise operated under a multiple objective framework, while a private enterprise simply had to maximise a single objective function subject to the relevant constraints. For this reason, a public enterprise had a greater need for sophisticated mathematical planning techniques.

Srinivasan asked whether EDF took technological uncertainty into account in planning, for example, such as that introduced by the potential availability of fusion energy. *Boiteux* answered that up to now the analysis of this type of question had still not reached the stage of formal economic analysis, and that there was, therefore, more reliance on intuition. A sort of minimax strategy was used to protect oneself against the worst conceivable future situations.

8 Thoughts on the Role of Public Holdings in Developing Economies: INI's Experience in Spain

Tomás Galán
DIRECTOR OF PLANNING, INSTITUTO NACIONAL DE INDUSTRIA, MADRID

I. INTRODUCTION

State intervention in the economy through public enterprise, that is, by means of an active and direct participation in the production of goods and services, is an economic and political issue which generally leads to controversy. Historically, this kind of State intervention has taken many forms; both its relative overall level and its sectorial scope have been very varied, thus reflecting the present controversy about the relative roles of public and private enterprise in a private property economy.

This chapter limits itself to one of the elements of this issue, state participation in productive activity, principally industrial, by means of companies involving state participation. For this purpose, I deal with the thirty-six year's experience of the *Instituto Nacional de Industria*, (INI) in Spain.

My objective is to deduce from this particular experience some general propositions which can contribute to the formation of an economic theory of state holdings, or at least of its basic components. This ambitious task will not be completed in this chapter. However, it may be appropriate to offer an economist's thoughts based on knowledge of a reality about which he has acquired perspective. These thoughts are the result of frequent discussions with my colleagues of INI's Research Department (*Dirección de Estudios*) to whom I am deeply grateful, especially Rodrigo Keller, Director of the Department.

The two main issues examined in this paper are (i) the politico-institutional features of the concept of a public holding; (ii) the socio-economic and financial effects that this holding can and should have on the economy of a developing country.

This discussion will use as its frame of reference that introduced by property rights theory. This approach will enable us to analyse the second issue in terms of the first, that is, as a function of the structural and institutional rules which govern and control the conduct and functions of the public holding.

The objective of the paper consists of demonstrating the capacity of a public holding (whose institutional rules will be specified) to achieve significant socio-economic objectives in a medium-sized developing country.

II. A FEW ELEMENTS OF THE PROPERTY RIGHTS APPROACH

Every economic system consists of a set of rules which affect the behaviour of decision-makers. Any agent in the system who contributes his effort hopes it will be compensated by some reward, broadly defined. In each economic system therefore, there exists a system of rights which basically regulate the way in which this effort is adduced and the form in which the benefits generated are appropriated by the agent. Thus, specific forms of behaviour can be deduced from the system of rights, which is the result of incentives and penalties imposed by the system itself.

On another level, stability of the system's performance can only be guaranteed by a collective decision on a system of rights suitable for the pursuit of social objectives. This implies the necessity of superior rights assigned to what we shall call the state.

In the economic fields (production, investment, consumption . . .) activities exist whose characteristics make it easy to define the effort and the process of appropriation of benefits by each agent. In these cases, it is possible to control such activities through 'exclusive and transferable' rights, that is, through private rights. This is true of those activities which do not generate externalities (either beneficial or detrimental).

However, activities do exist which generate beneficial and detrimental externalities, or situations characterised by high costs of information or high costs of transaction. In these cases, it is difficult to equate the effort of each agent with his appropriation of earnings. As a consequence, the simple use of a system of exclusive and transferable rights may not only lead to an accumulation of value added which conflicts with the social objectives of the country, but also to a non-optimal allocation of resources for the achievement of the general economic objectives of the country.

There is fairly widespread conviction that in developing countries the system of 'exclusive and transferable rights' has not produced satisfactory results from the economic and social points of view. In production this system of rights corresponds to private enterprise, in which the owner (the capitalist in our western world) has three basic rights: (i) the appropriation of the surplus, (ii) the right (suitably adapted to each case) to examine the composition of the human team in charge of the management of the firms, and (3) the right to 'sell' the abovementioned rights.

When the economic power which the possession of those rights entails is injurious to or insufficient for achievement of the social objectives, when the generation of the surplus at the same time entails unregulated damage to third parties or the opportunity to generate wellbeing for third parties, for which no financial compensation is possible so that the opportunity is inadequately utilised, then the best possible solution to existing socio-economic problems cannot be attained. In other words, there are rewards and penalties which are inappropriately designed and which, therefore, have unsatisfactory effects upon resource allocation. There are also objectives of a social character which are not expressed in market terms and which therefore do not attract resources for their achievement.

There is general recognition that an economic system working on a basis of exclusive and transferable rights, leads to situations not desired by society. In fact, in every country there is a wide variety of corrections, going from the most controversial, those affecting freedom of international trade, liberty of transaction in the capital market or labour hiring, to special regulations relating to the performance or commencement of certain activities. These forms of interference have been added to those that are more traditional, using special taxes, tax rebates and even financial incentives.

This means there are actions which are classed within a system of non-exclusive and non-transferable rights; these relate to collective rights or rights of 'control' which are normally identified with state authority.

However, there are activities which do not fit into the framework of control rights, but which, when left to a system of exclusive and transferable rights, are not carried out efficiently in terms of the social and economic objectives of the country. For those activities a new system of rights has to be devised between the two already mentioned.

Public enterprise fits into a system of 'exclusive and non-transferable rights'. Public enterprise, since it belongs to the state, does not give rise to the problem of attribution of particular surpluses to particular economic agents who are not necessarily interested in achieving the social and economic objectives. Public enterprise does not need to protect itself or prepare itself for (in economic terms, it need not anticipate) the transfer of its activity or the sale of its rights. (This point is relevant when calculating the efficiency of public enterprise, since it may yield positive internal returns without necessarily being larger than those of other activities with which it may compete in the market for assets.)

Indeed, public enterprise must fit into the field of exclusive rights, as it is to perform an activity whose results must be identifiable and measurable, and its assessment, not its attribution, will affect the valuation of the team exclusively entrusted with the management of its resources.

III. PUBLIC ENTERPRISE IN GENERAL

In western countries with market economies, state intervention is motivated by the deficiencies of the market in two different fields: (i) the distribution of wealth and income; and (ii) the dynamic sectorial equilibrium of the economy.

The available intervention instruments which may be used for these two purposes have comparative advantages whether one objective or the other is pursued. These advantages are derived both from technical features (such as scale economies) and from institutional properties (flexibility of decision, information properties, etc.).

There are many forms of intervention which can be adapted to a wide range of collective needs, from the fiscal system, one of whose aims is a fair distribution of fiscal charges, to incentive measures to stimulate private initiative, whose main objective is to direct economic activity. Public enterprise falls within this range as direct state production activity, and it should be assessed for its comparative advantage in achieving the social economic objectives entrusted to it.

Public enterprise has traditionally pursued the objective of improved distribution and sectorial equilibrium. When public enterprise is designed for fiscal purposes, selling above cost in order to acquire revenues from consumers, or when, on the contrary, it is used as a means to channel subsidies to users, its main objective is redistribution, even though it is sought through an activity that should be characterised by productive efficiency as well.

In terms of its role in dynamic sectorial equilibrium, public enterprise has been assigned the task of stimulating strategic and leading sectors for two different reasons:

(a) the decision not to leave activities related to security, defence or national independence to private firms;
(b) the inability of private enterprise to perform tasks requiring great financial outlays or subject to high risks in recovery of capital.

In both cases the problem is to provide a substitute for free market initiative, because it is inefficient in allocating resources to some particular activity, or because it is intended to reduce detrimental externalities or to foster beneficial externalities.

The objective of this chapter is to show that among the economic activities that generate externalities there are some for whose management the best institutional arrangement is the public enterprise.

Before continuing, it is convenient to point out that a principle that should govern state intervention in the productive process through public enterprise, when its purpose relates to sectorial dynamic equilibrium, is that its management of an activity should give rise to the capacity to generate a surplus that can be reinvested, at least in an amount sufficient to permit repayment of invested national capital. On the other hand, if the public enterprise is operated exclusively to promote income redistribution, it should not be forgotten that, since it uses scarce real national resources, it must remunerate these resources, that is to say, it must also generate a surplus. If there are other methods of intervention that can lead to the desired redistribution it is probably not appropriate to pursue this goal by means which require the use of scarce resources.

Consequently, public enterprise should be used primarily to pursue the second goal of state intervention: improved dynamic sectorial equilibrium of the economy. This does not imply that the distributive effects of an activity should be ignored, but it means that its main purpose lies in another area. This purpose is improved production of goods and services and, there, economic rationality is a necessary requirement.

Public enterprise must satisfy some objectives of a general character, but subject to constraints derived from the requirements of economic rationality. The interplay of these two elements determines the scope of activity of the public enterprise; the former modifies the aim of maximum profit as the only criterion, the latter demands a degree of economic efficiency.

It is assumed that in every instance management will satisfy an internal rule which requires it to minimise the cost of any particular output combination and to seek to maximise monetary profits. This constitutes the operating efficiency of a public enterprise which is already in operation and will be highly dependent on the administrators' professional quality and training.

Thus, what we want to emphasise here is the preceding (*ex ante*) definition of efficiency in the public enterprise at the time the desirability of its establishment is decided.

It seems clear that the public enterprise should generate an economic surplus for reinvestment. But it is convenient to specify its expected components. The supporting feasibility analysis should be expected to show a positive internal return, permitting recoupment of the funds to be used by the firm. If the expected rate of return is greater than the cost of capital, economic efficiency will appear to be guaranteed, even from the market's viewpoint. Nevertheless, the public enterprise may be economically efficient, even if its expected rate of return is lower than the cost of capital, as long as 'social benefits' not capable of provision by the market are obtained and are wanted by society.

The evaluation of these 'social benefits' in quantitative terms presents difficulties which have not yet been solved. It is impossible to impute a monetary price to values which are outside the market; but some relative prices may be estimated on the basis of the values of available substitutes. A system of indicators, evaluating in relative terms the social interest in the creation of beneficial externalities or the elimination of detrimental externalities, will permit a comparison of the social benefits which a public enterprise is likely to generate along with other benefits desired by society.

The less the difference between the expected rate of return of the public enterprise and the cost of capital, the less will be the 'social profits' that the company will have to show and the more easily it will pass the opportunity cost test for the resources it will require. Thus, the less the difference between the expected rate of return – measured in monetary terms – and the cost of capital the less will be the opportunity costs required to obtain the social benefits to be pursued by the public enterprise.

The calculation and decision problems arising from these issues require a specific institutional setting. The differences between public and private enterprise justify behaviour that follows both positive and normative rules. In fact, private enterprise is based on the three rights described in section II, within the exclusive and transferable rights system. What enters the calculation of its profitability is the value of the possession of those rights which, when they can be transferred freely, should be capable of monetary quantification, in transaction terms.

Some of the rights which pertain to public enterprise are not transferable, either for technical reasons (transaction or exclusion costs giving place to non-exclusive rights) or as a result of political decisions. As they can only be the subjects of collective or political transactions, they cannot be measured in monetary terms. Another valuation system is then needed, whose expression is political in nature, and which reflects the values of the society.

It can be assumed that this valuation will depend on the objectives of the activities of the state, defined by the government and parliament. To the extent that the desired results of the public enterprise are in theory appropriated by the country as a whole or by its social groups, according to rules instituted by the country, it must be the country itself which evaluates and controls the management of the entity administrating the enterprises.

For this purpose it is necessary to establish an institutional system and instruments to guarantee that such a system works in the same way as the market which evaluates and controls the activities of private enterprises in terms of their monetary results. By the definition of public enterprise the market alone cannot be left to direct its activity, rather, other institutional controls have to be arranged for it; instruments that, generally speaking, require unified action by government and parliament.

Up to this point, we have sketched some specific features of public enterprise which do not start from an allegation of necessity of interference of the state, but rest on a definition of the property rights which permit the public enterprise, operating through exclusive and non-transferable rights, to attain various social objectives stimulating external benefits or deterring external damage, whose results are more satisfactory than those based upon maximisation of monetary yields through the market.

This requires an institutional mechanism that complements the automatic market mechanism and obtains from both government and parliament the necessary specification of objectives and the designation of its mission.

IV. INDUSTRIAL PUBLIC ENTERPRISE HOLDINGS

When the state participates in industrial production it does so mainly, if not exclusively, for sectorial dynamic balance. By this is meant the creation of a sectorial or intersectorial structure coherent with long-term socio-economic objectives and consistent with available resources, technology and demand characteristics of the country; all this subject to an efficiency requirement, that is, of surplus creation (national growth and development).

Normally there are measures adapted to the pursuit of multiple objectives such as employment generation, international competitiveness, guarantee of basic supplies, national independence, etc., which impose obligations that the market, exclusively relying on private initiative, cannot satisfy effectively.

A medium-sized industrialised country such as Spain, encounters specific and interrelated problems, which require the intervention of public enterprise. These are traditional technological backwardness and inability, because of size, to introduce new techniques domestically in every area of development; and a domestic market of insufficient size to permit the full benefits of economies of scale of certain basic industries, or even attainment of the minimum scale required technically, with the consequent danger of excessive penetration of foreign capital, or external dependence. Also, because of size, there is considerable interdependence among the activities of different sectors, mainly the strategic ones (power, iron and steel, etc.). That is to say, in planning terminology, marginal projects are non-existent in many areas.

When there is neither public enterprise nor efficient state intervention in a developing country, the market yields structurally inefficient basic industries, fails to produce advanced technology sectors needed for medium-size manufacturing industry, and substitutes foreign private enterprise (multinationals) for national initiative. If these consequences are considered undesirable, public enterprise should correct them.

This all requires state intervention to be designed with the following elements in mind:

(a) the necessity of joint planning, to take account of sectorial interdependences;

(b) the need to gather large volumes of financing for a few activities;

(c) the necessity of bearing risks and of repaying them with efficiency and equity in the long run;

(d) the necessity of correcting social distortions caused by concentrated industrial development.

The traditional institution that many developing countries have used to deal with these elements has been national economic planning, in many cases expressed in a development plan imposing more or less compulsory objectives.

It is possible to distinguish two types of development activities with different characteristics: first, social and infrastructure activities (public services) whose 'demand' is inherently domestic and has (virtually) no external beneficiaries; second, economic and industrial activities which are necessary for the country and whose growth is, at the same time, dependent on international economic and technological conditions.

The first of these can be planned for the long run without great risks. The second should be planned for the long run but with continuous revision and adaptation to the changing international environment. Accordingly, the first can be controlled by large and powerful institutions on a national scale, since flexibility is not necessary (direct administrative management). For the second, besides economic and financial power, the managing institutions must have great flexibility and capacity for initiative (public enterprise).

Once these working conditions are satisfied, we may ask what are the characteristics of a public holding (such as INI), what is its usefulness in facing the problems that have been described, and what is necessary to guarantee its good performance.

The characteristics of such a public enterprise are:

(a) State ownership, permitting it to serve as an instrument of policies with general (long-term) social-economic objectives;
(b) participation in firms which are run competitively as mercantile firms, thus permitting initiative, flexibility, efficiency and decentralisation;
(c) diversification of its portfolio among several sectors, so that risks are offset to some degree;
(d) a significant share of domestic economic activity (no less than 10 per cent of the Gross Industrial Product), permitting it to serve as a dynamic stimulus in various particular sectors as well as at a macroeconomic level.

For a public holding to attain its potential the following provisions are required:

(a) it should be run in accord with economic profitability criteria, including in this calculation its service to the general interest and to attainment of national policy objectives;
(b) it should be under effective control by the government (which forms national policy) and parliament (representing the general interest);
(c) it should produce and supply the necessary information for such effective control;
(d) it should provide well-organised information and management instruments that permit not only *ex-ante* evaluation, but also rational making and implementation of decisions and reporting of results. That is, it needs an efficient and modern system of management planning and control.

The institutional articulation of all these elements is most important as a guarantee of efficiency. There are four institutional elements required for the system of objective-planning, decision-implementation and follow-up of results:

(a) the parliament, that represents and defends public interest;
(b) the government, that proposes and carries out social and economic policies;
(c) the public holding, including its experts, managers and technical directors of the programmes corresponding to the established policy;
(d) the market system and private initiative, as a competitor in the same social-economic process.

The institutional problem, which is a matter of organisation theory, consists of the assignment of duties and responsibilities to each one of these. When the public holding has an important effect on the national economy, derived from its volume, the institutional problem presents very special qualifications. Experience shows that a decision-making process based on two poles, namely the government and the management of the holding, does not lead to efficient service from the national point of view. In fact one of the two instances will tend to dominate the other. The example of INI in Spain is suggestive. There were periods of great independence of the management of INI, that was not subject to a coherent scheme of political guidelines. More recently, its exclusive dependence upon the government has induced the government, which faced economic and social problems with immediate pressure, to compel INI to undertake quick solutions, inappropriate to its long-term role as a balancing influence.

Since a difference in purposes is likely to arise between both decision centres, a third influence is required at the parliamentary level in order to define national guidelines and represent those general interests, not satisfied by market forces alone, which in substance are the justification for the existence of a public holding.

The various control elements can then be articulated as follows:

(a) the parliament dictates general socio-economic rules and guidelines and decides upon matters involving serious issues;

(b) the government serves as interpreter of the parliamentary guidelines and acts as decision-maker on plans proposed;

(c) the market serves as a counterbalance for the economic activity of the public firm, spurs its efficiency and always provides an institutional option;

(d) the public holding is the organisation having the required technical and economic information in disaggregated form and having at its disposal information at two distinct levels, (i) it has a complete and coherent picture of the situation as specified by the guidelines of government or parliament. It is able to evaluate the results of employment of additional resources in a manner consistent with optimal results and efficient management of the entire enterprise, and (ii) the holding companies, in addition, have detailed economic information about their particular problems and specific options.

For their operation to be efficient the interplay of these elements must be co-ordinated by operational instruments. These include: a planning, information and management control system permitting co-ordination between the holding and the firms in which it participates; an external system of control of the group activities, operating in two ways; (i) through *ex-ante* control, that is, the approval of plans, with explicit evaluation of goals to be achieved and instruments to be used, and (ii) through *ex-post* control, that is, periodic reporting of the results of the actions undertaken by the plan and in adaptation to current circumstances; a degree of managerial autonomy, within limits set by *ex-ante* and *ex-post* controls, allowing sufficient flexibility for a changing environment; total equality between private and public firms in their working conditions in the market (financing, tax incentives and burdens) with the necessary compensations, explicitly given for those activities not demanded of private enterprise, when public firms are required to serve extra-market social objectives.

Equality with the private firm is the means by which the market exerts control over the management's autonomy; public controls evaluate and demand accounts of activities for which the market offers no reward.

One should not undervalue the important role of some instruments which seem to be neutral. Specifically, modern strategic planning and management control systems together with the use of social profit and loss acounts, in a broad sense permit governmental and parliamentary decisions to be carried out with efficiency.

J. K. Galbraith[1] strongly emphasises the degree of independence within large private groups, which the 'technostructure' manages to retain before the scattered shareholders, whose only possible option is to continue to hold on to their shares or to sell them. On the other hand, when a public holding is explicit about its functions, objectives and strategies, its management is completely subordinated to the guidelines decided by the state, which can neither transfer its property rights nor waive its authority.

INI now has an articulated system of four-year sliding plans for each firm and a quarterly management control process to follow up the implementation of the programmes. A set of indicators (now being used in some pilot experiments) is under study as a means to evaluate the contribution of each firm to the country's social-economic system as a step in the establishment of a social balance sheet for each firm.

The next step will be the establishment of a social balance sheet for the entire enterprise as a starting point for the elaboration of INI's long-term strategic plan.

In fact, the government has to approve INI's plans in advance; but the functions and schedule of objectives for a coherent policy consistent with the pertinent parliamentary debate are not defined.

V. SOME ECONOMIC-FINANCIAL ISSUES ARISING FOR A PUBLIC HOLDING

So far the institutional issues affecting a holding have been discussed. Though some general remarks about the economic reasons for intervention have been

---

[1] J. K. Galbraith *Economics and the Public Purpose* (Boston, Houghton Mifflin, 1973).

offered, it is necessary to explain some facts about the holding's economic and financial behaviour.

First, in a developing country, a change in sectorial structure is essential for maintenance or acquisition of comparative advantages and penetration of the international market as a means to equilibrate its trade and technological balances. If this is not done, the country will be subject to foreign dependence both economically and politically.

Moreover, a developing country must increase its growth, reducing the share of agriculture and increasing the share of industry in its national product. The strain of such dynamic adaptation implies the need to expand markets, to acquire technology and to provide funds.

The first two issues have to be studied for a world with great international competitiveness and aggressiveness but, at the same time, with significant market imperfections in the form of imperfect information and limited competition. Hence, in order to break out of a stationary situation with insufficient industrial development, countries must rely upon a large and powerful national group relative to the national economy whose development it serves. This, as already noted, is a sound reason for the establishment of a public holding.

But it is in the gathering of funds that the public holding may play a still more crucial role, as its size and diversity permit it to obtain the best interest rate conditions available in the financial markets, including the international financial markets. On the other hand, since it is a state organisation it can obtain funds from the national budget, with effective political control of the expenditure. It must be pointed out that the use of public funds by an industrial holding produces additional funds if the principle of surplus creation is complied with, thus reducing or compensating for inflationary effects of public spending, at least relative to other spending activities.

However, the most serious impediment to growth in developing countries is the structural scarcity of saving. Interest rates are high for two reasons: the scarcity itself and the rigidity of capital markets in which the problems of security of loans and coverage of risk are more difficult than in developed countries. In these circumstances, funds for small investments of a commercial and industrial type are abundant, while funds for large industrial investments are not within the capabilities of domestic private initiative.

The large public holding offers guarantees that permit the acquisition of volumes of funds and financing conditions that are more favourable, and it can undertake large projects with lower profitability than the small businesses that are more common in these countries.

In fact, the public holding can undertake investments in plant and equipment of an optimal size from the technical point of view, anticipating a market not yet available in the form of effective demand but which it is hoped to achieve within the foreseeable future.

A public holding is thus a dynamic influence able to increase effective demand for capital, thanks to its capacity to make long-term forecasts of the different markets and technologies and also because of its capacity to anticipate the market in undertaking projects of adequate technical size; and thanks to its diversification, it can undertake projects with long maturation periods.

This ability to anticipate the market in order to achieve adequate size is no doubt a source of economy which should be considered in evaluating the lower monetary profitability of such projects relative to those of alternative projects.

The public holding is also able to attract savings from within the country as well as from abroad, not only because of the interest rate it is able to pay but also on the basis of other incentives such as greater security.

Consequently, a public holding can be an efficient way to increase the level of investment and the country's economic rate of growth. INI in Spain has experienced significant growth throughout its thirty-six years of existence, moving parallel to the growth experienced by the Spanish economy.

TABLE 8.1   EVOLUTION OF INI

	1950	1960	1970	1976
Assets value of INI firms (in million current pesetas)	–	61,826	502,264	930,000
Industrial product in Spain (in million pts.)	111,302^a	203,335	744,322	1,748,564
Share of agriculture on total working population	48.8%	41.7%	29.1%	20.0%
Per capita current income (pesetas)	4968	18,664	64,737	166,277

^{a}In 1954.

VI. THE NATIONAL INSTITUTE OF INDUSTRY IN SPAIN

Finally, it is useful to describe INI briefly in relation to the issues discussed here, since it forms the framework of experience from which these have arisen.[1] This also provides an opportunity for an assessment of INI as an instrument of Spanish economic development policy.

(1) Summary description of INI

INI is an autonomous agency of the Spanish State Administation under the Ministry of Industry and Energy. Its commitment is to manage as a holding and in accord with national objectives, the sharing, acquisition and sale of capital shares in firms with the legal status of corporations. Its main institutional characteristic is that it is a hybrid between public enterprise

---

[1]This is not the place for a detailed description of the economic activities of INI.

(because it is held by the state), and private enterprise (since its corporations are legally subordinated to private law and they act in accordance with the market system).

At present INI holds shares in 66 important firms in the industrial and service sectors and indirectly, through the former, in over 200 other firms. The holding represents more than 10 per cent of the country's gross industrial product, 5 per cent of industrial employment and 16 per cent of industry exports. Its capital assets amount to 11.000 million dollars. In 1977 the group's investments constituted nearly one-third of the capital formation of the industrial sector.

Considered by sectors, INI is seen to account for very significant shares of industries in basic production: oil refining (33 per cent), power (16 per cent), steel (45 per cent), aluminium (56 per cent), pit-coal (62 per cent), shipbuilding (92 per cent), trucks (about 50 per cent, depending on types).[1]

The 66 firms also cover a wide range of activities in addition to these, including foodstuffs, paper, fertilisers, engineering, tourism, aircraft manufacture, air and sea transport, etc.

Its magnitude and variety are the bases of its power as an instrument for the pursuit of objectives such as:

(a) anticyclical action at macroeconomic level;
(b) reorganisation of industrial sectors;
(c) contribution to regional balance;
(d) stimulation of employment;
(e) speeding up and preservation of strategic sectors.

Its dual institutional character as a 'public-private' organisation and its counterpart in the combination of control and autonomy in its activities find their operative instrument in the planning and management control system established two years ago. This system is composed of (i) the long-term strategic plan defining the philosophy and duties of each firm in accordance with industrial policy. This plan is at the heart of the planning criteria of the holding unit; (ii) the activities planning system with its internal management control adapted to the strategic plan, comprising a four-year plan, a one-year operative programme and a quarterly control review by management; (iii) in addition, in the future, the planning process will incorporate an information system on the social consequences of INI's activities which is consistent with the 'Social Accounting' concept.

There is now under discussion in Spain a Public Enterprise Statute which will largely determine the control society will exercise over INI. The Institute is prepared, or in the course of preparing, to satisfy the requirements that will be

---

[1] The outputs of INI firms in 1977 were: oil refining 18,000 tons; electric power 15,600 million Kw; coal 4,800,000 tons; steel 5,150,000 tons; aluminium 140,000 tons; industrial vehicles 35,000 units; shipbuilding 1,700,000 G.R.I.

imposed on it. This preparation is being carried out mainly by the planning system described above.

One cannot avoid discussing INI's financing system since it is one of the essential means of attracting and channelling national savings toward activities serving national objectives. At present INI's financial sources are: own resources (22.5 per cent) including state contributions charged to the Budget, and INI Reserves; external resources (77.5 per cent) including bond issues, and loans from domestic and foreign capital markets; and those of the group of affiliated firms are: own resources (35 per cent) including self-financing, and capital furnished by INI or private partners; external resources (65 per cent) including domestic and international loans, and direct state grants.

The yearly investment volume of INI's controlled group of companies is more or less equivalent to one-third of Spanish industry's gross capital formation. The absolute figure reached in 1976 amounted to about 1400 million dollars and in 1977, to 1660 million dollars.

The sectorial distribution of these investments is shown in Table 8.2.

TABLE 8.2   INVESTMENTS OF INI 1976–7

		1976	*1977*
Energy		66.2	64.5
Steel and metal–Metallurgy		10.6	9.9
Mechanics and shipbuilding		12.9	12.3
Transport		10.9	5.9
Non-energy mining		0.8	0.7
Chemistry		7.3	4.2
Foodstuffs		1.2	1.3
Services		1.0	1.2
	Total	100.0	100.0

(2) Evaluation of INI's current situation and activities

A full evaluation of the extent to which INI has contributed to the objectives of economic and industrial policy and, in general, to accumulation and balanced growth, would require a study in depth, which would be rather complicated, on account of the difficulty of defining causes and effects. However, some simple criteria may permit an approximative view.

In the first place, from the investment viewpoint the INI group has, throughout its history, sustained a steady growth in its total investment level, independent of fluctuations in industry's capital formation. Particularly, in slack periods, INI investments have not diminished though the conditions of its firms were disadvantageous, and it has always proposed a very stabilising depreciation policy. This means that it has served as a significant anticyclical instrument, since its investment volume is a substantial part of capital

TABLE 8.3   NATIONAL, INDUSTRIAL AND INI GROSS INVESTMENT (1971/76)

	Millions of constant pesetas (value 1970)					
	1971	*1972*	*1973*	*1974*	*1975*	*1976*
INI's investment	39,625	43,875	38,569	47,978	55,991	54,575
Gross industrial investment	149,030	164,988	188,119	195,543	181,296	167,323
Gross national investment	638,472	737,179	842,483	904,688	860,231	835,878

SOURCE National Accounts and INI Reports.

formation in industry, its diversification can induce demand in many economic sectors, and its preponderance in basic industry enables it to maintain high levels of activity in strategic sectors with long-term significance. This also constitutes proof of the generic capacity for capital accumulation by the Spanish economy.

As may be seen from Table 8.3, real national and industrial investment in the last few years has declined while INI's has generally maintained its growth.

These statements are necessary conditions for an argument that INI has contributed to the achievement of the basic objectives for a holding of its character. But they are not sufficient conditions because the fact that it accumulates productive equipment does not mean that it is contributing to the general efficiency of the economy. The contrary could be the case: excessive accumulation in deficient sectors with little or no overall profitability, to the detriment of private initiative, and/or a transfer of saving to an institution which, because of its political backing can risk inefficient investments.

But one can provide arguments against such conjectures: first, INI's record shows it to be an efficient financial entity. One of the ways to estimate efficiency from the point of view of the market system is profit margin. When an institution has a low margin, so long as it does not incur protracted losses, it contributes better to the system's economic efficiency. This criterion can be applied to financial institutions. Table 8.4 shows the gross margin between financial revenues and expenses in the last few years of several types of Spanish financial institutions.

TABLE 8.4   GROSS MARGINS IN SEVERAL SPANISH ORGANISATIONS, 1971–77

%	*1971*	*1972*	*1973*	*1974*	*1975*	*1976*	*1977*
INI	0.32	−0.21	0.40	0.70	0.49	0.30	0.35
ICO	−0.06	0.11	0.14	0.14	0.11	−0.09	−
Official loan entities	0.2	0.3	0.5	0.8	1.1	1.2	−
Commercial banks	7.7	7.4	7.4	6.9	7.1	−	−
Industrial banks	4.1	3.9	3.2	3.7	3.7	−	−
Savings banks	3.7	3.7	3.8	3.7	4.0	−	−

It can be seen that INI has a much lower gross margin than other types of institutions except for the *Instituto de Crédito Oficial* (ICO). This means that the basic objective of accumulation is promoted rather better by INI than by other institutions mentioned. That is, it channels domestic saving efficiently and directly to investments and does so steadily for long periods.

It must be shown that those investments yield true positive economic profits. It is clear that this must be demonstrated in detail by sectors, in comparison with other competing firms, and in terms of the industrial policies they pursue. But that is clearly beyond the scope of this chapter. A simple argument may, however, prove sufficient for present purposes.

At times of insufficient demand in certain economic sectors INI has increased its production, accepting risks that private initiative did not assume. The immediate result of such action may, depending on the case, be an increase in the self-sufficiency of a strategic sector, the substitution of imports or the favouring of a new type of consumption. In nearly all these cases, INI has maintained or increased its production levels, but simultaneously the sector's private production also increased. This means that at best, INI has fostered the development of private initiative while at the same time maintaining its own growth capacity in that sector; at worst it means that INI was able to compete with the private sector without cutting the ground from it. In either case, it is sufficient evidence of its competitiveness. Of course, this expansion of domestic production may be due exclusively to protection against foreign countries which leaves sufficient margin for an expansion of both public and private firms. But if, after some time, once the country's needs are met, the sector is able to export, it is clear that INI's competitiveness relative to the private sector also extends to the international market. This is the infant industry argument in a very simple form. The reasoning is that INI can demonstrate its efficiency by promoting infant industries which if they are successful, may after some experience, compete abroad, leading the country to what in this report has been called balanced growth.

This view, only expressed theoretically in the preceding paragraphs, can be corroborated by several significant cases of intervention by INI in Spanish industry. Without denying that in some other cases there may have been failures, Table 8.5 indicates how basic sectors of the economy have reacted to INI intervention. We are not trying to demonstrate by this that INI's intervention has always been optimal, but that at least its contribution to a balanced development process has been beneficial both to INI and to the private sector, with the only true difference being that INI has taken the initiative in triggering the expansion.

One can summarise the process described by the magnitudes shown in Table 8.5 as the following normal sequence of events: low production in some sector at some particular period; significant INI intervention with strong subsequent growth of that sector; slow reduction in INI participation in the sector, with absolute growth of INI production; beginning of exports.

TABLE 8.5 VARIOUS PHYSICAL OUTPUTS – SPAIN AND INI (1950–76)

TABLE A   Petroleum (metric tons) (1950–76)

Year	Spain	INI	INI %
1950	1,071,276	268,968	25.1
1951	1,284,613	354,674	27.6
1952	1,690,740	883,942	52.3
1953	2,340,477	1,483,561	63.4
1954	2,818,455	1,821,863	64.6
1955	3,131,981	2,027,179	64.7
1956	3,563,419	2,158,057	60.5
1957	5,214,973	3,245,950	62.2
1958	6,048,341	3,972,758	65.7
1959	6,283,167	4,001,197	63.7
1960	6,274,658	4,024,033	64.1
1961	7,027,479	4,718,249	67.1
1962	8,615,864	5,520,207	64.1
1963	9,599,676	5,705,590	59.4
1964	11,702,731	5,839,330	49.9
1965	13,197,862	6,065,699	45.9
1966	16,483,330	7,705,317	46.7
1967	21,726,074	8,336,998	38.4
1968	27,437,363	9,046,665	33.0
1969	29,239,508	9,166,467	31.3
1970	32,019,848	11,217,963	35.0
1971	34,919,697	12,028,854	34.4
1972	37,477,567	12,188,887	32.5
1973	43,513,570	14,043,766	32.3
1974	44,916,744	14,685,080	32.7
1975	42,115,277	13,352,379	31.7
1976	50,960,417	18,900,344	37.1

TABLE B   Steel (thousands of metric tons) (1958–76)

Year	Spain	INI	% INI	INI exports
1958	1560	80	5.1	–
1959	1823	288	15.8	–
1960	1919	417	21.7	–
1961	2339	642	27.4	–
1962	2311	649	28.1	–
1963	2765	685	24.8	60
1964	3150	681	2x.6	48
1965	3515	650	18.5	0
1966	3847	803	20.9	24
1967	4512	1171	25.9	0
1968	5083	1307	25.7	12
1969	5982	1727	28.9	–
1970	7394	2170	29.3	–
1971	8025	2402	29.9	–
1972	9530	2856	30.0	–
1973	10,808	4920[a]	45.5	–
1974	11,476	5187	45.2	220
1975	11,091	5145	46.4	740
1976	10,989	4992	45.4	1386

[a]Acquisition of Uninsa.

TABLE C   Aluminium (metric tons) (1949–76)

Year	Spain	INI	INI %	INI exports
1949	813	153	18.8	–
1950	2507	1407	70.3	–
1951	4203	2955	70.3	–
1952	4476	3071	68.6	–
1953	4453	3067	68.9	–
1954	4902	3600	73.4	–
1955	10,729	9366	87.3	–
1956	13,601	10,904	80.2	–
1957	14,727	10,386	70.5	–
1958	15,831	10,561	66.7	–
1959	22,642	16,231	71.7	–
1960	28,968	22,466	77.6	–
1961	37,105	26,105	70.3	–
1962	44,450	27,000	60.7	–
1963	46,000	28,000	60.8	–
1964	49,700	29,200	58.5	–
1965	55,000	28,289	51.4	–
1966	63,679	36,417	57.2	–
1967	78,182	41,782	53.4	6370
1968	89,322	42,513	47.6	5985
1969	106,351	57,004	53.6	–
1970	119,926	71,304	59.4	1620
1971	125,848	78,548	62.4	2927
1972	143,241	77,913	54.4	658
1973	160,376	91,285	56.9	281
1974	188,795	107,218	56.8	–
1975	210,385	122,872	58.4	1773
1976	209,879	120,600	57.5	1789

TABLE D   Cars (units) (1953–75)

Year	Spain	INI	INI %	INI exports
1953	1345	1345	100.0	–
1956	17,478	10,590	60.6	–
1957	23,225	14,072	60.6	–
1958	32,626	22,560	69.1	–
1959	37,763	28,056	74.3	–
1960	39,732	31,073	78.2	–
1961	53,227	33,920	63.7	–
1962	67,304	38,484	57.2	–
1963	79,432	45,291	57.0	–
1964	119,510	72,779	60.9	–
1965	154,994	87,651	56.5	–
1966	249,405	120,877	48.5	–
1967	273,524	158,294	57.9	503
1968	310,556	175,751	56.6	1034
1969	368,991	218,275	59.1	3567
1970	442,159	280,280	63.4	34,990
1971	448,527	254,322	56.7	54,849
1972	601,120	335,340	55.8	55,167
1973	706,818	358,504	50.7	78,729
1974	706,758	361,272	51.1	57,112
1975	–	328,806	50.0	62,626
1976	–	347,057	–	75,744

TABLE 8.5   Continued

TABLE E   Industrial vehicles (units) (1965–76)

Year	Spain	INI	INI %	INI exports
1965	83,245	25,104	30.1	–
1966	92,495	31,167	33.7	–
1967	89,347	26,369	29.5	967
1968	81,902	25,275	30.8	468
1969	80,608	24,757	30.7	880
1970	85,440	27,244	31.9	1270
1971	76,701	21,788	28.4	1968
1972	94,658	32,008	33.8	1422
1973	115,593	38,113	33.0	3238
1974	132,321	43,714	33.0	3705
1975	117,540	40,896	34.8	5424
1976	113,215	34,728	30.6	3446

Discussion of Dr Galán's Paper

Dr Nyers said that Dr Galán's paper contained both general statements about public enterprise and specific remarks about the experience of Spain, and this dual character was interesting. He said that in developing countries public enterprise played an important role not only in the provision of public services, but also in the promotion of industries which the market failed to enter, because they required very large investments, or were new and risky. He said it was important that public enterprise be financially self-sufficient, and did not drain resources from other sectors of the economy. He considered the role of INI in Spain useful in that it co-ordinated investment and growth among firms in different sectors of the economy. But he said there was a temptation to increase central control over these firms unduly, which could lead to problems of bureaucracy. The best solution was an intermediate one between complete decentralisation and too much centralism. Finally, he said that he thought workers' participation was essential for good performance of a public enterprise. The socialist countries were currently experimenting to find the best form of workers' participation in management.

Mr Stoffaes agreed that one of the roles of public enterprise was to develop sectors which private capital neglected, because of risks involved or high capital-intensiveness, such as steel, petrochemicals, energy, etc. But he said other means exist of expressing public priorities and industrial policy, such as the granting of tariff protection, public subsidies or guaranteed orders. These could also work under private enterprise. Which was the most efficient instrument? He cited four examples from France to show that one could not decide clearly. The computer and electronic components industry received subsidies and government orders, but showed no great success so far. The oil industry was a public enterprise and successful. Aerospace was also public, but failed with the Concorde. Dassault, which built military aircraft, received subsidies and guaranteed orders and was successful. There was no systematic pattern. Success depended on the detailed relationship among the state, the trade unions, and the capitalists. Public enterprises in declining sectors (such as coal, shipyards, railway, post office, etc.) generally have trouble in reducing excessive employment because of the trade unions. The management of public enterprises has to be shielded from government interference. This requires responsible and strong personalities. He concluded by citing two examples of market failure which might call for public enterprise even in the absence of a natural monopoly. The first example was the pharmaceutical industry. Under its social security programme, the French government picked up the bill for medical drugs, and so the market did not work. The pharmaceutical firms took advantage of this by spending too much on advertisement and too little on genuine research to improve their products, putting products which only appeared to be new on the market in order to conceal price increases. This situation might call for a government takeover, not just price regulation, despite the absence of increasing returns to scale. The second example was military procurement, the military-industrial complex, where private enterprises benefited from public expenditures. Public officials had a tendency to spend government funds more easily than people spent money out of their own pockets. In the United States as well as in France, laws required military purchases to be made from domestic companies, and so prevented foreign competition and created an artificial monopoly. Here too, he said, a government takeover might be required to avoid overpricing, inappropriate technological changes and political interference.

Mrs Martínez-Tarragó said that throughout the debate so far public enterprises had mainly been characterised as being 'worse' than private enterprises, because they showed less profits and interfered with the functioning of the market mechanism. But she wondered what sort of private enterprises we were thinking about. Her contention was that public enterprises should be evaluated in terms of a worldwide process of increasing concentration demonstrated by the constant growth of corporations. So what we are facing is a world dominated by large firms, in which planning is used extensively. We are far away from free market forces. Therefore, the problem lies not in the size and nature of private as contrasted with public firms, but in the economic, social and political effects of both types of enterprises.

The success of the firm may not promote the stability of the economy at a macro level, and certainly may not serve some basic social needs. There is plenty of evidence of such lack of correlation both in developed and in less developed countries. Considering that the planning of large corporations pays little attention to the needs of the national economies, one can consider this as an increasingly important argument in favour of public enterprises.

Dr Pryke said that Galán's paper listed many useful things that the state could do in the economy. But that was not sufficient. It was necessary to go to actual experience to see whether the state had indeed behaved in the way it should. Recently, he said, governments had shown a preference for quick solutions to short-term problems which were contrary to a country's long-run interests.

Lord Kaldor said that arguments could be given in favour of either private or public enterprise. The conclusions were different depending on whether one considered private enterprise as natural, as in the United States Constitution, so that one had to make a case for public enterprise as a departure from the norm, or whether one considered public enterprise as natural and had to prove that private enterprise was more efficient. He was in favour of giving public enterprise the benefit of the doubt, simply because it avoided the social cost of consumption out of profits and the making of investment decisions by a small minority, for their own benefit, which is not necessarily the social benefit.

Professor Srinivasan countered that Kaldor's assumption that public enterprise represented the interests of the masses while private enterprise represented the interests of the capitalist class was open to question. It depended on the class composition of the power structure.

Galán responded to Pryke by saying that INI was self-financing and showed financial profits, and did not drain public funds. It had made a positive contribution in accelerating the development process. He found a public holding company preferable to interference in the economy carried out by the Administration. Such government intervention had two possible outcomes. Either the companies which received subsidies prospered, and were left in private hands or they went bankrupt in spite of subsidies, and were taken over by the government. This raised the delicate question of whether previous subsidies should be deducted from the compensation for nationalisation. As an example of an industry that benefited from indirect public subsidies, he mentioned that 80 per cent of the electric utilities in Spain were in private hands. The government regulated electricity rates, and set them at a level sufficient to allow the utilities to expand to meet future demand. The utilities showed high profits, but the investment, for which consumers paid through high tariffs, did not take place. The companies allocated their profits in a way that did not satisfy the public interest. The subsidies did not induce the companies to do what the government wanted. Some form of public control was necessary in these cases. And a public holding company, such as INI, could control such enterprises much better than a ministry or state department. He concluded by saying that there were two purposes to public enterprise. The first was political, and included tasks such as creating employment, improving the income distribution and balance between regions, etc. The second was to create a surplus and accelerate economic growth. It was sometimes necessary for a new industry to bear losses for a limited period until demand could expand and the enterprise reach the profit level of activity. This deterred private investors and called for public investment. INI's role was more of the second type.

9 The State Holding System in Italian Economic Development

V. Ajmone Marsan[1]
INSTITUTO PER LA RICONSTRUZIONE INDUSTRIALE, ROME

I. THE GESTATION PERIOD

Italy was a latecomer among European countries which in the nineteenth century followed the lead of England in industrialisation. The first great industrial upswing during which growth was especially rapid in the producer goods sectors and in power production only started in 1896, coinciding with the turning point of an international cycle and the ensuing upsurge in economic activity both in Europe and in the United States. The subsequent period of rapid industrial expansion lasted for a good decade and saw the creation, virtually from nothing, of important new industrial branches requiring very large investments. Given the lack of capital accumulation within industry itself or from other sources, a crucial role in the financing of this development fell upon the banks.

This is a central theme of Gerschenkron's pioneering studies[2] of continental European industrialisation, showing among other things the many features which Italy's early industrial growth shared with that of other relatively backward countries of nineteenth-century Europe. In this context Gerschenkron stresses the importance of the techniques of investment banking, as evolved in Germany, which were imported into Italy in the middle of the 1890s with the direct participation of German banks. These so-called 'mixed' banks combined the self-liquidating activities of a commercial bank with the provision of finance, including venture capital, for the long-run investment needs of industry. In the latter role the bank established a link thanks to which

[1]The views expressed by the author in this paper do not necessarily reflect those of the organisation for which he works.
[2]A. Gerschenkron, 'Notes on the Rate of Industrial Growth in Italy, 1881–1913', *Journal of Economic History* (December 1955), reprinted in *Economic Backwardness in Historical Perspective* (Cambridge, Mass., 1962), pp. 72 ff.

'not only capital but a good deal of entrepreneurial guidance was channeled to the nascent and expanding enterprises'.

In drawing a parallel with the German experience, Gerschenkron, however, points to the fact that whereas in Germany industry after 1900 gradually succeeded in freeing itself from 'decades of tutelage', so that its association with the banks was no longer a 'master–servant relation' but rather a 'cooperation among equals'; the same was not true of Italy. The author's conclusion is indeed that 'it would be difficult to discover in Italy any *serious* signs of a growing independence from the banks on the part of the industrial enterprises ... Their absence in pre-1914 Italy is not surprising and must be taken to reflect the belatedness of the country's industrialization effort'.[1]

This significant deviation from the 'German' model which the eminent Harvard historian detects in the initial phase of Italian industrialisation was amply borne out by the subsequent evolution of the country's industrial growth, and helps to explain the peculiar type of public enterprise which Italy eventually developed.

Already after the fast progress recorded between 1896 and 1906, the depression of 1907 ushered in a period of slow growth, extending until the outbreak of the First World War and marked by the crisis, first, of a major bank and, shortly after, of a group of steel companies, all of which required the direct intervention of the Bank of Italy. These early salvage operations at public cost revealed the inherent weakness of a situation in which the 'mixed' banks had become the main source of financial capital for industrial enterprise. The banks had been all too ready to take an equity stake in new firms and offer bridging finance until such time as market conditions became suitable for the placing of the companies' shares with the public.

Although this practice, at least initially, had the ultimate purpose of expanding the base for the bank's 'normal' commercial operations (especially by acquiring the role of sole purveyor of credit to the client firm or group),[2] the banks thereby became heavily dependent on the behaviour of a stock exchange which was still in its infancy and highly volatile. This induced the banks to purchase more industrial shares in the course of support operations on the stock market. Inevitably the banks' commitment with client firms tended to reach the point where a retreat could no longer be envisaged, thus transforming *de facto* the banks' position into that of holding companies. This was a far-reaching change, which forced the Italian mixed banks to perform an entrepreneurial role for which they were not really fit, if only because the capital they had locked up in industry largely exceeded their own equity and was for the most part their depositors' money. The banks' attitude was inevitably influenced by this inner conflict which limited their readiness to take long-term risks and – when confronted with a firm's crisis – confined them to

---

[1] *Ibid.*, pp. 88–9.
[2] This is borne out by the recent findings of A. Confalonieri in his monumental work *Banca e industria in Italia, 1894–1906* (Milan, 1974–76), see vol. III, pp. 459 ff.

trying to 'minimize the consequences of a mistaken venture'.[1] The overriding fact to consider is that the banks had to cope with the scarcity of entrepreneurial forces of the country and the limited amount of risk capital that existing entrepreneurs could independently accumulate for holding control over industrial ventures requiring much larger investments than in the earlier phases of Europe's industrial revolution.

To complete the picture one must add that the banks, being themselves quoted on the stock exchange, resorted during periods of pressure to heavy purchases of their own shares through specially created subsidiary companies (which the banks again financed with depositors' funds), thereby indirectly becoming their own controlling shareholders. That such a vulnerable structure could not survive for long is hardly surprising.

The postwar crisis of the 1920s was marked by severe economic difficulties and a few banking crises which led to fresh rescues by the Bank of Italy and the consequent transfer to it of controlling interests in important industrial firms. The final blow to the system came with the onset of the worldwide Depression of the early thirties. In 1933 the Istituto per la Riconstruzione Industriale (IRI) was created as a statutory agency, at first of a temporary character, but was soon (1937) converted into a permanent institution for the management of industrial enterprises having the form of joint-stock companies regulated by ordinary company law.

IRI took over from the mixed banks all their industrial stock and related credits together with the inherent losses; this prepared the ground for the banking reform of 1936 which put an end to mixed banking in Italy. One important result was that the commercial banks which – given the already mentioned interlocking of shares – fell under IRI's control, were from then on free to extend credit 'on behalf of the whole Italian economy and not of the limited number of enterprises with which they had become involved'.[2] The massive size of the salvage operation which was carried out may be measured by considering that the sum total of credits which the Bank of Italy – as a result of successive bank rescues – had immobilised directly or indirectly in industry and which were taken over by IRI in 1933 amounted to no less than 48 per cent of the total currency circulation of the time.[3]

Thus the management of industrial enterprises by the State was institutionalised in 1937 when IRI was established as a permanent agency. Thereafter the system has continued to expand as a result both of internal growth and of new rescues and acquisitions (far in excess of the altogether negligible number of firms sold back to private enterprise) and this not because of any deliberate nationalisation policy by the Italian state, but essentially to compensate for the inertia or the unwillingness of private entrepreneurship in

[1] *Ibid.*, vol. II, p. 412.
[2] P. Saraceno, 'The Italian System of State-Held Enterprises', *Journal of International Law and Economics*, No. 3, (1977), p. 407.
[3] P. Saraceno, *L'Istituto per la Ricostruzione Industriale – Origini, ordinamenti e attività svolta*, Report to the Minister for Industry (Turin, 1956), p. 14.

the historical context in which the country's industrial development had to proceed: an attempt, in Gerschenkron's terms, to achieve a 'substitution for missing prerequisites'.[1] And, indeed, the conclusion which Saraceno, the greatest authority on Italian public enterprise, considers most in accord with the fact of Italian economic history before and after the creation of IRI is that 'during the eighty years of existence of the industrial system, the type of public action which today goes under the name of state-held enterprise was in evidence for more than fifty years'.[2]

II. FOUR DECADES OF DEVELOPMENT

The evolution of the state holding system up to the Second World War coincides with that of IRI. The new agency, given the nature of the operation which led to its birth, acquired at one sweep from the banks all their industrial shareholdings, including both loss-making and profit-making enterprises. It could therefore rely from the start on a relatively large pool of experienced managers which became an important asset for the subsequent development of the group.[3] The first four years, 1933–36, were devoted, on the one hand, to the sale of most holdings in small-scale firms and, in terms of sectors, in the electrical industry, textiles, agriculture and real estate; on the other hand, IRI started the reorganisation and financial consolidation of its larger enterprises. As early as 1933 the agency grouped its three telephone subsidiaries under a sectoral subholding company (STET) which was followed in 1936 by a second specialised subholding (FINMARE) for the management of the shipping companies. In both cases new long-term strategies and investment plans were laid down and the necessary finance secured through the issue of convertible bonds. These were the first steps toward an organisational structure which was to be extended to other sectors and become an important instrument of decentralised management of the large and diversified group IRI has to govern. The subholdings, which are ordinary joint-stock companies, also play a useful role as suppliers of finance to their subsidiaries with resources derived from borrowing and share issues on the capital market.

In 1937 a third subholding organisation (FINSIDER) was set up along with the launching of a large-scale investment programme for the steel sector, including the construction of an integrated shore-based plant in the Genoa area. Although the new unit could not be completed before the outbreak of the war and was subsequently dismantled by the Germans, the implementation of the project and of the strategic design which justified it were to become one of

[1] *Economic Backwardness in Historical Perspective, op. cit.*, p. 358.

[2] 'The Italian System of State-Held Enterprises', *op. cit.*, pp. 411–12. Saraceno argues these points extensively in his important work, *Il sistema delle imprese a partecipazione statale nell'esperienza italiana* (Rome, 1975), pp. 31–3.

[3] This has not been the rule in other countries. However, comparable cases are to be found in Austria, where the state industry was the result of the overall expropriation of German firms after the Second World War, and in Portugal, where it occurred as a consequence of the nationalisation of the banking system in 1976.

the earliest achievements of IRI after the end of the war. In the three-year period 1937–39 a first rationalisation plan was also carried out in the engineering sector.

As a result of these actions, by 1939 the value of IRI's interests in the five major sectors (steel, engineering, telephones, shipping and electric power) accounted for 90 per cent of the total, against 57 per cent in 1934, a good measure of the restructuring and selective development policy pursued by IRI in a brief six-year period. In national terms, the group had a dominant position in the following lines of manufacturing: pig iron (77 per cent), steel (45 per cent), shipbuilding (80 per cent), arms and ammunition (50 per cent), heavy electrical machinery (39 per cent); it was fairly important (between a fifth and a fourth) in other engineering lines; as to services, it controlled the telephone network of the northern and west-central regions and about 90 per cent of Italian passenger liner shipping. Altogether about 170,000 persons were employed in the IRI group in 1939, three-quarters of which belonged to the steel and engineering sectors.

The outbreak of the war led to a rapid expansion of IRI's war production (in the engineering and shipbuilding firms employment rose from 70,000 to 100,000); at the same time severe damage was inflicted on the steel and shipping sectors. Both these circumstances were bound to cause serious difficulties when the fighting ended.

The postwar period is best analysed by distinguishing three phases. The first came to a close in 1953 and was dominated by the postwar reconversion problems of IRI's engineering and shipbuilding sectors, which were further aggravated by the fact that IRI was called upon to rescue five private engineering plants in Northern Italy. Conversion plans were entrusted to a newly-created sectoral subholding (FINMECCANICA) and had to be carried out without adding to the unemployed; this and the reparation of the substantial war damage suffered, involved the agency in an aggregate loss of about 700 billion lire at 1976 prices. This notwithstanding, the contribution of the Treasury to IRI's capital endowment fund was highly discontinuous and altogether limited to a bare 10 per cent of the needs. From 1948 IRI embarked upon long-range investment programmes, among which the reconstruction of the coastal steel centre interrupted by the war was of major importance. This decision was based on the view that, although Italy had no indigenous sources of most raw materials, it was possible to establish a competitive steel industry based on imported coal and ore. The successful implementation of this strategy was the precondition for the great expansion of the Italian engineering industry in subsequent years. The growing steel requirements of the country could hardly have been met cheaply in a stable way through imports of finished steel; nor could steel producers have relied on regular imports of scrap to be used in non-integrated plants. The early adoption of this policy enabled Italy later on to face the European integration process which started with the Coal and Steel Community in 1953. In addition, it became possible with time to locate important extensions of the steel sector in southern Italy.

A new field of activity was added to the group in the immediate postwar period, when IRI started two airlines, one in partnership with British (ALI), the other with American interests (Alitalia).

After 1953, as Italy joined the European Coal and Steel Community, a second phase may be said to have begun, lasting until 1963, when the rapid expansion of the Italian economy was halted for the first time. In this decade IRI's steel sector had to face the challenge of competition in the newly tariff-free European market. The group's major decision was the building of a new integrated steel plant in the South (Taranto); with a capacity of about 3 million tons, it ranked then among the largest in Europe. With the completion of this project in 1964 southern Italy was endowed with the most important and modern segment of this basic industry. Two initiatives of these years were linked with the rapid growth of motoring in Italy. In 1959 the construction of the *Autostrada del Sole* running from Milan to Naples (755 km) was initiated, marking the entry of IRI in the toll-motorway field, on a concessionary basis. In 1961 Parliament approved the first ten-year Motorway Plan and IRI was entrusted with the construction and management of about two-thirds (the rest was assigned to private concessionaries) of the 3200 km national network. The large capital resources required were raised – apart from a small contribution from the state – through bond issues guaranteed by IRI. The second venture was the transfer in 1960 of the production of Alfa Romeo motor cars to a new plant at Arese (Milan) with a planned initial capacity of 100,000 cars a year. In the old plant production had been of the order of 10,000 units per year. In the shipbuilding sector a major rationalisation programme was launched which was accompanied by the establishment of a new sectoral subholding (FINCANTIERI) to which all shipyards were transferred from FINMECCANICA in 1959. The decline of the passenger-ship market which had been the major outlet for IRI yards in the past and the consequent conversion to a far less labour-intensive type of shipbuilding required a gradual reduction of employment against strong union resistance. This delayed the progress of the plan to specialise individual yards and improve productivity, which could not be completed until the late sixties. In 1957 IRI acquired the control of the two remaining private telephone companies, operating in central and southern Italy, and was thus assigned the entire telephone network under concession, including all the urban and most of the domestic trunk system (the rest being run by a state agency). Also in 1957, with the incorporation of ALI in Alitalia, the management of air transport was unified after the withdrawal of the foreign partners.

In the decade 1953–62, prior to nationalisation of the electricity sector, the generating capacity of the group's power stations rose from 7.2 to 17.1 billion kWh, an increase of 138 per cent (150 per cent in the South) against a little more than twofold increase in the remaining private and municipal electricity groups. The first Italian nuclear power station was built by an IRI company and started operating by the end of 1963.

1959 saw the creation of IFAP, a management development centre, primarily for the group itself: IFAP's activity acquired an increasing importance for meeting the management training needs, arising from the expansion and diversification of the group in a period of rapid technical progress and of far-reaching changes in industrial relations.

A second state holding, ENI (Ente Nazionale Idrocarburi), was set up in 1953, at the beginning of the period under review, with the task of exploiting indigenous oil and gas resources and of searching for foreign supplies. ENI gave a new impetus in Italy to mining exploration and the construction of methane pipelines. Abroad, the quest for additional oil resources led to an agreement in 1957 with Iran whereby ENI radically revised the contractual terms which until then regulated the exploration and extraction of crude oil in the producing countries, by associating the Iranian oil agency on a 50/50 basis in the concessionary company. In the same year a similar joint venture was concluded in Egypt. In step with the growth of natural gas output in Italy and of petroleum extraction abroad, the Group expanded vertically, first in refining and distribution, then in the production of synthetic rubber and fertilisers for which a new plant was built at Ravenna. The discovery of hydrocarbon deposits in Sicily and Basilicata made it possible for ENI to locate important chemical projects in the South (Gela, Pisticci).

This rapid expansion of the ENI group in the first decade of its existence was largely self-financed, thanks to the profitable exploitation of natural gas deposits in the Po Valley, where the group was given exclusive rights of exploration.

The experience acquired in the field of oil and petrochemicals induced ENI in 1954 to continue the operation of an engineering plant in Tuscany which had been abandoned by private capital. The factory became specialised in the design and construction of equipment used in the exploration, extraction and transport of hydrocarbons, a line of production which was to expand with time, leading to the setting up of a new production unit in the South.

In this period ENI also entered the nuclear sector, carrying out exploration activities in the field of uranic minerals and embarking on the construction of a nuclear power station at Latina. Finally, the group equipped itself with a tanker fleet which reached almost half a million dwt at the end of 1963.

The years after 1963 and up to the present are marked by a growing instability of the Italian economy and, after 1973, by the structural imbalances created by the oil crisis. This new phase started for IRI with the withdrawal from the electricity sector following its nationalisation in 1962. The problem of how to use the compensation paid to the former electricity companies – which were eager to preserve the large number of individual shareholders to which a fair prospect of returns had to be ensured – was resolved by investing, in part, in the group's telephone and steel sectors and, in part, in the development of the South. This was put into effect by transforming SME, one of the major electricity firms of the group, into a holding company which used a large part of the compensations for the entry into new sectors, mainly food and confectionery. Given the strong presence of foreign multinational groups, SME adopted the line of purchasing majority holdings or 50 per cent stakes together with private partners in well-known Italian firms (Star, Motta and others). A new group was thus formed in a relatively short time on a sufficient scale to be able to start new ventures in the South.

During these years a great impulse was given to the electronics sector, which is handicapped in Italy by inadequate public support to R & D. IRI's electronic interests were placed under control of STET, in order to exploit the important link with telecommunications (also controlled by STET), which can secure a growing outlet for electronics and stimulate innovation. In this period IRI also took over SGS, the largest Italian enterprise in its field (electronic components) which had entered a crisis after the withdrawal of the American group that first promoted it. The sales of IRI's electronics companies rose in volume more than threefold from 1967 to 1976 and employment reached 43,000 persons, of which 4500 were in R & D laboratories; five new plants employing 19,000 workers were located in the South. In sum, the intervention of IRI enabled Italy to share in the worldwide expansion of a strategic sector for a modern economy. In this context the setting up in 1969 of a software company (ITALSIEL) must also be noted. This company, in which other state holding agencies as well as major private industrial groups and large banks were associated, now has a staff of almost 1000, four-fifths of whom are technicians; it is carrying out a considerable amount of work both for public administration and enterprises to which it offers an alternative to the traditional dependence in this field from the suppliers of hardware.

In 1967 the construction near Naples of the Alfasud motorcar plant with a planned output of 1000 vehicles a day was approved. It employed 15,000 persons by the end of 1973; to this must be added the 13,000 persons working in local ancillary factories, mostly private.

In the steel sector the centre of Taranto was enlarged to a capacity of 10 million tons; plans were made for the construction of a new centre in Calabria, which is now being delayed by the world steel crisis.

In 1966 all enterprises of the steel and engineering sectors working in the area of plant design and construction were grouped in a new company (*Italimpianti*) which has become an important supplier, at home and abroad, of engineering know-how and a vehicle for increased exports of machinery and components by the group as well as by private Italian industries.

In 1969 the reorganisation of all plants operating in the field of power-generating equipment, both conventional and nuclear, was undertaken. The design capacities of the group were strengthened and licences obtained for light water reactors. In 1972 a new company (NIRA) was set up with ENI and private firms to participate in joint international projects for advanced, including breeder, reactors.

In 1966 IRI and FIAT founded the SGM company which built a new diesel engine plant in Trieste where the production of three previous factories in Turin (FIAT), Genoa (IRI) and Trieste (IRI) was concentrated. Again IRI and FIAT joined forces in 1969 to locate a growing share of the aircraft production of the two groups in the South. However both of these joint venture agreements were short-lived, as Fiat decided to withdraw when the prospects of the two firms deteriorated (and losses were recorded) mainly as a consequence of the world oil crisis. Thereafter the IRI group has taken over, as sole shareholder, the full control of these enterprises.

In the shipbuilding sector IRI in 1971 had to engage in the rescue, after its bankruptcy, of the only extant large private group (CNTR) with four yards employing over 8500 persons. A complete restructuring of the shipping sector was launched in 1974 providing for the winding up of international passenger lines and the development of new regular freight services as well as bulk cargo transport. In the area of infrastructural activities, where the group first entered the field of toll-motorways, a large private construction firm was purchased from the private sector and new units created, among which were one for building an urban motorway for the Naples metropolitan region and one for the operation of Rome airports. All these enterprises were grouped in 1970 under a special sub-holding (ITALSTAT). Among the objectives of this reorganisation was that of placing at the disposal of the state and local authorities a technical unit capable of acting as main contractor for the carrying out (normally with private participation) of large infrastructural and residential building programmes. This role has proved important also for its export potential, as the group has been bidding successfully for some of the world's largest construction projects, especially in developing countries.

The commitment of ENI to cover the energy requirements of the country provided a strong incentive to intensify mining exploration abroad. Several long-term contracts were concluded to secure the supply of crude oil and gas and the construction of international oil and methane pipelines was undertaken, the former for the supply from Italian ports of foreign refineries (from Genoa and Trieste to Switzerland, Austria and Germany) and the latter for providing links with foreign sources of supply (Holland, the Soviet Union and Algeria). At the end of 1976 the ENI group operated in mining prospecting and production in twenty-three foreign countries (compared to only seven in 1963). At home ENI added offshore prospecting to that on the mainland: about half of the group's production of natural gas comes at present from marine deposits. In this period the network of methane pipelines was more than doubled, reaching an extension of more than 13,000 km.

In the nuclear field ENI was assigned the task of operating in the various phases of the fuel cycle, in agreement with IRI which is engaged in the design and construction of reactors.

Finally, petrochemical production and the related activities of plant engineering were stepped up, the latter through the work of a specialised company (SNAM Progetti). In 1963 ENI entered the textile sector through the acquisition of Lanificio Rossi which provided an outlet and possibilities of experimentation for the production of synthetic fibres; a plant for the manufacture of clothing and a large cotton textile factory in the South were added later on as a result of rescues.

A third state holding agency EFIM – established in 1962 – was first entrusted with a number of formerly private minor engineering firms which had entered *de facto* into the public sphere during the postwar reconversion crisis, when they became entirely dependent on financing from a public fund created *ad hoc* in 1947. Operating both directly and in association with private interests through the intermediary of the subholding INSUD, EFIM gradually extended its activities to other sectors, mostly with middle-sized enterprises. The aluminium sector is an exception; in addition to constructing two plants in Sardinia, the agency acquired from the Montedison group (see below) the latter's considerable interests in this field. In collaboration with ENI, EFIM constructed in the South a plant for the production of sheet glass employing 3000 persons. An important activity of the group is railway rolling-stock manufacture, which together with other transport equipment (for instance helicopters, produced in joint-venture with a private partner) are grouped under the subholding Breda Ferroviaria.

A number of projects were undertaken by EFIM in agriculture and food products, all located in the South where the agency also started the construction and management of a series of holiday villages.

In 1971 a fourth state holding organisation (EGAM) was entrusted with the responsibility for a few mining and metallurgical enterprises previously directly owned by the State; other interests in special steels and minor engineering were transferred to the new agency from the IRI group. The scope of EGAM's activities grew further with the acquisition of more holdings from Montedison.

The latter group was the outcome of the merger, in 1964, after the nationalisation of the electricity industry, of the largest private chemical concern (Montecatini) with Edison, formerly among the strongest electricity producers in Italy, but with interests in many other sectors. From 1968 the Government decided to come to the rescue of the new group, which faced serious losses and problems in a number of its activities (predominantly chemicals and mining). IRI was asked to increase its equity holding[1] and ENI acquired one through open market purchases, after which both agencies joined the 'committee of control' which runs the Montedison group and in which the most important private stockholders share voting rights equally with ENI and IRI.

To aid in the difficult rehabilitation process of Montedison and in the hope of avoiding a complete takeover, various state holdings were involved in what were more or less salvage operations. Thus EGAM acquired all the mining and metallurgical interests of the group except the aluminium sector which, as already seen, was transferred to EFIM. IRI, in turn, acquired from Montedison its food industries (Alimont), with some ten firms representing one of the most important complexes in this sector. The total size of these operations is

---

[1] IRI acquired a minor shareholding in the Montecatini group as far back as 1934 in connection with the initial bank rescues.

indicated by the fact that they involved some 25,000 persons, out of a total of 142,000 employed by Montedison prior to the transfer.

The above summary description of the salient facts of over forty years of existence of the Italian state holding system shows that rescue operations required by the Government and autonomous expansion through investment and diversification combined in bringing it to its present size and structure. The part played by the two motive forces varied over time and for each individual state-held group. Rationalisation plans have been a major concern of the holding agencies and this led also to the transfer of subsidiary companies from one group to another. With the sharp deterioration of general economic conditions in recent years, the need for restructuring increased together with the difficulty of achieving it, because of union and local resistance. But as Saraceno rightly stresses, the system today represents 'a structure which has some coherence' and must be considered 'a considerable improvement over the initial haphazard assortment of enterprises which entered the public sphere because they had been abandoned by private initiative'.[1] In 1977 the problems of organisation of the state holdings system became the object of a wide debate and the Government formulated a series of proposals for a partial redistribution of sectoral responsibilities among state holdings, implying among other things the dissolution of EGAM. The latter was approved by Parliament so that, at present, the system is grouped under only three state holding agencies whose size can be measured by the following figures:

	IRI	*ENI*	*EFIM*
Consolidated assets, at the end of 1975 (million $)	16,650	5750	1450
Value added in 1975 (million $)	5900	2200	400
Workforce (at the end of 1975) in thousands	519	100	44

The workforce of the three groups was equal to 6.5 per cent of total Italian non-agricultural employment (excluding Public Administration). The groups' share in domestic value added was slightly over 7 per cent (rising to roughly 15 per cent for industry, transport and communications); their fixed investment in the five-year period 1971–75 was equal to about 16 per cent of the national total (25 per cent in the manufacturing sector). In the South, where 19 out of 55 million Italians live with a per capita income that is about 40 per cent below the national average, state-held industry created in the same five-year period 63,000 new jobs in the manufacturing sector, equal to over one-half of the total increase in southern industrial employment from 1971 to 1975.

The above figures show that in overall terms the bulk of Italian economic activities are within the private enterprise sector. At the same time it appears that the state holding sector has been growing faster in the seventies than warranted by its share in total employment and value added, particularly so in

[1] *The Italian System of State-Held Enterprises, op. cit.*, p. 411.

the South. However these general indicators must be supplemented by consideration of more qualitative and structural aspects to obtain a better picture of the system's importance. Thus a typical feature of the state holding system is that it is organised in large-scale multisectoral groups. In this connection it should be mentioned that Italy has, by European standards, an industrial structure in which small-scale enterprise is far more predominant, whereas the number of large industrial groups in the private sector is extremely limited. State-held groups are indeed among the very few Italian large-scale enterprises appearing toward the top of the list of the largest European companies. It may thus be said that they provide Italy with an essential component of an advanced industrial system.

State-held companies, moreover, are concentrated in specific sectors where they play an important role, such as in steel (about two-thirds of Italian output), energy (about 40 per cent of total supply of primary sources) and non-ferrous mining; to this should be added almost nine-tenths of shipbuilding and, in engineering, about two-thirds of electrical (including nuclear) and non-electrical equipment manufacture, as well as of aerospace production. The system accounts for 20 per cent of the Italian chemical output (mostly heavy) and about a third of the electronic industry (excluding the 'consumer' field, from which it is absent). State holdings also control a large section of the Italian telecommunications network, most of air transport, the radio and TV national broadcasting company, one-quarter of the freight maritime fleet and over one-half of toll-motorways. The share is much lower in other lines of production (food and confectionery, textiles, cement, glass and paper) and in the construction industry.

Finally, three of the largest banks (with about a fifth of total deposits of the Italian commercial banking system) are controlled by IRI, to which they were transferred in 1933. The banks' position within the group is however unique in the sense that no privileged access to their resources is afforded to IRI companies. This is proved by the share of the three banks' credits extended to the group which is entirely proportionate to the relative weight of IRI enterprises within the Italian productive system.

III. MAIN INSTITUTIONAL FEATURES AND PERFORMANCE OF THE SYSTEM

Italy's history as an industrial nation and the progress she has made towards the dual goal of full employment and balanced regional development are linked in many ways with the growth of the state holding system. The specific role it has played is summed up by Saraceno as that of providing the state with 'a team of managers' which the state can rely upon in order to solve problems of industrial development such as are 'continuously and unpredictably' raised by the growth of an economy in a market environment.[1] This explains why, for the

[1] *Il sistema delle imprese a partecipazione statale nell'esperienza italiana, op. cit.*, p. 55.

carrying out of its productive activities, the system has left completely intact the existing legal forms of enterprises. The adoption of the joint stock company module clearly determines the operational criteria for a businesslike management of state-held companies, opens up the possibility of private equity participation both as a source of financing and as a means for industrial partnerships, makes the turning over of a state-held firm to private enterprise a relatively simple operation, when it becomes expedient in the interest of public policy. Also important, in the same logic, is that the state, as a rule, gives up any idea of sectoral monopolies as well as of a strict and permanent boundary line for public sector activities (e.g. utilities, 'basic' industries, etc.); instead it lets its enterprises operate side by side with private enterprises in the same sectors, applying equal treatment to all of them. This is in order both to preserve a climate favouring efficient and dynamic management in the public sector and to avoid any undue dampening of private enterprise growth.[1]

Also characteristic of the system is the recourse to the group form of organisation, operating, as already seen, on a broad front of manufacturing, service and construction activities. To the normal advantages which large groups derive from scale economies in finance R & D, marketing, development and utilisation of managerial talent, etc. there must be added those linked with the economies of diversified growth, in terms of quicker and more effective responsiveness to new opportunities and new needs, when these arise. Thanks to their multisectoral structure the Italian state-held groups have thus been able to contribute more than they otherwise could have done to the survival and expansion of new lines of activity often of strategic value (electronics, nuclear engineering, etc.), to the promotion of regional development and to the restructuring of declining industries without loss of local jobs. As large and diversified groups they have also started to compete successfully on the world market for complex capital projects. Finally, they have helped to check the extension of dominant positions of multinational groups (software, food industry, etc.).

The question arises as to how the entrepreneurial function of the system is made to serve the goals of public policy, which is the *raison d'être* of state-held enterprises. Finding a solution to this problem which is both workable and free from inner contradictions is obviously of crucial importance to a sound functioning of a mixed economy. The definition of a coherent framework for decision-making in the Italian state holding sector has indeed not been the easy result of a ready-made formula, nor has the application of the normative model, once defined, always been consistent.

The first theoretical formulation grew out of an effort made within the

---

[1] It is for this reason that, for instance, IRI confidently accepted, in 1953, the entry of Italy in the European Coal and Steel Community with the consequent exposure of its steel subsidiaries to unprecedented competition. It is worthwhile mentioning that Britain refused then to join the Common Market; the fact that at the time the steel industry had been nationalised was not without influence on such a decision.

leading state-holding agency, IRI. It was in fact necessary, given the altogether vague language of the relevant acts of law[1] to derive by implication a satisfactory model of behaviour for both the managerial and the political roles. It is not really surprising that the clarification was achieved at the holding agency level, i.e. at the interface between the two spheres, political and entrepreneurial. The construction of the conceptual model is due to the rigorous thinking of Professor P. Saraceno, who has been a key figure in IRI since its birth.[2] In his approach Saraceno's starting point is that at the enterprise level of the state holding system management must remain motivated by profitability in order to maximise efficiency and initiative in the pursuit of the political goals which the holding agency must serve. There would be no problem at all, if the achievement of the public goals did *not* involve additional costs which the going market prices will not cover. That this may be the case can be seen from the example of the integrated ore-based steel industry which IRI created with regard to its long-run potential contribution to the growth of Italian industry, but which has also been profitable in business terms (while private enterprise did not feel attracted, given the smaller capital requirements and quicker returns offered by steel plants using scrap). But in other cases, public activities may well be subject to constraints involving a financial burden, which however cannot be ultimately carried by the state-held company, if it is to preserve its entrepreneurial role in a market environment. So the costs of non-economic goals must be met by the holding agency, which can rely for this on the 'endowment fund' it is awarded by the state. The fund may be considered as a form of equity capital and as such it performs the normal role of risk capital in any enterprise. In fact, the state enters it in the budget as an expenditure on capital account and, according to the agencies' statutes, it will be remunerated when profits are available. It will also have to bear any losses due to unforeseen market reverses or to managerial incompetence.

It would, however, conflict with the equity capital function of the fund if it were in advance and deliberately exposed to absorption in losses originating from the pursuit of social objectives. In Saraceno's normative model, if and to the extent that non-commercial costs have to be met, this may be obtained by accepting a less than full return on the fund or, at worst, no return altogether. Saraceno's conclusion, then, is that the endowment awards by Parliament must be sufficient to allow the holding agency to offset the non-commercial costs in

---

[1]Law No. 1589 of 1956 which established the Ministry of State Shareholdings confines itself to the curt prescription that state holding agencies 'operate according to criteria of economic viability (economicità)'. As to the holding agencies' statutes, those of IRI and ENI are silent on the matter of operational rules, while that of EFIM (created in 1962) mentions the 'economic viability' criterion.

[2]See, among the many writings by Professor Saraceno on this theme, *Lo Stato e l'Economia* (Rome, 1962), and *Il sistema delle imprese a partecipazione statale nell'esperienza italiana, op. cit.*, of which the article appearing in the *International Journal of Law and Economics, op. cit.* represents an abstract.

the way described; by the same token, the size of the fund, as contributed by Parliament, sets an upper limit to the social costs to which the state holding may be subjected. This is why the parliamentary debate on the request by Government to increase an agency's endowment fund – which usually takes place when the investment programmes of state-held groups undergo the recurrent yearly review – is one of the most important stages of the decision-making process, as it is then that Parliament decides on the desirability of that part of public expenditure which represents the cost of such government policies as are carried out by the state holding system.

Different decision levels are involved in the process described. The formulation of social goals and policy objectives is placed squarely where it belongs, i.e. in the class of political decisions. They are handed down to the state holding agencies which must ascertain in advance whether the objectives are attainable by subsidiary enterprises without damaging their profitability. This stage of the process involves both companies and parent agency in estimating the feasibility and costs of alternative proposals for meeting the social objectives, which are seldom clear-cut, and are more often multiple and conflicting. The final solution is therefore the result of successive approximations in which both the political and the enterprise level must co-operate. The role of the state holding agency is essential in the process as it must (a) make sure that the constraints of a political order remain within limits which are compatible with the survival and progress of the enterprise involved, (b) quantify the extra costs, if any, entailed by such constraints and (c) make known to the Government the additional endowment funding which may be needed to offset such costs.

Point (a) above implies that non-commercial costs must be of a temporary nature, in the sense that the agency must be persuaded that with the managerial resources of the group it controls – and with the outside conditions which the government should create in order to promote its policy objectives – it will be possible gradually to eliminate such costs and make the enterprise stand on its own feet. The time horizon for realising a return on investment may well be long, implying at times the progressive creation of external economies (as with enterprises which are located in backward areas) or a thorough restructuring of a plant and even its conversion to new lines of production. But profitability must appear to be eventually achievable.[1] This opens up the difficult chapter of rescue operations of which the history of the state holding system offers many examples. Experience has shown that not all rescues are to be rejected, but that certain preconditions for a successful rescue must be present, such as a potential for synergistic integration in the rescuing group and, most of all, a scale of operation that is efficiently manageable. This generally rules out small enterprises, which notoriously cannot be run successfully as subsidiaries of a

---

[1] A permanent non-commercial cost is conceivable outside of manufacturing industry and is typical of certain service activities of a monopolistic nature. In these cases, however, the normal solution is straight subsidisation of the operating enterprise, public or private, in the framework of a concession.

distant head office in the context of large groups, either private or public.[1]

As to point (b), Saraceno stresses that the isolation of the element of social cost, prior to any decision, should be followed by an assessment, once the decision is carried out, of the actual cost incurred. This allows both government and parliament to exercise their constitutional roles with regard to this particular class of public expenditure. The initial estimate must clearly be the result of a subjective judgement by the management of the relevant state-held enterprise, but this is just one of the many similar judgements that managers continuously have to make in the conduct of their enterprises.[2] After the event, non-commercial costs may well prove lower or higher than initially expected (which again is a normal occurrence in business management); if this is the case, the agency's fund will earn correspondingly greater or lesser returns or even suffer an (unintended) loss.

The important result of this approach is that it allows the manager of the state-held enterprise to get on with his job and strive to maximise the return on capital, a goal which – given the constraints imposed by political directives – implies the minimisation of non-commercial costs. The conditions therefore exist in Saraceno's model for not abandoning the profit and loss account as an indicator of the efficiency of management and for applying the price mechanism and the profit motive to state-held and to private enterprises alike. This is certainly a condition which must appeal to a competent manager and thus help him to attain the all-important objective of attracting capable executives for state-held enterprises. Needless to say, in this context, that the holding agency must be free to appoint company managers selected on the basis of their professional ability and experience, who are therefore motivated by the success of their companies and reluctant to see them making a loss.

Notwithstanding an early, albeit not explicit, acceptance of Saraceno's logical construction by the Italian Court of Accounts, a state organ which exercises its supervision and control over the operations of all state holding agencies,[3] it must be admitted that the application of the principles on which the state-held sector's delicate balance depends has been far from consistent. In fact the system has had to get along in recent years without clear-cut directives, while the pressure of economic and social necessities was giving rise to growing constraints and stresses, for which the State made available little of the needed contribution.

---

[1]In 1971 the Government set up a special company (GEPI) charged with the major objective of assisting sick firms of relatively small size. By the end of 1976 GEPI controlled 116 companies employing 42,000 persons, having succeeded in turning back to private enterprise no more than 22 companies with 7500 workers.

[2]This point is discussed in the report of an *ad hoc* consultative committee set up by IRI in 1976 to enquire into the 'loss areas' present in the group. See *Rapporto conclusivo del Comitato tecnico-consultivo per le aree di perdita* (IRI, Rome, 27 October 1976), pp. 19, 25.

[3]See *Relazione della Corte dei Conti al Parlamento sul controllo degli enti sovvenzionati dallo Stato per il periodo 1951–1960*, published by the Italian Chamber of Deputies in 1963. For a comment see Saraceno's article in the *Journal of International Law and Economics, op. cit.*

It must be recalled that ever since the end of the 1960s the entire industrial system in Italy has been facing growing difficulties caused by fast-rising labour costs and underutilisation of plant; the latter was due at times to a lack of demand but more generally to the gap between potential and actual productivity stemming from workers' resistance to mobility within the factory, to overtime work, etc. Notwithstanding the efforts made to redress the balance, the overall result has been disappointing, expecially for large concerns and thus particularly for state-held enterprises.

When the shock of the oil crisis came, the state holding system for many reasons proved relatively more vulnerable. To begin with, the companies more closely connected with transport (motor car production, shipping and shipbuilding, airlines and aircraft manufacture) were immediately exposed to the direct impact of the sharp rise in oil prices. The subsequent economic recession and the inflation that accompanied it had effects just as bad on other sectors, such as steel, chemicals, most investment goods, and non-essential consumer goods (confectionery, etc.) as well as construction. At the same time there was the continued delay of one of the positive repercussions expected of the crisis, namely the launching of the nuclear power station programme, which the Government had several times announced and which the IRI and ENI groups had prepared for with sizeable investments in their engineering and nuclear fuel companies. This is not the only sector in which the economic crisis hit the state holding system at the closing stage of a large investment programme started years earlier and resulting in large productive capacity increases. This applies to steel, chemical fibres, electronics, motor cars, telephones and toll-motorways. By itself, this aggravated the economic consequences of the fall in demand which for certain industries was worldwide (steel, shipbuilding, etc.). Add to this that a large share of the new investment was located in the South where conditions for the operation of industry are generally more difficult, even when the existing financial incentives are taken into account. Indeed, the fact that these incentives are still insufficient to compensate for the local external diseconomies is revealed by the very limited private enterprise investment which flowed during these years to the southern regions.

All the above factors combined in slowing down the growth of cash flow generated from operations while the capital requirements of the state-held groups continued to expand, sharply increasing the need for outside funds in a period of growing paralysis of the capital market and of generally restrictive monetary policy. The failure by the state, pressed by the need to redress an increasingly unbalanced budget, to respond to this situation and secure the funding requested by the holding agencies at each annual review of their investment programmes, was bound to have crippling effects on the financial situation of the whole sector.

Already in earlier years the endowment funds constituted a very minor proportion of the total capital employed by the state-held groups, averaging 10–12 per cent over the fifties and sixties. Adding to this the amount contributed by private minority shareholders and by partners in joint ventures, the share of equity in overall capital invested was roughly equal to one-third in the fifties and early sixties, falling to about one-fourth after 1963, mainly as a result of the stock exchange crisis which followed the nationalisation of electricity. That this situation contained long-term dangers was to become evident when the inflationary crisis of the seventies broke out: at its peak, after the oil crisis, the cost of the only outside source of finance available in practice, i.e. bank credit, rapidly soared to levels in excess of 20 per cent and even now (November 1977) is still equal to 17–18 per cent. This has sharply revealed the weakness which lay hidden beneath the precarious equilibrium of the pre-inflationary years, when borrowing seemed for some time attractive because of a much more favourable tax treatment of interest than dividend payments. Figures for the IRI group of companies, on a consolidated basis, show that in 1968 the ratio of equity to total capital employed was equal to 27.6 per cent, against an average of 50.7 per cent resulting for a reasonably comparable sample of private companies.[1] Since then the situation has deteriorated for both types of companies and by the end of 1975 the above ratios had dropped to 34.4 per cent in the private sector and 18.5 per cent for IRI companies. IRI's Annual Report for 1976, in commenting on these figures, notes that the recapitalisation needed merely to raise the IRI group ratio to the still unsatisfactory average level recorded by private companies would be of the order of 3000 billion lire. Even assuming a 5 per cent return on equity, this would produce a net saving in capital costs of some 300 billion lire. Clearly, the burden imposed by the lack of equity financing was a concomitant of the insufficient and delayed endowment funding by the state (no contribution at all has been made over the last two years) revealing a complete disregard for the dangers inherent in a sharply rising gearing ratio. The crisis, however, having brought the system near to a financial breakdown eventually induced both parliament and government to take steps which are meant not only to redress the situation but to create safeguards for the future. These safeguards altogether appear to move in the direction of the rational decision-making rules described in Saraceno's normative model.

Thus Law No. 675 (August 1977), while awarding a still very limited endowment fund increase to the three state holding agencies, has for the first time established[2] that the investment programmes of the state-held groups, when submitted by the government, 'must indicate separately the burdens which for any reason bear upon any investment project and are not otherwise offset by financial aids offered by the state'. At the same time the new law explicitly states that the endowment fund awards are intended 'for the financing of investments and . . . for offsetting any indirect costs'. The need for a prior isolation of the element of social cost, so that Parliament may decide with full

---

[1]See, Mediobanca, *Dati cumulativi di 757 società italiane, 1968/75* (Milan, 1976).
[2]See Law No. 675 of 12th August 1977, Article 12.

knowledge, is here clearly asserted. On the other hand the government, in its annual Economic Planning Report for 1978, submitted to the Chambers in September 1977, recognised that 'the problems of capital structure are more acute for state-held than for private companies . . . a distortion of direct concern to the state who is the owner, through the holding agencies, of the controlling stake in the enterprises of the system'. Whereupon the Report concludes that 'the State should not fail to make its contribution, which will have to be in proportion to the objectives pursued'.[1] The prospects opened up by these official pronouncements have led some to conclude rather sadly that, obviously, 'things had to get worse in order to get better!'.

The overall picture which can be derived from the present state of the whole of Italian industry has long-term implications difficult to assess. In fact the situation described for the state-held sector appears to be only slightly better for most large industrial concerns. This at least is what emerges from a further comparison published in IRI's Annual Report for 1976, which shows that the performance of IRI companies, measured by the ratio of gross return to total capital employed over the period 1968–75, was generally not lower than in a sample of about 700 private companies, even though far from satisfactory for both IRI and private enterprises.[2] What these figures seem to point to is that the accumulation of productive capital in Italy still cannot be seen as an autonomous mechanism, nor is it possible to overcome such deficiency with conventional policies of demand management. Saraceno argues this persuasively when he writes that 'the policy of demand support, as the principal means to foster a process of expansion, is unimaginable in an economy which does not yet have an effective growth mechanism'.[3] Pursuing this point, the author recalls the fact that the support afforded over the years by the Italian state to the process of capital accumulation for the most part had to be directed, with each recurrent crisis, to the northern regions from which modern industry, after its take-off toward the turn of the century, proved unable to spread to the rest of the country. As a result the vast southern area, notwithstanding the productive investment which the state holding system has located there during the past two decades, still has not developed an independent industrial base capable of solving its employment problems.

[1] *Relazione Previsionale e Programmatica per l'anno 1978* (Rome, 1977), (published by the Italian Senate), p. 43.

[2] The ratio used divides the sum of net return on equity plus net interest paid on borrowed capital, plus amortisation by total capital employed plus the amortisation fund. The showings for the two groups of companies are the following:

	1968	1969	1970	1971	1972	1973	1974	1975
IRI group companies	8.0	8.4	7.7	7.2	7.4	8.9	9.5	8.3
Private company sample	8.1	8.0	6.9	5.3	5.1	9.0	11.5	7.7

Source: Mediobanca, *op. cit.*

[3] P. Saraceno, *Inziativa privata ed azione pubblica nei piani di sviluppo economico* (Rome 1959), p. 6.

All considered, one can hardly dispute Saraceno's conclusion that Italy is still at present 'more comparable to the economies of developing countries than to those of the industrially advanced.[1] A circumstance which by itself implies that in the future the state holding system still has to play a durable role; its effectiveness, however, must depend on the ability and readiness on the part of the state to support the state holding sector with consistent overall policies and with an adherence to decision rules which will avoid the disruption of the framework needed for a sound functioning of the system and, with it, of the mixed type of economy which characterises Italy.

[1] *Ibid.*

Discussion of Dr Marsan's Paper

Mrs Martínez-Tarragó said that Dr Marsan's paper had summarised in a clear and interesting way Italy's experience with public enterprise. The macroeconomic objectives pursued by the public sector had been the generation of employment and the promotion of balanced regional development. The social objectives were determined by the government, as a political decision. The role of the State Holding System was, according to Marsan, (a) to insure that the restrictions of a political nature remained within the limits imposed by the interests of the enterprise, (b) to quantify the social costs of a project and to assure that they were of a temporary nature, (c) to try to minimise social costs, and (d) to use profit and loss accounts as a gauge of the enterprise's efficiency. The treatment of the subject was very interesting, but opened a series of questions.

Martínez-Tarragó said there seemed to be a contradiction in the paper between the (macroeconomic) objectives of public enterprise and its (microeconomic) evaluation of performance, as she would go on to explain.

Classical microeconomic theory was based on certain assumptions, which implied that what was good for the enterprise was good for the economy as a whole. The invisible hand took charge of it. But history, especially in recent times, had shown that the underlying assumptions were not fulfilled. The individual countries and the world were suffering from similar and recurring problems of unemployment, inflation, growing concentration, internal and external imbalances, insufficient growth rates and growing inequality, especially on a worldwide level. In comparison with the paradisiacal world of the small businessman and free competition, what we now had was growing domination by a handful of large firms which used planning to a fantastic degree, but only to serve their own interests. Given this state of affairs, irrespective of the interests they represented, governments recognised as a condition for political support for themselves, the need to make economic systems work better and to offer greater wellbeing to society.

The traditional instruments available to states to influence the economy had not always been capable of counteracting the system's incapacity to achieve objectives beyond those of the firm. Public enterprise was the most direct instrument for state intervention. Its existence was justified only if it contributed to the fulfilment of the conditions necessary to assure proper functioning of the economic system; and to satisfy these conditions, the purpose of public enterprise always had to be an increase in benefits for the majority. One should say here that what is good for the majority is good for minorities, which is not necessarily true the other way round.

What is lacking is a microeconomic theory consistent with a macro theory that does not spring from the assumption that the system dedicates itself, on its own initiative, to the achievement of social objectives, as there is not a necessary harmony between the firm's private interests and the interests of society. If private enterprise were capable of paying attention to objectives other than its own profits, there would be no need for public enterprises. Attempts to compare private and public enterprise would seem superfluous. Both are economic agents, but their *raison d'etre* is different, and the criterion for measurement of their efficiency should be different. The profit criterion is in itself a false standard, because profit cannot be accepted as an end but, at most, as a means.

Once we have a theoretical foundation on the micro level, one can use this frame of reference to analyse any specific situation; the point of reference would always have to be on a macro level and the objectives would have to be social and not private ones, since in the final instance they are not in conflict with private benefits, but are the only guarantee of permanence of the latter.

In the situation of permanent crisis in which three-quarters of mankind is living, we should not ask whether public or private enterprise is more profitable but, rather, which can best fulfil society's macroeconomic objectives.

The preceding formulation of the problem implies the need for a sort of national plan, with specific goals for each sector, such as to guarantee a dynamic equilibrium. This would doubtless present difficulties, as private investment cannot be planned, but certain sectoral proportions will have to be maintained.

She considered this point to be vital for the analysis of the problem and regretted that Marsan's paper, that reaped the rich experience of the IRI, had not mentioned it in relation to the Italian experience.

Martínez-Tarragó concluded by saying that a country without a national management, without well-qualified technical personnel, with inadequate public service would have neither successful private nor successful public enterprise. Public enterprise, with its multiplicity of objectives, constituted a greater challenge, and if dedicated men and women were available, it should attract the best administrators and the best economists, the best 'businessmen', and not the other way around as Marsan had suggested.

Mr Sánchez said that IRI's experience was interesting for a developing country such as Mexico, because IRI had not only entered traditional public service sectors, but had promoted economic growth by investing in fields in which the economy lagged behind. Mexico was suffering from an investment strike. It needed such an instrument to overcome the shortfall in investment.

Professor Sacristán Colás thought that too much attention had been given so far to comparison of public and private enterprise on the basis of microeconomic criteria. He agreed with Martínez-Tarragó that macroeconomic criteria, concerning themselves with the welfare of the masses, were more important.

Dr Pryke said he was impressed by the success of IRI. He wondered whether it had something to do with the weakness of the Italian government which kept political interference at a relatively low level, compared to other countries. He said that the approval of construction of a steel plant in Reggio Calabria after riots had taken place there corresponded to British tradition.

Mr Stoffaes pointed out that Britain, France and Italy had different forms of public enterprise. In Italy there was a State Holding Company, in France public enterprises were supervised by ministries, and Britain had theoretically autonomous public enterprises, which went to the treasury when they needed money. He raised the issue of the formal relations between the government and public enterprises – how instructions were given in each case, by whom, and to what extent firms could resist public pressures. He asked whether this could explain differences in success.

Dr Marsan said it was essential that parliament be informed of the true costs of a project when it reached a decision, even though politicians sometimes wished to be deceived. For example, if the public voted funds for a school or a bridge, it would have to know how much it cost. If parliament wanted to tell Alpha Romeo to move to the South, in order to create employment in a depressed region, it would have to know what amount of subsidy was needed, for how long, and it could then decide rationally whether the honourable goal was worth the cost. Nationalised industries should contribute cost estimates, but then leave the decision to a political process. Market costs were relatively easy to determine, while social costs were much harder to estimate. The managers of public enterprises should not concern themselves with social goals, but take them as a constraint given from outside and then try to maximise profits within these limits. Even if a manager was told that he could not dismiss any workers, he could still maximise profits under that constraint. As an illustration, he mentioned that even the state-owned French firm, Renault, had diversified from cars into machine tools and agricultural machinery, in order to increase its profits.

Marsan also said that one of IRI's advantages was its large size and diversification into several industries. This permitted it to undertake modernisations without dismissing workers, by offering them employment in its other branches. Direct investment by the government in industrial sectors or geographical regions which lagged behind was preferable to the granting of incentives to private industry to do so, he said. In spite of subsidies for investments in the South of Italy, most private investment took place in the North. On the other hand, some of the firms that benefited from these subsidies made excess profits. Subsidies were usually either too low, having no effect, or too high, leaving excess profits. If a public enterprise made excess profits, it could use those funds to finance additional investments.

Finally, he stressed the importance of objective criteria for evaluation of a firm's efficiency. He mentioned a story told by Oskar Lange, who said that the Polish government wanted to reduce coal prices in order to help the steel industry. But the managers of the coal industry protested, because they did not want to look inefficient. A firm's efficiency ought to be judged by objective criteria, not by political or personal whims. If managers could not exercise their professional skills, it was hard to attract good people.

10 Enterprises in Hungary Before and After the Economic Reform

Rezsö Nyers
HUNGARIAN ACADEMY OF SCIENCES,
and
Márton Tardos
INSTITUTE FOR ECONOMIC AND MARKET RESEARCH, BUDAPEST

I. INTRODUCTION

For better understanding we must begin by distinguishing between a socialist economy and a mixed one: an economy organised on socialist lines is essentially different from and cannot be identified with a mixed economy organised on a capitalist footing. In an economy operating on socialist principles the foundation rests on a planned economy relying on state and co-operative ownership, although the market plays an important role too. At the same time, in a socialist economy where the market relations are well-developed, certain similarities with mixed economies will emerge, as will be described later.

Before reviewing the progress and problems of the Hungarian economy, it seems necessary to survey briefly the general course of development of socialist enterprise, to trace the changing status of enterprises in the socialist countries. Certain aspects of the Hungarian case can be understood and evaluated correctly only in the context of the European socialist countries. The evolution of Hungarian socialist enterprise is closely linked to the history of the development of socialist enterprises in Eastern Europe. The socialist type of economy was introduced into these countries in the years following the Second World War and the circumstances of their birth, its substantive and formal features, have greatly affected their later fate.

II. STAGES OF DEVELOPMENT OF SOCIALIST MANAGEMENT IN EASTERN EUROPE

The Eastern European Peoples' Democracies started to lay the socialist foundations of their economies in 1948–50 by nationalising their extracting and manufacturing industries, their wholesale and foreign trade as well as the banks, while the socialist transformation of agriculture took place later and gradually.

The initial stage of development was characterised by the fact that the new socialist countries relied on Soviet experience, they employed what was, essentially, the Soviet economic mechanism, both in organising the enterprises and in shaping the system of economic controls. Reliance on the Soviet example was advantageous in several respects. It meant adopting many tested forms and methods of organisation, and the countries adopting them were not compelled to learn many things at their own expense. They took over four basic characteristics of the Soviet model oriented towards rapid development: the two forms of socialist enterprise, i.e. the state-owned firm and the co-operative; the direction of enterprises by means of central plan-instructions in the interest of raising the volume of output; the allocation of materials, investment goods and major products in kind; and the central fixing of prices, neglecting demand and supply. In their early years they achieved significant results in attaining and then surpassing the prewar levels of output, primarily by means of better utilisation of productive capacities, rapid increase of employment and high rates of accumulation.

The second stage of development may be reckoned to have lasted from 1953 to 1964. This period was characterised partly by changes in the Soviet economic policy and partly by the emergence of 'adaptation disturbances' in some of the Eastern European countries, connected with the adoption of the Soviet model. Such disturbances occurred in the GDR, Hungary, Czechoslovakia and, to a lesser extent, in Poland. One of the causes was that in using the Soviet model the special characteristics and circumstances of these national economies had not been taken into account sufficiently. The adoption of the system and its methods of control had neither been sufficiently deliberated nor debated democratically. Another problem was due to the fact that these smaller countries were much more dependent upon foreign trade than the almost self-sufficient Soviet Union and needed different economic methods on this account as well. In order to surmount these troubles the organisation of enterprises and the methods of economic control were modified in various ways, but the measures taken were not basic and proved later to be insufficient. It was only in Yugoslavia that development took a different course, but this had other, deeper reasons. It should be noted that the economic growth rate remained high throughout the whole period, while growing difficulties beset the realisation of economic equilibrium.

The third stage of development may be reckoned to have started in the mid-sixties with the wave of economic reforms in the socialist countries. In this period we can no longer speak of a simple adaptation problem, but rather about the changing conditions of growth, requiring for the rational utilisation of resources another and different mechanism. Some of the countries, and later all of them, including the Soviet Union, entered a period of intensive development. The growing, changing and diversifying needs of the population came to the fore in economic development, while the resources needed for extensive development were being exhausted. The reforms differed among countries – their national peculiarities having been given greater attention – but their general pattern can be outlined clearly while keeping this diversity in mind: central control had to be made more flexible; the autonomy, material motivation and initiative of the enterprises had to be increased; the central allocation in kind had to be more or less replaced by commercial methods; and the market mechanism had to be activated. The differences may be explained not only by varying economic circumstances, but also by the disparate acuity of the reform policies.

The similarities in the organisation and management methods of current socialist enterprise are attributable to the anchoring of the planned economy in social (state and co-operative) ownership, and to the much smaller role now accorded to short-term (annual) plans. Medium-term plans have unequivocally come into focus and long-term planning has begun to develop. However, there is an abundance of variants. The most characteristic differences include the Yugoslav self-management system and the socialist market economy accompanying it; small-scale agricultural production in Poland; and the Hungarian economic mechanism, more flexible than the others, not restricting the autonomy of enterprises to the principle of independent accounting, but extending it and building it into the system of their planned economy.

Following the introduction of economic reforms we may now witness the process of consolidation of the new methods. The results achieved are weighed against the emerging difficulties and there are several signs indicating that we have not yet reached the end of the reform period.

III. ORGANISATION OF ENTERPRISE IN THE MULTISECTOR HUNGARIAN ECONOMY; SUCCESS AND CONTRADICTION OF ENTERPRISE CONTROL BETWEEN 1950–68

Initially the socialist national economy of Hungary consisted of three socio-economic sectors: the state, the co-operative and the petty-commodity-producing private sector. This multisectoral nature of the economy has persisted throughout the later period of development and even characterises the situation today. Of course, in two and a half decades intersectoral proportions have changed substantially, and though the organisational solutions within particular sectors have changed in many respects, a significant integration process has taken place.

The state enterprises play a dominant role in industry and are preponderant in trade. They have an important role – but do not constitute a majority – in agriculture and in some services. In this sector ownership rights are exercised by state organs; they appoint the manager of the enterprise who is responsible to the agency appointing him. The state enterprises are highly specialised and it is not characteristic of them to pursue activities outside their line. The state enterprises have two different basic forms, the centrally supervised enterprises and those subordinated to local administration. This distinction assumed significance after the reform of 1968.

The co-operatives are organisations based on voluntary membership, having the character of self-management; they elect their leaders themselves and the latter are responsible for their activities to the members. The size of the co-operative sector has shown strong growth from the initial period up to the present, though their share in total employment has not changed much in recent years. The co-operatives are preponderant in agriculture, they are an important minority in trade, in the commodity-producing industries their share is relatively small, but is again considerable in the services.

Petty commodity production was still the economies' largest sector in 1950, but dwindled by the mid-sixties, particularly in its traditional forms. From 1.5 million independent peasant farms 120,000 farms remained outside the co-operatives after fifteen years, the number of private craftsmen and artisans fell from 200,000 to about 70,000 and that of private retailers from 47,000 to about 10,000. This process was the result not only of economic and administrative restrictions, but also of the economic expansion of the socialist sector that took place in the course of economic competition. Simultaneously with this process new forms of small-scale production occurred in agriculture. One and a half million small farms emerged; they are not primarily in competition with the two socialist sectors but have rather established a particular division of labour with them.

In what sense is economic entrepreneurship limited and restricted in Hungary, and what is the situation regarding the freedom of enterprise? The creation of a private enterprise based on wage labour is prohibited by law. Thus, freedom for capitalist enterprise is entirely absent. But, in the original sense of the word, the Hungarian socialist enterprise never lacked freedom entirely. And at the end of the sixties the economic reform expanded the possibilities for entrepreneurship on a socialist foundation.

(1) State enterprises can be founded, alongside the central state agencies, by local autonomous agencies of state administration using their own funds or resorting to credit.

(2) The law makes the foundation of co-operatives dependent on the will of those desiring association and on the compliance of the co-operative with legal prescriptions. The law also permits the co-operatives to associate with one another with the aim of founding joint enterprises (normally serving the co-operatives). After 1968 more than 1500 such enterprises were established. The activities of co-operatives are regulated by the state using economic and financial tools, but they do not deprive the co-operatives at all of their freedom of decision on essential matters.

(3) There is no law hindering the activities of private craftsmen and retailers. The issuing of the required licence is the right of the local councils, which can judge an application for a licence on the basis of the needs of

the population. The only legal restriction is that craftsmen and retailers must not employ more than two workers.

(4) There is no restriction, nor is a licence needed for small-scale production and the selling of commodities based on family labour either in agriculture or in handicrafts.

Owing to its multisectoral nature the Hungarian economy may thus even be termed a mixed one, all the more since this is reflected in the interplay of economic interests. Different interests seek to assert themselves even in a socialist economy, they have an effect on economic life and even on the political one. However, an economic mechanism exists that partly plays the role of reconciling interests and partly establishes priorities among the differing interests in terms of the general interests of society. The interests of society are projected by the national economic plan and the market is regulated by the latter.

Information about the sectoral distribution of the Hungarian economy may be obtained from the Statistical Yearbook of Hungary for 1977, in which the data for 1976 are published. From among them we present here those on the sectoral distribution of enterprises and employees (see Table 9.1).

It follows from the data that in industry the following enterprise size is characteristic: state enterprises with 1800 employees, co-operatives with 300 employees and artisans with 1–2 employees. In agriculture, state enterprises on average have 1100 employees, co-operatives 400 and the individual farms are based on family labour. In trade the state enterprise has, on average, 1000 employees, co-operatives have 400 and private retail trade is, in general, based on family labour.

It should be noted that in agriculture a further form of activity beyond those listed above exists: that of small farms relying on part-time work. A considerable number of them are linked to a certain extent to the co-operatives, a smaller number to the state farms, but about half of them are operated by people whose main occupation is not in agriculture. In 1975 1.6 million such small farming plots were recorded in the following distribution by strata: workers 23 per cent, co-operative members 13 per cent, intellectuals 7 per cent, retired (pensioners) 14 per cent and non-employed 43 per cent (a large proportion of the latter are dependents of members of co-operatives).

So much for the sectoral situation; in the following discussion we wish to draw a picture of Hungarian economic policy.

In the economic policy of the period prior to the economic reform two stages should be distinguished: the years 1950–56 and 1957–67. The economic policy of the latter stage is not an organic continuation of or improvement upon that pursued in the former stage, but its critical revision. The economic policies of both stages were based on socialist principles and yet they differed strongly from one another, so that in the final analysis the former proved to be erroneous in the stage in which Hungary found itself, while the latter proved essentially correct. The difference between the two economic policies showed

TABLE 10.1   SECTORAL DISTRIBUTION OF HUNGARIAN ENTERPRISES

Economic branch	State sector			Co-operative sector			Petty-commodity-producing private sector	
	Number of enterprises	Number of employees	Share of employees %	Number of enterprises	Number of employees	Share of employees %	Number of employees	Share of employees %
Industry and construction	952	1,807,000	82.3	1009	319,000	14.5	69,500	3.2
Agriculture and forestry	179	199,800	19.6	1800	720,000	71.1	95,000	9.3
Trade	317	323,000	65.0	394	144,000	32.5	12,000	2.5
Public services	700	473,000	100.0	–	–	–	–	–
Economy total	2148	2,802,800	65.0	3203	1,331,000	30.9	176,500	4.1

SOURCE *Statistical Yearbook of Hungary*, 1977.

up not in the rate of economic growth, but in the shaping of the economic structure and, generally, in the nature of growth.

In 1950–56 the government pursued an economic policy aimed at attaining full employment and a lasting increase in the dynamism of investment. These aims were appropriate but the measures were exaggerated and the methods incorrect from three points of view. First of all, the national economic plan forced an ever higher rate of economic growth, but restricted the growth of consumption by shifting important assets from the sphere of consumption into the production of investment goods. Second, it also forced industrialisation by restricting agricultural investment and shifted assets from there into industry. Third, it encouraged autarky by stimulating the domestic production of an ever greater number of products.

All these mistakes were aggravated by a rigid, over-centralised control of the economy and an almost utter neglect of market relations. Finally, economic growth, though considerable, was smaller than planned, the employment target was met and the dynamism of investment increased; but the equilibration of the economy deteriorated, the drive toward autarky led to a temporary lag behind international technical development, living standards improved almost entirely as a consequence of expanding employment, and real wages per earner hardly increased.

Economic policy between 1957–67 was characterised by greater realism, and by increased attention to the available possibilities. In those years the lopsided orientation towards accumulation (investment) was replaced by an attempt to raise both investment and real income simultaneously. Beside that of industry, the development of agriculture was assigned due importance. Participation in the international division of labour became an aim. In the plan, targets issued to enterprises, productivity and profitability were also given greater emphasis in addition to the volume of output (turnover). The methods of economic control became more flexible, the enterprises were given a smaller number of obligatory plan indicators from above and the rigid restrictions on the price system were eased: it became a principle that prices should adjust to costs. This economic policy resulted in greater economic efficiency and less economic tension than had been the case earlier and found more favourable political acceptance among the populace. But it preserved some contradictions of economic life, which later increasingly called for solution.

In the final analysis, between 1950–67 highly important social objectives were attained in Hungary. Unemployment was completely and permanently abolished, the share of wage earners within the population increased from 44.1 to 46.1 per cent (now 48.5 per cent). The share of accumulation within national income increased from 14 per cent to 25–26 per cent, and was also stable in character. The growth rate of national income rose from the annual 3 per cent of the 17 years before the Second World War to 5.4 per cent, and growth of foreign trade increased, from the old rate of 4 per cent to an annual rate of 10 per cent.

By the end of the stage under discussion the bulk of the tensions and undesired accompanying phenomena of the first stage ceased, but certain contradictions stubbornly remained. They were the following:

(1) The structure of production did not adapt itself with sufficient flexibility to the quickly changing pattern of demand of either personal or productive consumption or of exports. This caused some loss of income, surplus stocks in some products and shortages in others.

(2) There was strong import pressure in the economy, and relative to it interest in exporting was weak; the productive sphere was not aware of external market effects, the balance of trade was not in equilibrium, and, with occasional wide fluctuations, a tendency toward deficit appeared.

(3) In the enterprise sphere, the proportion of enterprises utilising their resources with low efficiency was large. Material motivation toward good work was minimal, the poorly performing enterprises did not feel any disadvantage nor the good ones any advantage from the difference in their performance.

(4) Democratic methods in economic life were increasingly advocated: the workers wanted to participate in part of the activity of their enterprise, local political bodies concerned themselves more and more strongly with the economic future of the enterprises operating in their areas, they wanted to know what, why and how things were to be done, and consumers raised more and more criticisms and requests. All this was in conflict with the rather narrow zone of freedom of action available to managers, which was all too narrowly circumscribed by central decisions.

In the democratic atmosphere of Hungarian political life these contradictions did not remain hidden, they were not declared 'political taboos', though such measures had a small number of adherents. Finally, the political balance tilted in favour of reform, in favour of creating a new kind of relationship between enterprises and central control.

IV. CENTRAL PLANNED REGULATION AND MARKET RELATIONS IN THE SOCIALIST ECONOMY

As it has everywhere else, the founding of a socialist economy in Hungary necessitated discarding the capitalist economy. The basis of management was created, as has been mentioned, by large-scale nationalisation. At that time central control accorded only a complementary and subordinate role to co-operative ownership relative to ownership by the state.

When working out the economic reform, we had to face a particular contradiction. How can one conceive of an organisation of the, mostly state-owned, enterprises that is comparable, and not only formally, to the separation of enterprises operating in a market economy, but still permits planned control and regulation of the economy?

These two goals may seem particularly contradictory if we consider that the reform of the highly centralised system of control based on instructions under the plan was carried out in Hungary at a time when, in the market economies, the role of state interference was unequivocally strengthened and when, because of the internal contradictions of market processes, there was a growing opinion that in countries with non-socialist systems it was socially useful to replace the market forms by an internal set of hierarchical organisations.[1]

Those preparing the Hungarian economic reform, when discarding control by means of plan-instructions and advocating the increased use of forms of self-regulation, never believed that the market would spontaneously guarantee social efficiency of management or that large organisations should be replaced in every field by small companies, corresponding more closely to the ideal conditions of atomistic competition.

The studies preparing the reform[2] and the documents describing the bases of the regulations in 1968, as well as the articles evaluating them[3] discussed a centrally regulated market. Although the documents had not unequivocally clarified what the creators of the reform meant by planned regulation of the market, it is certain that they had not forgotten about those social objectives (beneficial and detrimental externalities) which cannot be expressed by spontaneous price movements under the influence of demand and supply. The most important hallmark of planned control of the economy is that the reform always extended only to those fields of management where experience had proved that, in the interest of efficiency, the aim should be increased adaptability to demand. This was indeed important in those fields where the frequent changes of demand and a rich assortment of products are very important, and where, precisely for this reason, needs cannot be satisfied without rapid adaptation of producers to changing demand patterns, even if they have been using the results of the best predictions.

This field of management may be termed the sphere of competition. We believe that there is no exact limit to the expansion of the competitive sphere. It is, however, certainly appropriate to consider as part of the sphere of competition the production of manufacturing and agricultural commodities as well as their trade at home and abroad. In these fields the pattern of enterprises, the competition among them, the possibility of letting imports compete with domestic production, do create market conditions. Competition may extend to

---

[1]The seemingly most authentic comprehensive work about the problem is by O. E. Williamson: *Markets and Hierarchies: an Analysis and Antitrust Implications* (The Free Press, New York, 1975).

[2]F.i. György Péter, *A gazdaságosság és jövedelmezőség a tervgazdaságban (Efficiency and Profitability in the Planned Economy)*, Közgazdasági- és Jogi Könyvkiadó (Budapest, 1966).

[3]Béla Csikós-Nagy, *A gazdaságirányitási reform küszöbén (At the Threshold of the Reform of Economic Control)*, Közgazdasági Szemle, No. 3 (1967); *Ő évvel a gazdaságirántitási reform után (Five Years After the Reform of Economic Control)*, Gazdaság, No. 2 1973); Rezső Nyers, *25 kérdés és válasz gazdaságpolitikai kérdésekről (25 Questions and Answers about Problems of Economic Policy)* (Kossuth, Budapest, 1969).

the production and trade of the most important raw materials (coal, crude oil, electric energy, etc.) or part of them, but, depending on economic conditions and political value judgements, these may be eliminated from the competitive sphere. That decision, of course, will have significant consequences.

Naturally, not all economic activities are characterised by such differentiation and constant change in needs which are so difficult to survey that a hierarchical organisation of activities and determination of tasks for more specialised units would disturb efficiency. In an ever-widening area of the economy, in the production of public goods and services, such as road building, water supply and other infrastructural outputs, conditions are generally such that social needs can be better satisfied in a well-organised system of institutions with planned central control than if it were done by competitive enterprises. In fact, it is probable that with enterprises competing in these branches many external economic effects (not affecting price) would be left out of consideration and this would result in social damage.

Another characteristic underlying planned control is that, in our view, in the wide domain of economic activities that we called the competitive sphere there is the objective possibility for the state not only to create competitive conditions for its enterprises (even after almost full nationalisation), and to operate them on the market as autonomous, profit-motivated, economic units, but also to regulate these activities centrally on the basis of a plan. The most important precondition for such control is a uniform regulatory system that is consistent with the national economic requirements and their changes. This requires, first, the use of taxes and the valuation of basic resources, such as labour, fixed and circulating assets and foreign currencies. Second, central control must be able to use preferential credit support, to those industries which can trigger accelerated development of the entire economy. Further, it can levy taxes on activities with socially harmful side-effects, e.g. the excessive concentration of industry in Budapest, environmental pollution, etc.

But even with these provisos we have not yet bridged the contradiction with which the discussion began. When the decision was taken to introduce Hungarian economic reform, the necessity of changes was deduced from the following facts:

(1) that the central organiser cannot sufficiently know the pattern of expected economic needs;
(2) the standards of information about the alternative economic possibilities of production are inadequate because of the complexity of relations between enterprises, the uncertainty of estimates and the biases of the sources of information;
(3) the central organiser is therefore unable to evaluate quickly and unequivocally, in a way that is consistent with the requirements of social efficiency, information of doubtful value about needs and production possibilities.

On this basis those who carried out the reform reached the conclusion that instructions formulated by the central organiser and compulsion of enterprises to carry out these instructions together with moral and financial inducements to meet these obligations are not sufficiently effective methods of economic control. Experience indicates that control through plan-instructions is not efficiently adaptable to changing needs. The fitting of supply to demand is so weak that it causes not only direct losses, but, indirectly, even greater ones. Dissatisfaction with work essentially damages the enthusiasm and initiative of both managers and employees. Let us confront this line of reasoning with the market criticism found in the literature about organisations. These begin by recognising that differences in efficiency between particular productive and management institutions are decided not mainly by the technology used, but by the quality and costs of carrying out the economic transactions. Analysing the experience of market economies, this literature states that the participants behave in a manner involving limited rationality if information is imperfect. Among other things, the market may be imperfect and weak because economic pressures are weak, there is cheating in the course of negotiations, the negotiations themselves become protracted and the atmosphere deteriorates, all of which damage the efficiency of these transactions. They therefore reach the conclusion that it is frequently expedient to substitute large organisations for the market and that government limitations on large corporations need not involve compulsion.

What is common to the Hungarian idea of the reform and the analysis of organisations is that they approach the efficiency of the organisational–institutional order on the basis of transaction costs. A similar idea is that the decisive elements for the evaluation of the system of institutions is the uncertainty of the future and the adaptability to changing conditions. At first glance, however, their conclusions seem to be utterly divergent. One of them rejects the compression of the entire economy into one hierarchical system, the other considers hierarchy to be more efficient than individual markets. Yet the conflict between these two statements, each of which seems to be convincing in itself, though not yet satisfactorily resolved, is smaller than it would seem at first sight. The advocates of Hungarian economic reform do not deny the possibility that large organisations may promote the rational solution of some problems, and even expressly rely on large organisations. What is denied is only the expediency of controlling the entire economy as a single large organisation and the rejection of a role for small, quickly-adjusting enterprises alongside the large ones. At the same time, the adherents of organisational hierarchy did not claim the expediency of an organisation comprising the whole economy, or that the state should guarantee a monopoly position to any large organisation (hierarchy).

As regards the centralisation or decentralisation of development decisions, even after implementation of the reform, the discussion in Hungary continues to be sharp. There are economists who believe that adaptation which relies on profit motivation is justified when the problem is the utilisation of existing productive capacities or the improvement of earning conditions in the short run, but think that the system of profit-oriented decisions is a poor mechanism for the control of investment. Those advocating the centralisation of investment decisions set out from the assumption that the central organs will know the social interests better than the individual enterprises and will take into account the external effects which influence the development of the economy but do not appear in expected profits. Those in the other camp refer to the poor level of information available to the central organs, and, therefore, wish to hand the right of decision to the enterprises, while informing them about the general social interest with the help of uniform state regulation.

In the discussion about the quality of information both parties may be right. It may easily happen that there is no way to decide unequivocally whether in the vertical flow of information it is the stream going up or the one going down that is likely to be freer from disturbances. Nevertheless, we believe that there are strong arguments, beyond those usually discussed, that speak in favour of decentralisation in development decisions in the competitive sphere – with adaptation to well-defined state preferences. First of all, it should not be forgotten that long-run economic efficiency is not attributable mainly to an *ex ante* optimal allocation of inputs. We refer here, in addition to Hungarian experience, to production function computations performed by Solow, Denison and others which prove that 50–80 per cent of the increment of GDP is a consequence not of increased inputs of resources, but of residual factors. In this, in our opinion, a role is played not only by the allocation of assets – it is also profoundly affected by the way the leading, responsible specialists adapt themselves to unexpected changes in economic conditions as they carry out the investments that were decided upon and during the operation of a new project. This adaptation is surely an important element in what is called X-efficiency.[1]

But, in order for the leadership of the enterprise adequately and continually to adapt itself to the changing circumstances which frequently deviate from those on which the plan was based, it is necessary first of all that it have full responsibility for the implementation of the investment. However, if this responsibility is divided between management and the central agencies, because the manager's requests have not received consent or because he has to deviate under external pressure from his original ideas in the execution of the development project to such an extent that he can no longer regard the realised project as his own, his behaviour will change significantly. In this case it is better for him to proceed as an honest official, not fighting like a lion for the success of the project. Such differences in the behaviour of enterprise managers, can result in substantial differences in the efficiency of development.

These differences cannot be simply bridged by more successful harmonisation of the views of leading agencies. Each of the contradictory opinions regarding development projects may be sensible in itself. The

---

[1]H. Leibenstein, 'Allocative Efficiency versus X-Efficiency,' *American Economic Review* (June 1966) 392–415.

differences are frequently attributable to differing judgements of partly
uncertain possibilities and to differences in the roles of the experts judging the
problem. Thus it can easily happen that several alternative decisions may lead
to solutions of identical value – if implementation is successful.

The weakness of the system of central decisions is generally not that it yields
incorrect judgements, but that they are unable to formulate their valid
judgements in practical terms consistent with the details of enterprise
management and that they have no possibility of enforcing the actual
requirements.

The second group of arguments in favour of decentralised development
decisions is related to the fact that the participation of the state or the centre is
described in the discussions in an idealised form. It is dealt with as if it were the
manifestation of a single, central will. In practice – at least in Hungary –
interference by the centre in the problems of development takes the form of
pressures from many institutions, frequently in sharp debate with one another.
The supervising Ministry, the National Bank, the Development Bank, the
Ministry of Finance, the National Board of Technological Development, and
frequently even different departments of these institutions represent particular
opinions, rational in themselves, until a decision on development is finally
reached in the Council of Ministers, which, often, none of the state organs
considers as its own. Such participation of the central agencies in development
decisions is not only extremely complicated and slow but, for lack of proper
harmonisation of interests, it is frequently not suited even to represent the
internal rationality of a central decision. In addition, there are complex
economic processes – affecting several industries – which can be overseen only
by the enterprises.

The third line of reasoning argues that it does not seem advantageous for the
highest state agencies to take upon themselves direct responsibility for
industrial, agricultural and commercial development decisions whose outcome
is uncertain by dint of their internal properties. The incomplete success of
development or, in some cases, its unavoidable failure, sometimes presents a
temptation to the government which it is difficult to resist. The task of
economic regulation can provide the government with such powers that it finds
itself in a position to prevent even the greatest failure from becoming manifest.
As a matter of fact, maintenance of an unsuccessful enterprise by budgetary
and other means, thus slowing down or rendering unnecessary its adaptation, is
most disadvantageous for society.

Acceptance of the arguments in favour of delegating development decisions
to the managers of autonomous enterprises does not call into question the
necessity of enforcing central preferences on economic policy in the
competitive sphere of the economy. The central agencies must not neglect
planned selection of those industries whose creation or accelerated
development will trigger a definite increase in the total performance of the
economy with high probability.

When dealing with this possibility, practice in the socialist economy frequently makes use of ideas which are proposed by many authors for the developing countries.[1] A task awaiting solution is the design of procedures that enforce central decisions formulated to accelerate development and protect new industries while weakening neither the creative powers of enterprises nor their adaptation to the changing conditions of production.

V. REFORM OF THE ECONOMIC MECHANISM: A QUALITATIVE CHANGE IN THE ECONOMY

The decision to undertake a fundamental revision of the Hungarian economic mechanism had been taken at the end of 1964 and the reform itself was introduced in the beginning of 1968. The preparation thus took three years and consisted of three consecutive stages: critical analysis of the existing system, formulation of the principles of the reform and, finally, the elaboration of government decrees and regulations. In the first two stages about 130 economists, jurists, technical experts and economic leaders participated, in the third one the number of participants trebled. The uncertainty factor, unavoidable when such major changes are being made, was surely present, but, thanks to the wide participation of theoretical and practical experts, there was no question of risking a 'leap into the dark'.

In the course of the critical analysis it was necessary to determine the sources of the apparent deficiencies and contradictions. Further, it was necessary to judge whether there is some deeper, more systematic reason for the problems behind the apparent chain of concrete causes. It was necessary to weigh whether there was validity to the view that the prime cause was the basic moral stand of the workers, or the 'liberalism' of central planning. Against these views the critical analysis by experts uniformly concluded that the final and basic source of the many problems lay in the system of economic controls and management. From this it followed that a partial change was insufficient and it was necessary to strive for fundamental changes.

The analyses clearly showed that the emerging problems of efficiency were not caused by the socialist ownership relations, that it was possible to work with greater efficiency both in state enterprises and in co-operatives, and that the changes essential for this purpose can be initiated by basic changes in the circumstances of enterprise management. The many other deficiencies could be fought successfully by reform of the mechanism.

The question emerged whether enterprise profitability was of major or minor importance in a socialist economy. There can be no doubt that in a socialist economy decisions taken independently of enterprises may in some cases strongly affect profitability. This may happen, e.g. when, for some important reason, central price policy fixes some price lower than is justified on economic grounds alone, or when some of the enterprises receive a small share of the

---

[1]See e.g. A. O. Hirschmann, *The Strategy of Economic Development* (Yale University Press, New Haven, 1958).

centrally allocated investment funds and can thus develop technology and raise productivity only to a small extent. In the economic science of the socialist countries there emerged two views regarding the profitability of enterprises. According to the first only the profitability and overall efficiency of the economy as a whole is important, while enterprise profitability may have only a restricted role and importance. However, the second holds that national income depends closely on enterprise profitability, and economic efficiency demands a strong profit-motivation of the enterprises. At the end of the sixties and the early seventies the Hungarian economic experts unequivocally adopted the latter standpoint, but it should be noted that those adhering to the first view are still with us, and recently they have again emphasised their doubts.

No doubt, in the practice of a socialist planned economy the urge for and the possibility of profits is smaller for the enterprises than it is in a capitalist one. If profitability is low, they may be induced to ask for a revision of the plan indicators in the directive system, and in the case of indirect control they may ask for price, credit or tax preferences, and thus the pressure is weakened. The possibility is also smaller because part of the development funds – in the directive system of control almost all of them – are collected by the state from the enterprises and then redistributed. But this hardly puts the socialist system at a disadvantage against the capitalist market economy, since in the long run the social loss due to cyclical fluctuations is much smaller in a socialist economy and this more than compensates for the differences in enterprise profitabilities, if they are not too large. In the final analysis, the fact that the urge and scope for profitability are smaller for objective reasons does not diminish, but rather increases, the importance of profitability in a market regulated by a national economic plan.

For an understanding of the nature of the reform in the socialist countries it is necessary to know that they are motivated not so much by the wish to transplant market economies into a socialist environment, but rather by the coming to the fore of those schools of socialist economic theory that seek to build the socialist planned economy on the wide-scale use of market and monetary relations. This is against the school which expects to carry out the principles of socialism by gradually pushing back the market and monetary relations, regarding them as capitalist institutions, and by expanding the direct central allocation among products – which in their view is a more socialist institution. The latter school has had a decisive voice in economic practice in the USSR since the early thirties and, after the war, also in the East-European socialist countries, but the tensions caused by concerns over efficiency and quality increased the standing of the reform school. The alternative is thus not whether 'we should apply capitalist or socialist methods', although even the so-called new left is of this opinion, but whether we can better carry out socialist management on the basis of market relations or with the aid of direct product allocation.

Let us return after this brief digression to the Hungarian economic reform. In the final analysis, the reform is a complex made up of six basic principles, each of which is important in itself, but they simultaneously constitute an interrelated system and the content of each principle is related to all the others. This package of principles is made up of the following:

(1) *The persistence of the multisectoral nature of the economy in the long run.* This means that it is not in the interest of society to restrict the co-operative sector, to 'develop' the co-operatives gradually into state enterprises and thereby to establish a uniform form for socialist ownership. State enterprises have proved to be the most expedient form in large-scale mass production, in wholesale and foreign trade. The greater flexibility of co-operatives in shaping the pattern of production, their relatively bolder risk-taking, and the more direct form of democracy in the co-operatives makes their operation advantageous in a specific part of the economy. Similarly, it is rational to maintain, even in the long run, small-scale private economic activities in a role complementing the socialist sector, particularly in services and small-scale commodity production: only in some areas is the socialist sector competitive in satisfying such needs; in other fields it has proved to be cumbersome and expensive. Precisely on this account, the principles of the reform stressed that from the point of view of state regulation the state enterprises and co-operatives should be treated comparably – it is inappropriate to adopt economic rules that are more favourable to the state enterprises. The principles also include the proviso that the relative proportions between sectors should not be determined by abstract political positions, but should be left to develop as a function of economic efficiency and competitiveness.

(2) *Turnover of materials and products on a commercial basis.* The earlier method of central allocation, of delivery and purchasing obligations, in which price played almost no role whatsoever, was to be abolished. Effective demand was thereby to influence the composition of production, and, in comparison with the earlier situation, there seemed to be an increased prospect for harmony between the patterns of production and demand. Earlier, central planning had determined the production pattern of enterprises (by major product categories), the allocation of materials and the conditions under which buyers had to take over the products. Only between retail trade and consumers were relations of a fully commercial nature. It hardly occurred in deliveries within industry or between industry and trade, rather, the directives controlling physical exchanges were dominating. The physical exchange character of the calculations created such an artificial climate that economic calculation lost its true importance and surpluses and shortages occurred but were covered up by centralised allocation, the system of obligation to accept deliveries. The shift from a centralised allocation of materials and products to a commercial basis promised the elimination of bureaucratic administration on the one hand, and the elimination of 'over-insurance' of enterprises – the accumulation of large inventories – owing to the uncertainties of supply on the other.

(3) *Flexible state price policy, gradual assertion of value relations in prices.* Earlier, in principle, all prices were established by the state, but in practice the

central organs were incapable of following either the changes in costs or those in demand and supply. Under the new principles prices were to express the effect of three factors: actual inputs, the value judgement of the market and preferences of the state. Transition to the new price policy necessitated a wide-scale revision of prices on 1 January 1968, when the new price mechanism took effect.

(a) The government agencies informed enterprises in advance about the preliminary magnitudes of production, turnover and profit taxes; the new import prices and the rate of profit they had to calculate on their assets. The prices calculated on this basis constituted the initial prices which were then finalised after negotiations with buyers and on the basis of knowledge about the preferences of the state.

(b) Enterprises were permitted to set about 80 per cent of producer prices free from any restrictions and about 20 per cent within government restrictions.

(c) Some staple consumer goods were given preference by the state by means of price subsidies, while consumption of some luxury goods (beverages, tobacco, etc.) was discouraged by levying taxes on them. Right from the start the aggregate sum of subsidies exceeded the sum of price-reflecting turnover taxes.

(d) The new state regulations fixed about 50 per cent of consumer prices; the prices of almost 25 per cent were allowed to move subjects to an upper limit, and somewhat more than 25 per cent were declared to be free.

(4) *Close economic links between production and foreign trade activity.*
Prior to the reform, the foreign trade exporting and importing enterprises rather than acting as links, served to isolate producing enterprises from foreign markets because the domestic prices of products could not be related to the export or import prices expressed in foreign currencies. The foreign trade enterprises constituted a separate branch, planning in isolation from producers and settling their accounts with the state separately. There was no requirement specifying what domestic inputs could be used to earn foreign exchange. The reform brought three substantial changes:

(a) Some of the producing and trading enterprises obtained the right to export or import directly, mainly in the case of special products. The aim was to comply better with the requirements of foreign markets, to make better use of the export opportunities.

(b) For accounting relating to foreign trade transactions, a uniform foreign exchange coefficient was introduced calculated from the full value of the domestic inputs necessary on national average to earn a unit of foreign exchange.

(c) These productive enterprises, which produced substantial quantities for export or processed much imported material but which were not given the right to transact foreign trades independently, established common interests with the specialised foreign trade companies – mostly in the form of commission contracts – and came into contact with external markets in this way.

(5) *Creation of the possibility of autonomous action by enterprises under uniform government regulations and use of material (financial) interests.* Earlier, the state organs had 'addressed' to every enterprise separate plan-indicators which had been obligatory and left very little scope for autonomous enterprise decisions. With such detailed direction by the plan it was impossible to allocate tasks and means correctly among the enterprises. A characteristic 'plan bargaining' process developed between the ministries and the enterprises: the ministries sought to increase the size of the tasks and to reduce the inputs available to carry them out (this is how they hoped to comply within the targets assigned to their branch); while on the contrary, the enterprises made efforts to reduce the scale of their tasks and increase the inputs to be put at their disposal. Critical analysis disclosed that this sort of relationship had worked against a really good utilisation of their opportunities by the enterprises. Instead, it seemed expedient to permit enterprises to define their tasks by themselves through a locally optimal combination of production factors. For this purpose the following measures were adopted:

(a) In medium-term planning uniform economic regulations were used, valid for the entire sphere of enterprise and some for particular industries were spelled out and issued to the enterprises before the start of the period of the plan. These included: a plan for central price measures, rules relating to taxation, investment regulation, wages and incomes, the magnitude of the profit tax and tasks deriving from interstate economic agreements devolving upon the enterprises. These constitute the financial links between central control and the management of enterprises, called upon to mediate the efficiency requirements of the national economic plan for the enterprises.

(b) The enterprises were expected to draw up their short- and medium-term plans themselves. They were also offered a real possibility of preparing a long-term enterprise strategy based on their circumstances and opportunities. The assumption was that the aggregate of enterprise plans would come near to meeting macroeconomic objectives even in this manner, and possible deviations would not be greater than or different from what can be expected from a realistic 'counter-plan'.

(c) The earlier, centrally established and rigidly enforced 'production profiles' were abolished, the central organs determining only the scope of activity of the enterprises. It became the right of the enterprises to expand into directions linked to their scope of activity (production of spare parts, complementary activities, stockpiling, trade, designing, construction, transport, etc.) in so far as they could perform them at a profit.

(d) The enterprises were permitted to build up their own development funds from depreciation allowances, from a centrally determined share of profits, as well as from technical development funds accounted for among costs. The enterprises could decide for themselves on the use of their development funds. As a result of this change about half of all productive investment is now decided upon by the enterprises. The other part is decisively influenced by state agencies and banks.

(e) The state guarantees that the earnings of enterprise workers will not fall below the level already attained, but the raising of earnings depends on an increase in profit. A relatively greater part of the incomes of executives (20–25 per cent), and a relatively smaller part of those of workers (8–10 per cent) depend on profits. The enterprises may cover the greater part of the costs of social and cultural activities from pre-tax profits according to centrally determined norms.

(6) *Assertion of the democratic rights of workers in the operation of the enterprise.* The Hungarian economic reform affected the development of economic democracy in two respects: by creating enterprise autonomy it broadened the scope for democratic methods and it brought about new forms of co-operation between economic leaders and workers in the enterprises.

(a) The management of enterprises has become a meritorious partner of trade unions in concluding collective agreements in enterprises, since the scope of its authority expanded. Acknowledgement of the right of co-operatives to self-management freed them from the tutelage of the territorial and national federations of co-operatives, so that the members could now exercise their democratic rights.

(b) Through their trade union representatives the workers regularly participate in discussions of enterprise plans and design of development strategy. The forums for this purpose are the production meetings on different levels. The plans of co-operatives are decided upon by the general assembly.

(c) The trade union organs within the enterprise have obtained the right to have a say in matters affecting working conditions. They participate as equal partners of management in deciding on general rules affecting employment and wage payment, may put in their veto against measures infringing upon collective agreement or a legal prescription, and also have the right to check upon the observance of legal rules affecting the workers.

(d) In the wake of the reform concerns and ideas related to the operation and development of enterprises, as well as the relations between the enterprise and its development, received much greater publicity than was the case before.

As a result of the reform, the economic environment of Hungarian enterprises has changed since January 1968. The activities of enterprise executives and working collectives are no longer restricted merely to execution of the plan received from the centre, they have become more diversified, encompassing also the evaluation of alternative courses of action. Nor is central control restricted to planning the national economic processes. A special role for market regulation has evolved. The basic importance of central planning has persisted, but greater attention is devoted to harmony between physical and value processes and, in general, to efficiency and quality.

In the final analysis, we may state with justification that with this reform the socialist Hungarian economy has entered a qualitatively new stage of development.

VI. THE NEW METHOD OF CENTRAL CONTROL AND ENTERPRISE AUTONOMY, AND THEIR ECONOMIC AND SOCIAL EFFECTS

One can generalise from this experience by observing that while the Hungarian economy has allowed room for enterprise autonomy, it has preserved the character of planned development. In fact, as has been pointed out by scientific investigations carried out by the Committee for Economics of the Hungarian Academy of Sciences, conformity to plan has even improved. The planning from two directions, from that of the national economy and that of the enterprises, has not opened the road to spontaneity. The main data characterising economic growth under the national economic plan and the aggregate of enterprise plans have come sufficiently close, while the enterprise plans themselves are much more realistic than the earlier plans deriving from central allocation.

A characteristic feature of the present Hungarian system of economic control is the fact that the national economic plan has preserved its determining role in defining the direction of economic development as a whole, while the operative control of the economy has proved to be capable of applying the tools of price, monetary, commercial, and foreign exchange policies in the interest of planned development.

It has been proved by experience that application of the old system of centralised plan-instructions at the end of the sixties was not the best method for stimulating economic growth or for securing economic equilibrium, at least not in the case of Hungary. After the reform economic growth accelerated, equilibrium conditions improved and the social effects of the growth process became more favourable. The situation after 1968 may be characterised by the following facts:

(1) The legal workweek was reduced in 1968–70 to 44 hours from 48, meaning a loss of capacity of almost 10 per cent, which was

counterbalanced by the gradual growth in productivity. This factor moderated the rate of growth.

(2) Despite this effect, between 1968 and 1976 gross national product increased by 6 per cent annually on the average, in constant prices, against the rate of 5.4 per cent prior to the reform.

(3) Real wages per earner also increased at a faster rate than before, by 3.5 per cent p.a. between 1968 and 1975 as against the former 1.7 per cent. Equilibration on the consumers' market essentially improved, and this was a factor having a generally advantageous effect on living conditions.

(4) The wider price changes instituted at shorter intervals than before were a new factor affecting the population. As inflationary pressure appeared in the Hungarian economy prices tended to rise, and the regulating role of government price policy manifested itself in braking actions, not in price stability, since the latter would not have been rational. Between 1968 and 1975 the consumer price level increased by 3.5 per cent annually on the average, while the wage level rose by 7 per cent. In this situation the living standards of every stratum of economically active persons increased in the medium run, but in the short run a transitory decrease may have occurred in some strata because not everyone obtained wage rises each year.

(5) The balance of trade of the country was in equilibrium between 1968 and 1973, with some annual fluctuations – the difficulties being related to certain countries. The price explosion of the world market changed this situation and introduced a new foreign trade problem.

(6) The dynamism of investment was maintained after the reform; this partially explained the fact that, with other elements of efficiency improving, the utilisation of assets ('capital productivity') did not improve significantly. Between 1970 and 1975 GNP per unit of assets engaged increased by a mere 1 per cent. Equilibration of the investment market improved only partially and transitorily. The improvement in efficiency of investment has not been satisfactory. The reform has been unable to solve this problem with the means presently available.

(7) We deem the change extremely important, highly appreciated by the members of Hungarian society, which consisted of the adaptation of supply to demand, which increased the economy's efficiency in satisfying needs and reduced the number and value of articles in excess demand. This represents a substantial difference in the performance of the economy which has so far, unfortunately, not lent itself to national income and efficiency computations.

While the state and enterprise system of social policy considerably improved and had a highly favourable effect on the political atmosphere, there were two circumstances which produced undesirable effects: one was the increased mobility of labour and the other the growing differentials between earnings, depending on stratum and performance. These two factors caused tensions that still persist today, and the dilemma of Hungarian economic policy both now and in the future is that, on the one hand, the structural changes of the economy require substantial flows of labour and wage differentials depending on performance (and qualification), while, on the other hand, political public opinion expects minimisation of both of these.

To what extent have the principles of the reform been followed in practice? The answer is that they are followed substantially but not entirely and not always consistently. In this context reference should be made to the economic phenomena called 'brakes' by Hungarian economists at the introduction of the reform.

The changes in the world economy in the last five to six years have been a great test indeed for the viability of our system of control, particularly because the Hungarian economy is linked to the world economy to a high degree and by strong ties. In 1975 the value of exports amounted to 39.5 per cent of the GDP and the weight of foreign trade continuously increases. 62.8 per cent of exports went to the socialist countries (within and outside the CMEA), while 37.2 per cent went to the capitalist and the developing countries.

From the viewpoint of the Hungarian economy three effects of the changes in the world economy have to be emphasised: the acceleration of inflation on the world market, the explosive changes in relative prices and the sharpening of export competition.

Acceleration of inflation on the world market first reached Hungary when it possessed a mechanism for warding off the infiltration of external inflationary pressures, but an active exchange rate policy was only the initial stage in its armoury of tools. In 1973 about 30 per cent, and in 1974 70 per cent of the external rate of inflation had to be neutralised with the aid of so-called 'financial bridges'. As a result, relative domestic prices deviated more and more from the external ones and thus the orienting force of the price mechanism was greatly weakened. This situation again pushed to the fore the question whether we should not free ourselves from the harmful effects of world inflation by returning to the rigid price system in force prior to the reform, and thus make domestic prices independent of external ones.

The world market price explosion had a strongly adverse effect on the terms of trade of the Hungarian economy: between the levels of import and export prices an adverse margin of 17 per cent emerged, beginning in 1974. This completely claimed the annual GDP increments of 6 per cent of several earlier years. Though it occurred with a time lag and only to a minor extent, deterioration of the terms of trade also appeared in relations with the socialist countries. We had to decide how to adapt ourselves to the new world economic situation. In this context, two problems reappeared to which an answer had already been given by the reform, but which again demanded an answer in the new situation. (i) Could we not diminish import requirements substantially by shifting toward a strongly protectionistic production policy in both raw materials and finished products? (ii) Was it not possible to increase self-sufficiency quickly within the CMEA and to narrow down relations with the capitalist world economy?

Owing to the depressed state of export markets, the conditions besetting Hungarian exports became difficult precisely at a time when the deterioration in the terms of trade could be partly counterbalanced by an increased export drive. For an annual 5–6 per cent growth of GDP an annual increase of 10–12 per cent in exports had to be attained in the non-socialist market, but the unfavourable business situation endangered the attainment of this goal. How should we have adapted ourselves to this situation? Should we have pushed to the fore the raising of the competitiveness of exports or, rather, the reduction of imports and its substitution by domestic production? This was how the alternatives for action were formulated.

As a result of the export problems, the years 1974–75 were a period of waiting, whose dilemma was as follows: should we develop the reform further or correct some of its essential principles? Scientific and practical-political investigations were conducted on this issue. From the analysis of the situation it followed unequivocally that the maintenance of a growth rate of about 5 per cent p.a., as well as the gradual but fundamental modernisation of the production pattern and, finally, the securing of external equilibrium as basic objectives could not be attained either by narrowing world economic relations or by increasing self-sufficiency within the CMEA. The main objectives required the Hungarian economy to adapt itself more flexibly to the conditions of the world economy. This statement clearly speaks for a more consistent application of the principles of the economic reform.

In 1976–77 new steps were taken to enforce the principles of the reform. The domestic prices of significant imported products were adapted to their foreign trade prices, and this raised the rate of inflation temporarily to 4–5 per cent. A further essential step was that, making progress on the road of an active exchange rate policy, the National Bank of Hungary worked out the 'commercial' and 'non-commercial' rates of exchange of domestic currency, and these are now operating as true rates of exchange in their respective fields. At this time the process of expansion of central restrictions has already stopped, in fact some of them which proved to be superfluous have been lifted. All that, however, does not yet guarantee that economic control will 'keep pace' with events.

A more consistent enforcement of the principles of the Hungarian economic reform raises the issue of promotion of economic efficiency, of further development of the reform. In this framework answers must be found to the following questions:

(1) Can the internal market price proportions be made to approximate those on the world market with the aid of the price and foreign exchange mechanism? What deviations are necessary?

(2) What methods are needed in regulating earnings, the movement of

labour and investments with a view to greater flexibility of product patterns in industry?
(3) How can we eliminate the 'overheated' nature of the investment market and create equilibrium in this market by means of central regulations?
(4) To what extent and in what manner should we make room for vertical integration (in research, development, production and trade) in big companies, in the interest of better organisation of enterprises?
(5) What economic institutions are necessary for Hungarian enterprises also to work successfully in international ventures?
(6) What advantages can be attained in state control of socialist enterprises by easing the present rigid division by industries and in what form is this possible?

VII. ACHIEVEMENTS AND INTERNAL CONTRADICTIONS OF THE HUNGARIAN ECONOMIC REFORM

Though there were several internal and external economic factors that prevented the reform from exerting its accelerating effect, it can nevertheless be stated that the reform was essentially successful.

The most important fact is that we succeeded in regulating the economy centrally in conformity with the plan despite the elimination of the rigid plan-instructions which had fettered the adaptability of management. The experience of the Hungarian economy furnished an important lesson showing that control by directive is not the only possible form of economic management after socialist nationalisation, and that one can rely on autonomous enterprise decisions. Our experience adequately proves that evolution of objective price and monetary relations and successful adaptation is feasible in an economy operating with many independent decision centres.

One of the most important areas of change in the adaptability of management is the striking change in enterprise relations. The system of material allocation, which unavoidably simplifies and narrows the range of available commodities and, thereby hampers the role of demand, has been replaced by widely ramifying relations among enterprises. Thereby, a green light has been given to the satisfaction of the actual needs of final users, foreign and domestic, by permitting even minor changes in demand to be taken into account.

These achievements notwithstanding, we cannot rest satisfied with the results. There are two main reasons for dissatisfaction. On the one hand, we are aware that the actual achievements in increasing the rate of production and efficiency as well as in adapting to demand have lagged behind their potential. On the other hand, the changes in external markets occurring in the wake of the price explosion and affecting Hungary disadvantageously have not only overwhelmed the beneficial effect of the changes, but also annulled the total increment in national income (at unchanged prices) in the last four years.

Evolution of the successful processes initiated by the reform was hindered by the fact that stimulation of the activities of enterprises in a country where the bulk of the enterprises are owned by the state is a complicated task likely to encounter contradictions. The root of the contradiction lies in the double task the state performs: on the one hand it regulates the functioning of the enterprises, while on the other hand, as owner, it is responsible for them.

The Hungarian programme tried to solve co-ordination and harmonious implementation of the two tasks without essential institutional reforms, relying on the system of organisation developed earlier. As a matter of fact, the centre recognised that it possessed neither the information nor the information-processing ability sufficient for continuous, smooth and elastic control of enterprise activities. But, to eliminate such deficiencies it was believed sufficient to renounce control by plan-instructions that were rendering enterprise behaviour particularly rigid and directly hindering development of enterprise adaptability. Many important details about the methods to be used for the central regulation of economic activities remained unclear. The leading agencies of the national economy naturally insisted on the retention of several procedures from the old institutional system, even though they did renounce control of means of plan-instructions. Yet they continued to confine managements to the framework of the old hierarchic organisation, in which the division of labour between enterprises had to develop along predetermined paths.

Such a development of relationships between the central state agencies and the enterprises can be explained in terms of three closely interrelated causes. The first group is related to the power structure. The internal inertia and conservatism of a hierarchical system does not readily release the formally free enterprises from the chain of earlier established relations. The most important form of resistance to the new type of management is manifested by the sectoral Ministries. Exploiting the slogan of selective economic development they have frequently done everything to conserve their own positions. The opportunity for this was provided by their right to supervise enterprise activities and to appoint enterprise executives and determine their remuneration.

The second group of causes is economic in nature and is related to the objective obstacles to the introduction of a competitive situation. It should be clear that where a chronic deficit restricts the scope of competition for imported goods and where there are but few enterprises, the result of bargaining among enterprises will be dependent on chance and the tactics adopted to improve bargaining positions, and may cause substantial social harm. To this we may add that artificial obstruction of the evolution of market forces must lead to an increasing number of cases in which the interests of the enterprise and those of the national economy clash, and this will necessitate direct state interference. It can be shown simply that whenever prevailing prices do not adequately reflect the conditions of demand and supply, when elements of international economic relations are unknown to enterprises, then, even with regulations that are otherwise well-designed, the interests of enterprises may unequivocally run counter to some interests of the state. This again supplies a persistently recurring argument for restoration of the system of central decisions.

The third group of causes is constituted by the methods of regulation actually instituted in Hungary. These methods, which impede rationality in social decisions and are closely related to one another, were mainly introduced deliberately under the impetus of the forces just mentioned.

1. Relative stability of producer prices was considered a basic requirement for several reasons. These included the successful policy of the government which was intended to avoid inflation and rapid rises in wages at any cost, despite world market inflation. The steady and regulated improvement of living standards with consumer prices increasing at a rate not exceeding 2–4 per cent p.a. required a rigid producer price system that did not react adequately to changes in conditions of supply and demand nor to those in world market price ratios.

Several other factors also acted in this direction. The rigidity of the price system was promoted in order to prevent the profit motive from disrupting smooth internal economic relationships; to permit 'objective' evaluation of the success of enterprise efforts on the basis of profits in some annual or five-year period, and to prevent the *profit motivation* of working collectives from resulting in income differentials, considered in some leading social circles to be incompatible with the value of labour performed. Stability of the price system was accomplished, first, by fixing some domestic producer prices and, second, by controlling a wide range of prices to an extent that produced practically the same consequences as the fixing of prices. In addition, the export earnings and import expenses of the enterprises were reckoned not in terms of a uniform system of exchange rates, but in terms of commercial rates of exchange modified by government subsidies that varied by enterprise and industry. This substantially reduced the income differentials between state enterprises, but simultaneously reduced the information content of external relations from the viewpoint of the national economy.

The conflict between price stabilisation and the allocative role of prices was believed to be resolved by occasional modification of prices. Prior to the world market price explosion, a revision of producer prices at five-year intervals was provided for, but this could not be sustained. After 1971, in 1975, and also in 1976, partial price revisions had to be carried out. But the revision of prices at certain intervals has not proved to be successful. This was not only because the influence of changed conditions was transmitted with a time lag, but mainly because when considering the adjustment of prices the prime objective was not clearing of the market but constraining of enterprise profits. This dominated the production and distribution of the particular groups of products, on the basis of decisions by the central financial bodies.

2. To minimise the role of conflicting social interests within the enterprise, extremely strict prescriptions were used to control personal incomes (wages). The average wage (after 1976, in some enterprises, the wage-bill) was made dependent on the profit of the enterprise. This had the result that enterprises which could not increase their profit from one year to the next, or whose

development strategy would have required a shift involving a transitory decline in profit or perhaps a loss, could raise wages only if the central agencies accorded them exceptional treatment in agreement with the supervising agencies.[1]

3. The size of the amount remaining in the hands of the enterprise for investment purpose was limited by such rigid rules that major investments could be started only with the aid of credit made available by the National Bank of Hungary (the central bank). In practice such credit could be acquired by the enterprise only with the consent of the supervising Ministry. This resulted in a situation in which investment was possible only if it corresponded to the development preferences of the pertinent sectoral Ministry. Thus, expected profitability was pushed into the background when the decision was made.

As a result, instead of by market prices – as contrasted with regulated prices and their bias – essentially all developments were regulated by so-called government preferences. This entailed the allocation of more credit to industries whose development plans required funds exceeding the amounts they had available, without being able to favour those industries which do have a role in accelerating social progress and therefore deserve the preference.

These three characteristics of financial–fiscal regulation together led to a situation in which, even after the abolition of plan-instructions and their compulsory fulfilment, the economic autonomy of Hungarian enterprise did not develop satisfactorily and administrative methods continued to dominate in state control. Thus, autonomous enterprises, working on the principle of profit motivation as formulated in the documents of the reform, have so far failed to emerge. Instead, we have enterprises which, owing to the established organisational set-up and the regulations in force, interpret for themselves the expectations of the leading social agencies and try to conform to them.

In the meantime, the enterprises continue to bargain with the leading agencies, in accord with their special interests, over modification of prices fixed or controlled by the state, over tax exemptions, and over special budgetary funds or credits. Their immediate interests, of course, influence their behaviour in the bargaining process, as well as the information supplied to the centre about their business opportunities. This bias has hampered the rationality of the decisions of central agencies.

The established order of management is appropriately distinguished from the regulated market economy on one hand, and, on the other, from control through plan-instructions as occurred before 1968. In practice, enterprises are controlled by the central organs, by the 'visible hand', without use of the directive methods of immediate control.[2]

A uniform, hierarchical organisation of the economy and regulation

---

[1] The system of so-called 'wage preferences' extended over the whole economy. A very large proportion of industrial enterprises obtained individual wage preferences.

[2] The expression derives from E. Neuberger, who first used it to describe the system of management in Yugoslavia up to 1965. See E. Neuberger and W. J. Duffy, *Comparative Economic Systems, a Decision-making Approach* (Boston, London etc., Allyn and Bacon, 1976).

differentiated by enterprises and the treatment of managers as functionaries, fulfilling national economic tasks, have become, willy-nilly, important characteristics of Hungarian management.

The reason why, ten years after the start of the reform, we have not made better progress in achieving enterprise autonomy and central regulation in practice cannot be found exclusively in the internal social tensions related to the divided powers of decision and income differentials just described. The explanation is related to the world market price explosion, the reduced capacity and readiness of socialist partners to supply raw materials and other such factors and has caused a deterioration in the economic situation of the country. These brakes on the economic development, though they intensified the craving for new methods of control and management designed for greater economic efficiency, also increased the caution of responsible authorities in dealing with the institutional system of the economy and its control – and the emergence of new forms – consistent with the spirit of the reform.

Many people ask whether, with such limitations, it was worth instituting the economic reform. We believe that the answer is affirmative in spite of justified doubts. Though, because of world market events unfavourable to Hungary and the internal causes discussed above, we cannot report that spectacular changes have resulted from the reform; still the statistics of the last ten years have shown modest, but not negligible results. First, the increase in national income has been attained with a reduction in the use of particular inputs, above all labour; second, the productive machinery has succeeded in adapting itself much more effectively to demand conditions, thus users in both the foreign and the domestic market are better satisfied with the product of Hungarian labour than they were before. Unfortunately, we are also aware that with the world market price explosion the beneficial changes emerging between the two years, 1968 and 1972, have succumbed to stagnation, at best. Even more important, we are also aware that because of deteriorating world market conditions, improvement experienced up to now is insufficient to provide the prerequisites for further improvement in living standards and for the safeguarding of economic stability.

VIII. WHAT LESSONS CAN BE DRAWN FROM THE TEN-YEAR HISTORY OF THE HUNGARIAN ECONOMIC REFORM?

We believe that there are four fields in which general lessons can be gleaned from the Hungarian experience – lessons which can be used in the control of every nationalised system of enterprise.

(a) Competitive conditions and price system

The first and most important conclusion is that in those areas of the economy in which demand changes swiftly, the needs of buyers cannot be satisfied successfully if the economy is not based on autonomous, profit-motivated enterprises. But these can function successfully only if the state does not exempt them from competition with domestic firms or potential, foreign partners, and if the state does not undertake to solve any economic difficulties that emerge at the expense of the budget. In such a competitive situation the autonomous enterprises must be fully informed about the system of prices and taxes as well as any subsidies, all of which influence the performance of the enterprise, and they, themselves, must find their way of adaptation. The efficiency of the system requires that when results are unfavourable, the enterprise executives should not be allowed to turn to the funds of their powerful owner, the state budget. It is only under such strict conditions that working collectives and their appointed leaders may be expected to devote great effort to an efficient use of the means made available to them, for personal success depends on it.

For efficient evolution of enterprise autonomy everything must be done to make financial regulations rational and clear. With consistency in prices and financial reforms, the development of such a price system may be promoted – as is presently planned by government agencies in Hungary – one which will correspond to better social values and costs than the present one, and which will be directly affected by external demand and supply on foreign markets mediated by proper rates of exchange. Thus, the role of financial regulators in bridging the difficulties of particular enterprises will essentially diminish. But this is not sufficient. All beneficial effects of the price reform may quickly evaporate if the state does not strictly adhere to the principle that the prices system and budget should be modified only if the global situation of the economy requires it, and only if these modifications are enforced in a uniform manner for every economic unit. All this means that the state must permit prices to be affected directly by the changes in internal conditions of demand and supply, and even modification of administratively regulated prices, in response to changes in demand and supply, are only temporarily delayed. The anti-inflationary policy of the state, a response to concern over the price level, must not be extended by trying to stabilise producer price ratios. If the government considers stability of nominal prices of some staple foodstuffs to be a political objective, it can carry this out during the final sale of the commodity in question, by budgetary means, to avoid disturbance of the adaptation process in production and realisation. From this it also follows that the state must not bridge difficulties of individual enterprises using the means of the state budget.

(b) Wage control

To resolve the tensions inherent in wage control is a task almost as difficult as the development of the price system. The dilemma still awaits solution. One must yet decide whether to maintain the Hungarian practice under which managers of state enterprises economise on wages only to the extent required by the centre through wage control. For it is now considered a greater success if they can pay high wages than if profit is increased, among other things, by reducing wage costs per unit of output. The handling of the problem is complex because of its social implications. If saving on wage costs is declared a task of enterprise executives, the conflict between management and workers will become overt, and this is usually avoided in the practice of Hungarian enterprise control.

If Hungarian economic leaders were pressed only by the first problem, a simple solution could be provided for the problem of wage control: frugal management of wages could be delegated to the managers in a manner similar to its responsibilities over other cost elements. The special rules regulating the outflow of wages could be dispensed with. But the central Hungarian agencies believe that the possibility of sharpening conflict within the enterprise is politically intolerable. Their view derives support from the fact that in modern market economies even the governments of the leading industrial countries are frequently forced to control wages. Presumably social conflicts within the enterprise in these countries are also diminished thereby and are replaced by negotiations amongst manufacturers, trade unions, and the government. The behaviour of capitalist enterprises may also be characterised by the fact that whenever they can shift cost increases resulting from increased wages to the user, they frequently desist from taking upon themselves the conflicts likely to result from a brake on wages.

The task is particularly difficult in the case of socialist, state-owned enterprises. Rationality of management seems to demand that enterprise executives increasingly take upon themselves the task of managing wages and economising on wages; thus the rigidity of wage control can be eased as progress is made in this direction. By all means one should avoid transforming debates about wage control, bargaining between the enterprises and central agencies, into a factor determining the success of management.

Another problem which awaits solution is the determination of the means by which the necessary central control of wages is most expediently carried out. The cause for concern is that increases in wages cannot always be expected to parallel productivity and efficiency. Growing demand for some categories of workers frequently necessitates a wage increase, and, for social reasons, this cannot be counterbalanced by reductions in the wages of other categories. As is well-known, wages are rigid downwards. The problems of wage control become even more complicated if shifts in relative wages are accompanied by a rise in the consumer price level. On such occasions a general rise is required, even in those factories which prove incapable of raising their profits at the time of the price rise. Thus, the smooth operation of a considerable portion of enterprises can be secured only if they are not prevented from raising wages only on the basis of their economic performance and in direct proportion to it.

We do not see any possibility of solving the problem without conflict. In the last two years we have, with some success, been experimenting with the establishment of specified bounds within which wage rises are not precluded, with a progressive tax levied only on a wage rise exceeding them; in many cases this method has proved to be prohibitive.

(c) Investment allocation

It is difficult to find ways to bring entrepreneurial spirit to life simultaneously with planned, central regulation of investment and the execution of government preferences. An outline of the possible solutions may be interesting even when the government has not put these issues on the agenda.

A solution can be found in a felicitous separation of the administrative functions of the state from its economic ones. In our opinion, the task is to create an institution, or system of institutions, that enables enterprises to acquire the assets (capital) necessary for its development as a function of its expected efficiency. The institution or system of institutions fulfilling the functions of a capital market can play its role consistently only if functions other than express business activity are renounced. Thus, such an agency cannot claim simultaneously to represent all state interests. It also seems to follow that holdings, independent of one another, or organisations similar to conglomerates should take over the role of state supervision of enterprises from the hierarchically organised sectoral Ministries.[1]

An institution for the allocation of funds necessary for developments with special priority is also needed. But institutional provisions are required to prevent the allocation of these assets from impairing the autonomy of enterprises and to prevent the granting of preferential credit from exceeding the amounts earmarked for the purpose and from becoming sources of inflationary pressure. The best solution seems to be for the state organs to grant preferential credit under predetermined conditions and as lump sum grants. The granting of this support must not amount to the central agencies' taking over responsibility for development, by declaring that in case of failure no further credit will be granted to help in overcoming the difficulties.

(d) Appointment and control of executives of state-owned enterprises, working relations within the enterprise

One of the key problems for success in the activities of state-owned enterprises, as of any firm, is the selection of executives. An issue that needs theoretical exploration is the degree to which the executive should be held in dependence after being appointed.

---

[1] Relevant literature makes proposals for diversified forms. See Sándor Balázsy, 'Az irányító szervezet továbbfejlesztése' ('Improvement of the Control Organization'), 1970, mimeo; Sándor Kopátsy, 'A vállalati tevékenység komplex és többéves értékelésének problémája' ('Problems of Evaluating the Activity of Enterprises in a Complex Manner over Several Years'), *Pénzügyi Szemle* (1969), No. 9, 929–37; Márton Tardos, 'A gazdasági verseny problémái hazánkban' ('Problems of Competition between Enterprises in Hungary'), *Közgazdasági Szemle* (1972), No. 7–8, 911–26.

We believe that in answering this question two assumptions must be accepted. One is that, by its very nature, management of firms involves great risks. Second, success and failure usually do not become clear in short periods, but only over a longer time horizon.

It follows from these two assumptions that, provided we have been circumspect in selecting the manager, he must be accorded considerable trust. Acknowledging that the manager has been appointed to lead a risky enterprise, his entrepreneurial skill and not his administrative talents must be relied upon, and adequate preconditions for this must be created. It should be recognised in their work that peaks are to be expected to alternate with troughs, and boldly soaring paths frequently require long and tedious preparation.

Managers and their leading associates can carry out this task successfully only if they enjoy the support and trust of those appointing them. Thus one can argue the expediency of a long-term agreement between the supervising authority as owner and the manager, so that the latter may work in security and carry out his development ideas in an atmosphere of trust.

From the viewpoint of the efficiency of management it is also highly important to clarify what behaviour is expected of the executives of state enterprises when particular enterprise interests conflict with state or global social interests. The problem is highly significant because such conflicts occur in every system of management; and, unfortunately, on account of the weaknesses of regulation, in Hungarian economic practice they are more frequent than is desirable.

Two extreme viewpoints have emerged here. According to the first, managers should always back the social interests and ignore local ones. The second opinion is that the interests of the state, of society, cannot be judged from the position of the manager; and, therefore, he cannot be expected to determine the social issues nor to identify himself with them.

We believe that there can be no unequivocal choice between these two views, only a pragmatic approach may be advised. One cannot deny that government regulation works well if, as against the Hungarian practice of recent years, it does not build on the identification of enterprises with the interests of the state, which have not been and frequently cannot be exactly defined. Accordingly, it should avoid forcing them to undertake social tasks influencing business results detrimentally or even asking them to do so, lest it should allow them to put the blame for the lack of achievement on such 'voluntarily' undertaken tasks. On the other hand, a manager may be expected to proceed in his relations with the central agencies as a good businessman. In times of transitory troubles he will not strive to exploit his partner, knowing that the basis of safety is mutual advantage. Thus, in conformity with his own long-term interests, he will not strive after every petty, short-term advantage in the maze of the complicated system of government regulations.

There are still many unsolved problems in social relations within the enterprise. A widespread discussion is emerging in Hungary about the problems of extending so-called factory democracy. It would be premature to sum up the conclusions; for the moment the following seem to be clear:

(1) management of the enterprise is, in fact, the task of a broad collective of executives, in which the harmony between sharing responsibilities and the justified, hierarchial relations must be found;

(2) in the interest of successful work, enterprise management must rely on the active contribution and support of the entire working collective for interpretation of the economic tasks and negotiation of the means for their implementation;

(3) it is particularly important to stimulate such active co-operation in establishing general, working conditions;

(4) nevertheless, healthy, intra-enterprise, social relations demand the active work of trade unions, separated from management, to defend the interests of workers.

Discussion of Paper by Drs Nyers and Tardos

Mr Vuskovic said that the information provided by Dr Nyers and Dr Tardos in their paper was enormously valuable to readers in Latin America who were interested in planning. It helped them to see the nature of the changes in the Hungarian economy in the right perspective. Foreigners had little direct knowledge of what was taking place in Hungary, and often received distorted versions, claiming that Hungary was returning to a capitalist market system. Such reports were used as arguments against economic planning in Latin America. He now saw the meaning of the changes, that they were intended to improve the effectiveness of central regulation of the market, and not to lead to a return to a spontaneous market economy.

Vuskovic then considered the applicability of the Hungarian experience to Latin America. He concluded that the two regions were at two different stages in their development. Whereas Hungary was trying to decentralise decision-making, to introduce market mechanisms into a planned socialist economy, he judged that the Latin American countries with their dependent capitalist economies ought to move in the opposite direction, towards more planning and central control. He wondered whether it was possible to begin with a more flexible system, as was the aim of the Hungarian reform, or whether this could be achieved only after the central planning mechanism had matured. He listed a number of reasons why more central guidance might be needed in an initial planning phase. There were great differences in productivity levels among enterprises, which would cause large wage differentials in the absence of some central co-ordination. The maladjustments in the current income distribution had also helped to produce wasteful consumption patterns, which ought to be redressed. Was it feasible to introduce a flexible system from the start, or was it first necessary to go through a period of strong central control, so that flexibility could be permitted later? He said this was not just an academic question, but that he was motivated by the Chilean experience. While Cuba had been successful in the introduction of socialism, Chile had failed. The Allende government sought not to create a strong central planning body. The autonomous enterprises in Chile lacked control by the government. He said these enterprises should have received more guidance. Planning was the objective of the popular government, but it did not succeed in carrying it out. The principal merit of the paper by Nyers and Tardos was that it did not simply advocate planning, but described concrete strategies for the successful execution of planning. Although there were great differences between the situations in Hungary and in the countries of Latin America, he expected to find many applicable elements in the paper.

M. Dreyfus said that he, too, had been very interested in the paper. In his view the most difficult aspect of the reform was the determination of the proper equilibrium between the centre and the enterprises. If prices were fixed by the centre, then no self-financing by the enterprises was possible. Enterprises might refuse autonomy, even if they were offered it. To what extent were enterprises free to invest? He asked how these problems had been solved in Hungary.

Lord Kaldor said Dreyfus had touched on the crucial point. Industrial autonomy was inconceivable without the ability to reinvest profits. He was convinced that the greater part of investment should be undertaken by successful enterprises. The state should also control a portion of investment by creating *new* enterprises. He asked how enterprises were formed in Hungary, and how they were closed when it was appropriate. He also mentioned that decentralisation had gone farthest in Yugoslavia among the Eastern European countries. Firms were free to choose what they produced, and how much they wanted to invest. He said that when this system was introduced, it had serious consequences, as many enterprises went bankrupt and employment was reduced. But after an initial learning period it was improving. He asked whether in the long run that system wasn't better than the one in Hungary.

Dr Sacristán was particularly interested in how external balance of trade was achieved. Was this done through barter agreements, or through multinational planning?

Professor Minian was concerned that Hungary's expansion of trade with the West would make it increasingly dependent upon the economy of the West. He asked how socialist planning was made compatible with Western trade, and how Hungary could isolate itself from the effects of business cycles and inflation.

Dr Pryke asked at what point the introduction of more market freedom should stop. What were the useful functions of the centre? Was it simply to exchange market information, as in France, or more than that?

Dr Marsan asked whether Hungary had now, or was planning to set up, holding companies encompassing several enterprises in different industries. He did not want to act as salesman of his organisation's own system, he said, but he thought that diversification was a typical way for an enterprise to develop, and the state should also exploit this. A parent holding company exhibited a sort of *superadditivity* in that it was more than the sum of its components. One of the advantages of a holding company was its ability to select good managers. It could decide which people were most useful in existing enterprises, and select those who should be assigned the responsibility of setting up new enterprises. Such decisions had to take into account expertise and professional experience, and could not be made well at a bureaucratic level. Middle management, which was an important group, would not willingly accept unsatisfactory appointments. He mentioned that, for example, in the Italian national oil company ENI the top manager was appointed on the basis of the judgement of middle management. He also said that a holding agency could be a good conduit for the submission of proposals for new enterprises to the political authorities. It had the capability of evaluating social preferences (among objectives such as income distribution, regional balance, technological independence, balance of payments, etc.) and their financial feasibility.

Professor Barkai favoured decentralisation, even of investment decisions, and suggested that investment credits be auctioned off to the firms bidding highest. These credits could consist of the fraction of the GNP set aside by the government for investment purposes, and also of foreign credits, if foreign debts were politically acceptable.

Professor Vickrey warned that decisions concerning investments and operating expenses should not be separated. As a bad example he mentioned that in New York new subway tunnels were being dug, but no funds for operation of these lines were in sight.

Dr Nyers stressed that Hungary was not moving toward capitalism. It was only progressing toward more flexibility in the socialist economic system. The traditional image of socialism was one of rigid central planning. But this was not valid. Flexibility was not a monopoly of the capitalist system. He found the Yugoslav system to be an interesting experiment, but said its aims were different from those of the Hungarian economic reform, and Hungary would not move toward the Yugoslav system. In reference to Pryke's question on how far decentralisation should go, Nyers said that it would certainly not reach the free market system. Hungary wanted to decentralise what the state could not do well. Earlier, the state wanted to do certain things which it could not do very effectively, as it turned out. For example, the state could not fix all prices, only those of some basic materials and the retail prices of some essential foodstuffs. For some other prices it could give enterprises a zone within which to act freely. Replying to Marsan, he said that Hungary had some agencies mediating between enterprises and the government, but not all enterprises belonged to one of them. This would, however, introduce a third level of decision-making, which was sometimes excessive. He mentioned that generally there are no intermediate bodies between enterprises and economic ministries.

Dr Tardos said that Nyers had been one of the principal authors of the 1968 Hungarian economic reform. He emphasised that Hungary wanted to retain central control and planning of the whole economy but to combine it with decentralised decision-making in a large part of the economy. In answer to Pryke he said that the principal tasks of the centre were to formulate an overall plan, to fix the rate of accumulation, to play a conscious role in the international division of labour, and to set up an active exchange rate policy in order to increase economic efficiency. Responding to Minian, he added that trade with Western countries had not imposed a burden on Hungary, but had enabled it to better use its own resources. To Sacristán he said that Hungary had made efforts to increase its exports, especially to industrialised countries. Western markets had difficult requirements, but it was necessary to find areas in which Hungarian skill and knowledge could compete effectively. Regarding the questions of Dreyfus and Kaldor, he said that in the allocation of investment funds among enterprises, the central government has maintained the determining role through the issue of credits. It is assumed that both the discounted future profit and government priorities should provide guidelines in credit allocation. In practice, however, state interference often had an arbitrary character. There was some self-regulation by firms investing retained profits. Using the opportunity of state preferences, managers had the possibility of asking the state for new funds, and the government had the temptation to subsidise failing state enterprises. There have been obvious shortcomings in this policy. He expressed his opinion that it should be clearly conveyed to managers that they would not receive any grants if they ran into difficulties. He agreed with Marsan that Hungary could learn from the experience of the Italian state holding companies. Such firms in Hungary, in his view, could allocate funds to the most efficient enterprises. This mechanism would serve the allocative role of a stockmarket, whose importance was stressed by Barkai. He also emphasised that sometimes there was a conflict between governmental objectives and efficiency. The desire to improve adaptation of production to consumer demands made central planning and control more complicated. But the Hungarian people appreciated the improved quality and greater variety of goods. He was impressed by the remarks of Vusković, but, since they were so specifically directed to Latin America, he was unable to offer specific comments.

11 The Efficiency of Public Enterprise: Lessons of the French Experience[1]

Pierre Dreyfus
DIRECTOR EMERITUS, RÉGIE RENAULT

I. THE ISSUES

The question we have before us is whether in countries with a market economy, whether already developed or still developing, public enterprise is comparable with private enterprise in terms of economic efficiency.

This leaves aside the implications of a deliberate policy transforming a free market economy into a socialist one. This always involves a very considerable enlargement of the public sector on essentially political grounds, even if the approach is gradual.

Even if we limit ourselves strictly to economic aspects in comparing the efficiency of public and private enterprise, we have to make up our mind first about what we mean by efficiency.

So far as private enterprise is concerned the answer is clear. A private company sets out to make as much profit as possible, which, in practice, means paying the highest possible dividends to shareholders. Even if this can be achieved only by generating social utility, the latter is not itself the purpose of the firm. For public enterprise the issue is less simple. Here we must make a distinction between firms producing a public service, in which case efficiency must be measured in terms of general economic and social utility, and industrial companies with public ownership, which operate in a competitive market.

A firm of the latter type has a pilot function. In working for its own expansion, it must also aim at the growth of the national economy, and to this end needs to earn a profit so that it can cover the costs of its expansion through its own resources. But it need not necessarily aim at maximum profit, much less at maximum dividend distribution, if the state, as its shareholder, is prepared to let it take risks for the sake of national economic development.

[1]Translation by Elizabeth Henderson.

II. ORIGINS OF PUBLIC ENTERPRISE IN FRANCE

To address ourselves more specifically to the question of the efficiency of public enterprise, we need to know what precisely are the government's intentions in setting up a state-owned firm. This depends largely on the historical context in each country. Our discussion, I know, is meant to cover the experience of many countries, especially in Europe; for my part, I propose to talk here only of the case of France, with particular reference to public enterprise in a setting of competition.

In France, the idea of state-owned enterprise is by no means socialist in origin. It goes back to the time of Louis XIV, three centuries ago, when the creation of industries in an essentially peasant economy and in the absence of appropriate private enterprise, was conceived of as a means of enhancing the wealth and power of France. This is how the Royal Manufactures came into existence – ironworks and shipyards, factories making glass and porcelain, tapestries and textiles. They were generally very efficient; one of the survivors, Saint Gobain, now in private hands, is currently one of the leading companies of France. They had no monopoly; they served as pilot enterprises, stimulating the economy, assuming risks for the sake of development of the Kingdom's economy as a whole, and sometimes exporting. In short, they created a living tradition in France.

The establishment of public enterprise under the monarchy was not part of any grand design or systematic policy. In France it was not until the twentieth century, after the First World War, that the idea arose that there is a case for transfer to national ownership, which means in practice to the state, the major service industries of a modern economy. In placing large sectors of the economy, transport and energy, for instance, under public control the intention was to create an efficient base for the development of the economy as a whole.

I do not propose to discuss here whether in fact these services were so managed as to achieve the original purposes, and, in particular, whether in fact public enterprise proved to be efficient. I note in passing that the French National Railways, SNCF, compares very favourably with railways abroad and specially with private railway companies in the United States, from the point of view of technical productivity achieved by such means as modernisation of traction, reorganisation of administration, improved working arrangements (while traffic doubled between 1950 and 1976 the size of staff fell by one-third, in spite of a reduction in working hours), and adjustment to market requirements.

Thanks to the efficiency of this branch of public enterprise, railways in France continue to hold their own in relation to other forms of transport, such as private cars and buses. In contrast, in the United States, for example, the Federal Government has had to step in to make passenger transport by rail profitable enough to prevent its collapse in cases where this would have caused serious damage (around the great cities of the Northeast, for instance).

Other reasons for nationalisation of certain sectors of the economy became apparent, and this was followed by action, in France during the last thirty years. It was felt that nationalisation would help the government to defend itself against undue pressure from certain firms or groups of firms in some sectors, and help to provide means to stimulate the economy.

The idea that it is the duty of government to keep the economy in good health by an overall plan is steadily gaining ground in France. This implies more sophisticated planning of the sort that has been practised in France, and involves keeping an eye on industrial developments in separate sectors and sometimes even in individual firms.

If this line of thought should prevail, it may well lead to an enlargement of the public sector even in competitive branches of industry. We must remember that, until very recently, France was still much more a country of farmers than the rest of Northern Europe. French private banks had not, on the whole, acted to stimulate rapid industrialisation, as happened in Germany for example, where, in addition, bankers and industrialists were much more inclined than their French counterparts to accept the high risks of capitalist entrepreneurship.

How else is the absence of French private firms from many innovative industries to be explained except on the hypothesis that private management tended to adopt the attitude of a prudent family man, more anxious to husband his resources than to launch new ventures? Yet at a time when traditional French industries are threatened by the products of developing nations, France simply cannot afford to avoid the innovative industries.

If private enterprise fails to meet the challenge, if it cannot or will not make the effort and assume the financial risks involved in making such industries pay, then the government will find itself under increasing pressure to fill the gap through public enterprise.

But will public enterprise prove efficient? Let us see what clues we can find to the answer by looking more closely at the performance of two public-sector companies, Renault in motor cars and Elf in oil, which have been in operation long enough for their experience on an international scale to be a matter of public record.

III. THE CASE OF RÉGIE RENAULT

Take first the case of Régie Renault, the successor of a limited company called Usines Renault, which was confiscated in 1945 on charges of collaboration with the Germans. The text of the law says no more than that the Régie is to carry on the business of its predecessor exclusively in the interests of the nation and, more generally, to develop in the national interest the industrial concern entrusted to it.

But the new management at once took a more concrete view of its task. It felt that the French economy in the interwar period had suffered from Malthusianism and from excessive caution on the part of private industrialists, encouraged in this attitude by a long history of strong protectionism. What was needed in 1945, it was argued, was not only to rebuild the ruins of war, but to purge the nation of its lazy habits. And so, the managers of Régie Renault assumed a pilot function for their company. They meant it to become the pioneer of a new dynamism in France; it was to hasten French industrial progress and brave international competition, and in so doing to carry along the company's suppliers and induce its rivals to follow suit.

Régie Renault had no special privileges whatever, or any legislated advantage over its competitors. On the contrary, at its birth in 1945 it had no resources of its own and no reserves, and for eighteen years thereafter it received no finances from its shareholder, even though one-third of the plant had been destroyed by air raids. It needed a lot of courage to expand an enterprise whose resources were often stretched to the limit and whose margin of reserves was negligible. Foreseeing a boom in motor cars, Régie Renault seized the opportunity in 1945 and launched itself upon a path of bold expansion. At that time it was one car manufacturer among many; in 1975 it was the leading French car manufacturer among four still surviving. Its assets have quintupled in the last few years, yet only some 10 per cent of the costs of the company's expansion since 1963 was covered by the state as sole shareholder; the rest came from self-financing and from borrowing on a scale comparable to its leading private rival.[1]

What is more, the company's growth was made to serve policies of national interest. To begin with, ever since 1945 all new jobs created were located elsewhere than at the Billancourt factory in Paris, in response to the pressing requirements imposed by inter-regional planning ('aménagement du territoire') in France. Régie Renault adopted this policy well before any government machinery was set up to encourage and possibly to subsidise the establishment or relocation of factories and offices in distressed or backward regions of the country. Now private enterprise is doing as much in this line as Renault, but it was public enterprise which set the pattern, as it should.

In the social field, too, Régie Renault often led the way, although here its pioneering role was somewhat hampered by the need to remain competitive. In any event, the company's liberal attitude toward trade unions has always been remarkable.

From the outset, Régie Renault set itself ambitious export targets. As early as 1955 the company decided to aim at exporting half its output, a proportion until then unheard of in this branch of industry. It pursued this aim in spite of difficulties due mainly to French inexperience and to the great expense and the long period of time needed to build up a distribution network. Rival car manufacturers have since imitated this export drive to such good purpose that by now Peugeot and Citroën together have probably drawn abreast of Renault, which, however, remains the leading seller of motor cars in the European Economic Community.

[1]According to *Fortune*, Régie Renault ranks fifty-fourth among the world's largest companies, including American corporations.

The fact that Renault's French rivals successfully imitated it in exports simply means that in this field, too, public enterprise has served as a pilot and acted as pace-setter.

Lastly, the company, anxious to deploy its resources and its experience to benefit the nation, undertook a difficult policy of diversification. It branched out mainly into two fields of great importance for the French economy: commercial vehicles and machine tools. In these industries private enterprise had failed to secure for France its proper place and it seemed only natural that public enterprise should devote a special effort to them, even if initially there was no certain prospect of profit.

More than once Régie Renault was induced to set up subsidiary companies, generally in order to help solve some national employment problem. The state, to be sure, did not ask the company to assume risks which might impair its competitiveness, yet often wanted it to move into areas where private enterprise had been unwilling to venture. In such cases the state, no doubt, hoped that Régie Renault would be able to do what was asked of it without detriment to itself, and the company's management often eventually took the same view and went ahead. But sometimes the managers refused to go along with some government request, when they felt that the proposed venture had no chance of success, however much effort was put into it.

In the case of Régie Renault, then, it may be said that public enterprise has efficiently served the nation's interests and that it compares favourably with private enterprise.

IV. THE CASE OF FUEL: ELF-AQUITAINE

In the oil industry, a sector of key importance for the French economy, public enterprise, in the shape of Elf-Aquitaine, likewise seems to be carrying out the government's intentions very efficiently.

France is rather poor in energy resources. Its coalmines are for the most part difficult to exploit, its main hydro-electric resources are already fully utilised, and there is little oil and natural gas. The rapid pace of industrialisation in recent years has brought to the fore the balance-of-payments problems caused by mounting imports of raw materials, especially oil.

The French government has long felt a threat to the country's independence in having to rely wholly on foreign sources for its supply of hydrocarbons. This is why after the First World War France demanded, and obtained, part of the Iraqi oil interests confiscated from Germany. This was the point of departure for the expansion of Compagnie Française des Pétroles. A state monopoly of oil imports and refining was established by law in 1928, and its administration delegated to private companies. Then the government set up a number of public and semi-public bodies and industrial companies for prospecting in metropolitan France and in French territories overseas, for exploiting such deposits as were found and, eventually, for refining and marketing them. But it was not until a good deal later that the state began to play a direct and active part in this important field. This took place in 1966, when Elf-Erap – transformed in 1976 to Elf-Aquitaine – was set up with 70 per cent of its capital owned by the state.

The French oil industry is a good example of co-existence of public and private enterprise. The market is dominated by subsidiaries of the seven big multinational oil companies, which pursue their own goals; then there is the French Total group (Compagnie Française des Pétroles), with a majority of its holdings in private hands; and finally the state company Elf-Erap. To assess the latter's efficiency and success is therefore a matter of special interest.

The French oil industry got off to a late start. Without state intervention French capitalists would probably have been in no hurry to invest in this field, one more example of their lack of enthusiasm for venturing into activities whose capital intensity and risks are high. The only major private concern, the Compagnie Française des Pétroles, owed its growth to resources obtained through government action. But its expansion followed the familiar pattern of French capitalism; for instance, it was prudent to the point that the company hesitated a long time before it took steps to diversify its sources of supply, in spite of the fact (or, perhaps, because of it) that its Iraqi oil was so lucrative.

This is no doubt why the French government decided to set up Elf, while on the face of it they might have rested content with the existence of a French oil company in which, moreover, they had a large, though still a minority, stake.

Though a late-comer, Elf-Erap and its successor Elf-Aquitaine pursued a dynamic policy of exploration and acquired large interests abroad, especially in off-shore oil.

Elf also developed its refining capacity very quickly and, at 45 million tons per year, now accounts for one-quarter of the French market, the same as Total. The company has also done much useful work in scientific and technical research, and has built up an efficient distribution network.

Like Régie Renault, Elf also diversified. It did not do so to a much greater extent than its French rival, Total (Compagnie Française des Pétroles). At present, for instance, it already occupies an important position in pharmaceuticals, and it is branching out into other chemicals and into non-ferrous metal mining.

Elf's story definitely is one of industrial success achieved in a very short time. Again, like Régie Renault, it discharged a pilot function not only in the key sector of oil, but also in other fields where the French economy urgently needs a new approach. Public enterprise in this case has proved highly efficient in terms of national utility no less than the criteria of private capitalism.

V. THE ROLE OF GOVERNMENT IN FRENCH PUBLIC ENTERPRISE

In both cases discussed above the efficiency of public enterprise is attributable to the high degree of responsibility and freedom accorded to the management of the companies concerned.

Government control over state-owned companies in France takes many different forms and is largely a matter of history. But here a distinction must be made between public utilities and other firms.

The former have much less independence, for some government control is exercised over the quality of the service itself, over the rates charged for it and, in varying degrees, over investment and wages. Major decisions of many kinds are subject to prior government approval. If the government decides that rates must be kept so low that the company experiences a loss, state interference assumes fatal proportions. Everyone agrees that there is too much interference, and everyone keeps saying that it must be brought to an end. One solution often recommended is a system of programme contracts under which the government sets general targets and undertakes to provide finances for special requirements, but for the rest leaves management largely free to run the company's affairs at its discretion, within the terms of the contract. But, invariably, short-term economic conditions thwart the best intentions and make it hard to introduce, let alone maintain, sound economic management in this part of the public sector.

In the case of public enterprise in a competitive market state intervention is usually much more discreet. Let us see, again, what happens at Renault and at Elf.

To take Régie Renault first, the government appoints the Chairman-General Manager, who is then free to make his own appointments to senior posts. The Board has a majority of members representing government departments and also includes representatives of the workers. However, while the powers of the Chairman are not enumerated, those of the Board are, and by this very fact are restricted. They are still important, though. Decisions on the investment budget, for instance, are reserved to the Board. State control (through government ministries and the Audit Office) is exercised *a posteriori* and, in cases of serious conflict, the only solution is the Chairman's resignation or dismissal.

Now let us see what actually happened in the relations between the government and Régie Renault. The choice of the first Chairman in 1945 proved a happy one and was very quickly accepted as such by the company itself. When he died in 1955, I was Vice-Chairman of the Board of Directors, where I sat as the representative of the Department of Industry; I was appointed head of the firm at the request of the company's own staff. And when I retired in 1975, the government chose as my successor one of the senior managers, again in the light of the company's needs as expressed by its own staff. Note the remarkable continuity of management, interrupted only by the death of the first and the retirement of the second Chairman, throughout a period of changing politics when indeed, the Republic itself was transformed.

The company's general policy, its choice of products and markets, its financial policy and its labour policy were always decided by the Chairman-General Manager, assisted by his own staff and by the Board of Directors. The latter sometimes needed some persuasion, but in the end never refused to go along with any major project. Before any new project is undertaken or any major risks assumed, the matter is always explained to the ministries concerned, but when all is said and done the government has always allowed the management its freedom of action. This freedom drew additional strength from two circumstances. The first was that the all-important choice of product was one that could not be made by anyone other than the company's own management, and that on the whole they chose well; and the second circumstance, largely a consequence of the first, was that Régie Renault never had to ask the government for financial aid. When the government in 1963, eighteen years after the company was created, offered to increase its capital so that it could expand faster, Régie Renault gladly took advantage of this supplemental opportunity, but could have gone on perfectly well coping with its own problems.

Renault has since 1955 had a system of five-year planning, with clearly-defined targets for the company's own expansion simultaneously designed to serve the national interest. This has helped the government in defining its industrial policy for the engineering sector. And from the moment in 1963 when discussions started on the issue of new capital funds, there have been regular talks, especially with the Department of Industry and the Finance Ministry, which have led to what may be described as quasi-contractual relations between the company and the state.

As a state-owned company, Régie Renault has always tried to conduct its affairs in the national interest, but for its part the government never defined what the national interest was in this context, or at most gave a bare outline of it in the National Plan.

To sum up, it can be said that the facts have proved the appropriateness of a system under which Renault's management has a very large measure of autonomy and under which the company's and the government's policies are co-ordinated by constant exchange of information, so that both are in a position to make quick decisions when they are needed.

In the case of Elf, as in that of Renault, a major part of its success can be attributed to the very large measure of independence enjoyed by the company's management. And this independence in turn is justified by the background and experience of its Chairman (who, as an official in the Department of Industry, was responsible for fuel policy in the post-war years) and senior executives, by their competence and their personal contacts with government officials, as in the case of Renault, and by the company's financial success.

However, unlike the engineering industries, the energy sector, and more especially the oil sector, has long been, and continues to be, one to which government devotes much thought. Elf's independence, therefore, goes hand in hand with an active government policy, with close co-ordination maintained by a joint committee responsible for major decisions. It is this unity of purpose between government and public enterprise which explains both Elf's freedom and its success so far.

However, what has been said of Renault and Elf does not apply to all public enterprise in competitive branches. State-owned companies in France differ widely as regards their legal status. But beyond its institutional set-up, the efficiency of any one firm can be judged only in terms of the degree of freedom the government wants to give or can give its management.

In banking, there has been no problem of management and the government has never had any comprehensive plan to use the public sector for purposes of a deliberate credit policy. For this reason there is little government interference with the management of the nationalised banks. For their part, the latter have produced no new ideas for overall policy.

In sectors where problems of financial balance loom large, often just because of state ownership, government interference has greatly reduced the autonomy and efficiency of management, thus aggravating their problems. An example is aviation.

VI. SOME IMPLICATIONS OF THE FRENCH EXPERIENCE

One lesson to be learned from the experience of nationalised industry in France is that, regardless of legal status, public enterprise must pay its way if it is to play its proper part. Another lesson is that the best system for enabling a state-owned company to take care of its own requirements, and at the same time to serve the imperatives of national development and the national interest, is a quasi-contractual system. By this I mean a system under which government and company management jointly lay down general objectives, specify their reciprocal obligations and define certain indicators calling for a possible revision of the contract.

The institutional powers conceded to the head of the company or to its Board of Directors and, within the latter, to representatives of government or of workers or users, or of other groups, may be more far-reaching or less, varying from case to case. But in all cases the choice of personnel, though it cannot always be divorced from political considerations, must be based on competence and responsibilities must be distributed so as to permit quick and clear decisions.

In any case, while the choice of top executives for public enterprise certainly does have its problems, the same is true of private enterprise. In a country like France where family firms are still frequent, nepotism is more of a danger in the private than in the public sector. A good many of the largest private concerns in France are actually headed by former civil servants, which at least suggests that their counterparts in the public sector should not find their recruitment problem more difficult.

VII. CHARACTERISATION OF PUBLIC ENTERPRISE IN FRANCE

In France, there is a coherent philosophy behind the nationalisation of the services and industries which make up the economy's infrastructure, such as rail transport, electricity and gas, coal (in part), oil and aviation. The same applies to the nationalisation of a large part of the banking system, with a view to the distribution of credit in accordance with requirements of the national interest.

By contrast, the growth of the public sector in heavy industry and in manufacturing has been haphazard and followed no overall design. Direct state intervention in these fields has often been prompted by a wish to make good some failure of private enterprise, or to contribute to the rapid development of new industries or the adoption of innovative techniques. In these circumstances government surely should have a general strategy covering a span of many years.

After the war, state intervention was largely designed to help France overcome its gap in industrialisation. Now, since 1973, it occurs in the name of what the planners call redeployment, reorientation or restructuring, and involves many individual companies and entire branches of industry. It varies in degree, ranging from simple aid to nationalisation, depending on the capacity of private enterprise itself to respond to the challenge facing the country. What, we may wonder, will happen to the steelmasters and the shipbuilders in the traditional sector? And what will occur, in industries using advanced technology; electronics, especially components and computers (the state has backed mergers and private agreements, but one cannot really be sure that this is sufficient to safeguard the national interest in this field); fine chemicals and pharmaceuticals?

It would be well if the government's strategies, worked out with the help of the appropriate technical ministries, were embodied in an overall economic plan. This should outline long-term goals, so defined as to be both feasible and compatible with one another. Public enterprise strategically located at a number of key points would serve to guarantee that everything possible was done to attain national objectives and would serve as a leader in economic growth.

Such a voluntarist approach is doubtless the most appropriate in countries where private enterprise has often done an inadequate job. It has the advantage that it does not merely assist ailing or declining industries, but takes the offensive and looks beyond the domestic market to an expanded international role.

A sustained effort, planned for the medium- and long-term future, mobilising all national resources to the utmost degree, is obviously required in countries where the balance of payments threatens to fall into structural deficit, either because they are poor in raw materials, including oil, or because their industry is deficient.

Public enterprise geared to the national interest is often the most effective weapon in these cases, provided it is organised on the right lines. That this can be done is demonstrated by the recent history of France.

Discussion of M. Dreyfus' Paper

Lord Kaldor said he agreed completely with what M. Dreyfus had said. He asked about the reasons for the French success. Before the Second World War France's industrial production had been about two-thirds of Great Britain's and its living standard had been lower. Today it was just the reverse, with France producing about one and a half times as much as Britain, if not more. France's wages had been lower, now they were considerably higher. France was a success, Britain a failure. He said he was not surprised by this. He saw the basic reason for the difference in past experience in the fact that France had used planning, while Britain had not. In 1946, Jean Monnet set up the *Commissariat du Plan* of which he, Kaldor, was also an adviser for a time. He became an enthusiastic advocate of the adoption of a similar overall plan for Great Britain, of getting individual firms in different industries together to work out an optimal investment plan to their mutual advantage. But this proposal was badly received. He was regarded as a 'madman' who wanted planning – by the bureaucracy in Whitehall. Events had now proved that France was right and Britain was wrong. An important aspect behind this difference lay in the quality of manpower. France had a long tradition of outstanding civil servants, trained in special schools like the École Polytechnique. Britain, on the other hand, had graduates of Oxford and Cambridge who had specialised in Latin and Greek. If instead they had specialised in high-grade engineering it would have been more useful, as the success of France and Japan had shown. Their leading civil servants were very good administrators. But he knew of no British civil servant who had subsequently made a big career in business. French industry used to be in the hands of family firms, which had been unimaginative, and France fell behind. Then the State began to promote industrial activities and changed the situation. He agreed with Dreyfus that private enterprise receiving instructions from the government was not the same as public enterprise. Governments always issued prohibitions of one kind or another, but it was not possible to get something positive out of many negatives. What France had done could be copied by other countries, if they had people with the right technical qualifications combined with integrity, tradition and an *ésprit de corps*. Without trained manpower, reforms like the introduction of public enterprises could not transform the economy. The great difficulty with public enterprises in less developed countries was corruption. It could be eliminated only by creating a cadre with a spirit of integrity. This could not be done overnight. Another example of a country that did well was Germany, because it had a reservoir of highly trained and able manpower. Its reconstruction after the war was carried out mainly by private enterprise, but with public enterprise it would probably have been the same.

Dreyfus thanked Kaldor for his favourable judgement of France, but also pointed out that France owed its freedom to Great Britain.

Dr Galán said that qualified management was a necessary condition for successful public enterprise. But there were two additional conditions, namely the existence of a market in which public enterprise had to compete, and a regime of parliamentary democracy. There were two criteria for success of public enterprise, one microeconomic and the other macroeconomic. Microeconomic success depended on capable managers, who clearly sought to minimise costs, without having to be told to do so. But macroeconomic success, which was even more important, depended on the functioning of the market and the existence of government policies that represented the public interest.

Professor Baumol proposed that the discussion focus on two questions: (i) Apparently there was something France had done right. What could Latin America learn from it? What, concretely, was transferable? (ii) What were the limits of public enterprise, if any? Should the entire economy be public, only some of it (and, if so, how much), or none at all?

Dreyfus said it was important to have democratic planning. Even if it was not very scientific, it could still be very effective as long as it addressed the right goals and had financial support. He also said that the selection of capable top managers in public enterprises was crucial. They did not have to be specialists in every field, but should have the intelligence required to choose good engineers, planners, financial analysts, etc.

Kaldor said he found that enterprises were successful when people were motivated by a co-operative spirit. The failure in Britain was due to the alienation of the working class from managers and capitalists. The so-called Bullock Committee had been appointed to find ways to improve the situation, and had prepared a series of proposals, which were no more radical than what already existed in West Germany. But they were received with contempt and unanimously rejected by the managers of industry. Hatred and dislike plagued the British economy. The same situation might be found in Latin America, where there were enormous differences between classes. In Germany, workers identified with their enterprise and realised that their future was interlinked with it. He asked how such a co-operative spirit could be encouraged.

Professor Barkai attributed the success of public enterprise in France to the fact that it was composed of large entities which were led by sophisticated managements. But many developing countries had a shortage of trained managers.

Dr Sacristán said that Mexico realised that in order to develop it was necessary to industrialise. It had set up the *National Financiera* as an organ to promote industrial development. But many successful Mexican entrepreneurs decided to sell their firms to multinational corporations. This created an imbalance. The public preferred to consume imported products, and Mexico had a large foreign debt. There was a shortage of qualified managers, and appointments to public enterprises were often made on the basis of political connections. The ministry of planning was now trying to train more people, and the situation was gradually being improved.

Professor González said, in reference to Kaldor's statement about the importance of well-trained management, that this had some importance, but should not be overstressed. He pointed out that when Mexico nationalised the oil industry in 1938, most of the foreign technicians left and people with little training had to take over their functions overnight. Nevertheless, the level of production was maintained. He also said that after the land reform of 1910 agricultural output in Mexico experienced a great increase, although many of the peasants who received land were illiterate. He said motivation was more important than formal training. Regarding Kaldor's point on co-operation between workers and management, he said that in Mexico unions were represented in the government and thus became part of the power structure, while in France there had been serious struggles between workers and the government.

Dreyfus replied that periods of peaceful co-existence between workers and management alternated with periods of intense disputes, and this constituted a sort of game which both sides had agreed to play. But, basically, the unions were willing to make the system work, and this was the reason for France's success. He considered periodic struggles a healthy phenomenon, and said he hoped they would continue, even if France acquired a socialist government. He stressed that the purpose of an enterprise should be to make people happy, not simply to put out machines.

Addressing the question of how far public enterprise should extend, Dreyfus said that this was essentially a political, not an economic question. There were many different views, and they depended on the time and the country. At present, the majority in France thought that the amount of public enterprise was sufficient. But the French Communist Party wanted to extend the public sector considerably, in order to give France a new industrial orientation. There were also voices calling for a new protectionism. France had strong tariff protection from 1929–33. But if it were reinstituted today, Renault would have to dismiss 50,000 workers. The socialist party preferred to take more modest steps and to work within the limits of available capital.

Kaldor said that in Germany, for example, there was not a big difference between private and public enterprise. The managers of large private industrial enterprises were appointed by a board of supervisors, which consisted of bankers and representatives of the workers. Plans of the firm were discussed between the managers and large banks, which in Germany played the role of the Italian state holding company IRI. If these companies were to become public, little would change. This was even more true in Japan, where the managers of large private enterprises followed the 'administrative guidance' of ministries. In Britain and the United States, things were quite different. Firms were formally controlled by shareholders, but this control operated in a peculiar way. They were under constant threat of being taken over by another corporation through the purchase of a majority of their shares, if the value of their shares fell too low on the stock market. The stock market was considered an advantage by some economists, since it kept managers on their toes to prevent their companies from being bought up. But this form of pressure made managers concentrate on short-term profits, to the neglect of longer run considerations. This was a bane of British industry. The United States had an equally bad record of productivity growth in the last twenty years, but it had started from a higher base.

Dr Marsan said that there was still a difference between control by large banks and control by the government. A bank, for example, would never request a company to rescue the Palermo shipyard.

Professor Arancibia maintained that the special problems which beset the less developed countries, particularly those of Latin America, had as yet not been considered sufficiently in the discussion. The significant role which the state has had to play in our economies is attributable to a number of factors which are found to be fundamentally associated with certain distortions produced by the functioning of the market, among them the weakness of domestic private industry and its limited capacity to contribute effectively to expansion of production. The severity of concentration, limitation of entry, the inelasticity of supply of essential goods, and the necessity of supplying the population with basic services, such as education and health care, are among the reasons which underlie the need for expression of activity by the public sector. In addition, two types of problems have exercised an influence of primary importance: on the one hand, private firms' incapacity for, or lack of interest in, activities with large capital requirements and slow returns, such as the basic industries, so that for them the only remaining alternatives are public enterprises or transnational firms; on the other hand, public initiative has had to take under its care and absorb the losses of private firms which have fallen into bankruptcy in order to avoid aggravation of the already serious unemployment situation or to assure the survival of industries or activities upon which entire regions of the country's interior are dependent. Thus, we are not dealing with invasions by the state of area appropriate for private enterprises but, rather, with responses to serious internal problems and with the preservation of national independence in strategic economic areas. Nor is there more validity to the view suggested earlier, that the state should undertake the risk of initial establishment and then transfer its control to the private sector, because if the state is prepared to supply resources sufficient to acquire a firm which is already productive it would be more useful to devote these to the inauguration of new activities, thereby enhancing the productive capacity of the economy. Finally, it must be noted that in many of our countries a significant portion of the private sector seems to be more disposed toward consumption than toward investment, more inclined to venture its earnings in speculation than on the means of production. Besides, the transfer of firms into the control of transnational corporations is by no means infrequent, with the capital transferred outside the country by the seller. In turn, the transnationals obtain substantial returns by using their equity to promote their own objectives with no regard for the policies and needs of the country in which the firm is located. Under these circumstances, and with no apologies about unexplored elements of the issues, we have only claimed to have shown that the upsurge of public enterprise in the region is not an arbitrary phenomenon, but has been a result of the evolution of our economy, of obstacles to the process of domestic industrialisation, and of the need to attend to the urgent requirements of large segments of the population.

Mr Stoffaes disagreed with an earlier statement by Dreyfus saying that SNCF, the French national railways company, was one of the most efficient enterprises. He objected that it was protected from competition from road transport by quota regulations, that it nevertheless had large deficits, and that, if tariffs were increased, this would shift more traffic to the road.

Dreyfus replied that this was a result of government policy which insisted on low tariffs. If one said that it did poorly, one would have to explain what efficiency meant. Was Peugeot more efficient than Renault because it showed a higher rate of profit? That was easy for Peugeot, since it did not take any risks. By investing less, one would get higher profit rates. Renault had created 100,000 new jobs in rural areas, while Peugeot did not. Renault also paid higher wages and served the national interest in many other ways. The role of public enterprise was to serve the public interest while remaining balanced financially. One thing that Peugeot had learned from Renault was that planning was useful.

Dr Pryke said it would be wrong to consider French public enterprise as a uniform success. Air France, for example, was not very efficient. He said that SNCF did efficiently what it did, but did the wrong things, such as keeping lines open which should be closed from an economic viewpoint. He advised that Latin American countries, in order to make their public enterprises efficient, should give them as little credit as Renault had received.

Marsan said he was not shocked by the deficit of SNCF, if it did its accounting in the same way as a private enterprise, looking only at its own revenues and expenditures, without taking into account the benefits it provided to the public through its services. It also generated income from French engineering firms by purchasing rolling stock from them.

Dreyfus ascribed SNCF's deficit primarily to its artificially low tariffs. He said that because of imminent elections, the government had not wanted tariffs to increase and had preferred a deficit, which could be made up after the elections were over. It might not be possible to justify SNCF's failure to close unprofitable lines, but it was difficult for it to resist the public authorities as long as it incurred deficits and received government financing to cover them.

Baumol agreed that inadvisable public pressure upon firms was a crucial issue. In the United States, he said, private regulated firms were subject to identical pressures. For example, there, too, railroads were prevented from closing down routes which could not cover their costs. It was not easy to find ways to deal with natural monopoly which did not open the way to unjustifiable restrictions upon pricing, exit, entry and other portions of the firms' activities.

Part Three
Studies of Relative Efficiency

12 Public Enterprise in Practice: The British Experience of Nationalisation during the Past Decade[1]

Richard Pryke
UNIVERSITY OF LIVERPOOL

INTRODUCTORY

Public corporations and their subsidiaries now account for some $13\frac{1}{2}$ per cent of the UK's gross domestic product. Several of the undertakings have only recently been transferred to the public sector (shipbuilding, airframe manufacture, British Leyland and water), and others are too small to warrant attention. This paper will discuss the performance of electricity, telephones, coal, British Rail and the other major nationalised industries which appear in Table 12.1. They contribute about $9\frac{1}{2}$ per cent of the GDP, whereas companies and unincorporated businesses are responsible for 61 per cent.

I. PRODUCTION

Are the nationalised industries efficient? One obvious test is whether they are able to satisfy demand; whether they have been successful in marketing and product development; and whether, in areas where there are alternative sources of supply, they have managed to maintain their market shares.

BSC and the Freight Corporation, which are subject to direct competition across the whole range of their business, have both sustained a large decline in market share. In 1968, the first full year after steel nationalisation, BSC's sales of steel were equivalent to 106 per cent of home market deliveries; by 1976 the figure was only 87 per cent. Some reduction was probably inevitable but, due

[1]I have largely confined myself to the past decade partly because the previous period has already been covered in a number of studies and partly due to lack of space. The latter consideration also explains (a) the absence of references; (b) why there is no description of the way in which the productivity and price figures were calculated; (c) why the theoretical foundations on which my analysis rests have not been laid bare; and (d) the omission, except for where they were vital, of explanations, qualifications and supporting evidence.

to its production problems, BSC has constantly had to restrict its sales. As a result exports have fallen, imports have increased, the private sector has expanded and BSC has established a reputation as an unreliable (and not particularly high quality) source of supply. The Corporation had to restrict exports between 1968 and 1970 and found it necessary to import large tonnages to supplement its own production in 1969 and 1970. But it was in 1973 that the problem of steel supply became most acute. Demand was high but the Corporation's output was 5 per cent lower than in 1970 and 3 per cent less than that of its predecessors during 1965. Because of the lack of steel, output was held back in construction and a considerable burden was imposed on the balance of payments. In 1971 the UK's net exports of steel totalled £200m, but by 1976 they were £134m. Although this was a year when the demand for steel was exceptionally low, BSC was still having some difficulty in meeting its customers' requirements.

Between 1968 and 1976 the volume of traffic carried by road haulage undertakings which mainly operate for hire and reward increased by about 25 per cent. However, there was a reduction of around 10 per cent in the work performed by the NFC's general haulage and special traffic companies. In the parcels field private carriers have been gaining business at the expense of the Corporation and the other public sector carriers, partly because the latter have a defective pricing structure.

Apart from the Steel Corporation and NFC most of the nationalised undertakings are the sole suppliers of their principal products. However, there are usually some areas and activities in which they face direct competition. Here they mainly appear to have been losing ground or have failed to gain new business. For instance, the Post Office's parcels traffic has been seriously eroded and until 1976 it did not, because of union opposition, carry unaddressed communications, of which there is a huge volume. The Electricity Boards' revenue from the sale and installation of appliances rose by only 39 per cent between 1971 and 1976, whereas the turnover of privately owned radio and electrical goods shops increased by 81 per cent, excluding television hire. There has also been some reduction in the Gas Corporation's share of the market for gas appliances. BR's shipping division has been outstripped by its competitors on the short sea routes. In 1968 BR earned 42 per cent more revenue than European Ferries and the Irish state-owned B and I Line. By 1976 the combined turnover of these two concerns was 24 per cent larger than BR's.

When we turn to the products for which the nationalised industries are monopoly producers the position is more complicated. The postal services have made little use of selective price reductions to stimulate traffic which could be handled at little extra cost, e.g. direct mail advertising which forms a much larger proportion of mail in America and Japan than it does in Britain. The National and Scottish Bus Groups, which possess local monopolies, have a very poor record in marketing and product development. They do not vary their fares either between routes or between peak and off peak periods, and have been slow to revise their timetables and routes, although some progress is at long last being made. BR has a much better record. There has been a marked improvement in the quality of its Inter-City services which has generated new traffic, since 1968 charges have been varied from service to service and considerable use is now made of concessionary fares in an attempt to fill empty seats. However, the High Speed Train is being introduced about three years behind schedule and the Advanced Passenger Train will be at least five years late. Although there has been a considerable reduction in freight traffic this has been due to the loss of wagonload traffic, which was almost inevitable, and BR has had considerable success in building up its trainload traffic. Gas, electricity and telecommunications have all been successful in developing the use of their products. The two latter industries have off peak tariffs and the waiting time for a new telephone, which was about 6 weeks in 1966, has now been reduced to about 10 days.

II. PRODUCTIVITY

To be regarded as efficient the nationalised industries must do more than satisfy demand: they should employ the minimum quantity of resources to produce the goods and services they provide. Table 12.1 shows the way in which output per unit of labour has been changing in the public enterprise sector and in manufacturing. Between 1963 and 1968 most of the nationalised undertakings made substantial gains in labour productivity. The only industries where there was a rise of less than 3.4 per cent per annum were the postal services (−0.2 per cent p.a.) and the buses (−3.0 per cent p.a.).

During the period 1968–73 productivity continued to increase at a very rapid rate in gas, electricity, telecommunications and airways, and at a moderate rate in NFC; but none of the other industries did better than +2.6 per cent p.a. There was a marked deterioration in the productivity growth rate for BR (from 5.7 per cent to 2.6 per cent p.a.); for steel (from 4.2 per cent p.a. for the industry to 2.5 per cent p.a. for BSC); for coal (from 3.5 per cent to zero) and for the postal services (from −0.2 per cent to −1.4 per cent p.a.). Although the nationalised buses did much better than previously, the rise which they secured (2.2 per cent p.a.) was insufficient to offset the reduction between 1963 and 1968.

Because the economy has of late been so depressed it is difficult to find a period after 1968–73 which does not give a misleading impression. Perhaps the best one to take is 1971–76, as both 1971 and 1976 were years of recession, although the amount of spare capacity was considerably larger in 1976. Over this period there was a substantial reduction in labour productivity in posts (−1.8 per cent p.a.), on BR (−1.7 per cent p.a.), at BSC (−1.6 per cent p.a.) and in coal (at −1.3 per cent p.a.). In buses there appears to have been a modest increase, but this is misleading as output per worker was at a very low ebb in 1971. Between 1968 and 1976, which in the case of buses is a more

TABLE 12.1   PERCENTAGE GROWTH PER ANNUM IN LABOUR AND TOTAL FACTOR PRODUCTIVITY

	Output per equivalent worker[a]			Output per unit of labour and capital	
	1963–68	*1968–73*	*1971–76*	*1963–68*	*1968–73*
British Airways	7.9	7.8	8.7	8.7	6.5
British Gas	7.4	10.9	8.1	–	–
Telecommunications	6.7	7.8	6.8	4.7	4.6
British Rail	5.7	2.6	–1.7	3.3	0.9
British Electricity Boards	5.5	8.8	3.2	0.7	
Steel Industry/BSC[b]	4.2	2.5	–1.6	2.7	0.2
NCB: deep-mined coal	3.5	–	–1.3	–	–
National Freight Corporation	3.4[c,e]	4.0	2.3	–	–
Postal services	–0.2	–1.4	–1.8[e]	–	–
National and Scottish Bus Groups	–3.0[d]	2.2	1.5	–	–
Manufacturing	4.9	4.3	2.9	3.7	2.9

[a] The number of workers was adjusted so as to allow for the decline in hours worked by manual workers.
[b] BSC's iron and steel activities.
[c] Output per man year in the Transport Holding Company's road haulage subsidiaries.
[d] Figure for Tillings and Scottish Bus Groups.
[e] Output per man year.

appropriate period, productivity only rose by 0.6 per cent p.a. When the economy revives, the productivity performance of some of the nationalised industries will probably look more satisfactory. However, it is doubtful whether the situation will be transformed, if only because it was already evident before the energy crisis that labour productivity was stagnant or falling over a large part of the public enterprise sector.

Labour productivity has the obvious weakness that no allowance is made for the use of capital. Estimates of total factor productivity have therefore been made wherever reasonably reliable figures for the gross capital stock are obtainable. Instead of using the (low) profits which the nationalised industries actually earned as the weight for capital, I adopted an opportunity cost approach and estimated the profits that they would have had to make in order to cover their replacement cost depreciation and to earn a return of 10 per cent on their net assets at replacement cost. For the labour weight I used their actual staff costs during my base years, which were 1963 and 1968.

It can be seen from Table 12.1 that, except for airways during 1963–68, total factor productivity increased less rapidly than labour productivity. This was to be expected as economic progress normally involves a growth in the quantity of capital per worker. However, it is a matter for concern that BR and BSC, which both secured a modest rise in labour productivity between 1968 and 1973, had very little increase in total factor productivity (0.9 per cent and 0.2 per cent p.a., respectively). And electricity, which is a high flyer in terms of labour productivity, had a rise of only 0.7 per cent p.a. in overall productivity between 1963 and 1973. (The separate figures for 1963–68 and 1968–73 are misleading because of the build-up and subsequent rundown of capital work in progress.)

The picture which emerges is highly disturbing: the only nationalised industries where productivity is not stagnant or declining are the airways, telecommunications and gas. Moreover, performance appears to have deteriorated as coal, railways and steel used to have moderately high rates of advance.

III. EFFICIENCY

What must now be investigated is whether the industries where there is *prima facie* evidence of inefficiency have had scope to raise their productivity or whether, since gains in production and productivity tend to go hand in hand, they can be excused on the ground that they have had little or no growth in output.

Because of the demand conditions under which they have been operating it would be unreasonable to expect BR and the postal services to have made enormous gains in productivity. Nevertheless, the poor productivity performance of so much of the public enterprise sector cannot be explained away by reference to its output. British Rail managed to bring about a considerable increase in its productivity between 1963 and 1968 despite the handicap of a 9 per cent decline in traffic. As we have seen, the postal services, BSC and the Freight Corporation would have produced more if they had made the most of the opportunities which were open and had not sustained a decline in their market shares. Although the Electricity Boards' output has been growing at above the average rate they have only managed to achieve a small increase in total factor productivity. Finally, there is no reason to believe that rising production has a beneficial effect on productivity in coal because inferior seams have to be worked.

What does help to explain the slow progress of so much of the public enterprise sector is that by 1968 some previous sources of productivity growth were drying up. In coal a very important contribution had been made by cutter-loaders, where installation was complete, and by self-advancing pit props, where it was far advanced. Furthermore, the benefit of the post-war programme of colliery modernisation and reconstruction, which was still being felt in 1963, had come to an end by 1968. Between 1963 and 1968 BR made considerable productivity gains through the replacement of steam by diesel and electric traction. During 1968 this process was completed and by then the more obvious measures of rationalisation, initiated in the Reshaping Report of 1963, had been carried through.

Nevertheless, as their own plans show, even coal and railways had ample scope for higher productivity. In 1969 the NCB forecast that output per manshift would increase by over 75 per cent between 1968–69 and 1975–76. It only rose by 5 per cent. There was probably an element of wishful thinking in the Board's estimate but, as we shall see, it did have solid reasons for believing that OMS would continue to increase rapidly. The financial forecasts which British Rail prepared for the Government's Joint Steering Group in 1967 appear to have assumed that rail employment would be reduced to less than 200,000 in 1974. A new estimate by work study staff in 1969 showed that the labour force could be cut to 201,000 by the end of 1974. At the latter date BR still had 233,000 workers.

Large gains in productivity and/or reductions in employment were also forecast for steel and posts. In 1966 the Benson Committee concluded that the steel industry could increase its labour productivity by 6.8 per cent over the period 1965–75. Its employment estimate for the industry implies that BSC ought to have had only about 160,000 *steel* workers in 1975. In September 1975 there were 180,500, although production was far lower than had been predicted. The Benson Committee was trying to show that there was no need for nationalisation and may therefore have been over optimistic. However, in 1969 BSC made a detailed estimate of its future manning requirements which indicated that its *total* employment should fall by nearly 50,000 to about 205,000 in 1975. At that date it still had 220,000 workers, although it produced only 17m tonnes of crude steel as against the 33m tonnes that had been envisaged. In 1972 it was forecast that the postal services would make a staff saving of 25,000 by 1978. Between April 1972 and April 1977 there was a reduction of 2,500!

That these industries have scope for greater efficiency is also clear from their inefficient use of labour and capital: Since 1968 the NCB has introduced cutter-loaders which are more productive and more reliable. Tunnelling has been partly mechanised and there has been a considerable extension of retreat working, which is more efficient than the normal advancing system. Despite this there has been a substantial decline in the productivity of workers engaged on tunnelling and no improvement in the utilisation of cutter-loaders. A study in March 1976 showed they were only at work for $1\frac{3}{4}$ hours per shift, i.e. a third of the available working time. One important reason appears to be a lack of motivation on the part of the labour force as a result of the elimination of piecework from 1966 onwards. The Board attempted from 1971 onwards to negotiate an incentive scheme with the mineworkers' union, because it believed that this would increase productivity by about 10 per cent. However, it was impossible to secure an effective system partly as a result of opposition from some union leaders and within the mining community, and partly because of the inhibiting effect of the Labour Government's pay policy. It was not until the end of 1977 that the NCB was able at long last to begin introducing productivity payments.

British Rail is highly inefficient. Large numbers of 'firemen' are still carried on diesel and electric trains and guards are retained both on passenger trains with power doors and on fully braked freight trains. On other freight trains they could be dispensed with by getting rid of loose coupled wagons: a process which was completed during the 1930s in other West European countries. It should also be possible drastically to reduce the number of drivers. This could be done by speeding up freight trains, which average only about $22\frac{1}{2}$ mph, and by increasing driving time, which averages around $3\frac{3}{4}$ hours out of an 8-hour turn of duty. Ticket collectors are unnecessary. The guard can do the job on Inter-City trains and ticket barriers can be installed on suburban routes. Moreover, there has, despite mechanisation, been a decline in the mileage of track per manual worker engaged on the upkeep of the railway system, and BR recognises that a large reduction could be made in white-collar labour. Save for the latter area the Board has not even tried to persuade the unions to accept the staff cuts and changes in working practice that are necessary, although it has at last tentatively placed guards on the negotiating agenda.

British Steel is overmanned and does not make proper use of its plant. A recent comparison between Llanwern and the Belgian Sidmar, which both make strip mill products, showed that the British plant had a third more workers per ton of crude steel capacity. However, this considerably understates the difference because, although Llanwern is slightly less modern, hours are shorter at Sidmar and it tends to make products which require more labour, etc. At Llanwern the proportion of white-collar workers was higher (32 per cent versus 22 per cent) even though Sidmar is an independent works. On the blue-collar side equipment tended to be more generously manned and so did the maintenance and service departments. One important reason is that demarcation lines are far stricter at Llanwern. Not only is Llanwern overmanned but less of its capacity is utilised. Poor use of plant is a general problem in BSC. During 1973 the Corporation only tapped its basic oxygen furnaces about 170 times per week, although the most efficient foreign producers were achieving around 250 heats.

There is also scope for raising productivity in the postal services. The mechanisation of letter sorting is still at a relatively early stage, although it was originally planned that it would by now have been applied to 75 per cent of all traffic. Nor, due to the opposition of its workers, has the Post Office applied the improved methods, devised in the late sixties, for measuring the volume of work at sorting offices and deciding how many staff are required. This is urgent as there was a rise of 15 per cent between 1967–68 and 1975–76 in sorting time per unit of mail. Postal work is concentrated at particular times of day but little use is made of part-time staff, although they are used extensively on the continent. Unfortunately, there is union opposition to their employment.

It may therefore be concluded that the NCB, BR, BSC and postal services all have considerable scope for higher productivity; and the same is true of the nationalised buses. What requires further examination is the performance of those undertakings which have had the advantage of rapidly rising output. My impression is that gas is reasonably efficient but that telecommunications has been less successful. It has failed to meet its manpower targets, its labour productivity appears to be signficantly lower than that of some foreign administrations, and it has fallen seriously behind in the introduction of advanced exchange equipment. Gas, on the other hand, deserves credit for the speed with which it has converted to natural gas.

IV. PRICES AND WAGES

The nationalised industries' productivity performance helps to explain the way in which they have raised their prices. As Table 12.2 shows, most of the undertakings increased their charges by less than the average amount between 1963 and 1968, but in contrast raised them more than average between 1968 and 1976. Coal, posts, steel and buses had to make very large increases because of the exceptionally rapid growth in their staff costs per unit of output. BR raised its charges somewhat more than average despite the escalation in its losses. This was due to the big rise in its unit staff costs. NFC, where there was a switch from a gross trading loss to a small trading profit, also made an unusually large increase in prices.

Electricity raised its prices in line with inflation and only gas, airways and telecommunications had less than the average increase. Their staff costs per unit increased relatively slowly but electricity experienced a very large increase in its fuel bill, primarily because of the enormous rise in the cost of coal. Gas, on the other hand, had the advantage that its unit fuel costs remained the same due to the switch to North Sea gas.

Unit staff costs would have increased less rapidly but for the exceptionally rapid rate at which earnings have increased. As Table 12.2 indicates the

TABLE 12.2   PRICES, STAFF COSTS, EARNINGS AND PROFITABILITY

	% Increase in prices[a]		% Increase in staff costs per unit of output	% Increase in average weekly earnings of manual men		Gross trading surplus as % of turnover[i]		Trading surplus after depreciation at replacement cost[i]
	1963–68	1968–76	1968–76	1963–68	1968–76	1968	1976	1976 (£M)
NCB: deep-mined coal	12.9[b]	295.5[b]	325.8	28.3	226.9	8.8[j]	8.4[j]	−25
BSC: iron and steel	7.5[b]	227.1[b]	241.5	35.7	229.1	8.6[k]	4.5[j]	−239[j,k]
British Gas	2.3[c]	51.9	96.6	39.0	220.4	18.0[j]	35.7[j]	365[j]
British Electricity Boards	22.0[c]	142.5	131.8	21.3	241.9	41.0[j]	25.9[j]	−26
British Rail	8.6	160.3	322.0	49.1	197.6	1.4	−22.0	−430
National and Scottish Bus Groups	45.9[d]	193.6	245.6	39.9[g]	213.2[g]	10.4	−3.5	−56
National Freight Corporation	20.2[e]	182.6	156.6[f]	–	–	−3.6	4.2[f]	−13[f]
British Airways	5.2	78.6	78.8	33.5[h]	172.3[h]	20.5[j]	14.1[j]	66[j]
Postal services	43.7	276.6	270.0[f]	38.8	200.8	3.6[f,j]	11.0[f,j]	110[f,j]
Telecommunications	7.6	125.0	79.7[f]	36.6	187.2	44.6[f,j]	52.0[f,j]	804[f,j]
Manufacturing	15.3[b]	144.3[b]	178.2			–	–	4009[l,m]

[a] Revenue per unit of output except where otherwise stated.
[b] Base weighted index. Wholesale price indices for coal, iron and steel and manufacturing.
[c] Excluding retailing, etc.
[d] The Tillings and Scottish Bus Groups' revenue per journey.
[e] Figure for Transport Holding Company's road haulage subsidiaries.
[f] Excludes supplementary pension fund contributions.
[g] Road passenger transport excluding London Transport.
[h] Air passenger transport.
[i] Including rent, except for companies; excluding subsidies, except those covering concessionary fare schemes on buses; and ignoring costs of closure.
[j] Financial year beginning in year shown.
[k] Year to end September 1968.
[l] Excluding stock appreciation.
[m] Industrial and commercial companies.

average weekly earnings of manual men rose more rapidly in the nationalised industries than in manufacturing between 1968 and 1976. The relatively large increase in weekly earnings has not been due to the way in which the amount of overtime has changed. Between April 1970 and April 1976 average hourly earnings, excluding overtime, increased faster in all of the nationalised industries for which there is information than they did in manufacturing.

The rapid rise during the seventies is partly explained by the fact that in coal and electricity average *weekly* earnings had lagged behind in the sixties. This was due to the productivity deal in electricity which drastically reduced the number of hours worked, and to the restraint which the NUM, then under moderate leadership, exercised with the object of preserving employment. Moreover, as a result of the Power-loading Agreement, which eliminated piecework, the growth in pieceworkers' earnings was exceptionally slow, especially in those areas where it had previously been highest. As a result, militancy replaced moderation and in place of local piecework negotiations there was a national drive for higher earnings, which resulted in two protracted and damaging strikes. In the other nationalised industries unions were concerned that they should not drop behind because of the Conservative Government's policy of pay restraint, which was initially brought to bear in the public sector. The result of this and of the general upsurge in militancy, which particularly affected the nationalised industries as one of the most strongly unionised sections of the economy, was a wave of industrial action. In 1971, 1972 and 1974 the nationalised industries with 7 per cent of all employment accounted for 40–50 per cent of days lost in strikes. The extent to which the public enterprise sector has contributed to wage and price inflation requires detailed investigation, but there is little doubt that during the period 1968–76 it was significant.

V. PROFITABILITY, PRICING POLICY AND SUBSIDIES

As a result of large price increases the nationalised industries' finances are now considerably more healthy than they were in the mid seventies. Nevertheless, the only undertakings which during 1976 earned amounts sufficient to cover their replacement cost depreciation were telecommunications, the Gas Corporation, the postal services and British Airways. The airways' net surplus was equivalent to 7.7 per cent on their net assets at replacement cost, and for telecommunications the figure was 7.2 per cent. At the other end of the financial spectrum were BR and the nationalised buses. Neither managed to meet its operating costs and both were heavily subsidised. BSC was also in serious financial difficulties.

Where nationalised undertakings face direct competition it is instructive to compare their financial performance with that of their private rivals. During 1975 the Freight Corporation had a trading surplus equivalent to only 0.7 per cent of its turnover, and this excludes National Carriers and Freightliners (which had large losses). Meanwhile the leading privately-owned road haulage contractors, with a combined revenue that was slightly larger, earned a profit of 5.0 per cent on their turnover. In 1976, which was a more normal year, the NFC, once again excluding National Carriers and Freightliners, had a profit margin of 2.5 per cent. However, the Transport Development Group and United Carriers which are two of the largest road haulage contractors in the private sector, earned 9.7 per cent on their turnover (compared with 8.6 per cent in 1975). The Electricity Boards' retailing and contracting side may be compared with Currys which is the leading private electrical chain store. During 1976–77 the Boards made a profit equivalent to 0.7 per cent of their revenue. Currys, with a turnover about half as large, had a profit margin of 8.0 per cent. BR's shipping services are another peripheral activity where comparisons are possible. In 1976 they sustained an operating loss of 2.5 per cent on turnover, but B and I made a profit of 3.5 per cent and European Ferries one of 9.2 per cent after substantial interest payments.

The fact that a large part of public enterprise production is sold at a loss would appear to show that resources are being wasted. It may however be objected that in the short run resources are not being misallocated provided that avoidable costs are being covered. However, in many cases losses have been persistent and there is no sign that they are being eliminated, e.g. in British Rail and the nationalised buses. Moreover, in coal and in other cases there is a substantial amount of output where even avoidable costs are not met.

It may be thought that BR should be subsidised because railways are a declining cost industry.[1] But this not only ignores the misallocation which the extra taxation involves, but also overlooks the fact that BR has been undertaking heavy investment because it believes its track capacity to be inadequate. Furthermore, for much of its traffic the revenue is insufficient to cover its direct costs. The provision of inherently unprofitable rail and bus services could be justified on the ground that if each passenger could be made to pay as much as he were prepared to, revenue would exceed costs, i.e. the consumers' surplus is greater than the deficit. However, this is often implausible because of the size of the losses, and cost benefit studies indicate that a large number of rural rail services have no justification.

The subsidisation of public transport may be regarded as beneficial because it is held that, especially in congested urban areas, the private marginal cost of using private transport is less than the social marginal cost. It is, however, extremely doubtful whether society benefits (a) because the divergence between the cost and the subsidised price of public transport is generally greater than the divergence for private transport; (b) because, as numerous studies have shown, lower fares are unlikely to cause any great shift from public to private transport, and increased traffic will mainly represent journeys that would not previously have been made; (c) because any transfer that does occur is likely to intensify congestion on commuter trains; (d) because any freight that is

---

[1] I have examined this and the points which follow in detail in *The Rail Problem* (with John Dodgson) and in my contributions to *A Policy for Transport* (the Nuffield Foundation).

attracted to the railways may well involve road collection and delivery; and (e) because subsidisation will hinder the adoption of preferable policies such as road pricing.

Another argument for producing at a loss is that it will not result in any waste of resources if the workers involved would otherwise be unemployed. At present there is general unemployment as a result of the Government's counter-inflationary policies. In this situation the maintenance of employment in the nationalised industries is likely to result in higher unemployment in the rest of the economy. Moreover, where, as in the case of BR's 'firemen', workers are wholly unproductive, no output will be sacrificed if they are made redundant. Similar considerations apply where production is continued at high-cost plants although if output were transferred to efficient works they would require little or no extra labour. This is the situation in steel (and probably coal) where at the Government's insistence BSC has delayed the closure of plants which it wants to shut. Such policies, however attractive they may appear, demoralise management and foster the feeling among workers that they do not have to accept industrial change.

Thus it appears that where nationalised industries are producing at a loss resources are in general being misallocated. Moreover, there is extensive cross-subsidisation within some of the profitable undertakings. In telecommunications large losses have persistently been made on the rental of apparatus and facilities. These are offset by the high profits earned from trunk calls. In the (inland) postal services the same rate is charged irrespective of distance or destination, despite the enormous variation in costs. It should however be noted that gas is at long last being sold to industry at a price more or less equivalent to that of oil.

VI. POOR PERFORMANCE EXPLAINED

It must be concluded that a substantial waste of resources is occurring within the public enterprise sector due both to technical inefficiency and to misallocation. The nationalised industries must not be judged too harshly because the private sector is also woefully inefficient. Nevertheless, even by British standards their performance appears to be poor. What is particularly disturbing is that the progress which was being made during the sixties has not in general been maintained. This is particularly evident in the area of productivity.

It seems clear that many of the nationalised industries have been badly managed. Examples of mismanagement abound. Much of BSC's planning has been very poor. The forecasts which it made in its Development Plan of 1971 were totally unrealistic (production of $42\frac{1}{2}$m ingot tonnes in 1980–81!). In the Corporation's strategic study of 1972 it was taken for granted that smaller works should be shut and the exercise was so conducted as to yield the desired results: the largest possible amount of big plant and the closure of medium-sized works. Time and energy have been wasted on administrative reorganisation. In 1970 plants were regrouped on a product basis, but in 1976 BSC switched over to geographical divisions. BR's first and second Corporate Plans were seriously overoptimistic, as was evident to the civil servants who vetted them. A policy of high investment was adopted in 1973, although it was clear that there was no economic case for much of the expenditure. During 1973 NFC embarked on an ill-conceived programme of expansion on the Continent from which it aimed to secure half its turnover by 1978. Most of the companies acquired were duds, and huge losses were incurred. Moreover, the National Bus Company manages to lose money on its express coaches.

The adverse effects of bad management within the nationalised industries have been compounded by the obstructive and restrictive attitude of their workers and the unions to which they belong. There are honourable exceptions. The electricians' union played a highly constructive part in the negotiation and implementation of the productivity deal of the mid-sixties. As a result the Electricity Boards secured a rise of 24 per cent in the workload per manual worker between 1967 and 1970. This shows what is possible where unions are co-operative, but as we have seen they have been obstructive in posts and coal. The same is true in railways and, to a lesser extent, steel. Although BR is to blame for not having tried to negotiate the changes in working practice that are obviously necessary, there is no doubt that ASLEF, the footplate union, would bitterly oppose the removal of second men. Indeed, it has recently succeeded in having co-drivers placed on high speed trains. In steel a series of productivity agreements have been negotiated but opposition within the unions has prevented their full implementation.

The Government has made its contribution to the industries' poor performance. During the sixties financial targets and economic guidelines, including marginal cost pricing and dcf, were laid down. Moreover, the Prices and Incomes Board devoted particular attention to improving their performance. Despite obvious weaknesses, this system of control had a favourable effect on performance. Unfortunately, the PIB was killed off in 1971; and the financial targets were rendered meaningless by mounting inflation, the policy of price restraint (1971–74) and the heavy subsidies that became necessary. In railways and buses large-scale financial support was adopted as a permanent measure. Under the 1968 Transport Act BR was provided with a relatively small subsidy to cover the losses on what were termed its social passenger services, but the rest of the system was intended to pay its way. No real attempt was made to make the Act work and in 1973 the Government decided that, rather than compel the Board to adopt unpopular policies, it would provide a virtually open-ended subsidy.

There is little doubt that these developments, together with an increasing amount of *ad hoc* intervention, have damaged efficiency. That subsidisation has an enervating effect is shown by the railways. Soon after BR was granted a permanent subsidy there was a dramatic reduction in productivity growth; and the decision to extend subsidisation was followed by a vigorous recruitment drive. Employment was pushed up by 8000 between the end of 1973 and

March 1975. It was only when the Board was told that there could be no further increase in passenger support that the labour force started to be cut back. And it appears that BR will, as instructed, eliminate its freight deficit during 1978, although it had been arguing that a permanent subsidy was necessary.

The various factors which account for the poor performance of so many of the nationalised industries seldom operate in isolation. On the contrary, they tend to reinforce each other. This is illustrated by what has happened in steel. The inherent weakness of BSC's strategic study of 1972 meant that it was only too easy for the Labour Government to pick holes in the associated programme of plant closure which the Conservatives had sanctioned. As a result the Corporation has been made to keep open plants some of which ought to have been shut. Another example of cumulative causation is the way in which the subsidies that BR has received have weakened management and this, in turn, has resulted in higher losses, greater subsidies and still worse management. The knowledge that subsidies are available has also made the railway unions even less co-operative than they might otherwise have been. Moreover, the obstructive nature of the unions has provided BR with a convenient excuse for inertia. Besides the particular cases that can be cited, there is one general way in which poor government has been responsible for weak management; constant *ad hoc* intervention in the affairs of the nationalised industries has made it difficult for Ministers to find first-rate men who are willing to run them.

To attribute poor performance to a combination of bad management, restrictive unions and Government failure begs the question of why the situation has deteriorated. There may have been an element of accident here. Some of those who were placed in charge of the nationalised industries during the sixties happened, like Beeching and Robens, to be men of outstanding ability. In contrast some of the more recent Chairmen have turned out to be very poor appointments. This has been true in the case of British Rail, the Steel Corporation and NFC. However, there have been more fundamental reasons why the performance of the public enterprises sector has deteriorated. One obvious cause has been the growing difficulties of the British economy. As a result the nationalised industries have been increasingly used as a tool for Government intervention and this, besides its adverse effect on their labour relations and finances, has led to confusion over the Boards' objectives and provided them with a ready excuse for failure. As unemployment has mounted it has become increasingly difficult for the industries to pursue policies which will lead to the loss of jobs, and Ministries have become less willing to enforce or even sanction them. Moreover, the greater power, growing militancy and increasing industrial conservatism of trade unions, has had an adverse effect on the public enterprise sector, where they are particularly strong. Their strength is due to the nature of the industries that have been brought into public ownership, to the way in which nationalisation raises workers' expectations, to the Boards' obligation to be model employers, and to the influence which the unions have over the Labour Party. Another factor which helps to explain the deterioration in the nationalised industries' record has been the growing power of environmentalists and the growth of the belief, to which economists have greatly contributed, that the social and private interests of the nationalised industries frequently diverge. This has encouraged the view that they should not behave commercially but need to be subsidised.

Discussion of Dr Pryke's Paper

Dr Pryke, in his opening remarks, offered a set of five hypotheses that he had inferred from his investigations:

(1) Nationalised industries did relatively worse than private industries when the economy performed badly because (a) union resistance to the dismissal of workers was stronger than in private industry, (b) politicians did not want to create unemployment, because of short-term considerations, (c) there was a temptation for *ad hoc* intervention, and (d) price restraints upon public enterprises designed to reduce inflation led to losses.

(2) Unconditiònal subsidies led to loss of control over costs and tended to escalate.

(3) Nationalised industries should be expected to cover their own costs. Problems of inequality should be tackled by other means, such as taxation and redistribution.

(4) New devices were needed to increase productivity in public enterprises – means such as productivity targets and five-yearly efficiency audits.

(5) Monopolies should be avoided where possible. If a nationalised industry was in competition with private industry, the government could let it contract if it did not improve its efficiency.

Dr Tardos said the crucial problem was whether nationalised industries were efficient. Pryke had reached a negative answer, and had provided many warning stories in his excellent paper. He had given a number of explanations for this, such as technical inefficiency, bad management, obstructive behaviour by workers, *ad hoc* intervention, etc. But this still left unsettled the fundamental reason for the factors inducing inefficiency. He did not want to blame Pryke for not going into greater detail; his paper offered a fairly concrete analysis. But even his results concerning the measurement of efficiency are not fully convincing and do not say much about ways of possible improvement and about the existing constraints. However, some people make statements of this type, not based on comprehensive scientific research but only on wishful thinking. In this connection he praised the careful empirical investigation in Savas' paper. But he said, even in this evaluation, the measurement of the population's satisfaction was lacking. It is conceivable that people may prefer waste disposal to be provided as a public service, rather than to have to solicit competitive bids and worry about the slightly higher cost. Tardos said he thought that for the explanation of the comparative efficiency of state and private business performances we should know more about the costs and benefits of economic activities. Moreover, we should understand more about the desires of the societies which do not select a social order on the basis of cost-benefit analyses alone. Finally, it is an even more important and promising task to explore what institutional changes are necessary for the improvement of both private and public economic performances than to give criteria for choosing between them.

M. Dreyfus said that large private enterprises also found it difficult to dismiss workers. *Pryke* agreed, but said it was a matter of degree. Private enterprise could at least be threatened by bankruptcy, but in a subsidised public enterprise this threat was removed. *Dreyfus* also said that in some areas, where scale economies were present, it was necessary to have a monopoly. But in those areas where a public enterprise was in competition with private enterprise, it was important that the public enterprise be given no special advantage by the government, so that it would not relax its efforts.

Dr Srinivasan said that the Indian government usually took over 'sick enterprises', to protect employment, and if a comparison of efficiency between nationalised and private firms were made, the outcome would probably be in favour of the latter. *Pryke* replied he had considered a fair spectrum of both growth (such as gas and airlines) and stagnating industries (such as railroads and postal services) in his survey. *Srinivasan* also pointed out that firms which were granted a monopoly through tariff protection from foreign competition manifested no cost discipline. Foreign trade could help make them more cost conscious.

Kaldor mentioned that Pryke had published a book in 1971 in which he sought to dispel the widely-held belief that public enterprise was less efficient than private enterprise. In the meantime he had completely changed his mind. For this he could either be taken *more* seriously, since he had been willing to advocate public enterprise only as long as the evidence supported it, or he might be judged simply to have leaped to the opposite extreme. It might be like disappointed love that had turned into hate. *Pryke* said he was aware of that danger, and had made an effort to avoid it, but the audience would have to judge.

Kaldor also offered as an explanation for the poor performance of the nationalised industries in Britain in the present decade, the fact that the Conservative government had forced them to hold back on price increases, and in this way had subsidised the private industries which bought inputs from them. *Professor Savas* objected that this was no excuse. A principal problem of public enterprises was precisely this – their vulnerability to such pressures.

Kaldor disagreed with a statement by Pryke that government efforts to maintain employment in the short run had led to higher unemployment in the long run. As the main reason for the high unemployment in Great Britain, he saw her entry into the Common Market. This had led to a great increase in imports of manufactured products from the Continent which penetrated the British market. The increase in exports to Europe was much smaller, because British firms were less competitive.

Professor Barkai agreed with Pryke's view that public enterprises should be financially self-sufficient, but with an important qualification. If a firm could use only its own profits to finance investments, this would hurt fast-growing industries, because they would be squeezed for funds. On the other hand, it would help maintain industries which actually ought to contract. He proposed that public firms should be allowed to issue stocks and bonds on a capital market, so that savings would flow to the most efficient firms as the highest bidders.

Professor Vickrey saw unemployment as the key factor in the poor performance of public enterprises. This problem would have to be cured before they could improve their efficiency. As an illustration, he mentioned that in New Zealand ticket takers on commuter trains were passengers on the way to their office, who were employed part-time. This was possible only because of very low unemployment. On the other hand, United States railroads had not been able to eliminate superfluous employees, the so-called practice of 'featherbedding'.

Pryke said the suspicion that the Conservative government had appointed less qualified managers to public enterprises than the Labour government was unfounded. Both had appointed men who were usually smooth and amicable, but have sometimes turned out to be hopelessly incompetent. He concluded by saying that there was no single cause for the poor performance of public enterprise in Britain, but there were many factors which reinforced one another. It was important to bring them to light so that remedies could be found.

13 Incentives, Efficiency, and Social Control: The Case of The Kibbutz

Haim Barkai
HEBREW UNIVERSITY, JERUSALEM

I. THE A PRIORI CASE AGAINST COLLECTIVES

Material incentives have been identified as the dominant motivating force of economic activity in Adam Smith's felicitous dictum on the subject: 'In civilized society [man] stands at all times in need of the co-operation and assistance of great multitudes . . . it is vain for him to expect it from their benevolence only. He will be more likely to prevail if he can interest their self-love in his favour, and show them that it is for their own advantage to do for him what he requires of them' (Smith, 1937, p. 14).

This presumption on the motive power of economic activity is taken for granted in industrial societies. And not only capitalist societies; Stalin's well-known statement of egalitarianism, in which he identified it as a 'petty bourgeois' concept, belies this notion. His opinion that payment by results, and hence wage differentials, are an integral element of the socialist, centrally planned economy, was put into practice in the Soviet Union in the early 1930s and has since been the rule in all centrally planned economies.[1]

If material incentives directly linked to performance are indeed the only, or at least the most effective way to induce economic agents to strive and to keep enterprises ticking, it follows that economic units which reject payment by results cannot survive. Thus collectives, and indeed any system run along collective principles, are doomed – sooner rather than later – to failure. Consequently, the kibbutz, which in its attempt to maintain equality has cut the direct link between an individual's contribution to production and the real

[1]This opinion was stated in the famous Six Point Speech delivered at a conference of managerial workers in June 1931. See Dobb (1957), p. 259; Baykov (1946), pp. 226–7; and Nove (1969), pp. 208–9.

income from which he benefits, cannot be considered viable.[1] If indeed such collective communities could persist at all it could be only as wards of some organisation ready to foot the bill. Even then their living standards would, in Smith's phrase, depend on the 'benevolence . . . of [their] brethren' and would, at best, be at the lower end of the income distribution.

II. THE KIBBUTZ VIABILITY DEBATE

During the spurt of Zionist resettlement activity in the 1920s about 25 kibbutzim appeared on the scene in the newly established political entity, mandatory Palestine. Their establishment, with its call on financial resources, immediately gave rise to an acrimonious debate about their viability. Two strains of reasoning, not always clearly spelled out, may be distinguished in the statements and arguments which led such people as the well-known sociologist Franz Oppenheimer, Elwood Mead (a leading American agronomist at that time) and many leading personalities in industry, business, and politics to conclude that kibbutzim were bound to fail.

The first of these two related yet distinct arguments, alluded to mainly by Oppenheimer and his followers, is an impossibility theorem of the Von Mises type applied to the collective as a microeconomic unit.[2] This suggests that the abolition of wages means that these units cannot set a price for the factor of production labour, which in turn implies the absence of a proper set of relative factor prices and, hence, the impossibility of an efficient allocation of resources.

Yet the rational–economic–calculation case against the kibbutz did not occupy the foreground of this debate. The opponents of the Zionist experiment in collective farming put the main burden of their case on the absence of incentives. The linchpin of their argument was the Smithian proposition that effort is positively and strongly related to material incentives. Since effort-related material benefits (and dismissals) are 'out-of-bounds', the performance of the human element in the collective must inevitably be below its potential. And below-potential performance by workers, management, and entrepreneurs *ipso facto* means that the whole organisation must be inefficient.

Referring to the inherent weaknesses of collectives, they dwelt on three features in particular: the absence of 'property ethics', leading to mistreatment

[1]The *modus operandi* of the kibbutz, which identifies it as a full collective (a socialist community) is summarised in Barkai (1977, pp. 7–10). What interests us here is the principle of equality – in the distribution of income – which involves the severance of the link between an individual's contribution to production and the real income allocated to him; behaviour is of course affected by the whole socio-economic fabric. The inherent problem of a public entity, whether run as an administrative unit or as a public enterprise, is evidently due to the severance of the link between rewards and effort at the entrepreneurial level and the rather tenuous link between them at the managerial level.

[2]Oppenheimer was of course aware of the Von Mises thesis, propounded in a well-known book published in 1920, but his contributions to the viability debate were published before the publication of Taylor's, and Dickinson's later rebuttal of the Von Mises thesis.

of stock and inventories; the absence of effort-linked rewards which penalises the industrious worker; and the consequent absence of managerial ability and entrepreneurial talent and drive. All of these, it was suggested, are manifestations of the fatal flaw of the collective – the feebleness of economic motivation, if not its total absence.

The prediction that *communistic colonies* were bound to fail in short order was forcefully expressed in a well-known document submitted in 1928 by Elwood Mead to the Joint Palestine Survey Commission. He voiced doubts about . . . 'the ultimate outcome of the experiment in communistic cultivation of the land and equal division of income', and came to the conclusion that 'the almost universal failure of such experiments elsewhere emphasizes the wisdom of so designing houses and farm buildings [to be built for kibbutzim] as to make them suitable for use by the cultivators of individual farms' (Mead, 1928, pp. 57–8; see also pp. 443–5).

Within the Zionist establishment even the supporters of the collective-settlement experiment entertained doubts on this score, and did not dismiss the incentive and differentials argument of the opponents. Yet having personal contact with the enthusiastic young pioneers who sought Zionist and socialist fulfilment in collective settlements, they believed and hoped that ideology might somehow substitute for material incentives. They therefore argued that the 'experiment', as they kept describing it, should be allowed a chance. Their attitude is expressed in the following excerpt from a speech by Ruppin: 'I do not know whether the kvutzot will, in the years to come, fulfill all the hopes of the Kvutzah[1] members. . . . In any case we have no right . . . to condemn the Kvutzot in advance and on a purely doctrinaire basis simply because they happen to represent something new. They should be given fair play and judged by their economic results. So far, our experience does not justify us in placing the Kvutzot above or below the Moshav Ovdim [cooperative settlements] as far as economic results are concerned.[2] Thus even the supporters of the movement, who fought tooth and nail to provide the minimum funds needed to give the kibbutzim a chance of survival, were doubtful about their future.

III. PERFORMANCE IN RETROSPECT

Population and living standards

The predicted failure of the collectives has not materialised, at least in the short-run period of 50 years. The prophecy of impending doom was made in the years in which the movement was still in its infancy, with a population not much over 2000 scattered in two score settlements. By now the kibbutz population is over 100,000 in 250 settlements. Current living standards simply cannot be compared with those of the struggling settlements of the 1920s. Per capita consumption has grown by a factor of 5 in the 40 years since 1936. A

---

[1] The earlier term for kibbutz.
[2] Ruppin (1936) pp. 162–3. See also pp. 155–9 and the article *The Kvutsah*, pp. 131–41.

reasonable guess would put it about six times what it was when the viability debate was at its height.

An even more significant indication, for this purpose, is afforded by a comparison of kibbutz living standards with those of the country as a whole. Estimates for the late 1960s and (preliminary) estimates for the 1970s suggest that kibbutz per capita income and per capita consumption expenditures were well within the sixth and seventh deciles of the respective distributions for the country as a whole.[1] This means that per capita income in kibbutzim was above $3000, Israel's average for the late 1960s.

The time pattern of productivity

The significant rise in population, the simultaneous and striking rise in living standards, and the place of kibbutz income in the countrywide distribution have, on the face of it, falsified the gloomy forecasts of the 1920s. Yet the contradiction between prediction and reality can perhaps still be explained in terms of the Smithian conceptual framework on which the prediction was based. The present high per capita income can conceivably be attributed to the comparatively high and arguably excessive capital intensities in the kibbutz production sector. If so, this would imply that the marginal productivity of real capital is low, or at least that its returns are below the alternative cost of marginal funds. It would also suggest that kibbutzim disregard the signals emitted by relative factor and product prices, since excessive capital intensities imply an improper response in terms of factor allocation.

These hypotheses can be tested by means of conventional production–function analysis, which allows for simultaneous estimates of factor elasticities and, hence, the derivation of estimates of marginal factor productivity and an index of total factor productivity. An extensive study of factor productivity in kibbutz farming and manufacturing, based on data for the whole population of the more than 200 settlements existing in the 1950s and 1960s, offers relevant information on this issue. The main results, obtained from several alternative variants of single-equation cross-section models, are summarised in Table 13.1.

Consider first the total factor productivity indexes for agriculture and manufacturing, which rose by 76 per cent (in 12 years) and 97 per cent (in 10 years), respectively [columns (4) and (7)]. These figures, which represent annual rates for rising overall efficiency of over 5 and 7 per cent for agriculture and manufacturing respectively, suggest that kibbutz performance in a rapidly growing economy has by no means lagged behind.

These data refer to only a decade out of the half-century of the movement's history, and cannot by themselves settle the issue. A comparison of marginal factor productivity in the kibbutz and the economy at large and an inspection of the time pattern of factor productivity offer more insight to the efficiency

---

[1] The very low values of the interkibbutz Lorenz inequality index indicate that the mean for the movement is a good proxy for comparisons with the countrywide distributions.

The data on living standards, on the comparative standing of kibbutzim within the community and on interkibbutz equality are from Barkai (1977), pp. 149–58 and Tables 8.5 to 8.8.

TABLE 13.1   INDICATORS OF PRODUCTIVITY IN AGRICULTURE AND MANUFACTURING

| | Agriculture[a] | | | | Manufacturing[b] | | |
| | Marginal product of | | | | Marginal product of | | |
	Labour (1958 IL/ man-year) (1)	Capital: real rate of return (2)	Land (1958 IL/ dunam) (3)	Total factor productivity (4)	Labour (1958 IL/ man-year) (5)	Capital: real rate of return (6)	Total factor productivity (7)
1954	3016	0.066	10.7	76.3	–	–	–
1955	4186	0.062	2.1	79.2	–	–	–
1956	4446	0.085	4.0	89.7	6318	0.082	82.2
1957	4550	0.108	7.2	94.9	5096	0.170	88.2
1958	5772	0.108	0.3	100.0	6422	0.266	100.0
1959	5304	0.107	3.3	99.5	5200	0.270	83.1
1960	6942	0.096	1.4	109.7	8684	0.215	99.5
1961	6968	0.116	8.2	118.0	9295	0.239	112.6
1962	7358	0.086	6.3	118.1	11,492	0.210	143.6
1963	8086	0.110	1.8	120.3	13,728	0.159	161.0
1964	9984	0.078	21.3	130.1	9958	0.247	139.6
1965	11,128	0.141	18.5	134.9	14,014	0.196	162.0

[a]The marginal product figures in agriculture were derived from a single-equation production-function model using the Cobb–Douglas equation equation $Y = AL^\alpha K^\beta V^\gamma$, where Y is gross product, L is labour input, K is agricultural gross capital stock, V is land, and A is a constant. The estimate is based on cross-sectional data for each of the about 200 kibbutzim.

The coefficients of determination for the regressions are within a range of $0.72-0.82$; all the coefficients for labour and capital are significant as the 5 per cent level, and most of them at 1 per cent.

[b]The marginal product figures for manufacturing were derived from a single-equation production function model $Y = AL^\alpha K^\beta$, where Y is gross product, L is labour input, and K is gross capital stock in manufacturing (excluding workshops; see note a to Table 13.2). The number of observations is substantially less than in agriculture. The estimate is based on data for all manufacturing establishments in kibbutzim: just over 50 in the mid-1950s and about 100 by the mid-1960s; this is adequate for purposes of conventional regression analysis.

The coefficients of determination are about 0.60, all the labour coefficients are significant at the 1 per cent level, and almost all the capital stock coefficients are significant at 5 per cent.

SOURCE Barkai (1977) see p. 198, Table 10.6, for column (4); p. 203, Table 10.7, for columns (1)–(3): p. 214, Table 11.1, for column (7); and p. 219, Table 11.3, for columns (5)–(6).

The data presented here refer only to one of a set of alternative models used to estimate kibbutz production functions. For details of the others see Barkai (1974) and forthcoming. For a discussion of the simultaneity issue and the use of the single-equation technique in the kibbutz context see Barkai and Levhari (1973), Barkai (1974), pp. 3–6, and Barkai (forthcoming).

issue. The marginal productivity of labour in kibbutz agriculture has grown by
a factor of about 3.5 in 12 years. Analysis of the marginal productivity of
capital figures easily refutes any facile explanation of this impressive
performance in terms of excessively high capital (and land) intensities. If this
were indeed so, one would expect declining or at least low levels of marginal
product of capital (and of land in agriculture). The vagaries of agricultural
production stemming from climatic effects do indeed show up in the rate-of-
return series and the marginal product of land series [columns (2) and (3)
respectively]. Yet the trend of the rate-of-return series is obviously not
downwards: although the 1964 entry is slightly below the 1956 figure of 8.5
per cent, it is evident that if a trend can be traced at all, it is a slightly rising
one. This is remarkable, since in the same period the capital/labour ratio in
agriculture more than doubled. Thus, although capital intensity, along with the
marginal products of co-operating factors did grow rapidly, real rates of return
which are stable or rise slightly hardly suggest excessive use of capital.

In manufacturing real rates of return shot up quite early, to a high gross rate
of almost 27 per cent, so that rates of almost 25 and 20 per cent in the last year
of the series are indeed lower than these. Nevertheless, neither the comparison
between the first and last entries, nor inspection of the fluctuations of the entire
period indicate a falling trend. Thus, very high gross real rates of return were
maintained in the very period in which capital/labour ratios in manufacturing
almost doubled. This means that in manufacturing, as in agriculture, the
rapidly rising marginal productivity of labour cannot be explained in terms of
'excessive' capital intensity.[1] This suggests that there was (rapid) introduction
of labour-saving technology in these two branches.

Productivity in a comparative context

Further insight on the efficiency issue can be gained from a comparative study.
Consider first net returns in manufacturing. These are derived from the real
gross rates presented above by deducting appropriate rates of capital
consumption. Even at 8 per cent per annum, net real rates of return (except for
the first year of the series) would still be 10 per cent or more.[2] This is indeed
satisfactory. The most relevant external yardstick for the rate of return and the
marginal product of labour are evidently the corresponding market prices.

---

[1]Data on factor ratios are presented in Barkai (1977) p. 196, Table 10.5, and p. 217,
Table 11.2. The marginal product estimates for land are much less reliable than the estimates for
the two other factors. The figures indicate that the marginal product of land was not rising in the
period when the marginal productivity of the two other factors was rising quickly. Labour input
in agriculture hardly rose between 1956 and 1965 (and in 1972 it stood at roughly the 1954
figure). Thus labour/land ratios did not rise in the relevant period while the ratio of capital to
land tripled during the period 1954–65. See Barkai (1977) p. 196, Table 10.5, and p. 190,
Table 10.1.

[2]An annual capital-consumption rate of 8 per cent assumes an average lifespan for real capital
stock (structures and equipment) of about 12 years in manufacturing. Such a rate is not low by
accepted standards.

These are the nominal rates of interest paid by kibbutzim for funds obtained in the commercial credit market, the real rates paid by the Israeli economy for commercial credits abroad and, finally, the real wage rates in Israeli manufacturing industry. A comparison of nominal rates of return (net real rates of return plus the annual rate of change in prices) with the rates paid by kibbutzim in 1956–65 shows that the former were higher. Even in the first year of the series presented in Table 13.1, the rates of return were slightly above the marginal rates paid by kibbutzim for commercial credits, and in all the subsequent years they were much higher.[1] The allocation of real capital to this branch was therefore not excessive or wasteful from the point of view of the kibbutz. Indeed, if anything, the figures suggest a shortage of capital, that is, that greater capital intensity was called for. Note further, that real net rates of return of 10 per cent and more are higher than the real interest rate which the Israeli government and financial institutions had to pay for foreign credit. This, of course, implies that the allocation of capital to kibbutz manufacturing did not cause waste from the social point of view either.

The value of marginal product of labour in kibbutz manufacturing in the same period was initially $1\frac{1}{2}$ times the average wage in Israeli manufacturing and had risen to about three times the national average by the mid-1960s.[2] The average wage payment is of course only a proxy for the more relevant specific wage rates (classified by industry and skill) with which comparisons should be made. But the substantial gap between kibbutz shadow wage rates and the average for Israeli manufacturing does suggest that the marginal labour productivity of kibbutz manufacturing of highly skilled operatives and technical personnel could hardly have been below the market rates for these specific skills.

The comparison of shadow wages and shadow rates of return in kibbutz agriculture with the relevant alternative rates yields similar results. Though lower than in manufacturing, the value of the marginal product of labour in kibbutz farming has, since 1954, been above the highest rate paid to farm workers. Initially, it was 20–30 per cent above the market rate and it was more than 60 per cent by the mid-1960s, which implies that labour productivity in kibbutz farming must have been higher than in the economy at large.

The simultaneously estimated shadow rate of return on capital does not justify attribution of the high marginal product of labour to excessive capital intensity. The net real rates of return, derived by deducting rates of, say, 3.5–4 per cent per annum for capital consumption[3] are undoubtedly below the rates

---

[1] Data on the cost of commercial credit are from Barkai (1977), pp. 174–5, Table 9.6, and p. 184, Table 9.9.

[2] See Barkai (1977), p. 221 and *Statistical Abstract of Israel* (various issues) for data on wages.

[3] This implies an average lifespan of capital stock of about 25 years. The lifespan of equipment is obviously shorter. Yet the lifespan of farm buildings, land improvement, irrigation networks, orchards, and similar capital stock in farming is much longer. Barkai (1977), p. 112, and Barkai (1969).

of return in manufacturing. Since 1956, the nominal net rates of return implied by these real net rates (Table 13.1) were similar to the marginal cost of commercial funds to kibbutzim. Similarly, the real net rates of return were on the whole no lower than the real rate of interest paid by Israeli financial intermediaries for commercial credits obtained abroad.

Similar results were obtained from other estimates of production functions which involve output instead of gross product (value added) as the dependent variable and therefore also raw materials as inputs.[1]

The efficiency of the kibbutz production sector has been the subject of several other studies based on variants of the neo-classical paradigm. These models were also subjected to empirical testing. Among others we may mention the Inbar–Peleg (1976) model which makes use of Baumol's hypothesis of revenue maximisation subject to a minimum-profit constraint as the basis of a behaviouristic model of the kibbutz production sector. This conceptual framework is used to formulate and test a Tobin–Markowitz rate-of-return risk model to explain the multibranch structure of kibbutz farming. Their findings suggest that kibbutzim are on the efficiency curve, though rather close to the origin, which means that they are high-risk averters. The findings of this and two other models (Goldschmidt, Levkowitz and Shashua, 1975, and Sadan, 1976), which use different samples of kibbutzim and different periods during 1936–73 are consistent with the results on kibbutz efficiency derived from our models (Barkai, 1977, pp. 205–7, and pp. 174–5, Table 9.6).

Efficiency in a dynamic context

Despite the remarkable performance revealed by the cross-section comparisons, the gap between marginal factor productivities in the two industrial branches, in particular between the real gross (and net) rates of return, may still leave some doubts on the efficiency issue. Paretian static conditions for optimal factor allocation require interbranch equality of factor returns. They also require equality of the firm's marginal rate of return with those of market alternatives. As the data presented in Table 13.1 indicate, this condition is not fully satisfied either.

Equilibrium conditions in the timeless static (formal) framework do require equality of factor productivities in all alternative uses and their equality with market alternatives. Time is, however, an essential factor in any real situation. Therefore, in a dynamic context, such as the one under consideration, interbranch inequality of factor returns is not necessarily inconsistent with welfare maximisation. Exogenous changes, which have a differential impact on various activities, recreate such gaps from time to time. What counts, therefore,

---

[1]This holds for results derived from estimates of production functions in agriculture which involve water as an explicit input variable. Water, which is the dominant constraint in a semi-arid country such as Israel, is heavily subsidised and thus rationed. The estimates do show that the marginal social cost of water is below the value of its marginal product in kibbutz farming. See Barkai (1974), pp. 25–30.

is not the productivity gap itself but the response to it. The test of dynamic efficiency relates to the nature of the response to interbranch inequality in marginal productivities. Optimal behaviour in such a context requires the channelling of resources into activities in which productivity at the margin is higher. In the kibbutz case, in which real net returns to capital and shadow wages have been persistently higher in manufacturing since the late 1950s, the situation called for relative expansion of this branch.

Table 13.2 shows that this was indeed the pattern of development. The first entries in the series, which show factor inputs, investment, and product in manufacturing as a percentage of agriculture, bring out the branch characteristics of the kibbutz economy in the 1950s. Although about 50 kibbutzim already had manufacturing plants proper, employment in them was only about 14 per cent of agricultural employment and required the services of

TABLE 13.2 FACTOR ALLOCATION – RATIO OF MANUFACTURING[a] TO AGRICULTURE

	Employment %		Capital Stock %		Gross investment %	Gross product %
	M & W (1)	M (2)	M & W (3)	M (4)	(5)	(6)
1954	20.6	–	16.6	–	5.7	–
1955	21.5	–	15.0	–	–	–
1956	25.9	13.8	16.3	6.2	–	7.3
1957	26.0	13.5	15.4	5.8	–	7.3
1958	26.6	15.2	16.2	6.3	11.2	8.8
1959	28.1	15.9	16.3	6.1	–	7.5
1960	31.1	18.6	17.1	6.9	–	9.6
1961	34.6	21.8	17.9	7.3	–	11.5
1962	38.5	22.6	19.6	7.9	–	15.4
1963	38.1	24.0	20.5	7.9	–	17.7
1964	47.6	30.6	23.3	9.5	–	18.1
1965	49.4	33.1	25.9	12.1	28.5	22.9
1970	85.3	54.0	–	–	95.4	(30.4)[b]
1972	102.0	65.3	–	–	111	–
1973	–	–	–	–	120	39.4

[a]M and W refer to manufacturing proper and workshops (for repair and maintenance), respectively. Since separate investment series were not available for the period before 1965, the gross investment ratios are given only for the combined M & W sector and therefore understate the relative decline of agriculture as the dominant industrial branch in the kibbutz. For the period after 1965 the M investment data are adequate and have been spliced to the M & W series on 1965; i.e. the ratios for 1970–73 represent the pattern of gross investment in manufacturing proper.
[b]Extrapolated from 1965 on the basis of output data.

SOURCE Barkai (1977) see p. 114, Table 6.2, for column (5); p. 190, Table 10.1, for columns (1)–(2); p. 191, Table 10.2, for columns (3)–(4); p. 192, Table 10.3, for column (6). The post-1965 data in column (5) and (6) are from *Kibbutz Industries Association Reports* (various issues; Hebrew).

a capital stock which was about 16 per cent of that of agriculture. The ratio of gross product in the two branches, about 7 per cent in the mid-1950s [column (6)], also brings out the absolute predominance of agriculture. The popular image of the kibbutz as a collective farm was at that time a reality.

Yet the investment series, which is the best indicator of where the wind is blowing, shows that by that time kibbutzim were already aware that economic rationality required a rapid restructuring of the branch (product) mix. As early as 1958, the ratio of manufacturing to agricultural investment was double the 1954 figure of 5.7 per cent. As can be learned from the series, manufacturing really took off in the 1960s. While (real) gross investment in agriculture was steady throughout the 1960s and 1970s, manufacturing investment grew by leaps and bounds, so that within seven years the investment ratio had risen to 30 per cent, and by 1972 manufacturing investment had overtaken gross investment in agriculture.[1]

The employment series, which is a flow series, shows a similar trend. By 1965 employment in manufacturing (M) had risen to one-third of agricultural employment, and by 1973 the ratio was two-thirds. Indeed, by then M & W employment had drawn level with employment in agriculture.

These figures and the corresponding (provisional) estimate for the gross-product ratio (for M) illustrate the fact that within twenty years the kibbutz has, indeed, responded rapidly to the pull of market forces. It has undergone an industrial revolution which has transformed it from a predominantly mixed-farming enterprise into an agriculture–manufacturing complex. The quantity series (employment, capital stock, investment and product) demonstrate that kibbutzim did respond to price signals in the manner called for by conventional economic criteria, and that they reallocated resources into the line of activity offering the higher factor returns.[2] The reallocation of resources and, in particular, the rapid introduction of labour-saving technology, which required substantial displacement of labour, proved comparatively easy because of the very nature of kibbutz organisation. It is the fusion of ownership, entrepreneurial and labour functions which, by eliminating the wage nexus, obviates the difficult social issue related to technology-induced unemployment.[3]

---

[1]Since good investment figures for manufacturing proper (M) are not available, we use a series for manufacturing and workshops (M & W). There is no reason why investment in the workshops component of M & W (which is also the smaller) should have grown more rapidly than investment in the M sector proper. The combined M & W ratio must therefore be at least similar to that of the M sector alone. Note further, that in agriculture a significantly greater fraction of gross investment is for replacement of existing capacity; i.e. net investment figures would show a more rapid growth of manufacturing capacity *vis-à-vis* agriculture.

[2]The results demonstrated here apply to the branch as a whole. Further evidence which applies directly to the operational units within each branch points in the same direction. Thus the high shadow wages in farming induced kibbutzim to change labour-intensive production techniques where feasible, and to *eliminate* branches, such as vegetable growing, where satisfactory mechanical substitutes for labour cannot be found.

[3]I am indebted to W. Baumol for raising this point in the discussion at the Conference.

These comparative and time-series studies of factor productivity and the pattern of response of kibbutzim to changing relative prices lead to the conclusion that the hypothesis that kibbutzim are economically efficient in the accepted sense of the term has not been rejected.

IV. ECONOMIC CALCULATION IN THE KIBBUTZ PRODUCTION SECTOR

The failure of the kibbutz predicted in the course of the viability debate of the 1920s has not materialised, and the opponents of that venture in collectivism have been proved wrong. Even the misgivings of its hesitant supporters in the Zionist establishment, who admittedly succeeded in keeping it afloat at a crucial time in their history, were wide of the mark. With the help of hindsight it is now possible to identify the presumptions, hypotheses and relevant omissions which are the source of that forecasting error.

Consider first the Von Mises impossibility theorem which rejects *a priori* the feasibility of Pareto-efficient factor allocation in a collective. It is well-known that Barone anticipated Von Mises in formulating the problem and showing that it can be solved – that is, economic calculation in a socialised firm is possible. The socialist planning debate, in which Taylor, Dickinson, and later Lange sparred with Von Mises, Von Hayek and Lionel Robbins (among others), has settled the issue of the feasibility of rational economic calculation. The last two admitted that conceptually (though not in practice) rational allocation is feasible in a socialist firm.[1] The constraints on such a unit allow the imputation of (scarcity) prices to intermediate products and factors of production (which the Von Mises theorem denies), as well as of final products.

Yet the Barone–Taylor–Lange proof that the market socialism genus of firm can operate on the basis of rational economic calculation does not apply directly to the kibbutz. First, the environment in which kibbutzim operate is not a fully nationalised economy. Second and more important, the Barone–Lange firm was not conceived as a collective – the wage nexus (and hence payment by results and differentials) is an inherent element of its *modus operandi*. The Barone–Lange model of market socialism assumes that market data, in particular, prices, are parametric to the firm. This property of all relevant market prices also applies to the kibbutz model, whose environment was assumed to be a market-economy. For our purposes the relevant difference between the Barone–Lange firm and the kibbutz is thus the virtual abolition by the kibbutz of payment by results.

To prove that a variant of the Von Mises impossibility theorem is not valid for the kibbutz either, it was therefore necessary to set up a formal model which does not assume *actual* payments of wages to kibbutz members. The analysis of such a model, which assumes that market prices of all factors are

---

[1]See L. C. Robbins (1934), p. 151, Hayek (1935), p. 207, and Bergson's classic survey article 'Socialist Economics', in Ellis (1948), pp. 428–39 in particular.

given, and at the same time that the supply of labour (to the kibbutz) is invariant to the wage rate (that is to say, it is ideologically determined), shows that its equilibrium conditions are fully consistent with Pareto-optimal factor allocation. The gist of the general equilibrium argument can be described simply for a partial-equilibrium model of the kibbutz labour 'market'. Technological data and market prices of products and of all inputs other than labour allow the derivation of a conventional value-of-marginal-product function for labour for each of the production branches of the collective. Their summation yields a kibbutz demand curve for labour, every point of which reflects the highest value of marginal product feasible for the corresponding quantity of labour. The points on this curve are evidently Pareto-efficient in the conventional sense. Thus, even though the quantities of labour supplied are invariant to wages, so that the 'ideologically' determined labour supply curve would be vertical in the conventional two-dimensional supply and demand diagram, the intersection of such a supply curve with that labour demand curve determines the Pareto-optimal shadow price of kibbutz labour. It is this shadow price which is to be used as a datum for what would be a Pareto-optimal interbranch allocation of labour and for the decision on how much kibbutz labour should be allocated to work in non-kibbutz firms, whose wages are a market parameter reflecting a possible alternative price for the allocation of kibbutz labour.[1]

The use of a 'shadow price' criterion for allocating kibbutz labour, which assumes efficient allocation of labour (and of all other resources), is fully consistent with the equality principle, since it functions as a planning device and not as a determinant of real income distribution. If, indeed, some of the critics of the kibbutz who predicted its rapid demise in the 1920s had in mind something akin to the Von Mises impossibility theorem, they were therefore relying on an incorrect premise. The *a priori* inefficiency argument is *invalid* in the kibbutz case, as it is for the Barone–Lange firm. Rational economic calculation is not precluded by the collective form of organisation.

V. THE MOTIVATION CONUNDRUM

The critics were, as we have seen, wrong in their forecast that the kibbutz would fail, and we have already pointed out that their implied 'economic calculation' argument is invalid. But they also used the 'lack-of-incentive' argument, to which, in any case, they gave more weight. It is obvious that Pareto-optimal factor allocation does not necessarily ensure efficiency in production. Performance can still be substantially below its potential if people do not pull their full weight as producers. In fact, the productivity data show

---

[1] The first approximation of this model for a multibranch kibbutz assumes a homogeneous labour supply which is fixed (in the short run). Successive approximations allow for labour heterogeneity and a varying labour supply in the long run. These refinements do not modify the conclusion stated in the text. See Barkai (1977), Appendix B, and Barkai (1972) in Vanek (1975), pp. 219–21.

that performance was undoubtedly much better than expected by the opponents of the kibbutz and even by many of its supporters. This may be attributed to their error in predicting the behaviour of the human element in the kibbutz environment.

Consider thus the incentive facet of the anti-kibbutz case, the proposition that the performance of individuals in a collective milieu does not come up to the standards which can reasonably be expected in a market-economy. In order to examine this proposition, a closer specification of the relevant variables is required. Performance level can be taken to be dependent on the personal capacity of each individual and on his 'degree of motivation'. This is what the critics seem to have had in mind.

To devise a technique of gauging motivation is of course a task better left to psychologists and sociologists. Yet, for our purposes, all we need is to conceive of a measure of the degree of motivation. This can be defined as an index ranging from zero, for absence of motivation, to unity, for the highest feasible motivation. The definition of the second variable, level of personal capacity, is simpler. The human capital approach to the analysis of labour supply offers an approximation to a (cost) measure of what might be meant by 'personal capacity'. A person's performance can then be specified as the product of these two independent variables:

$$\text{level of performance} = (\text{degree of motivation})$$
$$\times (\text{level of personal capacity}) \tag{1}$$

The product form of (1) has been devised to suggest that when motivation is zero, performance is also zero, whatever the person's capacity.[1] The main emphasis of the critics of the kibbutz was on the motivation component, though some of their statements suggest that they expected the level of personal capacity of individuals in collectives to be low on the grounds that 'energetic workers' would tend to leave sooner or later.

The specification of (1) underlines the implicit presumption of the critics that even outstandingly high values of the capacity component cannot compensate for very low values of the motivation index. If we do accept the simple motivation model specified in (1) as representing the verbal statements on this subject, it is necessary to explain why the motivation index did not have the predicted low values. The relevance of the other component of (1), personal capacity, must also be studied in this connection.

The fallacy which led the critics astray was, in my view, the assumption that material incentives affect the behaviour of all individuals as producers with the same intensity. The classical utility approach, which assumes diversity of

[1]The first factor on the right-hand side of (1) is a pure number, the second has the dimension of the unit in which it is measured (say a dollar figure of human capital); the dependent variable, level of performance, accordingly has the same dimension as the personal-capacity factor and is equal to or smaller than the latter. I am indebted to Liviatan (1977) for the notion of specifying performance level as a function of these two variables.

tastes, does of course suggest that some individuals may (in terms of effort) respond to non-pecuniary stimuli much more than others. But, in fact, non-pecuniary rewards were implicitly excluded as determinants of effort by those who relied on the lack-of-incentive argument.

Suppose, now, that the Smithian theorem does indeed apply to most people. That is, suppose that the economic effort of most, though not by means *all*, people is indeed entirely dependent on material incentives. This is still consistent with the possibility that there exists a group of people, making up a small fraction of the population, who might be ready to function at full stretch as operatives, managers, or entrepreneurs even though they receive no direct and differential material reward. Now, if such a select group forms a collective, there is no reason why the motivation index of each member should be reduced by collective life, as might indeed happen with a group of the same size chosen at random. In other words, the performance of a select group cannot be predicted on the basis of what one would expected from a 'typical' group.

Kibbutzim can be identified as such select groups. They came together, and are kept in existence, by what may be termed natural selection. Though their members are heterogeneous in many traits, their ideological motivation and thus their attitude toward payment by results is similar; that is, material reward is a comparatively minor stimulant to effort. The social mechanism which brought these people into the collective and which has kept them together is the principle of voluntarism.

A kibbutz is a community attempting to translate socialist principles into everyday practice, on the basis of *voluntary* membership. That is, people whose preference scales give a high weight to the effort–pecuniary income nexus would either not join the kibbutz in the first place or would leave it sooner or later. This process of natural selection is going on all the time, but it is relatively intensive in, say, the first five years of a collective settlement's existence. This involves great instability in the immediate post-settlement period and has a cost in terms of short-term efficiency.[1] But, in the long run, it is this selection process that ensures the survival of the fittest for that form of life. It has therefore been of major significance in maintaining strong motivation and, hence, the high performance level of individuals.

The process of selection has had yet another effect on labour and, hence, on individual performance and productivity. Those who are able to perceive the requirement that they do their best in the absence of a direct link between their contribution to production and the material reward presumably have above-average ability to comprehend a complicated set of abstractions. The process which selects a group of people who are comparatively unconcerned with the direct material reward of effort and abilities, therefore also raises the quality of

---

[1]This was an obtrusive feature in the 1920s when practically all kibbutzim were in the 1–7 age group. The critics frequently referred to it as a sure symptom of the approaching demise of the movement.

kibbutz manpower.[1] Quantitative data which measure the quality of manpower in terms of human capital underline this characteristic of the kibbutz (Barkai, 1977, pp. 97–101). Over the years this has reflected the process of natural selection and the deliberate social choice which has given very high priority to education and to training.

Furthermore, the comparatively high level of education is conducive to another important feature of the kibbutz: the equality requirement, which leads to the attempt to make all members share in managerial responsibility and has made the kibbutz an excellent training ground for work requiring enterprise and skill. The fact that membership is voluntary therefore increases both components of equation (1). Kibbutz members are of comparatively high ability; and they are also people whose response to non-pecuniary incentives is comparatively high.

Yet, though the natural selection process is of great significance, the effort to maintain work discipline does not rely only on it. Another control device, *informal* social control, in practice, works to maintain high motivation. This mechanism relies on community respect and approval, not necessarily formally expressed, for a good day's work and success in entrepreneurial functions. And *per contra*, community disapproval, also rarely expressed formally, is still a very powerful factor affecting behaviour, as anyone who spends some time in a kibbutz knows from personal experience.[2]

The effectiveness of informal social control devices depends crucially on the size of the community. (Note that the natural selection process also has implications for size.) Today, mean population is still about 500, which means that all adults know each other personally. Kibbutzim were, of course, much smaller in the past and, because of the importance of the informal motivation and control mechanisms, members and students of the movement always had doubts about their ultimate feasible size. Indeed, kibbutz agriculture and manufacturing are both still within the range of increasing returns, which means that pure efficiency considerations would dictate expansion.[3] However, the social control factor which has proved to be an important component of the complicated mechanism which makes the collective tick imposes a constraint on the size of the community. Obviously, further growth would force it to rely more on natural selection to weed out those less able to adapt themselves to the morés of the collective. This, of course, has been the trend in the past.

---

[1] This was much in evidence even in the 1920s. Thus Mead, a convinced opponent of the kibbutz, referred to 'sober, sensible ... [and] excellent ... men ... who, after long experience, believed most firmly that the kevotzah organisation was unquestionably the best'. (Mead, 1928, p. 444.) The belief that they are dealing with people of high personal quality was, of course, the major reason which convinced Ruppin and other establishment supporters to allow the experiment 'to go on for a while'.

[2] Censure in the general meeting or by a committee is very rare. Formal expulsions from membership almost never occur.

[3] The production function studies mentioned above clearly indicate this.

Even if the size of kibbutzim will in the future be less subject to constraints imposed by the informal control devices, the selectivity mechanism still implies that the dominant trait of the movement – that it is a minority and élite movement – is here to stay. It was this which the prophets of doom overlooked. What they failed to realise is that although the Smithian hypothesis has proved itself when applied to the 'typical' group of people, it is not necessarily applicable to the behaviour of a small self-selected group of people who are located several standard deviations from the mean of the distribution of the effort-reward nexus.

VI. CONCLUDING REMARKS

What can we learn from the considerable economic success of kibbutzim? Does it imply that public sector firms in which motivation is an important problem (and becoming more so owing to the increasing size of public enterprises) can follow the path traced out by kibbutzim? In particular, can a social control device be made to work in public enterprises?

In view of the absence of two critical characteristics, I doubt whether the kibbutz experience is applicable. First, those who work in public firms are not a naturally selected group. They regard themselves as employees of the enterprise, not as owners, managers and entrepreneurs. Furthermore, it is pay and differentials which are their direct and dominant stimuli. Secondly, the size constraint, which is important for the application of informal control devices, is also violated – public sector firms are usually large and must be run according to a set of formal rules.

Nor can the kibbutz experience be transferred wholesale to developing countries, as some people in them appear to believe. Obviously, the success of the kibbutz can be ascribed to specific historical circumstances, when an ideology fusing socialist ideals and national aspirations fired the imagination of a small and select group of comparatively highly educated people. This is not to say that no such group can come together elsewhere. Yet, in view of the great scarcity of educated and highly trained people in developing countries, I doubt whether this is a workable proposition.

If they are at all feasible, a more natural place for experiments in collectivism would seem to be the highly industrialised countries. It is in these countries that one finds large numbers of educated and highly trained people looking for an outlet from the consumerist trend of the last decades. 'Communes' have indeed recently appeared here and there, yet their chance of taking root and growing into a movement depends on their members' realising that success in production is the *sine qua non* of their survival. It was this truth, grasped by kibbutz members and leadership in the early days, which ensured that 'the kibbutz is an experiment which has not yet failed'.[1]

---

[1] This is how Martin Buber, a convinced utopian socialist, described the performance of the kibbutz movement in the 1940s.

REFERENCES

Barkai, Haim, 'The Kibbutz: An Experiment in Microsocialism', in *Israel, the Arabs and the Middle East* (Eds. Irving Howe and Carl Gershman) (New York and Toronto: Bantam Books, 1972), pp. 69–99. (Also published in a shortened version in *Self-Management: Economic Liberation of Man* (Ed. Jaroslav Venek) (Harmondsworth: Penguin Books, 1975), pp. 213–26.)

Barkai, Haim, *An Empirical Analysis of Productivity and Factor Allocation in Kibbutz Farming and Manufacturing*, Discussion Paper 748 (Jerusalem: Falk Institute, 1974).

Barkai, Haim, *Growth Patterns of the Kibbutz Economy*, Contributions to Economic Analysis 108 (Amsterdam: North-Holland, 1977).

Barkai, Haim, 'Productivity and Factor Allocation in Kibbutz Farming and Manufacturing', *Rèvue Economique* (May 1978).

Barkai, Haim and David Levhari, 'The Impact of Experience on Kibbutz Farming', *Review of Economics and Statistics*, LV (February 1973), pp. 56–63.

Baykov, Alexander, *The Development of the Soviet Economic System* (Cambridge: Cambridge University Press, 1946).

Bergson, Abram, 'Socialist Economics', in *A Survey of Contemporary Economics* (Ed. Howard S. Ellis) (Homewood, Ill.: Irwin, 1948), pp. 412–48.

Dobb, Maurice, *Soviet Economic Development Since 1917*, 4th edn (London: Routledge and Kegan Paul, 1957).

Goldschmidt, Yaaqov, Giora Levkowitz and Leon Shashua, 'The Influence of Return and Risk on Expansion of Kibbutz Agriculture', in *Issues in the Economy of Israel* (Eds. Nadav Halevi and Yaakov Kop) (Jerusalem: Falk Institute, 1975), pp. 323–38.

Hayek, F. A. (Ed.), 'The Present State of the Debate', in *Collectivist Economic Planning* (London: Routledge and Kegan Paul, 1935).

Inbar, Yitschak and Dov Peleg, 'Aspects of an Economic Model Pertaining to the Productive Sector of the Kibbutz'. M.A. thesis, Faculty of Social Sciences, Tel-Aviv University, 1976.

Lange, Oskar and Fred M. Taylor, *On the Economic Theory of Socialism* (Vol. 2 of *Government Control of the Economic Order*, Ed. Benjamin E. Lippincott) (Minneapolis: University of Minnesota Press, 1938).

Liviatan, Uri, 'Work Motivation of Kibbutz Members', *Hakibbutz veHataasya* (No. 2, 1977), 13–21 (Hebrew).

Mead, Elwood, *Report of the Experts Submitted to the Joint Palestine Survey Commission* (London, 1928).

Nove, Alex, *An Economic History of the U.S.S.R.* (London: Allen Lane, The Penguin Press, 1969).

Robbins, Lionel C., *The Great Depression* (London, 1934).

Ruppin, Arthur, *Three Decades of Palestine* (Jerusalem: Schocken, 1936).

Sadan, Ezra, 'Financial Indicators and Economic Performance in the Kibbutz Sector', in *Israel Economic Papers 1976* (Eds. Nadav Halevi and Yaakov Kop) (Jerusalem: Israel Economic Association and Falk Institute, 1976) (Hebrew), pp. 242–52.

Smith, Adam, *The Wealth of Nations* (Cannan edn) (New York: Modern Library, 1937).

Discussion of Professor Barkai's Paper

Professor Acosta asked whether the success of the kibbutizim in raising productivity and living standards had possible explanations other than the ideological fervour which had replaced material incentives. He wondered whether one could compare the kibbutz to a small-scale experiment under special favourable conditions, analogous to a greenhouse. The government had supplied infrastructure services out of general state funds. Machinery could be imported on credit with the interest rate kept below a preferential ceiling. Other physical inputs had also been subsidised. Under such conditions, neither a public nor a private enterprise could possibly fail. Mexico also had collective farms, called *ejidos*, which had a social structure similar to that of the Israeli kibbutzim. But the government did not have the resources to lead them to success.

Professor Barkai replied that the results he obtained were not due to special privileges that the kibbutzim had received. In his estimation technique, he had taken into account the level of technology used and the prices of productive factors and physical inputs. Moreover, the Israeli manufacturing industry had received the same kind of help from the government as the kibbutzim, yet the kibbutzim exhibited higher rates of return on capital.

Professor Baumol said the papers by Barkai and Savas complemented each other by showing places where conventional small-scale private enterprise was more effective, and where it was not. The self-selection of members in the kibbutzim led the most idealistic people to join, and the social pressure created in this way resulted in high levels of productivity. An additional reason for the success of the kibbutzim seemed to be much lower resistance to the introduction of new labour-saving technology than in an enterprise in which there was a separation between owners and workers. Attempts to introduce labour-saving automated equipment in American industries had been resisted by strikes of miners, dockworkers and others. This was understandable, since it meant that many workers were threatened with loss of their source of income. But in a kibbutz, where everybody benefited from increased output, there was every incentive to introduce labour-saving technology. This meant not only an improvement in static efficiency, but, more important, a *higher rate of growth* in productivity. And the growth rate was what counted ultimately. The secret for long-run growth may be an organic structure in which everybody knew he would benefit from technical change. This applied to small as well as large organisations. He hypothesised that one reason for the astonishing growth rate of Japanese industry was the Japanese custom that employees remain with their firm for a lifetime. Therefore, they presumably welcomed technical improvements, which they knew were not at their expense. There were things which could be transferred from one country to another, while others could not. It was very difficult to transfer idealism from one place to another. But institutional structures under which workers benefited from the introduction of more efficient technology, instead of suffering, were something that could be copied.

Professor Savas considered it important that Barkai's paper had disproved empirically an *a priori* theoretical hypothesis which had predicted that the kibbutzim would have to fail.

Dr Tardos asked Barkai what he expected regarding the future of the kibbutzim. Were they an interesting social phenomenon during a limited historical period or did he expect them to grow into a significant part of the economy of Israel in the future? Regarding the connection between the success of the kibbutzim and the discussion of the 1920s and 30s about the feasibility of socialism, he did not see a direct linkage. Kibbutzim represent only a small part of a market economy run mainly by private enterprises. The speciality of a kibbutz seems to be that it is interested in maximising value added, rather than profit, as would be the case with a firm in which the owner is different from the workers. The behaviour of an entity which maximises value added is more difficult to handle in economic theory than the behaviour of a profit maximiser. However, it has been shown maximisation of per capita value added in the neo-classical theory could lead by given assumptions to economic equilibrium. The successful performance of kibbutzim, demonstrated in Barkai's paper, shows only that a small portion of the economy can work successfully even without a connection between the individual work performed and the distribution of collective income.

Professor Vickrey asked whether there was a tendency for more skilful younger members to leave the kibbutz, and less able ones to ask for admittance, in order to benefit from the work of others.

Barkai said that just the opposite was observed. People who asked for admittance were generally among the most motivated and dedicated. On the question whether good managers or entrepreneurs tended to leave, he said that over their 50-year experience some very good people had left the kibbutz, but others also had joined and stayed. In serious cases of refusal to work, a member could be expelled, if exhortation remained fruitless. But this was extremely rare. He knew of only about half a dozen such cases in the entire history of Israel.

Professor Srinivasan pointed out that for social controls to work, collective units had to be relatively small. This limited the possibility of their expansion. Commenting on Baumol's suggestion that job security encouraged technical improvements, he said that in a full employment economy labour would not resist technical change either.

Mr González asked how decisions were made regarding the allocation of income between consumption and savings. *Barkai* said they were reached collectively, at an annual membership meeting, while day-to-day decisions were left to a core of elected administrators.

Dr Marsan questioned whether motivation was the result of a high degree of education of kibbutz members. One might, perhaps, suspect instead that motivation was the primary force, and that someone who was motivated would seek a good education. This was the old problem of which was first, the chicken or the egg. He also asked to what extent motivation was a result of social control and of participation in decision-making. Finally, he expressed some doubt about whether capital was allocated most efficiently if, as Barkai had said, work in itself was a source of gratification. In the Italian language the words for work and fatigue were identical. There was also a proverb that if one saw a man resting, one should help him. Generally, work was considered a social pain. If it was a gratification, what incentive was there to introduce labour-saving techniques?

Barkai said that in principle everybody should be able to perform every task in a kibbutz. But in practice this was not quite true. Managers did perform humble tasks as well, but usually for a relatively short time. Emphasis was placed on education and training on the job, through job rotation. He said that people who were not yet able to perform major functions when he left his kibbutz were now able to perform them very well. In reply to Tardos' question on the future of the kibbutz and what other societies could learn from it, he said that Israel's experience had shown that they could be efficient in every sense. Labour costs in a kibbutz were quite high, and some labour-intensive activities had been abandoned, on the basis of the usual marginal criteria. Kibbutzim were and are a minority élite movement. At present, 3.8 per cent of Israel's population lived in kibbutzim. The movement was at its peak in the 1940s, when it reached 6 per cent of the population. He said that there were no income differences between members. Some could earn ten times as much as others if they took a job outside. But for ideological reasons, all members made an effort. They also realised that one could distribute only what was produced. Concerning Baumol's comment he said that it referred to an important subject. A related issue was whether wages were to be considered a cost item or a benefit item. For a conservative, wages represented a cost (to the capitalist). For a socialist, wages represented income (to workers). From the viewpoint of profit maximisation, rational behaviour often dictated that people should be dismissed. But this would mean a loss of income to workers. A kibbutz had the advantage that it tended to maximise total output (or, more precisely, total value added), not profit. People were not dismissed, only shifted from one activity to another (e.g. from fruit growing to cotton planting). Mobility was not hampered by income considerations, since income of the individual was not related to comparative (marginal) labour productivity of the branch in which he was engaged. This was another source of increased efficiency.

14 Comparative Costs of Public and Private Enterprise in a Municipal Service[1]

E. S. Savas
CENTER FOR GOVERNMENT STUDIES, GRADUATE SCHOOL OF
BUSINESS, COLUMBIA UNIVERSITY

I. INTRODUCTION

Government expenditures in the United States have grown from 27 per cent of GNP in 1954 to 33 per cent in 1974, while the number of government employees grew during the period from 14 to 18 per cent of total non-agricultural employment. This growth has been accompanied by increasing concern about efficiency in government, and the drawing of invidious comparisons between the public and private sectors with respect to efficiency.

A number of reasons are advanced to explain why one sector should be better than the other in producing goods and services. Government agencies, it is argued, are better able to capture economies of scale, do not make a profit, generally do not pay taxes, and thereby are lower cost producers than their counterparts in the private sector. Often it is argued further that the quality of services provided by public agencies will be higher, because of greater dedication by public servants, greater responsiveness to the citizen–consumer, and more faithful attention to realisation of the basic public benefits that public goods are intended to provide.

On the other hand, critics of government agencies point to the general absence of competitive forces, personnel systems that – because of patronage and civil service – fail to relate rewards to performance, the use of political rather than economic criteria for making decisions on the type and timing of capital investments, budgeting processes and incentive systems that encourage agency growth, the lack of a market mechanism by which to measure agency performance, and a scale of operations that is often far from optimal.

[1]This material is based upon research supported by the National Science Foundation under Grant No. APR 74-02061. Any opinions, findings, conclusions or recommendations expressed in this publication are those of the author and do not necessarily reflect the views of the National Science Foundation.

The subject of public versus private production of services abounds with ideological overtones, and despite the considerable heat generated about this topic, there has been relatively little light shed on it. In particular, there have been few studies that have attempted to compare the performances of the public and private sectors in supplying the same specific service.

One service which lends itself to such a study is residential refuse collection. Both public agencies and private firms provide this service, and by its nature the service is more quantifiable than most services in which government is involved.

There are several institutional structures through which this service is supplied.[1,2] The principal arrangements used in the United States are municipal, contract, franchise, and private. Under *municipal collection*, a unit of the local government performs the service. In *contract collection*, the local government hires and pays a private firm to do the work. In *franchise collection*, a private firm is granted the exclusive right to provide refuse-collection services in an area, and the firm charges the customers it serves. Under *private collection*, the household arranges for service by any private firm and, as in franchise collection, pays the firm directly. Note that a particular city may utilise more than one of these arrangements.

A large-scale study of cities in the United States revealed that of cities larger than 2500 in population, 37 per cent had municipal collection, 21 per cent had contract collection, 7 per cent had franchise collection, and 38 per cent had private collection.[3]

A priori, one would expect certain cost advantages and disadvantages associated with each of these four institutional arrangements. As mentioned above, a municipal agency earns no profits and is not obligated to pay certain taxes. In addition, it generally serves every household in an area, and therefore benefits from economies of contiguity; that is, it has less non-productive travel time between pick-up locations than an organisation that does not service all households, all other factors being held constant. A firm providing contract collection service would have the same economies of contiguity as the municipal agency, incurs virtually no billing costs, but earns profits and pays taxes. A firm providing franchise service would have the same cost structure as a contract firm but, in addition, would incur the costs of billing its customers and would be expected to experience more bad debts (non-payment by customers) than would a municipal agency or a firm under contract to a city. Furthermore, if collection is not mandatory (that is, if households are free to subscribe to the service or to bring their own refuse to a disposal site), then the firm will not be able to capture the economies of contiguity. A firm that

[1]Young, Dennis, *How Shall We Collect the Garbage?* (The Urban Institute, Washington, DC, 1972).

[2]Savas, E. S., *The Organization and Efficiency of Solid Waste Collection* (Lexington Books, Lexington, Mass., 1977), Chap. 3.

[3]Savas, E. S., *ibid.*, p. 51.

provides private collection would have the same cost structure as a firm with a franchise for non-mandatory collection.

II. A STUDY OF US CITIES[1]

The cost per household for each of the major arrangements was studied. For municipal collection this was defined as the cost of service, regardless of the means used to finance the service – taxes or user charges. For collection by private firms, it was the price of service, again without regard to the means of financing. (Note that it was not necessary to obtain the *costs* to private firms, but only the *prices* they charged.) The cost to the household represented the cost of collection only; disposal costs were not included. The cost of collection was defined to include the cost of transporting wastes to a disposal site or transfer station, excluding all handling costs beyond that point.

Data collection

Cities with each kind of collection arrangement were selected at random after stratifying by population size and region. The cities were all drawn from Standard Metropolitan Statistical Areas (SMSAs) that (i) were entirely within a single estate and (ii) had a total population of less than 1,500,000. (These restrictions were imposed by the National Science Foundation, which supported the research.) A somewhat different method of data collection was employed for each of the arrangements.

Municipal service. Many comparative studies of municipal services utilise cost data reported in the municipality's published budget. While such an approach has the advantage of ease and simplicity, it is inadequate because accounting practices differ greatly among cities. To avoid this problem, the cost data on municipal refuse collection were gathered by on-site interviews, using a standardised cost-accounting format that was specially designed for this purpose. Two-person teams visited the selected cities and spent one to three days obtaining the detailed cost information.

It should be noted that many municipalities levy user charges for refuse-collection. These were *not* used to determine the cost of municipal collection; the latter was determined by examining expenditures, not revenues.

Contract service. Determining the cost to the household of contract collection was relatively straightforward. A sample of 165 cities with contract collection was selected at random (after stratifying by city size and region). Prices were determined by examining the contract documents, and by verifying the basic facts (price, service level, type of service, number of households

[1]Savas, E. S., 'Policy Analysis for Local Government: Public vs. Private Refuse Collection', *Policy Analysis*, Vol. 3, No. 1 (Winter, 1977), pp. 49–74.

served) with city officials by mail and telephone, and by conducting telephone interviews with the private contractors.

Franchise service.   A random stratified sample of 65 cities with franchise collection was drawn. Households in those cities were telephoned at random and asked the price they paid, the name of the firm providing the service, and the level of service received (that is, the frequency and location of pick-up). Then the firm was called and was asked about its rate structure (price for a given level of service), disposal costs, and operating characteristics, such as crew size, salaries, and type of vehicle used. (The prices quoted by the household and by the firm were virtually identical, differing by an average of only 1 per cent.) In addition, mail questionnaires were sent to the city government to learn about the procedures for awarding franchises and setting rates.

Private service.   A sample of 125 cities with private collection was drawn at random after stratification by size and region. Data were gathered as in the case of franchise collection, except that no contact with the local governmental unit was necessary beyond the initial determination that private service was the dominant method of collection in that community.

III. RESULTS OF DIRECT COMPARISON OF COST

Costs per household, with the level of service held constant, are shown in Table 14.1. For once-a-week curbside service, contract collection is the least costly, at $22.42, followed by municipal collection, at $24.41. Private collection is most costly ($35.91). For once-a-week backyard service, both franchise and contract collection ($27.48 and $31.63, respectively), cost less than municipal collection, which is $38.71 annually per household. Only for twice-a-week curbside service is municipal collection slightly less costly than contract collection ($28.83 compared to $29.14).

But even though service level was held constant in this analysis, the standard deviations are quite large, and the differences in means are not statistically significant. Part of the reason for the large standard deviations is that certain factors could not be held constant and tend to obscure the relationship between collection arrangement and efficiency. For example, there are regional differences in collection frequency, with higher frequency of service more common in the South, as one would expect in an area where both plant growth and putrefaction of food waste occur rapidly. Also, labour costs in the South are lower than elsewhere. Finally, contract and franchise collection are relatively uncommon in the South, and the sample could not be stratified simultaneously by size and by region. As a result of these three interrelated factors, the cost of high-frequency service in Table 14.1 is biased on the high side for non-municipal collection.

TABLE 14.1   ANNUAL COST PER HOUSEHOLD, BY ARRANGEMENT AND SERVICE LEVEL

	Service level											
	Once/week curbside			Twice/week curbside			Once/week backyard					
	Mean	Std. dev.	No. of cities	Mean	Std. dev.	No. of cities	Mean	Std. dev.	No. of cities	Weighted mean cost	Total no. of cities
Municipal	$24.41	$8.86	26	$28.83	$8.22	31	$38.71	$11.42	8	$28.28	65
Contract	22.42	8.98	30	29.14	10.79	23	31.63	20.39	4	25.78	57
Franchise	27.94	10.23	22	29.85	8.57	8	27.48	10.50	9	28.23	39
Private	35.91	7.96	27	38.71	12.32	9	46.24	10.87	9	38.54	45
Total	$27.54	$9.95	105	$30.30	$10.04	71	$36.66	$14.03	30	$29.82	206

IV. RESULTS OF A REGRESSION ANALYSIS

Because not all variables could be held constant in this manner, Stevens constructed an econometric model and fitted it by regression analysis in order to isolate the independent effects of the multiple variables.[1,2] The model relates the total cost of refuse collection in a community to the following independent variables: total quantity of refuse, quantity of refuse per household per year, wage rate, density (households per square mile), temperature variation, frequency of collection, and location of pick-up point.

For purposes of this analysis, cities with franchise collection were divided into two categories: those with mandatory service (where all residents are required to purchase the service) and those with non-mandatory service (where the resident has a choice of purchasing service from the single, franchised firm or else of hauling his own refuse to a disposal site). Mandatory franchised collection is structurally equivalent to contract collection, in that one firm services every resident in the area; the only difference is that the franchised firm incurs billing costs that the contract firm, which is paid by the city, does not. Non-mandatory franchised collection is structurally equivalent to private collection, in that the firm faces competition either from other firms or from self-service households and in general does not service every residence. The franchise category was therefore eliminated, and the cities with franchise collection were included within the contract or private category, depending on whether service was mandatory or not.

Stevens estimated her model in two ways: by using weight as a measure for 177 cities (including 91 with municipal collection, 34 with contract or mandatory franchise collection, and 52 with private collection); and by using volume as a measure of refuse quantity for 262 cities (92 municipal, 79 contract or mandatory franchise, and 91 private). The two approaches yielded mutually consistent results.

In terms of cost to the household, Stevens found that private collection was significantly more costly than contract collection. No significant difference was found between municipal and private collection for cities with less than 20,000 or more than 50,000 in population, nor between municipal and contract collection for cities with less than 50,000. But for cities of more than 50,000, contract collection was significantly less expensive than municipal collection: the cost per household for municipal collection in such cities was found to be 29 per cent (or 37 per cent) greater than the corresponding cost of contract collection, on the basis of refuse data in terms of tons (or cubic yards). This was significant at the 99 per cent level.

It should be emphasised that these data compare the *cost* of municipal service with the *price* charged by private firms. In order to compare the costs

[1]Stevens, Barbara J., 'Service Arrangement and the Cost of Residential Refuse Collection', in Savas, *Organization and Efficiency, op. cit.*, Chap. 8, pp. 121–38.
[2]Stevens, Barbara J., *Scale, Market Structure, and the Cost of Refuse Collection* (Center for Government Studies, Graduate School of Business, Columbia University, July, 1976).

of production on an equivalent basis, the prices of private firms should be adjusted by subtracting profits and taxes. This information was not obtained routinely from the private firms included in this survey, nor are industry-wide figures available. However, published reports of three publicly owned firms show average net profits after taxes of 5.9 per cent of sales revenues. With respect to taxes, several firms when questioned indicated that their federal, state, and local taxes and fees amounted to approximately 15 per cent of sales. If one combines these estimates and assumes that taxes and profits of private firms are equal to 20 per cent of the price charged, then one can conclude that the cost of production is 61 per cent greater for municipal collection than for contract collection. Price and cost comparisons are illustrated in Table 14.2.

TABLE 14.2   ANNUAL COST AND PRICE OF SERVICE, BY SERVICE ARRANGEMENT, FOR A CITY OF 100,000 IN POPULATION

	Municipal	Contract and mandatory franchise	Private and non-mandatory franchise
Price per household	$22.78	$17.64	$23.10
Normalised ratio	1.29	1.00	1.31
Productive cost per household	$22.78	$14.11	$18.48
Normalised ratio	1.61	1.00	1.31

NOTE Prices were calculated from Stevens' regression model (with coefficients determined from data measured in tons), using the following reasonable values of the independent variables:

Total amount of refuse: 45,000 tons per year
Annual amount of refuse per household: 1.5 tons
Wage rate: $600 per month
Density: 600 households per square mile
Temperature variation: 15°C
Collection frequency: once per week
Pick-up location: curb

V. OTHER STUDIES

The findings in the study by Savas and Stevens are corroborated by four other studies that were more limited in scope. Two additional studies, not corroborating the above study, are not inconsistent with it either: they failed to detect any cost differences between public collection and collection by private firms. Only one study found that public service was more efficient than private, and is inconsistent with the Savas–Stevens study. A search of the literature revealed no other empirical, cross-sectional studies that compared public and private refuse collection, although numerous investigations have been conducted in individual cities to determine whether that city should change from public to private collection, or *vice versa* (see, for example, Savas[1]).

The four studies that are consistent with the findings reported above were conducted in Connecticut, in the Midwest, in Canada, and in Switzerland.

Connecticut

Kemper and Quigley[2] carefully examined residential refuse collection in 101 cities in Connecticut, utilising data from the period 1972 to 1974. They relied on mail questionnaires, supplemented by telephone interviews and data compiled by a state agency. They, too, distinguished contract collection from private collection, and found that municipal collection was 14 to 43 per cent more costly than the price of contract collection, while the price of private collection was 25 to 36 per cent higher than the cost of municipal service. Although they do not report the level of significance of their findings, which were based on regression analysis, they conclude with the recommendation that cities should not provide the service themselves but should contract with private firms under competitive bidding (p. 73).

Midwest

A study of cities in Illinois, Indiana, Michigan and Ohio, conducted with 1974 data, compared the cost of municipal and contract collection in 83 medium-sized cities.[3] Data were obtained by questionnaire and by personal interviews, and were carefully adjusted to allow for commercial collection and to reflect all cost factors (as in the Savas–Stevens and Kemper–Quigley studies). The authors found that 'the costs of operating a solid waste collection system tend to be less for a private firm under contract to the community than for a municipally operated system. The typical or average city could reduce its costs by approximately 13 per cent by switching from a municipal to a private contract system'. This finding is statistically significant at the 95 per cent level.

Canada

Kitchen[4] conducted a study of 48 Canadian cities with populations greater than 10,000. He utilised mail questionnaires and verified many of the data

[1] Savas, E. S., 'Municipal Monopolies vs. Competition in Delivering Urban Services', in W. D. Hawley and D. Rogers (eds.), *Improving the Quality of Urban Management* (Urban Affairs Annual Reviews, Sage Publications, Beverly Hills, Calif., 1974), pp. 473–500.

[2] Kemper, Peter and John M. Quigley, *The Economics of Refuse Collection* (Ballinger Publishing Co., Cambridge, Mass., 1976).

[3] 'The Generation and Collection of Household Refuse in Cities', *Urban Affairs Quarterly*, publication pending.

[4] Kitchen, Harry M., 'A Statistical Estimation of An Operating Cost Function for Municipal Refuse Collection', *Public Finance Quarterly*, Vol. 4, No. 1, (January, 1976) Sage Publications, 56–76.

through telephone interviews. Private and contract collection were not treated separately, and therefore the comparison was between cities with municipal collection and cities with collection by private firms, regardless of arrangement. Regression analysis was used to estimate the effect of this factor. The finding, significant at the 95 per cent level, is that 'municipally run refuse collection tends to be much more expensive'.

Switzerland

Pommerehne and Frey studied refuse collection in Switzerland.[1] They obtained 1970 data from 103 cities using mail questionnaires. (While this would be an unsatisfactory method of collecting data for such a study among cities in the United States – see below – one cannot question this technique *a priori* in a study of Swiss cities; it may be that there is considerable uniformity of accounting standards and practices among municipalities in Switzerland.)

In the discussion, the authors refer to private collection in general, and make no mention of the distinction between contract and private collection arrangements as these terms are used above. One does not know whether only one of these forms is found in Switzerland or whether the two both exist but were lumped together for the purpose of the study. Coefficients were estimated for regression equations that predicted cost per household and cost per ton, with similar results: 'public production of refuse collection seems to be subject to higher average costs than private production'. This was true even if the five largest cities were excluded from the analysis. The findings were significant, usually at the 99 per cent level; however, they do not report the magnitude of the difference. The difference remained significant whether the comparison was made on the basis of cost of production (that is, excluding profits of private firms), or on the basis of cost of municipal service versus the price of private collection (which includes profits).

St. Louis

The two studies that are not inconsistent with the foregoing five studies, although they do not corroborate or reinforce the findings, were both carried out in St. Louis County, in Missouri. The earliest reported study that attempted to derive a cost function for refuse collection was carried out by Hirsch, in 1965, using 1960 data from 24 cities in St. Louis County, including the city of St. Louis.[2] (This was the smallest sample in the eight studies reviewed here.) One of the variables considered in his study was contractual arrangement;

[1]Pommerehne, Werner W. and Bruno S. Frey, 'Public Versus Private Production Efficiency in Switzerland: A Theoretical and Empirical Comparison', in Vincent Ostrom and Frances P. Bish (eds.) *Comparing Urban Service Delivery Systems* (Urban Affairs Annual Reviews, Vol. 12, Sage Publications, Beverly Hills, Calif., 1977), pp. 221–41.

[2]Hirsch, Werner Z., 'Cost Functions of an Urban Government Service: Refuse Collection', *The Review of Economics and Statistics*, Vol. 47 (February 1965), 87–92.

however, he did not distinguish between contract and private collection in his analysis – he lumped the two together and compared them to municipal collection.

Hirsch's regression analysis 'did not reveal statistically significant relations between costs and types of contractual arrangements'. However, it should be noted that he encountered certain data limitations in his pioneering study: he relied exclusively on mail questionnaires, only about one-quarter of the cities he sampled responded with sufficiently complete data, and the cost data included the costs of both refuse collection and disposal. There is no evidence that he received anything but conventionally reported budget data, or that any effort was made to design a standard cost-accounting framework.

Twelve years after Hirsch's work, Collins and Downes also studied the cities in St. Louis County, excluding St. Louis itself.[1] They selected a random sample of 53 cities, stratified by size, and obtained data from each by direct interviews with city officials and with officials of private firms. They differentiated contract from private collection and reported that 'no clear pattern emerges to establish any systematic cost difference between contractual and municipal systems', but observed that private collection seemed more costly than either contract or municipal collection.

Despite the commendable reliance on on-site data collection, the discussion reveals that, like Hirsch twelve years earlier, the study relied on published budget figures and did not attempt to derive municipal cost data according to a standardised cost-accounting framework. Savas has shown that budgets significantly understate the true costs of municipal collection[2] (he found that the latter costs an average of 30 per cent more than the budget indicates, and Kemper and Quigley found the same 30 per cent figure for 18 cities in Connecticut). In the light of these findings, it is perhaps understandable that the St. Louis studies did not find that municipal costs were higher than contract costs. Furthermore, by failing to distinguish between collection and disposal costs, an avoidable source of variation was introduced; this might have contributed to the fact that their regression equation explained only 18 per cent of the observed variation in cost. Further questions about the adequacy of the Collins–Downes data are raised by the anomalous finding that the cost per household does not vary with the frequency of service; numerous other studies confirm the plausible view that higher frequency of collection costs more.[3]

Another possible reason, of course, why the St. Louis studies found no difference between the cost of municipal and contract collection is that there *is* no difference in that locality.

[1]Collins, John N. and Bryan T. Downes, 'The Effects of Size on the Provision of Public Services: The Case of Solid Waste Collection in Smaller Cities', *Urban Affairs Quarterly*, Vol. 12, No. 3 (March, 1977), pp. 333–47.

[2]Savas, E. S., *Organization and Efficiency, op. cit.*, p. 200.

[3]Stevens, Barbara J., 'The Cost of Residential Refuse Collection', in Savas, *Organization and Efficiency, ibid.* Chap. 7, pp. 107–8.

Montana

The only study which found municipal collection to be less costly than private collection was conducted in Montana by Pier, Vernon and Wicks.[1] They were successful in obtaining usable data from 26 of the 62 cities in the state, after sending mail questionnaires to all the cities and private firms. They found 'greater governmental than private efficiency for garbage collection in Montana for all but very small communities'. Unfortunately, this study exhibits several serious methodological flaws which call the conclusions into question. (i) Like the St. Louis and the Swiss studies, this one relied entirely on budget data, a procedure which suffers from the shortcoming discussed above; (ii) no distinction was made between private and contract collection; (iii) the sample size was small and the response rate was relatively low, with unknown bias; (iv) location of pick-up site was not controlled for; one-third of the private firms but only one-sixth of the municipal agencies collected refuse from a location other than curbside or alley, that is, from a location that is more expensive to service; (v) the study was not restricted to residential collection; because each collector serviced an entire city, including all residential and commerical customers, it was assumed that the ratio of commercial to residential accounts was similar for private firms and municipal agencies; (vi) as Pommerehne and Frey point out[2] the study by Pier, Vernon and Wicks estimated separate production functions for the public and private sectors instead of a single function with a dummy variable for the two institutional structures.

VI. CONCLUSION

Three major studies have found that contract collection of residential refuse is less costly than municipal collection, and two additional studies that did not differentiate between contract and private collection found that collection by private firms is less costly than collection by a municipal agency. Two studies in the St. Louis area did not find a difference between public and private agencies, but the studies, as designed, were not as sensitive as the other studies. Only one study, with the serious faults discussed above, is inconsistent with the conclusion that the price of contract collection is less than the cost of municipal collection of residential refuse. This conclusion seems to be valid in the United States, in Canada, and in Switzerland, a remarkable cross-national consistency which suggests that some underlying principles may be at work.

Direct evidence as to the operational reasons for the higher cost of municipal collection is available from the study by Savas and Stevens. They found that compared to private firms performing contract collection, city agencies (i) used

---

[1]Pier, William J., Robert B. Vernon and John H. Wicks, 'An Empirical Comparison of Government and Private Production Efficiency', *National Tax J.*, Vol. 27, No. 4 (December, 1974), pp. 653–6.
[2]Pommerehne and Frey, *op. cit.*, p. 229.

larger crews; (ii) experienced higher absenteeism resulting from vacations, illness, and all other causes; (iii) served fewer households per hour; (iv) were less likely to utilise labour-incentive systems; (v) used vehicles with lower capacity; (vi) were less likely to use vehicles in which the driver can also work as a loader.[1]

These conclusions are supported by a 1967 study of refuse-collection operations in 234 cities. The study, by Ralph Stone and Company, was not primarily addressed to the issue of public and private service, but the authors nevertheless observed that[2]

> Public refuse collection systems in general have been slower than private collection systems to adopt new refuse collection technology such as smaller crew sizes, certain low-cost or high efficiency equipment types, and related system modifications . . . Current municipal collection systems are frequently characterized by: personnel with limited skills and work experience; high absenteeism; absence of promotion opportunity; and lack of public recognition of the collection worker's contribution.

In the absence of any persuasive evidence to the contrary, one is compelled to accept – at least tentatively – the conclusion that when collecting residential refuse government is less efficient than the private sector because of poorer management, which manifests itself in the failure to employ the most productive capital equipment and the failure to assign and supervise its work force appropriately. One can speculate that this difference in management is in turn due to the more fundamental factors discussed at the outset of this paper: the monopoly nature of municipal agencies, lack of adequate market feedback, poor personnel systems, political decision-making, and counterproductive incentive systems.

---

[1]Savas. E. S.. 'Policy Analysis', *op. cit.*, p. 72.

[2]Ralph Stone and Company. Inc., *A Study of Solid Waste Collection Systems Comparing One-Man with Multi-Man Crews*. US Government Printing Office. US Department of Health, Education and Welfare, Public Health Service. Bureau of Solid Waste Management. Report SW-9c. 1969. p. xx.

Discussion of Professor Savas' Paper

In his opening remarks, *Professor Savas* said that people had many different needs such as food, water, health care, etc. There were a great variety of institutional arrangements to satisfy those needs: pure public, pure private, mixed, contracting, franchising, subsidisation of producers or consumers, licensing, etc. The question was which institution was best to satisfy what needs, in what way it was better, and why. One could speculate about these issues, and that had also been done at this conference. But one should approach these questions empirically, not dogmatically, even though the latter approach was more productive in terms of published papers. So far there had been few truly scientific comparisons of different institutions. There were three criteria for comparison: efficiency, effectiveness and equity. Efficiency meant that inputs were converted into a maximum of output, without waste. Effectiveness meant that real needs were satisfied. Equity meant fairness in distribution, without discrimination among income classes, or by race, sex, age, etc. For such a comparison he had selected solid waste disposal, which was a public good that was supplied by the government in most cities. It was a clearly defined service, which could be evaluated easily. It would be much more difficult, for example, to compare the quality of different health care services. Three institutional arrangements had been compared in the study: (i) public enterprise (a municipal agency), (ii) private firms, which were selected by households on a competitive basis, and (iii) private firms that were hired and paid by the government. A measure of efficiency utilised was costs per household. *A priori*, one would expect the second arrangement to be more costly, because of economies of contiguity: it would be wasteful if, for example, five trucks ran down the same street, each picking up the garbage at a few households. Also, the cost of billing and collecting unpaid bills was higher, since government could insist on payment. Between (i) and (iii), one could think of advantages for each. Government could make full use of scale economies and operate at zero profits. On the other hand, the advantage of a contract to a private enterprise with a local monopoly was that it had to compete in the market in the process of obtaining the contract. His study had in fact shown that a contractual arrangement had lowest costs, while public enterprises were even more costly than private collection. In terms of the other two criteria, effectiveness and equity, the results were still being analysed, but initial findings indicated that the quality of service was the same. This would answer an earlier question of Dr Tardos regarding quality of service. A principal reason for the higher costs of public enterprises was that they used about 50 per cent more men for the same job, and had a higher rate of absenteeism. Wages were about the same. Some might object that inefficiency was justifiable because it created more jobs. But did anyone really perform a service to the public by being inefficient? This was not the right prescription for full employment. Rather, if higher employment were a goal, people could provide additional services, or services of higher quality, e.g. more frequent collection of garbage. What were the causes of inefficiency? It had been said that if government took some steps towards better management, it could do equally well. This was certainly true, but the issue was why it did not do so. A fundamental characteristic of government was the absence of competition. The result was that good performance (by workmen or by managers) was not rewarded, that decisions were made on a political rather than economic basis, that there were bureaucratic incentives for agency growth, that there was civil service ridigity and political patronage. If these conditions were absent, then public enterprise could be better at providing a service characterised by a natural monopoly. The issue, then, was not whether public or private enterprise was better, but the optimal role and extent of competition. Continuous competition in many public services was wasteful, because of scale economies (or economies of contiguity in public services such as garbage collection, water supply, electricity, telephone, etc.). A permanent monopoly was wasteful because of the absence of competition. And municipal services amounted essentially to a permanent monopoly, since the enterprises were never replaced except, perhaps, in a revolution. The best solution was *periodic* competition, which eliminated monopoly profits, and could still take advantage of the economies of scale or contiguity. In closing his remarks, Savas stressed the need for more empirical work, and said he hoped that there would be another conference on the same topic in about five or ten years, but with more empirical results and less dogma.

    M. Albert said that Savas had presented a very interesting document, because it attempted to provide objective results. This study was welcome, since some of the ideological digressions of the preceding days had shown how difficult it was to introduce rationality into the discussion. But did Savas completely escape precommitment? Albert warned against drawing excessively sweeping conclusions from the study, since it dealt with a specific sector in a specific country. The study had answered some questions, but raised new ones. Why did people often persistently choose the most expensive solution? Were there any considerations besides pure costs that had been overlooked, such as noise, cleanliness, etc.? Was the difference in Savas' results for small and medium-sized enterprises attributable to an inability of municipal enterprises to capture scale economies and Baumol's 'subadditivities'? Or was it that a certain critical mass was reached from the social viewpoint and that the personnel drew a rent from its relative strength in terms of wage levels and working conditions, and acquired a 'status' which the employees of private enterprises could not attain? Why did one not see the emergence of a nationwide 'US Refuse Company'? Where did innovation take place and how was it diffused?

    With regard to the measure of performance, Albert said one could judge results only in terms of the objective adopted initially. For example, if Renault had carried out tasks assigned to it by the government, this should be taken into account in an overall evaluation, and it should not be blamed for achieving lower profits than Peugeot. But it was often difficult to use the initial objectives as evaluation criteria, because they were rarely stated explicitly. M. Boiteux had made an effort in that direction by including a 'cost of failure to provide service' and by trying to introduce various externalities into the objective function used for planning purposes by Electricité de France. Only this type of analysis can permit an objective evaluation of large enterprises which takes into account both their *microeconomic efficiency* and their contribution to *macroeconomic objectives*.

Albert also emphasised the distinction between public ownership of an enterprise (nationalisation) and direct government control over day-to-day management decisions (*étatisation* or *gestion directe*). The latter was the worst formula one could imagine. For examples where 'public service' was used as a pretext to justify any decisions in advance, nobody was interested in competition. This was very costly, wasteful, and ultimately led to a degradation in the quality of service. An example can be found with some telephone services. Some municipal waste disposal services also fell into this category. Such services can be, at the same time, the worst and most expensive one can imagine, while the employees consider themselves more unhappy than those in other public or private firms. He thought that several contributions in this colloquium had shown the great dangers inherent in direct and centralised state management of enterprises, notably the very important paper by Nyers and Tardos. He thought that after some unsuccessful experimentation Hungary seemed to have found a better way to proceed. In contrast to government-managed enterprises, public enterprises under an independent management, such as Electricité de France or Renault, did well. He stressed that in order to perform well and to remain innovative, it was absolutely essential that a firm face a biological risk of extinction up to some extent, and through some process of natural selection. As Dr Marsan pointed out, the possibility of entry and exit should be maintained whenever it is possible, otherwise it lacked the incentive for efficiency.

He concluded by saying that Savas had made a systematic and well-documented contribution. He had achieved concreteness by dealing with an area in which the cost of service was a valid element of efficiency, though he reiterated that there was more to the notion of public interest than the cost of service alone. Stoffaes had dealt with more general public objectives in a large number of case studies in his book on 'Nationalizations', and Dreyfus' book was also important in this regard. If passion and faith, which unfortunately are rare goods, were adjoined to the goal of efficiency, then one could at the same time achieve *consensus* and *optimality*, something that economists' criteria were not yet able to measure very well.

Professor Srinivasan asked how government fixed costs were imputed to waste disposal services. The allocation of fixed costs was a difficult problem, and could possibly contaminate the results. Savas replied that private enterprise also had fixed costs, such as management overhead, and the same procedure was applied in both cases. Srinivasan also asked why the scheme of periodic competition did not permit the formation of a permanent monopoly. Savas answered that the costs of entry were relatively low. A single truck was enough capital to enter the business, and competition was working. Scale economies did apply up to populations of about 20,000 to 30,000, but not beyond 50,000 people.

Dr Galán said that public enterprise did have a role in meeting some national goals, but it was very difficult to determine what was best done by public and what by private enterprise. Savas' study had been clearly defined and relatively simple. But there were cases where many issues were interrelated in a complex way. Was Peugeot a better automobile producer than Renault because it had higher profits? Or was it inferior because it invested less? In such cases it was difficult to formulate a mathematical model and to use statistical methods to estimate its parameter values. Did this mean that countries had to wait before setting up public enterprises until econometric studies had proven their superiority? Governments often could not afford to wait. Economics was more than a pure science, and sometimes decisions had to be made on the basis of insufficient information.

Professor Baumol agreed with Galán that one could not always wait for conclusive studies before making a decision. But there was one thing which was even worse than postponing decisions, namely to rely *only* on judgement and to be unwilling to undertake *any* analytic study. It might be necessary to base some decisions on preliminary evidence, but once a thorough study had been performed, one should be prepared to learn from it and to revise mistaken decisions, if necessary. The issue was not to determine whether private enterprise was good and public enterprise immoral, or *vice versa*. The issue was to find how both can be made to work more efficiently and serve the public better. Even in the United States, the land of free enterprise, there was resistance to the introduction of competition in the provision of public services. There was a fear that immorality would otherwise take over. It was time to break down such superstitions.

Mrs Chávez gave an example of a successful public enterprise in Mexico. She said that Conasupo, a government operated retail food chain, had performed very useful services. For example, four years ago it had bought up a bankrupt private enterprise which produced edible oil. Last year it had made profits of over 100 million Mexican pesos. This year, the profits were expected to reach 200 million pesos. Profits were not the objective of the nationalisation, rather, the goal was to regulate prices in the edible oil market. If Conasupo returned this enterprise to private hands, the retail price of edible oil would almost double. She stressed that this did not mean that she was in favour of eliminating private enterprise, but public enterprise did have a role to fulfil in certain areas.

Dr Marsan said that in Savas' list of institutional arrangements one was missing, namely contracting to a public enterprise. *Professor Vickrey* mentioned that in California this did indeed exist. Several small towns contracted for police, fire department or library services with neighbouring jurisdictions, sometimes even on a competitive basis.

Dr Pryke said that there was a need for many other studies of this nature. He said that in Britain road passenger services were bad, because there were strong labour unions who had a monopoly. If they had to face competition, there would not be such a problem.

Savas said that he did not want to sweep to grand conclusions. There was room for many more questions. Refuse collection was different from power supply, and also different from national defence, etc. There was need for rational thinking. He said he would leave searches in the dark to others, and preferred to shed light where it could be shed. Other services which could be compared were, for example, cafeterias, computer services, tax collection, etc. In reference to Pryke's comment he said that unionisation was extensive both in public and private industry. But unions were better able to exploit a monopolistic than a competitive firm. There were more strikes in public services. If a private garbage collection firm were on strike, the city had the option of taking over the trucks, or of giving the contract to someone else. He added that as a result of his study, some cities had changed from municipal waste disposal to contracting of the task to private services.

Part Four
Toward Policy

15 The Rate of Growth of Real Wages and the Role of the State in the Economy

Antonio Sacristán Colás
PRESIDENT, CIDE, MEXICO

I. THE PROBLEM

The distinguished gathering present at this Conference will not miss the implications of the title of this paper. Stability in economic growth basically depends upon the stability of the growth of real wages in relation to the growth of output; therefore, the essential role of the state in economic life must be to ensure this stability.

However, we economists should clarify certain principles that may lead to superior economic behaviour. Therefore it may be useful to recall some of these principles which, although fundamental and well-known, are sometimes forgotten when dealing with specific issues – even more so in the issue which concerns us now, that of defining the proper relationship between the economy and government.

II. THE BASIC ROLE OF REAL WAGES

If we accept as the most general definition of equilibrium and stability the requirement that real wages increase in the same proportion as output per man employed (Golden Age), then there is no doubt that this should be the aim of all economies. The state should seek to correct deviations from this natural and logical principle of stable growth. A sounder theoretical meaning may thus be given to the vague expression, 'collective welfare', which is, indisputably, the mission of the state and the economy.

The rate of growth of real wages is, then, the clearest objective of economic policy. It is here that the real process of production and distribution converges with the monetary (and real) phenomena of the economy.

Real wages are determined by the ratio of labour to output (productivity), in which the technique is the determining factor (regardless of the 'quantity' of capital required by the technique), and *by the share of wages in output*.

On the other hand, prices are also determined by wage costs in production and by the share of profits, which in turn, determines the share of wages in output. The real wage is therefore the best yardstick for measuring value and the rate of growth of real output. It is this which permits us to see whether economic forces tend toward the fulfilment of economic objectives, or away from equilibrium, as the share of wages in output varies through changes in the share of profits.

This is not new, nor is it disputed, but it shows that disproportionate growth of profits in relation to output must alter prices and wages.

The formation and accumulation of capital is inherent in man, whether it be the primitive tools which first distinguished him from his caveman ancestors, or the most elaborate automatic equipment available today.

In the simple definition of capital as accumulated labour, the surplus product is given by the Wicksellian ratio which serves as the basis for his comments in 'Akerman':[1] γ/χ, where γ is the number of workers engaged in the production of capital goods, and χ is the number of 'free' workers who use the capital goods to produce consumer goods. As capital is clearly seen to be accumulated labour and human ingenuity, disproportion between the growth of profits and the growth of wages (an increasing share of profits) is inconsistent with the system.

According to the Wicksellian ratio, then, output is always proportional to labour, and the growth of output is determined by this proportion, while capital is measured in terms of its labour-saving capacity.[2]

This shows that a production function cannot possibly be used to determine the share of profits and wages in output, in accord with the neo-classical theory of marginal productivity. The wage depends upon the (non-marginal) productivity of labour. However, without a function of consumption out of profits independent of the production function,[3] it is not possible to determine the distribution of output between wages and profits.

III. ACCUMULATION AND GROWTH

Although they are based upon simple notions such as these, economic doctrines differ radically. It is not easily comprehensible how, starting from the same two premises, wages given at the subsistence level and an unlimited supply of labour, Ricardo and Marx reach such contrary conclusions.

---

[1] Knut Wicksell, 'Analysis of Akërman Problem', *Lectures on Political Economy*, Vol. I: *The General Theory* (George Routledge & Sons, London, 1938), pp. 293–99.

[2] This relationship is similar to Kaldor's technical progress function:

$$\frac{Y}{Y} \qquad \frac{K}{K}$$

growth of output per man relative to growth of capital per man.

[3] C. F. Nicholas Kaldor, 'Alternative Theories of Distribution', *Review of Economic Studies*, vol. 23 (1955–6).

The former postulates that the accumulation of capital will produce general welfare, and the latter that it will produce progressive pauperisation of the proletariat and self-destruction of the economic system.

Such a fundamental divergence divides the world into two ideologies that are economically and politically antagonistic. The growing and cumulative intervention of the state in economic life arises as the eclectic solution of these antagonisms, yet I believe that the explanation of this antithesis should be sought in the pertinent principles.

Neo-classicists criticise Ricardo because he has no theory of wage growth; and the orthodox economists criticise Marx because he assumed that wages would not improve, in spite of the increase in real output that makes accumulation possible.

Actually, both unemployment and inflation, the former as a cause and the latter as a consequence, are the expression of instability in distribution, preventing real wages from growing at the equilibrium rate. In this sense, both Ricardo and Marx are correct.

Nevertheless, economic analysis has brought to light a principle that can today be considered axiomatic: *the growth of real wages is not possible without capital accumulation; nor can there be capital accumulation without growth of real wages and other forms of remuneration for work.*

Yet this does not mean that the society we live in is actually governed by this simple principle, whether in the accumulation process or in distribution.

IV. THE NEED TO CONSIDER THE ROLE OF MONEY

In order to explain why this logical principle is not followed, it is necessary to bring money into the analysis. This was the great task of Keynes' *General Theory*.

If the wage rate is not given, one can neither determine the system of relative prices nor the rate of profits; and without the latter, it is not possible to determine relative prices and the wage rate (Sraffa).[1] Now, in order for either to be determined it is necessary to introduce money as a means of exchange, between goods and services of labour.

Without the existence of money, prices can only be determined by the assumption of 'perfect dynamic competition', an 'optimal Golden Age', or a 'golden equilibrium', in which there is zero consumption out of profits, so that profits are equal to the labour cost of accumulation, and wages increase according to the ratio γ/χ (productivity of labour as capital). *This is the only case in which it is possible to say that money is 'neutral'.*

V. RISING INTEREST RATE AS STIMULUS OF INFLATION

The introduction of money into the economic process makes instability in

[1] Piero Sraffa, *Production of Commodities by Means of Commodities* (Cambridge, Cambridge University Press, 1973).

distribution and prices possible. But it is not the increase in money in circulation that determines the rise in prices, as has so long been asserted by the quantity school, both in the traditional version (based upon variations in supply) and in the new version (related to variations in demand). This hypothesis is logically inconsistent on its own grounds, as it is not logically possible to establish a causal relation between an increase in money prices and an increase in money.[1]

In addition, it contradicts the axiomatic assumption of 'general equilibrium', since an increase in the demand represented by any of the equations implies a reciprocal effect in one or several of the others, to permit the equation of the *numeraire* to remain invariant, and the interest rate to be stable at the 'natural rate'.

In order for there to be excess demand in the system of relative prices as a whole, it is necessary that supply should not increase as demand prices rise. Furthermore, prices can rise only if one of the factors takes a larger share in output at the expense of the others, without necessarily having an increase in the quantity of money.

Therefore, what varies is precisely the system of relative prices, that is to say, the share of profits in relation to the direct cost of production, real wages.

The monetary determinant responsible for this discrepancy must be found in the cost of money, i.e. the interest rate, and not in its purchasing power, as we will attempt to show later on.

Even the creation of 'outside money' by means of increased public spending, which constitutes the prop of neo-quantity theory, can affect prices only if nominal wages or the proportion of consumption out of profits of the production sector does not decrease, thus permitting a greater proportion of spending for public services.

Consequently, the monetary explanation of price rises must be found in the determinants of the increase in the share of profits in relation to primary cost.

The world crisis of 1929 was illuminating for economic theory by showing that the interest rate did not have the stabilising effect in production and demand for consumption that the neo-classicists had supposed. It became obvious that it generated unemployment, and this made it practically impossible to fulfil the neo-classical assumptions regarding the stability of distribution. Unemployment alters the distribution of output, though it is impossible to attain full employment without stability in distribution.

The present world crisis, which is characterised both by massive inflation and by unemployment, shows that a more realistic hypothesis is that the interest rate has a positive, direct and cumulative effect on the inflationary process.

The explanation of this direct effect is that the cost-price of commodities increases with each exchange operation, through the interest that the banking

[1]See the author's 'Ensayo sobre la inconsistencia de la mecanización algebraica de la teoría cuantitativa', CIDE, mimeographed.

system charges, which is then incorporated into prices. The increase in prices then becomes the basis for new production and exchange operations, for which interest will again be charged; and so on.

Therefore, prices increase cumulatively at compound interest if the propensity to consume out of profits does not decrease at the same rate, so that the overall consumption out of profits does not increase in a higher proportion than the growth of income. It is hard for this to happen if the interest rate is not very low. The so-called *wage–price spiral then becomes a spiral of interest, profit, wage and price.* This explains the generally cumulative character of the inflationary process.

If banking policy then raises the interest rate in accord with the traditional idea that this combats inflation, far from correcting it, this will accelerate the inflationary process even more.

In itself, this would explain why a rise in the interest rate has no effect in correcting inflation, unless it produces such severe unemployment that it makes it possible for nominal wages to fall in a higher proportion than output.[1]

Since the bank rate of interest that the system charges for its intervention in exchange operations is usually the basis of financial markets, it is easy to understand why the present crisis is characterised by the demand for a *financial return higher than the real return on capital* (growth of output per man employed, in relation to the value in wages of capital goods or the marginal efficiency of capital, calculated in terms of the Keynesian money wage-unit). This explains both inflation and unemployment.

Such evidence appears sufficiently conclusive to support the hypothesis that there is a direct effect of interest rates on the inflationary process. This view is more logical and realistic than the hypothesis that an increase in the amount of money raises prices, and throws new light on the analysis of the effect of money upon the process of production and distribution. Since the simple dampening effect of the interest rate upon investment and effective demand is not sufficient to explain the inflationary process that accompanies both periods of expansion and recession, it seems to me that this can be considered implicit in Keynesian theory.

The direct effect of the cost of money on prices would have been easier to recognise had we not taken as a real fact the quantity hypothesis, based on the mirage of the creation of money which accompanies price rises.

If one takes into account the direct effect of the interest rate on prices, the consequence is radical. *Instead of concluding that an increase in the amount of money raises prices, we reach the opposite conclusion, that it is monetary restriction and high interest rates which raise the share of profits and, therefore, prices.*

The 'quantity of money – prices mirage' is similar to the optical illusion in seeing the sun revolving around the earth, from dawn to sunset. In order to

---

[1]See the author's 'The Rate of Growth of Real Wages and the Interest Rate', presented at a Seminar on Economic Theory and Policies for Growth, CIDE, mimeographed.

prove and appreciate the fact that prices move by themselves, it is sufficient to take a point of reference in the universe of economics other than the purchasing power of money. This can be nothing other than stability or growth of the ratio of prices to production costs; i.e. the real share of wages in output.

The quantity theory mirage persists because we have not given due consideration to Keynes' intuition that economic magnitudes should be measured in money wage-units;[1] this is the only measurement unit compatible with the principles of general equilibrium and aggregate effective demand as a function of the level of employment. If, in agreement with the *General Theory of Employment*, $L = L_1 + L_2$ is equal to $M_1 + M_2 = M$, then given M_1 as a function of employment, M, the amount of money, cannot increase more than income, unless there is an increase in the ratio M_2/M; i.e. of the interest rate.

A disproportionately large share of profits in relation to primary cost[2] causes external disequilibrium and gives rise to a sort of 'neo-mercantilism'.[3] A rise in interest rates cannot remedy this situation, however, for this tends to increase further the share of profits.

As the principle of general equilibrium also holds for the group of countries which engage in trade, international credits and so-called 'movements of funds' are nothing else than decreased purchasing power of currencies. These international financial assets are the expression of world inflation and are absolutely impossible to eliminate.

Besides having been shown as the immediate cause of the crisis, this provides empirical evidence for the hypotheses under consideration; that is, the effect of the interest rate and of the disproportion of profits on instability of production and prices. It makes one fear that a third aspect will be added to the crisis of unemployment and inflation; that is, severe financial crisis will result from a disproportion between financial returns and the physical productivity of the economies.

VI. THE ROLE OF THE STATE

Instability in the distribution of output between the factors of production, labour and capital, generally increases demands for state intervention in economic life. It also makes it possible to define the true reason for such intervention.

Increasing and cumulative intervention of the state in the economy is a fact that to some degree characterises every economy. It has undermined the classic principle of 'laissez faire', which sought to rely upon a series of natural economic laws independent of the arbitrary decisions of a sovereign.

The increasing intervention of the state as entrepreneur usually arises as an

---

[1]See the author's 'La asimetría en el efecto ingreso, la propensión al consumo de las ganancias y la "unidad salario en dinero". Contribución a la Teoría del Valor', CIDE, mimeographed.
[2]See M. Kalecki, *Theory of Economic Dynamics* (Unwin University Books, London 1954).
[3]See the author's 'The Rate of Growth of Real Wages and the Interest Rate', *op. cit.*

eclectic solution lying between capitalism and socialism; for the latter it is the way to self-fulfilment, for the former it is the hope of self-preservation. Therefore, the state's actions become vacillating and dependent upon the degree of temporal power of the political parties that advocate one or the other ideological tendency.

Socialists cry out for the nationalisation of enterprise as a commitment to party opinion, but without defining its aims very well. On the other hand, businessmen avidly accept and even ask for state aid in order to avoid sacrificing profits, even though these are inflationary.

It is necessary to seek, on the basis of fundamental principles, more objective reasons for state intervention in capitalism.

First, instability in distribution, a consequence of the inflationary effect of the interest rate and of the indeterminancy of the profit rate, generates demands for the socialisation of the means of production in the salaried sector. On the other hand, entrepreneurial activity slackens because of upward pressure on wages and the uncertainty that inflation produces, so that the state must itself become a producer.

Second, the inflationary process diverts investment toward techniques and areas of production which permit a degree of monopoly higher than the average, so that the general degree of monopoly is raised, while the real productivity of the economy and the growth rate of real wages are lowered.

It is assumed that the state, acting as entrepreneur, can better direct production and distribution, to yield a greater increase in output and real wages. But it is certain that if the state does not eliminate, or at least reduce, the causes of inflation that make for instability in the distribution of output between the factors, its actions cannot correct the accelerating tendency of the inflationary process. As a result, social inequality can be expected to continue or to become more acute.

The losses of the private sector must be absorbed by the public sector, and those of the public sector by the private sector. State action is usually thus converted into a means of transferring inflated profits to the entire community.

A very typical example is that of countries which nationalise banking or certain general services such as railways or electricity. If banking continues to be a lucrative activity, nationalisation of the banking system does not correct the problems of unemployment and inflation. The high cost of credit transfers the inflationary effect to the nationalised public sector, and the latter must transfer its losses to the economy as a whole by an inflationary rise in its costs and prices.

High financial and operating costs are supported by the general economic system through their unfavourable effects upon the growth rate of output and real wages; particularly if, in order to show profits, prices of services are raised.

More generally, one can conclude that public enterprise and state action will be more beneficial if real wages are made to reach or to approach their equilibrium level, both for its own sake and for its effect on the entire economy. It seems possible to estimate the efficiency of the state as manager by the rates of growth of real wages compared to the ratio of output to capital per man, and to that of the economy as a whole.

In accord with these considerations, it is necessary to make as precise as possible the *reason* for state intervention; that is, the most general function of the state in the economy.

The role of the state is to administer justice, and in the sphere of distribution of output between the factors, it is defined in terms of the growth of real wages. Growth and stability, both real and monetary, may be attained only if real wages grow in the same proportion as output per man employed.

The economic role of the state is to maintain stability in the distribution of output between factors, in terms of wages and profits, which the free play of economic forces cannot guarantee.

In order better to define the role of the state, we may allude to certain juridical principles. Roman law, which constitutes the basis for juridical relations in the western world, protects the ownership of goods acquired by the labour and industry of man. This principle implies that no one may be deprived of his rights or be constrained against his will 'without legal cause', i.e. without compensation freely estimated by the person who is under obligation. There can be no 'obligation without cause'. *Acquisition without cause is 'illicit enrichment', and so is revocable.*

On the basis of a just principle such as this, it is possible to construct a juridical theory of stability in the distribution of output among the factors of production (the *sum quique tribuere* of Roman Law).

Any increase in profits due exclusively to a rise in prices is illicit gain. In processes with greater return per man employed, either as a result of technical progress or of insufficient supply, disproportionate increases in profits relative to the increase in aggregate output may also be included in the concept of undue gain, if this does not serve to increase capital accumulation; for it has an inflationary effect upon prices through greater profit consumption.

This does not mean that those processes with a higher degree of technical progress, or greater productive efficiency, cannot yield rates of profit higher than the average of the economy. On the contrary, this is essential for an increase in production surplus and, therefore, for the growth of the economy and of real wages. What matters is that overall profits and accumulation should tend to be in proportion.

It is thus admissible for nominal wages not to increase proportionally in a case where productivity per man employed is higher than the average, if by this means the accumulation of capital and the later growth of real wages are stimulated.

The state must have not only the power but the mission of preventing illicit gains – by fiscal or any other means – in order to favour equitable stability in the distribution of output, which the free play of economic forces cannot guarantee. The so-called market system is not able to guarantee an increase in profits strictly proportionate to the growth of output, as the theory of free competition supposed. Not only is the legitimate share of wage-earners threatened, but growth and progress are slowed, causing inflation and unemployment.

This need for the state to guarantee stability in distribution does not necessarily imply restriction of the freedom of initiative in production or in the choice of production methods, as long as it does not provoke a change in stability of distribution of output between wages and accumulation. Naturally, this does not preclude the state from becoming a productive agent. Nevertheless, it is obvious that the state itself must not only submit to these rules, but that its intervention is justified precisely by its role in securing stability in distribution and the growth of real wages throughout the economy.

As a basis for these postulates, taking as an objective the growth of real wages, and as their central criterion that of output per man employed, one can seek more consistent methods for the planning of the economy, for the use of human, natural and technical resources and for the indispensable programming of international trade.

Planning could thus be made more dynamic than when supported only by the requirements of demand; differences between the free enterprise mechanism and state capitalism could be reduced; it would be possible to measure the multiplier more precisely; and finally, one could better understand the role of market imperfection as the obstacle to all planning, an imperfection primarily attributable to instability and lack of uniformity in the 'degree of monopoly'.

It does not appear feasible, in the present state of knowledge in economics, to carry out an *a priori* determination of the uniform profit rate, because this is in conflict with technical progress and the increase of productive capacity.

The only thing that government economic policy seems able to achieve is stability in the distribution of output, in order to render possible some degree of social justice and gradual convergence toward the absolute optimum (optimal Golden Age, or golden equilibrium), by means of progressive reduction in the proportion of consumption of profits.

VII. INTEREST RATES, STABILITY AND EQUITY

Definition of the functions of the state and of economic policies, as well as the valuation of public enterprise, must be carried out macro-dynamically by means of the growth rate of real wages and the growth of output per man employed, which are the determinants of both real and monetary stability.

Economic theory, both in its orthodox and critical forms, is gradually establishing rules of stability in economic growth, whose form more or less corresponds to those formulated in this chapter. However, the state not only has been unable to assure their fulfilment but has even contributed to the generation or acceleration of instability.

In its least controversial and most orthodox function in economic life, that of creating and managing currency, unfortunately, the state has generated cumulatively both inflation and unemployment by promoting high interest rates; and these are the expression of instability in the distribution of output between the factors of production.

In addition, governmental intervention in the international financial system through central banks is a decisive factor in the present world crisis of inflation and unemployment, which has had even more serious effects through financial crises in practically all economies.

Although it is not very easy to understand why economists still obstinately believe that monetary restriction and the raising of the interest rate favour economic stability, it is even more incomprehensible that, on the political side, they do not understand that the high cost of money is placing the economy and society in the hands of the profits sector, to the detriment of the welfare of the masses, which is the basic aim of democracy. When government is operated for and by the masses, minorities are also favoured; but when economic policy has profits as its principal aim, it is not easy to promote either the welfare of the masses or economic stability.

VIII. TOWARD APPROPRIATE POLICY

It is not easy to design a series of rules that must be accepted by governments dedicated to stimulation of economic stability through the growth of real wages. Nevertheless, we may list a few as examples for the task before us.

(1) Wage policy must favour nominal wage increases proportionate with the growth of output per man employed, in order to avoid a rising share of profits, rather than relating wages to profits, and the resulting tendency toward a wage-price spiral.

(2) Direct measures must be taken against unemployment by means that raise aggregate effective demand, thereby stimulating productive investment.

(3) Legal norms and measures must be designed to prevent 'undue enrichment', i.e. greater profits arising from higher prices, which the market system and free competition are unable to avoid.

(4) Economic policy should seek progressive reductions in the propensity to consume out of profits. It should also stimulate investment that yields maximum use of human, natural and technical resources, and of the saving which investment itself generates.

(5) There should be policies relating to exchange, commercial agreements and programming of foreign trade designed to attain equilibrium, since both surplus and deficit in the balance of trade generate internal disequilibrium. Financial policy must avoid the system of unilateral international credit and investment which, far from favouring them, actually damages both lender and borrower. To complete the foreign picture, it is necessary that institutions for international co-operation understand their role in controlling capital movements, which are as harmful for the country being drained of funds as for the one supposedly receiving them.

(6) Finally, and above all, the bank rate of interest must be driven considerably lower since, without this, it is practically impossible for other measures to achieve stability in the distribution of output.

It should be noted that this attempt to define the role of the state in economic life is equally applicable to the private enterprise system and to the mixed economy, regardless of the extent of the state's role as a productive agent.

In my opinion, it should be stressed that, whenever the state finds it necessary to assume entrepreneurial functions – because the private sector is not sufficiently dynamic or is not duly oriented toward activities which generate greater output and real wages – its actions must be consistent with stability in distribution, and must favour stability throughout the economy.

This chapter does not pretend to design rules or solutions, but only to show that although state intervention in the economy is widespread, we are still far from having a juridical and economic theory of its functions.

For the moment, it is possible to assert that the solution to the problems of productive growth and equitable distribution of output between consumption and capital accumulation does not lie in the simple transfer of the means of production to the state.

In any case, all production by means of labour and capital must first have a juridical and economic theory of distribution, in which the principal role of the state is to administer justice. It is difficult to conceive of a system that is not tripartite, consisting of wage-earners, entrepreneurs (public or private) and a government which makes certain that the wage sacrifice which is necessary for increased productive efficiency will eventually lead to the growth of real wages.

To the extent that the state fulfils its functions well, it can reduce the 'proportion' of expenditure on indispensable public services, and these may better contribute to increasing output and real wages. External stability and economic autonomy will also be more feasible.

I have always refused to believe in the inexorability of Marxist predictions because, it seems to me (as is assumed in this chapter) economic theory and a clearer view of the functions of the state can do much to correct instability in distribution and to raise the standards of living of the masses.

However, if we do not truly understand the role of the state in the economy, and if governments continue to imitate and even to aggravate the errors of the entrepreneurial system – which generate both internal instability in distribution and external disequilibrium – then a prediction of worldwide and self-propelling hyperinflation is not far-fetched. This peril, with all its consequences, has already begun to appear in almost all the economies of the western economic system.

Discussion of Dr Antonio Sacristán Colás' Paper

Professor Levhari said that Professor Sacristán's paper had focused on two questions, the role of the state in the determination of the real wage rate, and the effect of a change in the interest rate on prices. On the first point he said that the main issue was whether the profit–wage frontier could be pushed outwards, through technical progress, so that real wages could be increased without an upheaval. On the second point he said that Sacristán had considered the interest rate as a cost item which pushed prices up. On the other hand, Keynes had argued that a rise in the interest rate would reduce aggregate demand and thus reduce prices. He said that more empirical research was needed to support one view or the other. He then asked Lord Kaldor why he considered central planning always to be superior. He suggested that a comparison of the development of Austria and Hungary, which started off at a similar level after the Second World War, seemed to speak in favour of more decentralisation.

Kaldor replied that he never intended to suggest central planning always to be superior. He merely considered that there are some advantages inherent in public enterprise as well as advantages inherent in private enterprise; the advantage in public enterprise lay in the fact that it did away with some costs of capitalist production. The major cost item was the instability of investment by private entrepreneurs. Consumption out of profits was of relatively minor importance, at least in the developed countries. Consumption expenditures of capitalists also remained relatively stable, compared with investment expenditures, even in times of crisis, because they had reserves and could live on savings, rather than income, if necessary. Kaldor agreed with Sacristán that an increase in the interest rate was a cost item and contributed to inflation. He said that the primary cause of the current wave of inflation was the increase in commodity prices brought about by OPEC and the Soviet wheat purchases. This gave a further stimulus to inflation through commodity speculation. Low investment caused profits to be low, which in turn implied a higher share of wages in output. If in such a situation the central banks raised the interest rate in order to stop inflation, it was like administering poison to a severely sick patient in the hope that it would cure him.

Levhari interjected that if, as Kaldor had said, the cause of inflation was a cost push acting via rises in certain commodities prices, then an increase in interest reduces the desire to accumulate stocks of these commodities, helping to offset this source of inflation. *Kaldor* disagreed, saying that we suffered from demand *deflation*, rather than demand inflation. There were six million unemployed in the European community, because of lack of demand partly caused by the fall in capital investment. He saw a fallacy in the neo-classical position illustrated by Friedman's prediction in 1974 that the oil price was going to collapse within three months because of lack of demand. But this price increase has shown that it is cost factors, not demand factors, which determine changes in prices.

Professor Srinivasan doubted whether the disturbances of the early 1970s (OPEC, the wheat deal, etc.) could explain the current inflationary *process*. Temporary disturbances of that nature would only bring about a one-time shift in prices. The reason for the ongoing inflation was that monetary authorities acted to accommodate an ongoing inflation.

Kaldor replied by saying that inflation created its own momentum. Everyone wanted to keep up with the rise in prices by increasing his money income, which in turn caused further price increases and further demand for increases in money wages. Unless there were price and wage controls, or very high unemployment, the inflationary spiral, once started, continued. It was as if a body had been injected into space and continued on its path by its own inertia.

Mr Tello said that in less developed countries the cause of inflation was never excess demand, but price increases by manufacturers. Rather than expanding output, which would create more employment and increase demand, they resorted to price increases in order to maintain their profits in the face of restrictive monetary policies. These price increases reduce demand further, and lead to high unemployment and underemployment, with little purchasing power left in the economy. In this way entrepreneurs would ultimately tend to kill the hen that layed the golden eggs.

Sacristán summarised the main points of his paper and concluded by saying that a rise in the interest rate would result in more inflation and at the same time restrict investment. In this way it contributed to a reduction of both wages and profits.

16 Actual and Potential Pricing Practices Under Public and Private Operation

William S. Vickrey
COLUMBIA UNIVERSITY

I. THE DIFFERENCES BETWEEN PUBLIC AND PRIVATE ENTERPRISES

Many of the important differences between public and private ownership or management of large-scale enterprise show up in the pricing practices used in the sale of their products, in some cases even more significantly, though perhaps not as dramatically, as in the methods used for the determination of investment or the deployment of manpower. These differences are especially important in that in cases of natural monopoly, particularly where this relates to economies of scale, price policy decisions are logically prior to investment policy decisions, in that the desirability of a given investment cannot be properly determined without first deciding what pricing policy is to be followed in the utilisation of the investment. Some of these pricing practices seem strongly conditioned by the nature of the regime, others perhaps less so, but it is worthwhile just taking a passing look at some of these differences or perhaps simply tendencies.

II. LEVEL OF SELF-FINANCING

The classical case for public operation of enterprises having strong economies of scale is that if the efficient pattern associated with setting prices at or close to marginal cost is to be achieved, a subsidy is required, and while subsidy of a privately managed and owned operation is not impossible, indeed such subsidy exists in a fairly large number of cases, such subsidy is at least more likely to happen under public than under private operation. Indeed, in the case of private operations it is not unusual to find fairly heavy tax burdens placed on the operation, as, for example, in the case of the supply of electric power in New York City or special taxes imposed on telephone services. And while it is possible to find cases of publicly operated utilities being operated at a high profit as a form of taxation to provide revenues for the political entity concerned, these are comparatively infrequent.

Thus while one cannot lay down any universal rule, the general tendency seems to be for a publicly owned facility to operate under less stringent financial requirements than a comparable private one, whether this be expressed as relative freedom from tax burdens; access to low-cost financing; whether merely by the use of the public credit to minimise risk-premiums (Ontario Hydro); the use of tax exempt bonds (Port Authority of New York and New Jersey) or capital fund advances upon which less than a normal return is expected, or even no return (as seems to occur, according to Mr Marsan, in Italy, even for enterprises not having marked economies of scale and marginal costs substantially below average costs); or outright subsidies of various kinds (increasingly typical of urban transit operations in Western Europe and North America).

It would be erroneous, however, to describe such subsidies as exist as bearing any close relationship to the level of subsidy required to allow user charges to be brought down to a level appropriately close to marginal cost. In many instances subsidies to transit operations have been accorded only after it has become apparent that continued attempts to operate on a self-liquidating basis would have completely disastrous effects on the pattern of service that would survive under such a criterion. In others the subsidy has supervened as a result of a reluctance to allow rates to keep pace with the general rate of inflation, or as part of a general policy of holding down increases in the official cost of living index. In almost no case has the subsidy corresponded to any clear economic principle. Because of this lack of clear rationale, the amount of the subsidy has become a matter for negotiation among the interested parties and a factor in relaxing pressures for efficiency.

III. DEALING WITH INFLATION

Ways of responding to inflation have varied widely both on the private and public sides, but on the whole there seems to have been a somewhat greater tendency for publicly operated utilities to resist increases in prices, drifting into greater and greater subsidy in one form or another. While in many cases similar pressures affect privately owned utilities, most regulatory formulas call for at least some degree of keeping up with inflation and maintenance of a nominal self-liquidating posture. In some cases regulatory practice may even go further than this: a fairly typical regulatory formula in the US calls for rates to yield a fair return on a 'fair value' defined in terms of historical cost. In a growing utility, if depreciation charges are allowed on a straight-line basis in terms of book or historical cost (to say nothing of 'accelerated' depreciation), while at the same time a rate of return is allowed that is determined by reference to market rates that themselves include an element of inflation, there is the possibility of a degree of double counting that would result in rates being raised by more than a correct indexing for inflation would warrant. For example, a $1,000,000 asset with a twenty-year life will have a depreciation charge on a straight-line basis of $50,000 in the first year and an interest charge of $60,000 at a 6 per cent rate of return in constant dollars. If there is a generally anticipated inflation at a rate of 10 per cent per year, and as a result the equilibrium money rates of interest in the market move to 16.6 per cent $(1.10 \times 1.06 - 1.00 = 0.166)$, the capital charges under the usual procedures would be $166,000 of interest plus original cost straight-line depreciation of $50,000 for a total of $216,000 instead of the $110,000 without inflation, a gross overcharge. Correct procedure would be to combine the $166,000 interest on a nominal basis with a credit for appreciation from $1,000,000 to $950,000 \times 1.10 = $1,045,000$ for a net charge of $166,000 - $45,000 = $121,000 which is the equivalent of the previous $110,000 increased by 10 per cent for the inflation. Even if depreciation is on a 'sinking fund' basis with the rate of interest credited to the sinking fund raised to the market rate of 16.6 per cent, the fact that the calculations as ordinarily made posit a flat depreciation charge in money terms implies an excessive loading of the charges on the earlier years.

To be sure, this overcharging in the early years of the life of the asset will to some extent be offset by undercharging in later years, but for a growing utility the net result will be an overcharge. Another possible mitigating factor is that market interest rates may rise by less than the full equivalent of the inflation. The likelihood of a substantial overcharge remains, however, if the standard regulatory formula is carried out literally. Political pressures may cause regulatory commissions to shade matters a little and possibly increase the regulatory lag beyond the normal levels, but the likelihood remains that private regulated utilities will be allowed to overcompensate for inflation, whereas publicly owned utilities will tend to undercompensate.

IV. INTERNAL FINANCING

Closely related to depreciation accounting methods is the question of the degree to which funds for new capital investment are generated internally as against being secured externally from the market. Depreciation charges, properly computed, are a generally accepted source of such financing, which can even finance a modest degree of expansion, to the extent that the average age of the installed capital is increasing.

A second source consists of retained normal earnings. For a privately owned operation this may mean incurring a danger of greater difficulty in raising funds in the future on the basis of a history of low dividend payout. Financing by retained earnings has also been criticised in many quarters as having the effect of by-passing the test of market appraisal in the allocation of investment. And in many cases such financing has the effect of enabling shareholders to reduce, postpone or avoid entirely the individual income tax on their share of the retained earnings. For publicly owned enterprise the matter is more nearly a trivial question of accounting as between the operating agency and the government.

A third, more questionable source of financing, is the charging of rates in excess of what is required for a normal return on investment, in effect requiring current users to provide the capital to supply future services. In a publicly owned utility this may be managed in a manner that is not too inequitable, though in most cases it will significantly impair efficiency of utilisation of the service by driving rates further away from marginal cost. The effect in the case of a private utility will depend on the mode of regulation: where the regulation takes the form of limiting dividends in terms of capital paid in by shareholders or where the capital so financed is excluded from the rate base, the effect may be rather similar to what happens under public ownership. In many instances, however, this is not the case, and users are, in effect, being asked to finance capital expansion out of current rates, and eventually provide a return on this capital out of future rates. One form in which this can occur is where capacity under construction is put in the rate base immediately so that present users are asked to pay for it even though they can derive no immediate benefit from it, instead of the more appropriate procedure of capitalising the interest chargeable during construction so as to produce a more nearly correct value for the capital when it eventually becomes ready to provide services.

V. ROLLING IN OF RENTS

In many instances a service is provided in part through the use of scarce natural resources that command an economic rent which increases through time as the resources with the lower marketing costs are exploited and recourse must be had to sources involving higher marketing costs. For electric power we have hydro-electric sites, for gas we have natural gas wells and fields, and for transportation we have scarce road-space. Here, the way things work out may be as much a matter of the degree of integration in the industry as whether the industry is in the public sector, the private sector or straddles both.

In the case of electric power, private utility owners have not generally been allowed to appropriate, at least explicitly, the increased rents imputable to the hydro-electric sites as the value of the power they produce rises. Rather, these rents are required to be used, in effect, to subsidise the decreasing cost elements of the industry, particularly in the transmission phase but also in the distribution phase. In the case of gas, however, owners of gas wells have, in general, at least until the recent energy crisis, been allowed to retain the rents, and there has thus not been an industry source out of which the negative rents associated with the decreasing cost characteristics of transmission and distribution systems could be funded.

Generally, however, it appears that in areas where the gas production and distribution systems are in the public sector, there is some greater likelihood that means will be found of passing these rents through to consumers in lower prices, producing a result more nearly akin to that in the electric industry.

On the other hand, where the natural resource is in public ownership and there are no closely associated negative rent aspects of the industry to absorb the positive rents, there is often a reluctance to charge consumers a rent which does not appear on the books as an actual financial cost. There is also possibly involved a somewhat vaguely perceived application of the Marxist doctrine of the labour theory of value as a criterion for the pricing of publicly produced goods. Thus in India, in the 1960s, coal prices were set in part on the basis of an average of the explicit costs, so that the price of the limited supplies of high-grade coal were insufficiently above the price of relatively plentiful low-grade coal to balance demand and supply, with the result that a fairly elaborate rationing scheme had to be set up to allocate the limited supplies of high-grade coal among the various users.

VI. URBAN RENTS AND UTILITY SUBSIDIES

One area where a kind of rolling-in of rents should ideally be practised, but seldom is, is in the provision of locally oriented services having significant economies of scale, in the sense of a marginal cost below average cost. Here the high land rents that occur in urban areas can be thought of as being generated by the availability in the city of goods and services that are not equally available elsewhere on as favourable terms. To the extent that these goods and services are priced at low, marginal cost rates, the attractiveness of the city will be enhanced and the value and rent of land in the city will rise. Indeed, there is a theorem in urban economics that states that in an ideal economy in which all prices are set at marginal cost and cities are of optimal size, the land rents generated by the attractiveness of the city will be just sufficient, and no more, to finance the negative rents or deficits involved in the operation of the locally oriented, decreasing cost activities in the city at prices equal to marginal cost.[1] It would thus be appropriate for all urban rents to be 'rolled in' to reduce the price of decreasing cost goods and services in the city. Thus far, this has not been done to any significant extent, though there are instances, such as in Shaker Heights, Ohio, where some of the premium in the prices paid for lots served by a rapid transit line was used to help finance the rapid transit infrastructure. In other cases excess condemnation has been attempted as a means of helping to defray costs of a basic improvement to the infrastructure. This becomes difficult, however, in the case of services, such as bus lines, that do not involve heavy permanent fixed investments.

While one could conceive of monster capitalists developing entire cities along these lines – and even, given sufficient mobility of persons along the lines of the Tiebout model, being driven to the efficient mode of operation by competition among cities – most cities of any importance are sufficiently *sui generis* and cross-elasticities of demand are sufficiently short of infinite that

[1]W. Vickrey, 'The City as a Firm', in *The Economics of Public Services*, M. S. Feldstein and R. P. Inman (Eds) (Macmillan, London, 1977), pp. 334–43.

any such development would be unlikely to result in any close approach to the competitive norm. It is therefore incumbent on government at least to appropriate as much of these land rents as it can without leaving too little to the manager of the property as an inducement for good husbandry, and use them for the financing, not only of government services proper, but of the negative rents obtaining in the various locally oriented decreasing cost activities in the city, whether publicly or privately owned and managed. This brings up to an even more acute degree the problem of determining these subsidies in a way that will not have a deleterious effect on incentives for efficient management.

VII. DISTRIBUTIONAL CONSIDERATIONS

Recently there has been a spate of interest, in the US at least, in so-called 'lifeline' rates aimed at providing a basic level of service for residential customers at specially low rates, largely by privately owned utilities. The term 'lifeline' may be fairly apt for telephone service, where having a telephone on the premises may be a lifeline for summoning aid in emergencies, but in the case of gas or electricity the term is something of a misnomer. On the whole, one has the impression that special rates for distributional reasons have had a somewhat longer history in publicly owned utilities. In some cases, as at one time with the *Régie Autonome des Transports Parisiens*, subsidies from public funds were specifically aimed at making good the losses suffered by the Régie through such 'social' rates mandated by the government.

Actually, electricity rates have typically had rather substantial regressive patterns embodied in the usual form of declining block rates. Such rates were traditionally justified on the basis that low level usage was largely lighting and on-peak, with appliance usage associated with the later, lower-rate blocks more likely to be off-peak. This is over and above the block representing a crude approximation to a customer charge. This argument is no longer applicable where peaks are associated with summer air-conditioning usage. Another justification proposed for declining block rates is that the amounts sold at the various block rates are less price-elastic for the lower blocks than for the higher blocks, if only because the consumption sold at the higher block rates to customers using the lower follow-on rates is almost completely inelastic with respect to changes in the rates applicable to the earlier block, thus justifying the higher rates in terms of the Ramsey or 'inverse elasticity' type of rule. While it is sometimes alleged that inflation has increased marginal cost to the point where marginal cost rates would cover the revenue requirements based on historical cost, so that the Ramsey Rule would apply in reverse, if at all, in light of the above analysis of the way inflation can involve double counting, it is not at all clear that this rationale for declining block rates is obsolete.

At any rate, in this instance publicly owned utilities seem to have for a time used the same techniques as the private.

VIII. TIME OF DAY PRICING

It is in the field of time-of-day pricing that there appears to have been a fairly
sharp differentiation between private and public pricing patterns. Seasonal
pricing is of course well established in such competitive fields as resort hotels,
though even here not generally carried out to the extent that a perfectly
competitive model would indicate. In non-competitive areas, publicly owned
agencies have been well ahead of privately owned in using various methods of
controlling peak loads, whether by time-of-day pricing or separate metering of
controlled loads such as water and space heating. So-called 'interruptible'
power has been sold at concessional rates in both areas, but in the case of
privately owned utilities this seems often to have been, at least in part, a
discriminatory device used to justify concessional rates to special customers
rather than a cost-saving device: actual interruptions to such customers have
often turned out to have been far below the amounts allowed for in the
contract, and when interruptions actually take place according to the contract
customers sometimes complain that this is not in accordance with their
expectations.

Some of the resistance of privately owned utilities to time-of-day pricing may
be attributable to a kind of 'Averch–Johnson effect' according to which utility
operators would be motivated to adopt a price structure leading to higher peak
capacity requirements and greater capital investment, not only as a means of
general aggrandisement but in order to enhance the rate base on which they
would be allowed to earn a return that would exceed by some margin the actual
cost of capital, the margin being due either to the need for some kind of
incentive or simply an inherent allowance for the errors and uncertainties
involved in the regulatory process. In effect, peak use is subsidised at the
expense of off-peak use for the sake of justifying a higher level of investment on
which a net profit margin above the cost of capital can be earned.

IX. PUBLIC RELATIONS ELEMENTS

On the whole, in many areas there seem to be signs of a greater degree of
concern for good public relations with customers in the case of privately owned
than of publicly owned utilities, not always fully justified in terms of the overall
public welfare. For example, in the private segment of the telephone industry,
mainly Bell system companies, long-distance calls are charged for and listed on
an individual call basis, calling for fairly expensive additional apparatus,
whereas elsewhere most customer-dialled national calls are charged for on a
simple metered basis, by varying the time allowance per metering pulse. This is
not only a less costly method, but gives the user the opportunity to make very
cheap, simple message, brief calls, lowers the charge for 'wrong numbers' to the
point where it is hardly worth the caller's trouble in most cases to claim a
credit, and sharply reduces the number of occasions where it is worthwhile to
use an operator for a person-to-person call. In contrast, the Bell system until

relatively recently stuck to a relatively high minimum charge for the three-minute call with elaborate billing requirements, partly on the basis of a claim that consumers presented with an unitemised bill for an aggregate of message units would be unable to relate this bill to their usage, and would thereby be aggrieved.

In this case it seems that a desire to display technological virtuosity plus an Averch–Johnson motivated drive to expand capital investment have combined to produce a catering to a somewhat inchoate desire of customers at a cost that they might not have been willing to pay had they been presented with the alternatives in any realistic fashion.

Another aspect of public relations is the extensive 'institutional' advertising often engaged in by private sector companies attempting to justify various aspects of their operations and often more or less openly attacking the public sector.

X. TIMING OF CAPITAL CHARGES

In many cases where capacity is necessarily added in fairly large lumps, as with a bridge, a tunnel or a rail transit line, usage is way below capacity in the earlier years, with correspondingly low marginal cost, with sharply increasing marginal cost in later years as the demand begins to catch up with the capacity. In a world of certainty, at least, the efficient pattern of pricing would call for prices to be low or even zero in the early years, and to be advanced fairly sharply as the facility becomes congested, postponing the time at which an enlargement or duplication will be needed, with the price again dropping sharply as the new addition to capacity becomes available.

Neither public nor private operations seem to do very well on this score, in practice. Indeed a frequent occurrence is that as the indebtedness incurred for the construction of the facility is finally paid off, there arises a demand that the rates now be lowered by an amount corresponding to the amortisation no longer required on the financial books; this may even occur just about the time the rise in congestion would call for an increase rather than a decrease in the price.

In a world of uncertainty, it is perhaps understandable, but regrettable, that both private and public authorities are generally averse to thus deferring the amortisation of the capital investment to an indefinite future and perhaps even capitalising early deficits, over and above the 'underdepreciation', resulting from interest charges or fixed operating costs. This is perhaps more understandable for privately owned utilities, where investors would tend to be less willing to advance capital on terms such that there would not only be no dividends for an extended period, but not even any net cash flow in earnest of an eventual satisfactory return. Public agencies should, in principle, be able to take a longer view with less difficulty, but even here there is a distinct danger that economic rationality in the short run may stimulate political pressures that result in uneconomical long-run decisions, as when the expansion of a facility would be financed out of general funds while the particular beneficiaries would gain not only a better service but lower prices to boot.

XI. PROSPECTS FOR INNOVATIONS IN PRICING

Aside from looking at past experience, one can also speculate on the degree to which publicly owned and privately owned enterprise will be amenable to the introduction of new pricing structures and methods, some of which are capable of improving dramatically the efficiency of the operation.

(1) Simulated futures market in airline reservations

One such innovation with fairly dramatic potential would be the selling of reservations on long-haul flights on the basis of a simulated futures market, where the price of a seat for a given schedule on a given future date would fluctuate over time according to the relationship between the number of seats remaining unsold and the time remaining to departure. The effective price at any given amount would be calculated by taking the base price for the particular flight and applying a premium if reservations are running ahead of the normal rate, and a discount if they are lagging. In effect, the price would be calculated as $P = P_i f_j(t, s)$ where P_i is the normal price for flight i, t is the time remaining before departure, s is the proportion of seats on that flight already sold, and f_j is a function appropriate to the class j of flights to which flight i belongs, the classification being in terms of the time pattern of reservations normally observed for the flight type. Sale of reservations would normally be considered final sales, the passenger in the event of a change of plans being entitled only to resell the reservation at the price prevailing at time of resale.

Among the results should be an increase in load factors from the 45–55 per cent range to 85–95, permitting a corresponding reduction in the average fare level by 40 per cent; the almost complete elimination of occasions on which a passenger with an urgent need for a seat on a particular flight at the last minute cannot obtain a reservation, albeit occasionally at a high price (though rarely higher than present-day prices); inducements for passengers to shift their travel, where possible, to the less heavily demanded schedules, and opportunities for passengers with flexible plans to make trips at fares down to as little as 20 per cent of present fares; elimination of the need for charters in most cases; better utilisation of larger planes with lower seat-mile costs; better service to smaller towns through the ability to fill otherwise lightly loaded planes with through passengers who otherwise would choose non-stop flights; better distribution of large groups; and the like. Rough estimates indicate that the net gains attainable from such a procedure in appropriate areas would amount to at least 25 per cent of present gross revenues, and quite probably as much as 60 per cent.

It is not entirely clear what the relative prospects for an innovation such as this would be in cases where carriers are all private, all public or a mix of the two. Were there real competition among private carriers not subject to price regulation, one would expect something of this sort to be adopted first by one carrier, which would compel most of the others to follow suit or be at a disadvantage to the more aggressive. In an oligopolistic or cartelised industry, however, one might expect fairly strong resistance to the introduction of anything of this sort as being likely to lead to competition of a vigour that would be regarded as unattractive by the industry. Where there are airlines of both types, resistance might arise from fear on the part of the publicly owned lines that they might lose out against the greater flexibility of the private lines, and on the part of the private lines that they would be driven into an unprofitable position by the willingness of governments to subsidise their national airlines. This leaves cases where the publicly owned airlines are dominant.

On the other hand, in the case of local service or routes where there is only one carrier, such a scheme would create an incentive to cut back on service and drive average fares up. This would be difficult to resist or control in a private airline, but much less so for a public airline. On the whole, public operation seems to have the edge in terms of prospects for making use of schemes of this sort.

(2) Responsive pricing in lieu of interruptible power

Another area in which prices might be brought closer to marginal cost is in the pricing of electric power on short notice in terms of current supply and demand situations. One possibility is to invite customers to sign up for a responsive pricing scheme in which in the event of an unpredicted stringency the utility could raise the effective price to these consumers to whatever level is needed to deal with the situation, but the excess over the normal price would be placed in an escrow fund to be used to finance below-normal prices at other times to this same group of consumers. The escrow fund would be augmented by a bonus drawn from the savings made possible by the operation of the scheme in reducing the need for capacity required to deal with 'needle peaks' or reserves required to deal with outages. In this way it would be guaranteed that the subscribers to responsive pricing as a group would pay less in the aggregate for their actual consumption than they would have paid for this same consumption under the normal rates, and substantial numbers of users could expect to gain, on balance, from signing up.

Not only is there a potential for substantial saving in capital costs, and improvements in efficiency from not having to use gas-turbines and similar units with high operating costs, but there should be a substantial increase in the reliability of the service to all customers, including those not electing to reduce consumption in times of shortage. The distribution of cuts in power use among the various customers should be more efficient, given that these decisions would be made by the customer at the time rather than, as at present, largely by power company dispatchers who in the nature of things cannot be fully and adequately aware of the circumstances of the moment for each customer for whom a cut in service might be considered.

Given the reluctance shown in the past on the part of privately owned utilities to move significantly in the direction of time-of-day charges, it seems likely that the reception that they will accord such schemes as the above may be something less than fully enthusiastic, as predicted in part by the Averch–Johnson analysis. On the other hand, there are already indications of interest in something along the above lines on the part of Ontario Hydro, which at the moment is under strong pressure from the provincial government – from which it in effect secures its capital funds – to cut back on its programme of capital expansion. Here again, it would seem, public ownership appears to have advantages over private.

In effect, while neither private nor public operation precludes the effective use of any given pricing practice, there are differences perceivable in the practices that tend to be engaged in by the one type rather than the other. Neither form of organisation gets uniformly high marks for economic rationality, but on the whole the public operations appear to this observer to have the edge.

Discussion of Professor Vickrey's Paper

Professor Levhari said the sort of very flexible pricing mechanisms which Professor Vickrey had advocated would fit well in an Arrow–Debreu general equilibrium system. But the enormous information requirements of such schemes sometimes made them difficult to use in practice. The cost of introducing such pricing schemes also had to be considered and this might considerably reduce the advantages which they promised in theory. In practice, it was often necessary to devise second-best schemes, which struck an optimal balance between the cost of complexity and the gains from market efficiency. This applied both to public and private enterprise. The question was, which of the two was more innovative in this field. He also warned that regulated private utilities sometimes used pricing flexibility and discrimination among groups of customers to add to profits rather than to improve the cost–benefit ratio. So far as investments were concerned, public enterprise might have some advantage in that it was able to undertake risky projects on an expected value basis, and to take a longer view and apply the lower and more appropriate social discount rate, rather than a higher private discount rate.

Dr Pryke marvelled at the ingenuity of Vickrey's airline pricing scheme. But he thought the expected benefits were exaggerated because its destructive effect on charter flights had not been taken into account. Charter carriers typically operated with load factors close to 100 per cent, and therefore could afford to offer such low rates. If Vickrey's scheme were to increase the occupancy rate for scheduled airlines from say 50 per cent to 85 per cent, the gains would, indeed, seem enormous. But taking into consideration the effects on charter flights, the net gains would be much lower. This was an empirical matter, but he suspected that the benefits had been exaggerated. He also wondered what would happen if the consumers did not understand the scheme. What would be the welfare consequences? He felt the scheme was indeed of mind-boggling complexity for anyone other than economists. The same was true of the proposed scheme for electricity rates. What would a poor old company do about electricity rates that varied from moment to moment? Perhaps this was asking a bit too much. He was not sure what the consequences would be, but they struck him as inconsistent with an optimum. Regarding Vickrey's proposed use of a land tax to finance public services, he was concerned that it provided no incentive to reduce costs. The postal service might run down the same street half a dozen times a day and the electric utility might instal enormous underground pipes, if they were allowed to recover any costs.

Professor Baumol said that while he agreed with Pryke that sometimes one had to put up with pricing schemes that were not as sophisticated and flexible as theoretical considerations would lead us to advocate, he nevertheless thought that the points raised by Vickrey were of fundamental importance. He complimented him for turning the discussion away from the fruitless attempt to argue the virtues of one form of enterprise as against the other, toward the hard and important task of really designing mechanisms which could make one or the other approach work effectively and efficiently, and that was where the payoff was. That was where we were really going to have to do some work if a conference such as this one and its aftermath were going to make a real difference to anybody. He also wanted to ask two questions. In the case of electricity pricing it was clear that public enterprise had indeed been more flexible in its pricing policies than private. Was this also true in other areas? Secondly, he asked why, in Vickrey's view, airlines had rejected this sort of approach. He had himself advocated a simplified approximation to Vickrey's scheme, under which people could purchase *firm* airline reservations with the airlines obligated to serve these particular passengers. But if a purchaser of such a firm reservation did not actually turn up for the flight, some portion of his fare money would not be returned to him. Lower fares, without a firm reservation, would be available on a stand-by basis, and this again would lead to higher occupancy rates and lower costs per passenger. In addition, passengers would face less uncertainty. But there was apparently great opposition to even such a simple programme. He asked Vickrey whether he had any explanation for that.

Lord Kaldor said that to his knowledge British Airways had in fact introduced a similar scheme. People who wanted a reservation at a particular time, such as, for example, businessmen who had to attend a meeting at a specific hour, paid a higher fare than vacation travellers or others who were willing to take any flight during a selected three-day period, being notified 24 hours in advance of their flight.

Vickrey said that all these schemes did in fact go in the direction he was advocating. But he thought that the large variety of special fares now available involved as much complexity as his scheme. If an open market for theatre tickets of $5 and $10 could operate smoothly before the law clamped down upon it, he did not see any reason why the same system should not work for airline tickets that ran into hundreds of dollars, especially if it was done openly, in a systematic fashion, rather than underground. Addressing Baumol's question why airlines had been reluctant to adopt more flexible pricing schemes, he thought that, in general, large organisations were very rigid and opposed to innovative ideas, especially when they came from outside. For example, some years ago in an article, Julian Simon had advocated that in case of overbooking, airlines should simply pass around slips of paper asking people how much they would be willing to accept as compensation for having to wait for the next plane, and then pay the compensation to the necessary number of lowest bidders. Simon apparently had been more assiduous than he, Vickrey, in trying to peddle his scheme to the airlines and had gotten nowhere. Among other responses, he received a tongue-in-cheek letter from Pan Am describing how the scheme had supposedly been tried on a flight to Ireland with various disastrous consequences. Concerning flexible electricity rates, he said there were a great many ways in which companies and even households could save electricity at times when the rates were higher. Air conditioners could be operated at lower intensity, and elevators run at less frequent intervals. Even if people had to wait a little longer, this was much less serious than if an overloading of the network led to a black-out, and people were stuck in elevators for 48 hours, as had happened.

17 On the Implications of the Conference Discussions

William J. Baumol
PRINCETON AND NEW YORK UNIVERSITIES

I have been pleased and even surprised by the amount I have learned from this conference, and hope that this is also true of others. I have come away with a number of new ideas, and it has led me to change some of my previous views. That, to me, is as much as one can ever hope for from such an enterprise. A conference is not an activity which carries out research. It is an occasion which produces the agenda for further research. This is, indeed, what Lord Kaldor suggested in the letter in which he first described the objectives of the proposed conference, and I think it is precisely what it has been able to achieve. Of course, we did not arrive at nor did we intend to produce a set of firm and definitive conclusions. Rather, we sought merely to explore certain areas. Accordingly, let me try to list a few general interim conclusions which must themselves be considered as hypotheses that constitute items on the agenda for further research. By this I mean genuine research, undertaken with an open mind, whose outcome is not known in advance.

One of the general issues that loomed over the entire conference is the proper role of public enterprise and, in particular, the types of area, both in terms of countries and in terms of lines of industry, in which public enterprise is particularly apt to prove advantageous socially and efficient in comparison to private enterprise. Here, one conclusion is suggested by a comparison of our discussion of the small-firm activities (as in the case of garbage removal or the kibbutz) with the reports we have heard on the large nationalised firms – the producers of electricity and automobiles. There seems to be a marked difference in the relative performance of private and public firms in these two cases. In small-scale enterprise, it seems to be important to distinguish situations in which there is some special basis for reliance on idealism, on social pressure, on special enthusiasm. In such cases a non-profit-making enterprise and perhaps one which is publicly operated may operate with noteworthy efficiency. On the other hand, where one deals with firms whose mode of operation is, so to speak, business as usual, private enterprise is likely to have a marked efficiency advantage. There are a variety of reasons. First, it may be difficult to co-ordinate effectively the activities of many small enterprises, if it is desired to have them controlled by a single government agency. Second, in small private enterprises management and ownership may not be separated as in the giant corporations, and so one may still find the old-fashioned profit motive and its pressures for efficiency operating with full force. This, I think, is at least in part the explanation of the evidence of the persistent superiority of private enterprise in the removal of solid wastes that was reported by Professor Savas.

The case of large enterprises is quite different. Here the efficiency advantage of private enterprise, apparently, often disappears. One can easily find cases in which a public firm seems much more efficient than its private counterpart, as well as cases where the reverse is true. Thus, where large industry is concerned one must be pragmatic and be prepared to act differently from case to case in choosing between private and public ownership.

One is struck by the many similarities in the problems of large public and private enterprises. It has been pointed out here, for example, that in the large firm, whether public or private, the problem of bureaucratisation is a very real one. It can, it is true, be overcome by an effective management, but it need not be. This, indeed, may be one of the prime reasons it is so easy to think of examples of inefficient giants of both sorts. In both cases, one also encounters the problem of natural monopoly and the monopoly power that results from it. The temptation for governmental interference which is often well-intended but sometimes assumes irrational patterns one sees replicated for both types of firm. For example, our French colleagues have described such interferences in the setting of rates for railroads and airlines in France. It is easy enough to cite illustrations of that sort of irrationality in the United States, in its governmental regulation of private enterprise, which resemble the French examples in remarkable detail. There is also a very great similarity in the problems besetting motivation for efficiency in very large firms, public and private. In private large firms where there is separation of ownership and management, it is no longer clear that managers act anything like the profit maximisers of neo-classical analysis, and for this reason, as Lord Kaldor reminded us, one can no longer accept the presumption that the operation of these enterprises will bring them anywhere near their efficiency boundaries. Thus, weakening or elimination of the profit motive is an efficiency problem both for private and public enterprise. The primary issue, then, is not to argue which is better in this respect but to work upon the design of techniques, preferably automatic techniques, which can make the one and the other work with greater efficiency – to find means to deal both with the efficiency of managerial decisions and with the outlay of effort by employees, an issue raised by Dietrich Fischer.

Let me next draw several conclusions about some of the lessons for the institutional arrangements that seem to me to be suggested by our discussions as promising ways to encourage efficiency in these cases. First, and perhaps most important, it seems essential for the state to be prohibited absolutely from acting as rescuer of last resort. That is to say, firms must be made to recognise that they will suffer the financial consequences of their own folly or mismanagement. It must be remembered this is not an issue only for public enterprises. We have seen Lockheed rescued by the American government when it should not have been, just as we have seen public firms rescued in the same way. Such acts can all too easily become an open invitation to sloth, inefficiency and waste in management. This does not mean that one should oppose all public subsidies to industry. On the contrary, there are strong grounds for subsidy in many cases. But in granting these subsidies, each must be justified individually and it must never be granted in response to failure of the enterprise. They must be justified by beneficial externalities, or special tasks assigned by the state. But subsidies must never become a social welfare programme for industry. One must never confuse the virtues of social welfare programmes for individuals as an appropriate precedent for social welfare programmes for mismanaged firms.

A second lesson, and, I think, a relatively new idea that emerges from some of our discussions, is the need to institutionalise protection of workers from the costs of labour-saving technological change, not just for the sake of the affected workers, but as a means to facilitate the acceptance of innovation. Some of our discussion suggests that a major impediment to growth in Great Britain, perhaps in the United States and some other countries, is the resistance not only of management but even more of workers to technological innovation, particularly to labour-saving innovation. The other side of the coin is represented by Japan and the kibbutz where workers' jobs are protected from technological change. These cases suggest that so long as workers are not shielded fully from its burdens, we may end up with a most serious long-run inefficiency whose compounded costs to the community far outweigh the once-and-for-all costs of such guarantees. Thus, the second policy hypothesis that emerges from the discussions is the importance of institutionalising the protection of workers from the burden of technological change in both public and private enterprises.

A third important research task was suggested by Professor Vickrey's talk. Priority must be given to the search for devices which prevent financial gains from monopoly power and yet simultaneously provide rewards for efficiency. This has been one of the great dilemmas of regulatory policy because there is no easy way in which one can decide what portion of the return to a large firm, public or private, is ascribable to its monopoly power, and what part is the fruit of superior efficiency and enterprise. Consequently, there is always the danger that in seeking to prevent the former one will cut off the latter. Regulatory agencies have a tendency to force firms under their control toward a fixed rate of return which is judged to be fair and proper, in effect, seeking to guarantee that the firms will earn neither more nor less than this. But oft-repeated experience confirms that there is no better guarantee of managerial sloth, waste and inefficiency. For why should anyone lift a finger to produce more efficiently when rewards are fixed and independent of accomplishment, when poor performance brings in the same rate of return as exemplary operation?

Here let me offer a suggestion I have made before – an arrangement I call 'institutionalised regulatory lag'. What I have advocated as a means to prevent monopoly earnings while preserving incentives for efficiency is that the prices charged both by nationalised and regulated firms be subjected to periodic review at randomly chosen intervals. At each such review the prices of those firms would be assigned ceilings designed to permit those firms to earn no more than a competitive rate of return at that time. However, in periods between reviews, those firms would be invited, indeed encouraged, to increase their rate of return if they can do so without raising their prices (except in response to autonomous changes in cost). In, say, the five-year interval between its reviews if such a firm could cut its costs significantly, it would be permitted to retain the additional earnings that it thereby acquired. Thus it would receive the rewards of efficiency. But, as in the Schumpeterian process, these rewards would be temporary. At the next regulatory review, the prices charged by the enterprise would be lowered to correspond to the cost reductions that had been achieved. At that time, the full benefits of the cost reductions would be passed on to consumers.

Having provided some illustrative hypotheses about the areas of relative advantage of public and private enterprise, and having suggested some measures to encourage their efficiency, all of them suggested by our discussions, I would like to emphasise, in conclusion, that the major contribution of the conference, in my view, is the clarification of topics most urgently calling for future study. These include, first, the determination of the social, political and cultural circumstances which contribute to the success of nationalised enterprise. It has been suggested that in France circumstances seem to have been right, while in England they seem to have been wrong. It is important to look further into this conclusion, not because we want to criticise the one or congratulate the other, but because we want to learn from these experiences what *features* of the circumstances account for these results, so that others in turn can learn what to encourage and what to avoid when they themselves are considering the establishment of public enterprises. Second, we want to determine which spheres of economic activity make for success of nationalised industry. We want to be able to say, perhaps, that in electricity it is promising while in garbage removal it is not, rather than indulging ourselves in grand partisan generalisations. Third, when society adopts some overriding social goals, such as the creation of employers of last resort in periods of unemployment, as Mrs Martinez has reminded us, it is important to investigate the opportunity cost of the use of public enterprises for this purpose before it is decided to saddle them with this task. The question here is not whether it is desirable to find jobs for the unemployed; on that we are all agreed. Rather, the question is whether the nationalised enterprise is the most effective, efficient and desirable means for that purpose. Finally, I repeat what to me is one of the most important items on the agenda – the determination and testing of devices, preferably automatic devices, to enforce efficiency and stimulate innovation, while at the same time not inviting large monopoly profits. Economic research on this subject seems to me likely to be particularly important for policy. I suspect discussions such as ours will in fact have little influence on the future pace of nationalisation. The issue is much more likely to be decided on political rather than exclusively economic grounds, and it is perhaps right that it should be so. Economists are not the only ones who can contribute to that debate. Rather, where I believe we can contribute effectively is in helping to ensure that this decision, once made, is carried out in a way that yields social benefits as great as can reasonably be expected.

Index

Entries in the Index in bold type under the names of participants in the Conference indicate their Papers or Discussions of their Papers. Entries in italic type indicate contributions by participants to the Discussions.